GAME-THEORETICAL SEMANTICS

GAME-THEORETICAL SEMANTICS

Essays on Semantics by Hintikka, Carlson, Peacocke, Rantala, and Saarinen

Edited by

ESA SAARINEN
Academy of Finland

D. REIDEL PUBLISHING COMPANY

DORDRECHT : HOLLAND / BOSTON : U.S.A.
LONDON : ENGLAND

Library of Congress Cataloging in Publication Data

Main entry under title:

Game-theoretical semantics.

(Synthese language library; v. 5)
Bibliography: p.
Includes indexes.
1. Semantics – Mathematical   models – Addresses,   essays,
lectures. 2. Game   theory – Addresses,   essays,   lectures.
3. Predicate calculus – Addresses, essays, lectures. I. Hintikka,
Kaarlo   Jaakko   Juhani,   1929–   II. Saarinen,   Esa,
1953–   III. Series.
P325.5.M36G3   415   78–11855
ISBN 90-277-0918-1

Published by D. Reidel Publishing Company,
P.O. Box 17, Dordrecht, Holland

Sold and distributed in the U.S.A., Canada, and Mexico
by D. Reidel Publishing Company, Inc.
Lincoln Building, 160 Old Derby Street, Hingham,
Mass. 02043, U.S.A.

Printed in The Netherlands

TABLE OF CONTENTS

INTRODUCTION

The idea of borrowing concepts from the mathematical theory of games for the purpose of semantics is by no means new. Mathematically minded logicans have used game-theoretical semantics for spelling out the semantics of some infinitary languages ever since the early 60's (see Henkin, 1961). Other scholars, such as Lorenzen (1961), Lorenz (1961) and Hintikka (1968), have employed game-theoretical ideas for the analysis of some other formal languages. The main novelty in the essays of the present collection lies in the idea of using game-theoretical concepts for the analysis of natural language. Together with Hintikka's *The Semantics of Questions and the Questions of Semantics*, this collection makes available to philosophers, linguists, and other students of language and semantics the diversity of applications and results so far obtained in this approach to language theory. Most of the papers applying game-theoretical semantics for the analysis of natural language published to date appear here, with the exceptions of Carlson and ter Meulen (1978), Hintikka (1975), Hintikka and Carlson (1977), and Saarinen (1977).

This book is intended for two sorts of readers. It is intended on the one hand for those students of philosophy and linguists who, with little knowledge of logic and semantics, wish to become acquainted with the game-theoretical approach to semantics. On the other hand the present collection is intended for those scholars interested in or actively working on semantics who wish to compare the results achieved in game-theoretical semantics, and this approach generally, with rival theories (such as Montague grammar).

Hintikka's 'Language-Games', the opening essay of the present collection, discusses – as the title of the first section of the paper suggests – "semantical games as a link·between language and reality". This essay explicates the kind of theory of meaning which lurks behind the technical semantical games developed and applied in the other essays of the volume. Hintikka ties up his discussion with an evaluation of some central themes in Ludwig Wittgenstein's thinking. He concludes that the semantical games discussed in this volume "are at one and the same time designed as language-games in Wittgenstein's sense; they are games in the precise sense of mathematical game theory; they offer a handy tool for systematizing logical theory; and they give rise (in my judgement) to an extremely promising approach to the semantics of natural language''.

Hintikka's 'Quantifiers in Logic and Quantifiers in Natural Languages' provides an introduction to the basic ideas and concepts of game-theoretial semantics. It first discusses this approach as applied to first-order predicate logic and then to natural language. A student not familiar with game-theoretical semantics will find this paper helpful before tackling the more demanding and technical essays.

Hintikka's 'Quantifiers vs. Quantification Theory' was historically the first paper in the literature to discuss game-theoretical semantics for natural language. The main points of this paper are (i) to argue that English contains so-called Henkin-quantifiers (also called finite partially ordered quantifiers), and (ii) to sketch game-theoretical semantics for some natural language quantifiers, including the Henkin-quantifiers. The latter turn out to be particularly simple to handle on the game-theoretical model. In effect, all we have to do to spell out their semantics is to note that the relevant semantical games are games with imperfect information (to use a technical concept from mathematical game theory).

Hintikka's 'Quantifiers in Natural Languages: Some Logical Problems' is also, as the title suggests, concerned with a game-theoretical treatment of natural language quantifiers. This paper deepens and further develops Hintikka's earlier point of the existence of Henkin-quantifiers in natural language. Hintikka also presents and argues for his famous 'any-thesis'. This thesis says that (in a certain fragment of English) 'any' is grammatical in a given context X – any Y – Z if and only if the interchange of that occurrence of 'any' with 'every' results in an expression which is not identical in meaning with X – any Y – Z. This 'any-thesis' is interesting for a number of reasons, one of them being Hintikka's argument, based essentially on the 'any-thesis', to the effect that the class of grammatical (syntactically acceptable) sentences of English is not recursively enumerable, much less recursive.

Christopher Peacocke's 'Game-Theoretic Semantics, Quantifiers and Truth' is a comment on Hintikka's 'Quantifiers in Natural Language'. Peacocke tackles the foundations of game-theoretical semantics by asking for a motivation behind this semantical enterprise. Peacocke is especially concerned with the generalizability of game-theoretical semantics to other quantifiers of English, in particular to such 'non-standard' quantifiers as 'several', 'most', 'almost all', etc. Peacocke is doubtful of the possibilities of game-theoretical semantics in this area, and concludes that he has "failed to find compelling motivation that *both* makes essential use of the game theory *and*, as Professor Hintikka says, gives truth conditions identical with those of the classical account". In the second part of his paper, Peacocke criticises Hintikka's 'any-thesis', arguing that Hintikka's account of 'any' is not descriptively adequate.

Hintikka answers Peacocke's criticism in his 'Rejoinder to Peacocke'. In this paper Hintikka also sketches a game-theoretical account of some 'non-standard' quantifiers, called for by Peacocke.

In their paper 'Semantical Games and the Bach–Peters Paradox' Hintikka and Saarinen extend game-theoretical semantics to cover some typical uses of the definite article of English. They show that in the game-theoretical framework the so-called Bach–Peters paradox admits a straightforward solution. This paradox arises when considering certain sentences with crossing pronominalization between two different the-phrases (or other quantifier phrases).

In their paper 'Conditionals, Generic Quantifiers, and Other Applications of Subgames', Hintikka and Carlson put forward, for the first time in print, the idea of a subgame. (Subgames were first introduced in Carlson's unpublished Master's Thesis in 1975.) With the subgame-idea Carlson and Hintikka formulate a new type of semantics for conditionals, and use their theory to examine certain pronominalization phenomena involved in conditional clauses. Among other things, their treatment amounts to an explanation for the universal ('generic') force of the existential quantifier in sentences such as

If Larry owns a book he reads it.

In his 'Backwards-Looking Operators in Tense Logic and in Natural Language' Saarinen is occupied with giving a game-theoretical semantics of a new type of intensional operator which he calls 'backwards-looking operators'. These new type of operator, which could also be called *anaphoric* operators, can be handled naturally in game-theoretical semantics – a result Saarinen interprets as indirect evidence for the approach. He also offers examples of the new type of operators from the English tense system.

In 'Intentional Identity Interpreted' Saarinen analyses Geach's puzzle of 'intentional identity'. This puzzle arises when considering certain recalcitrant cases of the interplay of quantifiers, anaphoric pronouns and intensional verbs. As a framework of his discussion Saarinen uses game-theoretical semantics which he pushes further in various directions. He also offers an analysis of the various (semantical) ambiguities to which quantifier phrases are liable in intensional contexts, locating no less than five different sources of ambiguity.

In 'Ross Paradox as Evidence for the Reality of Semantical Games', Hintikka discusses the well-known Ross paradox which consists in the apparently strange logical force of natural language sentences of the form '*a* must do *p* or *q*'. Hintikka argues that the paradox is due to a pragmatic confusion between my (the defender's) moves in the relevant semantical game, and those of *actual* people, in this case *a*'s. This result Hintikka interprets as evidence for the reality of semantical games.

In his paper 'Urn Models' Rantala develops a new type of semantical interpretation for first-order logic. As a framework for his discussion Rantala employs game-theoretical semantics; it is indeed doubtful whether an equally natural treatment could have been presented in the customary Carnap–Tarski approach. The key idea in Rantala's analysis is to start from a stepwise evaluation process which proceeds from outside in, and to allow the relevant domain of individuals to *change* during that process.

To be able to explicate urn models one thus needs to use a semantical approach which assigns a non-trivial and formally explicit role to the concept of a stepwise evaluation process which proceeds from outside in. Game-theoretical semantics, unlike the usual Carnap–Tarski semantics, meets this criterion. (Also one of the main reasons why Saarinen's backwards-looking operators, and anaphoric phenomena generally, are naturally explicated in game-theoretical semantics is provided by the concrete role of an outside in stepwise evaluation process in game-theoretical semantics.)

Rantala's urn models are important because they make concrete model-theoretic sense of the philosopher's intuitive notion of an impossible possible world – i.e., a possible world which is in some sense possible and yet logically contradictory (logically impossible). The philosophical significance of Rantala's urn models is analysed in Hintikka's 'Impossible Possible Worlds Vindicated'. Hintikka points out that Rantala's work takes a long step by way of burying the difficulty of possible worlds semantics for propositional attitudes known as the problem of logical omniscience. This major problem is based on the observation that in customary possible worlds semantics for propositional attitudes (say for knowledge), whenever *a* knows that *p*, he also knows that *q*, provided *p* logically implies *q*. Since this principle is obviously wrong, many scholars have concluded from it that it demonstrates the inadequacy of possible worlds semantics for propositional attitudes. Given Rantala's urn models the situation essentially changes, however, and one can remedy possible worlds semantics for propositional attitudes so as to allow logically contradictory attitudes.

Important topics remain unexplored after the present volume. Apart from extending and deepening the game-theoretical analysis of those phenomena of natural language touched upon here, several interesting problems still remain to be studied.

One such problem is provided by the relation between game-theoretical semantics and the kind of theory of meaning advocated recently by Michael Dummett (1975; 1976). According to Dummett, "we know the meaning of a sentence when we know how to recognize that it has been falsified". Dummett's theory of meaning "links the content of an assertion with the commitment that a speaker undertakes in making that assertion; an assertion is a kind of gamble that the speaker will not be proved wrong". (Dummett, 1976, p. 126.) There are thus obviously some interesting interrelations between the kind of theory of meaning implicit in the essays of the present collection and that put forward by Dummett. It remains to be seen whether Dummett's theory and game-theoretical semantics can be tied together with more systematic links.

Another interesting problem that is not studied in this volume is the exact relationship between semantical games in the sense of the present volume and the dialogue games of Lorenz and Lorenzen. (See Lorenz, 1961; Lorenzen, 1961. See also Stegmüller, 1964.)

The history of game-theoretical semantics is also a much more fascinating topic than one might think *prima facie*. Indeed, Risto Hilpinen has located in an unpublished work the basic ideas of this semantical approach from no less a profound thinker than Charles Peirce. These ideas of Peirce's have been completely neglected so far, and are still unpublished.

Academy of Finland   ESA SAARINEN

BIBLIOGRAPHY

Carlson, Lauri and Alice ter Meulen (1979) 'Informational Independence in Intensional Contexts', in E. Saarinen et al. (eds.), *Essays in Honour of Jaakko Hintikka*, D. Reidel Publishing Company, Dordrecht.

Dummett, Michael (1975) 'What Is a Theory of Meaning?' in Samuel Guttenplan (ed.), *Mind and Language*, Clarendon Press, Oxford.

Dummett, Michael (1976) 'What is a Theory of Meaning? (II)', in Gareth Evans and John McDowell (eds.), *Truth and Meaning*, Clarendon Press, Oxford.

Henkin, Leon (1961) 'Some Remarks on Infinitely Long Formulas', in *Infinitistic Methods*, Pergamon Press, Oxford.

Hintikka, Jaakko (1968) 'Language-Games for Quantifiers', in N. Rescher (ed.), *Studies in Logical Theory*, Basil Blackwell, Oxford. Reprinted with revisions in Jaakko Hintikka, *Logic, Language-Games, and Information*, Clarendon Press, Oxford, 1973.

Hintikka, Jaakko (1975) 'On the Limitations of Generative Grammar', in *Proceedings of the Scandinavian Seminar on Philosophy of Language*, Filosofiska Föreningen, Uppsala, Sweden.

Hintikka, Jaakko (1976) *The Semantics of Questions and the Questions of Semantics*, (Acta Philosophica Fennica, vol. 28, no. 4), North-Holland Publishing Company, Amsterdam.

Hintikka, Jaakko and Lauri Carlson (1977) 'Pronouns of Laziness in Game-Theoretical Semantics', *Theoretical Linguistics* **4**, 1–29.

Lorenz, K. (1961) *Arithmetik und Logik als Spiele*, Doctoral Dissertation, Kiel.

Lorenzen, P. (1961) 'Ein dialogisches Konstruktivitätskriterium', in *Infinitistic Methods*, Pergamon Press, Oxford.

Saarinen, Esa (1977) 'Game-Theoretical Semantics', *The Monist* **60**, 406–418.

Stegmüller, Wolfgang (1964) 'Remarks on the Completeness of Logical Systems Relative to the Validity-Concepts of P. Lorenzen and K. Lorenz', *Notre Dame Journal of Formal Logic* **5**. Reprinted in Wolfgang Stegmüller, *Collected Papers on Epistemology, Philosophy of Science and History of Philosophy*, D. Reidel Publishing Company, Dordrecht, 1977.

ACKNOWLEDGEMENTS

Hintikka's 'Language-Games' first appeared in *Essays on Wittgenstein in Honour of G. H. von Wright* (Acta Philosophica Fennica, vol. 28, nos. 1–3), North-Holland Publishing Company, Amsterdam, 1976, pp. 105–125. It is reprinted here with minor changes with the permission of the Philosophical Society of Finland.

Hintikka's 'Quantifiers in Logic and Quantifiers in Natural Languages' first appeared in Stefan Körner (ed.), *Philosophy of Logic*, Basil Blackwell, Oxford, 1976, pp. 208–232. It appears here with the permission of the editor and the publisher.

Hintikka's 'Quantifiers vs. Quantification Theory' has earlier appeared in *Dialectica* **27** (1973), pp. 329–358 and *Linguistic Inquiry* **5** (1974), pp. 153–177. It is reprinted here with the permission of the editors and the publishers of these journals.

Sections 1–9 of Hintikka's 'Quantifiers in Natural Languages: Some Logical Problems' have appeared in Jaakko Hintikka, Ilkka Niiniluoto and Esa Saarinen (eds.), *Essays on Mathematical and Philosophical Logic*, D. Reidel, Dordrecht, 1979, pp. 295–314. Sections 10–19 of this paper have in turn appeared in *Linguistics and Philosophy* **1** (1977), pp. 153–172.

'Semantical Games and the Bach–Peters Paradox' by Hintikka and Saarinen has earlier appeared in *Theoretical Linguistics* **2** (1975), pp. 1–20. It is reprinted here with the permission of the editor, Professor Helmut Schnelle, and the publisher.

'Conditionals, Generic Quantifiers, and Other Applications of Subgames' by Hintikka and Carlson has appeared in Avishai Margalit (ed.), *Meaning and Use*, D. Reidel, Dordrecht, 1979, pp. 57–92. The paper is reprinted here with the permission of Dr. Margalit.

Saarinen's 'Backwards-Looking Operators in Tense Logic and in Natural Language' is a slightly extended version of its namesake in Jaakko Hintikka, Ilkka Niiniluoto and Esa Saarinen (eds.), *Essays on Mathematical and Philosophical Logic*, D. Reidel, Dordrecht, 1979, pp. 341–367.

Saarinen's 'Intentional Identity Interpreted' has been reprinted with some minor changes from *Linguistics and Philosophy* **2** (1978), pp.

151–223. Professor Robert Wall, Managing Editor of the Journal, has kindly granted his permission to reprint the paper here.

Hintikka's paper 'The Ross Paradox as Evidence for the Reality of Semantical Games' originally appeared in *The Monist* **60** (1977), pp. 370–379. It is reprinted here with a number of changes with the permission of Professor Eugene Freeman, Editor of *The Monist*, the Hegeler Institute, and the author.

Rantala's 'Urn Models: A New Kind of Non-Standard Model for First-Order Logic' originally appeared in *Journal of Philosophical Logic* **4** (1975), pp. 455–474. It is reprinted here with the permission of the Editor-in-Chief of the journal.

Hintikka's 'Impossible Possible Worlds Vindicated' is an extended version of its namesake in *Journal of Philosophical Logic* **4** (1975), pp. 475–484. It is reprinted here with the permission of the Editor-in-Chief of the journal.

Other papers appear here for the first time.

All the reprint permissions are gratefully acknowledged.

JAAKKO HINTIKKA

LANGUAGE–GAMES

1. SEMANTICAL GAMES AS A LINK BETWEEN LANGUAGE AND REALITY

What is it that ties together the two subjects figuring in the title of this section, language and reality? I shall not propose a general answer to this question, at least not on my own authority. Instead of putting forward a theory, I shall try to propose a model or paradigm for future theories falling within the purview of my title. I shall suggest that the most instructive actual examples of ties or links between a part of language and that aspect of the world which it can convey information about (or otherwise facilitate our dealings with) are to be found in what I have ventured to call *semantical games*. In order to arrive at this answer in a natural way, it is nevertheless advisable to start by considering some of the other answers to the same question. In fact, this paper is much less of an exposition of the theory of semantical games than an attempt to relate them to somewhat different approaches to the same subject, viz. to the different approaches Wittgenstein proposed at the different stages of his philosophical activity.

2. PICTURE THEORY AND LOGICAL SEMANTICS

How can we specify the meanings of the expressions of our language? How is a sentence of a language related to the part of reality it can serve to describe? One of the best known answers to the latter question is the so-called picture theory of Wittgenstein's *Tractatus*.[1] One of the most widely accepted types of answer to the former one refers to the recursive truth-conditions which are systematically used in the *logical semantics* associated with the names of Tarski and Carnap. A starting-point for my line of thought is found in the observation that these two theories (as they are often called) exhibit remarkable – and remarkably neglected – similarities and dissimilarities. The neglect is indeed remarkable. With the partial exception of Stegmüller,[2] no one has pointed out to my knowledge that there is a close similarity

1

E. Saarinen (ed.), Game-Theoretical Semantics, 1–26. All Rights Reserved.

between Wittgenstein's picture theory and the basic ideas of logical
semantics or logical model theory. This is the case even though both
parties of the comparison have been around for quite a while. The
Tractatus was published in 1921, while logical semantics was essentially founded by Tarski in the thirties, taken up and systematized by
Carnap in the forties, and built up into an integral part of technical
logic by Tarski and his collaborators in the late fifties.

One reason for the neglect is that the nature of Wittgenstein's
picture theory has often been obscured by an overliteral interpretation
of his terminology and imagery, especially by an interpretation which
takes the 'logical pictures' of Wittgenstein's *Tractatus* to be what he
himself disparagingly called in the *Blue Book* 'pictures by similarity'
(see pp. 36–37).

The basic idea of Wittgenstein's theory has been spelled out better
by Stenius than by anyone else.[3] The idea is that the ingredients of the
world are represented in the language by entities of the same logical
type. (Instead of 'logical type' Wittgenstein uses the stronger term
'logical multiplicity'; see *Tractatus* 4.04–4.0412, 5.475.) An atomic
sentence (Wittgenstein calls them 'elementary propositions' or
'elementary sentences', *Elementarsätze*) is true if the configuration of
these entities in the sentence matches the configurations of their
designations in the world. The truth-values of more complicated sentences are in the *Tractatus* assumed to be truth-functions of atomic
sentences, and their truth-values are hence determined by means of
truth-tables.

3. COMPARISONS

A comparison with logical semantics (model theory) shows a close
similarity. According to it, an atomic sentence will be true precisely in
the same circumstances as in Wittgenstein's picture theory. For instance, consider what the two 'theories' say of a simple two-place
relation (a relation 'in the world'). In a formal first-order language to
which Tarski-type truth-definitions apply in their simplest form, this
relation is represented by a relation symbol (say '$R(-, -)$') with two
argument-places. When looked upon in the right light, this symbol in
effect defines a two-place relation in the language, viz. the relation
holding between two expressions precisely when they fill the right
argument-places of the symbol. This relation in the language corresponds to the original relation it represents in the world. An atomic

sentence in which the two argument places have been filled by individual constants, say '$R(a, b)$', is according to logical semantics true if and only if the relation represented by 'R' holds between the individuals represented by 'a' and 'b' (in this order). But this happens precisely when the linguistic relation defined by the symbol 'R' obtains between the constants 'a' and 'b', that is, precisely when the sentence '$R(a, b)$' is a true picture of the entities represented by 'R', 'a', and 'b' in Wittgenstein's sense. Wittgenstein's picture theory of language thus comes very close to conceiving of all language on the model of first-order formalism (even though he objects in the *Tractatus* to some of the details of the *Principia* formalism).

It seems to me highly significant that the closest Wittgenstein comes in the *Tractatus* to giving us an actual example of an elementary proposition is to present a relational formula of formal logic. In fact, in *Tractatus* 3.1432 Wittgenstein comes rather close to saying what I just said, and in 4.012 he says in that the picture theory "is obvious" when applied to propositions in the usual logical notation. Wittgenstein's reasons for believing in the universal applicability of his picture idea were at bottom very closely related to his and his contemporaries' reasons for believing in the universal applicability of the symbolism of the *Principia*.

In logical semantics, too, the truth-values of more complicated sentences are determined recursively by means of clauses which in effect include the truth-tables of all propositional connectives. This is roughly analogous to the other one of "the two pillars of the *Tractatus*",[4] Wittgenstein's theory of truth-functions. The presence of quantifiers in model theory nevertheless creates important new problems. These problems and the new vistas their satisfactory solution opens are dealt with in an earlier paper of mine.[5] They will not be considered in the present essay. I shall not take up here the interesting historical question, either, of a possible influence of the *Tractatus* on the actual development of logical semantics.

4. HOW DO PRIMITIVE SYMBOLS REPRESENT REALITY?

There are interesting further similarities and dissimilarities between Wittgenstein's picture theory and logical semantics. One of the most important large-scale similarities is that in both theories the representative relationships between the basic elements of language and certain aspects of reality are not analyzed further in any way. In the *Tractatus*, this basic kind of representative relationship is called naming. It is being presupposed in all use of language, but not described in language. "Objects can only be *named*. Signs are their representatives. I can only speak *about* them: I cannot *put them into words*. Propositions can only say *how* things are, not *what* they are". (*Tractatus* 3.221.)

There is a partial similarity here with the fact that in model theory such notions as 'valuation' or 'interpretation' are not analyzed any further. For instance, a valuation will assign to each individual constant an individual member of our universe of discourse as its value and to each n-place relation a set of n-tuples of members of this universe, etc., quite as inscrutably as Wittgenstein's naming (or representative) relation in the *Tractatus*. (Cf. 3.22: "In a proposition a name is the representative of an object".)

In the *Tractatus*, Wittgenstein does not ask how these representative relationships are established in practice. However, in the *Blue Book* we find an instructive answer. "If we were doubtful about how the sentence 'King's College is on fire' can be a picture of King's College on fire, we need only ask ourselves: 'How should we explain what the sentence means?' Such an explanation might consist of ostensive definitions. We should say, e.g., 'this is King's College' (pointing to the building), 'this is fire' (pointing to a fire). This shows you the way in which words and things may be connected" (p. 37).

This kind of ostensive procedure of connecting 'words and things' is at its happiest when used to present the bearer of a (proper) *name*. It is therefore not surprising that in the *Tractatus* Wittgenstein frequently employs a terminology which applies most naturally to the relationship of particular objects to their names. *All* the basic building-blocks of the world are called by him *Gegenstände*, i.e., *objects*. "The configuration of objects produces states of affairs. In a state of affairs objects fit into one another like the links of a chain. In a state of affairs objects stand in a determinate relation to one another" (*Tractatus* 2.03–2.032). This has prompted a weird misinterpretation according to which the basic 'furniture of the world' consists according to the *Tractatus* entirely of things (logicians' 'individuals'). This interpretation is a wrong inference from a correct observation concerning Wittgenstein's terminology. That it is mistaken is shown most easily by reference to Wittgenstein's notebook entry on 16 June 1915: "Relations and properties, etc. are *objects* too". (*Notebooks* 1914–16, p. 61.) It is worth nothing that in the quotation from the *Blue Book* above Wittgenstein countenances ostensive learning of general terms: "We should say . . . 'this is fire' (pointing to *a* fire)" (italics added here). (Further remarks on this mistaken interpretation are offered in the Appendix below.)

In the *Tractatus* Wittgenstein does not speak of ostensive definitions but rather of *projections* of language on reality. What establishes these projections is not explained, however.

5. THE INSCRUTABILITY OF REFERENCE IN THE TRACTATUS

There is nevertheless a major difference between Wittgenstein's ill-named picture theory and logicians' model theory. The former is ill-named because for Wittgenstein it is not and cannot be a *theory*. It cannot be a theory because it is not expressible in language. Wittgenstein's reasons for thinking that it cannot be so expressed are the same as his reasons for the famous distinction between saying and showing. The relevant aspect of Wittgenstein's complex motivation seems to be the idea that we just cannot get outside our language. "The limits of my language mean the limits of my world" (5.6). And if my language is based on one set of representative relationships between the language and the reality, I cannot describe in the language a different mode of representation. We cannot 'make a picture' in the language of such a situation, for every picture already presupposes one definite system of representation of objects by names (cf. 3.203). Consequently we cannot think of such a state of affairs, either. (See 3.001.)

A brief exegetical comment may be in order here. Often, the main application of Wittgenstein's concept of *showing* as distinguished from *saying* is assumed to be to questions of logical form, e.g., to category-differences, rather than to questions concerning name-object relationship. Yet the latter relationship clearly falls within the domain of what can be shown but cannot be said according to Wittgenstein: "A name shows that it signifies an object, a sign for a number that it signifies a number, etc". (4.126). In fact, the natural thing here is to consider the inexpressibility (in the sense of unsayability) of logical form as a special consequence of the inexpressibility of name-object relationships. If in the last analysis we cannot *say* of a (primitive) name what it stands for, we cannot *say* what the logical type of the names object is, either. It may be that Wittgenstein wanted to restrict the term 'showing' to this special case of a sign showing or displaying its logical type. However, Wittgenstein's terminology is not the issue here. It may also be that 4.126 is primarily interested to claim only that the logical type of any object is shown by the kind of sign which stands for it. Yet this does not exclude that what an expression refers to likewise shows itself – "e.g. that it stands for a certain object, for no object, or the same object as some other given expression", to speak with Max Black.

As Black indicates, another special case of the wider phenomenon I have in mind is the impossibility of saying of a particular object that it exists or does not exist, as *Tractatus* 5.6 shows. This idea is in turn connected with Wittgenstein's idea that the limit of one's language are the limits of one's world.

Here we can perhaps see how the different doctrines of the *Tractatus* are connected with each other through the basic and puzzling idea of the unanalyzability and ineffability of the basic name-object relationships.

In any case we have here an extremely sharp contrast between Wittgenstein and logical semantists. For the deep leading idea of the latter is to vary systematically those very representative relationships which for Wittgenstein serve to define "the only language which I understand" (5.62). This comes up in an especially dramatic way in certain Tarski-type treatments of logical semantics.[6] In them the recursive clauses which characterize the notion of truth for quantified sentences involve themselves quantification over a class of different valuations of individual symbols, that is, over several different systems of naming of which our language always presupposes one *apud* Wittgenstein.

But even apart from such head-on collisions between the letter of Wittgensteinian and Tarskian ideas, there is a deep conflict between the spirit of the two. In terms of van Heijenoort's useful contrast[7] between theories of logic as language and theories of logic as calculus, Wittgenstein remains in the *Tractatus* irrevokably committed to the former, while all model theory pressupposes the latter. However closely the *Tractatus* account of how *one* privileged language works may agree (as far as atomic sentences and their truth-functions are concerned) with the model-theoretic idea of how *all* (formal) languages are related to reality, Wittgenstein refused to allow the variation which would have taken us from the former to the latter. It must be admitted, however, that this refusal has a point as long as logical semanticists have not offered a satisfactory account of those freely varying representational relations they are studying. Stegmüller is in any case quite right when he remarks (p. 182) that his "model-theoretic reconstruction of Wittgenstein's picture theory" presupposes the giving up of what Stegmüller calls Wittgenstein's 'absolutism'. Once this crucial admission is made, one can go even further than Stegmüller and wonder if any real difference remains between the two.

The problem cuts deeper than the question of the possibility of a metalanguage which Russell raised in his introduction to the *Tractatus*. For a believer in 'logic as language' will immediately apply to our metalanguage the same remarks he used to level at our alleged one and only home language. Ascent in a hierarchy of languages may help a logical semanticist who often finds himself unable to formulate his theories of an object language in this language itself. However, it does not solve Wittgenstein's problems, even though there eventually may be points of contact between the problems of self-applied languages and the Wittgensteinian questions.

6. WHAT HAPPENED TO THE PICTURE THEORY?

Wittgenstein's own progress beyond the *Tractatus* was in fact along entirely different lines. What they are is still not full appreciated, however. Often it is said, or implied, that one of the main changes was the giving up of the picture theory. However, this is scarcely compatible with Wittgenstein's approving appeal to a form of picture theory in the *Blue Book* (pp. 36–37). Even in the *Philosophical Investigations* pictures make a brief appearance (p. 11, note)[8] which is *prima facie* an approving one as far as the purely descriptive function of language is concerned. It the picture theory dissappears from the picture in Wittgenstein's later philosophy, it therefore is not because it was thrown by the board but because if faded away.

Further evidence for the compatibility of Wittgenstein's later philosophy with the picture idea is perhaps found in §290 of the *Philosophical Investigations*. There Wittgenstein warns us against thinking that 'word-pictures' (verbal descriptions of e.g. instruments) are like "such pictures as hang on our walls", which "are as it were idle". In other words, Wittgenstein is there saying, not that the picture idea is wrong, but that 'word-pictures' are not pictures by similarity.

7. LANGUAGE-GAMES AS THE LINK BETWEEN
LANGUAGE AND REALITY

What happened, then? One especially instructive way of looking at Wittgenstein's development beyond the *Tractatus* is to emphasize the role of his insight into the need of analyzing those very representational relationships between language and reality which were left unattended to both in the *Tractatus* and in logical semantics. They are not natural relations. They cannot be gathered just by observing the expressions of the language and by observing the world they speak of. A visitor from Mars – or a child learning to speak – can only gather them from the behavior of language-users. These representational relationships have as it were their mode of existence in certain rule-governed human activities. These activities are just what Wittgenstein calls *language-games*. They are what according to Wittgenstein creates and sustains the representative relationships between language and reality.

Perhaps the clearest single pronouncement of Wittgenstein's which shows the importance of the *use* of language as establishing the link between language and reality comes from *Philosophische Bemerkungen* (p. 85): "Unter Anwendung verstehe ich das, was die Lautverbindungen oder Striche überhaupt zu einer Sprache macht. In dem Sinn, in dem es die Anwendung ist, die den Stab mit Strichen zu einem *Maßstab* macht. Das *Anlegen* der Sprache an die Wirklichkeit".

The attribution to Wittgenstein of this idea of language-games as the mediators between language and reality (which I by and large accept) is one of the main theses of this paper. This thesis requires not only documentation but certain qualifications as well. Before trying to present them it may be in order to observe at once how this interpretation puts into a natural perspective several different features of Wittgenstein's later philosophy.

8. WHAT REALLY HAPPENED TO THE PICTURE THEORY

First, we can now understand what happened to the picture theory. It was not discarded, but it became increasingly irrelevant. Wittgenstein insisted very strongly that logic must not be based on anything more fundamental. (See *Notebooks* p. 4, cf. *Tractatus* 6.123 and *Notebooks* p. 2: "Logic must take care of itself".) Now in the *Tractatus* the picturing relations are in fact the rock bottom of our 'logic'. (Cf. Wittgenstein's expression 'Logik der Abbildung' in *Tractatus* 4.015.) Once the name–object relations are established, the only thing needed is to compare elementary sentences with reality. All that Wittgenstein finds himself called upon to say of the subject is: "Reality is compared with propositions" (4.05). In a particularly fascinating passage of the *Notebooks* we find Wittgenstein in the process of discovering his picture theory (entry 29 September, 1914; p. 7). His first comment on the picture idea is: "This must yield the nature of truth straight away (if I am not blind)". It did, indeed, yield straight away the *Tractatus* view of the truth of elementary sentences. The only reason why we do not find the same insistence on the rock bottom nature of the logic of picturing in the *Tractatus* is that Wittgenstein had meanwhile developed his theory of truth-functions, added another floor to the edifice of logic, and hence rendered the earlier formulation (in particular the use of the term 'logic') rather awkward. But they still apply to the 'logic' of elementary propositions in the *Tractatus*.

The language-game idea does not refute the theory of pictorial (isomorphic) relationships as establishing a link between elementary sentences and reality. (Otherwise it would refute logical semantics, too.) What it does to this theory is to deprive it of its primacy. Already in the *Tractatus*, the name–object relations were presupposed in all comparisons between language and reality. They were left unanalyzed, however, and their only function was to help to create such 'pictures' (elementary sentences) as could be compared with reality. (Hence Wittgenstein's insistence on Frege's principle that names have a function only in the context of sentences. (See *Tractatus* 3.3 and compare it with 3.2 and 3.263.) Their 'logic' could thus be taken to be part and parcel of the 'logic' of pictorial relations.

However, when the complex structure underlying these relationships is uncovered by the language-game idea, this 'logic' will not be the fundamental link between language and reality any longer. There will literally be "something more fundamental" than the pictorial relations. The logic of picturing will not be able to take care of itself. It will need the help of language-games. Nor can even elementary sentences be compared with reality without further ado. The comparisons will normally have to be mediated by the activities that instantiate the relevant language-games. Thus the picture idea retains its validity but loses its primacy.

9. WITTGENSTEIN VS. OSTENSION

Another feature of Wittgenstein's later philosophy which becomes understandable is his criticism of ostensive definitions. (Cf., e.g., *Philosophical Investigations* I, 26–32; pp. 12–16.) For we already saw that ostension is the likeliest competitor of language-games as a link between language and reality. If ostension were a viable link, a view entirely different from the language-game idea would result. All that we need to acquire our language would be a slightly more sophisticated version of the *Genesis* account (*Gen.* 2:19), for all that is needed would be to witness a sufficiently rich variety of samples of entities of different kinds, accompanied by appropriate gestures and names. (I have called this view, with a side glance to Russell, 'logical Adamism'.) To put the same point in another way, a semantically curious visitor from Mars would not have to observe long series of moves in complicated games. It would suffice for him to watch the relevant occasions of ostensive defining or ostensive conveyance of a name to another speaker.

Needless to say, Wittgenstein's criticism of ostension is convincing. Its details do not have to be recounted here. Its basic point could not be expressed more succinctly anyway: "... the meaning of a word is its use in the language. And the *meaning* of a name is sometimes explained by pointing to its *bearer*" (*Philosophical Investigations* I, 43, pp. 20–21). Elsewhere (*Phil. Inv.* I, 28) Wittgenstein points out in effect that an ostensive definition presupposes knowing the logical type of the concept to be defined. And *that* cannot be explained ostensively. Hence "an ostensive definition can be variously interpreted in *every* case".

Wittgenstein's criticism of ostension in the *Philosophical Investigations* is interesting also in a developmental perspective. It illustrates the truth of the point which was recently expressed by Anthony Kenny in the form of an answer to the question: How many Wittgensteins were there? As Kenny aptly put it, there may have been one Wittgenstein or several, but the right number is in any case not two. If one begins to split Wittgenstein's philosophy into different periods, the middle one has to be granted status of a separate stage ('the second Wittgenstein'). For the emphasis on ostension is found only in Wittgenstein's middle period, and hence the subsequent criticisms of ostension (for instance in the *Philosophical Investigations*) are directed primarily against his own middle period rather than the *Tractatus*.

However, one can turn the tables here. The distance between the *Tractatus* position view and the middle period emphasis on ostension is perhaps smaller than first meets the eye. Wittgenstein often discussed questions concerning the nature of semantical relationships by asking how these relationship can be learned. From this perspective, ostensive learning is only a genetic counterpart to the idea that the basic representative relationships between language and the world are simple two-term relations. Because of the simplicity these simple correlations of names and objects can (on the *Tractatus* view) be established by calling the learner's attention to the two terms of this correlation, in other words, can be taught and learned by ostension. Hence Wittgenstein's later criticism of ostension can be understood – as he himself does – as an indirect criticism of the *Tractatus*.

10. MISSING LANGUAGE-GAMES

Other main features of Wittgenstein's later philosophy likewise fall into a natural place in this framework. For instance, sometimes no language-game can apparently be found to provide a connection between a word and what it designates. In such cases, either we have an instance of language idling or else there is a language-game present in the everyday uses of the word which has not caught a philosopher's attention. Hence Wittgenstein's discussion of our terminology for sensations and his criticism of 'private languages'.

11. SOURCES OF CONFUSION

The importance of the idea of language-game in later Wittgenstein is obvious. However, my main thesis, that is, the role of language-games as the bridge between language and reality, is easily obscured by various misinterpretations and also by its being mixed up with other ideas of Wittgenstein's. Instead of trying to present direct evidence for the thesis, the best way of defending it may be to remove these potential sources of misunderstanding. For convenience I shall label them 'fallacies' even though some of them are not only genuinely Wittgensteinian doctrines but possibly even valid ones. They are fallacious only in so far as they obscure the important point I am here emphasizing. The 'fallacies' I will discuss may perhaps be labelled as follows.

(i)   The 'use as usage' fallacy;

(ii)   The 'use as usefulness' fallacy;

(iii)   The performatory fallacy;

(iv)   The 'mood and language game' fallacy;

(v)   The fallacy of utterances as moves in a game;

(vi)   The pragmatic fallacy;

(vii)   The holistic fallacy.

I shall discuss them briefly here one by one.

12. LANGUAGE-GAMES VS. USAGE

(i) Wittgenstein's idea that the *meaning* of an expression is its *use* is sometimes distorted to mean that meaning is somehow determined by *usage*, that is, by the *linguistic* use of the expression in question. Now this idea is certainly encouraged by some of Wittgenstein's own formulations, especially the ones in which he speaks of 'logical *grammar*' or of the use of a word '*in* a language'. It may also be valid and illuminating idea in some special cases. For instance, recently I have found myself arguing that the *whole* difference in meaning between the interesting English quantifier words 'every' and 'any' lies in something like a difference in the scope conventions governing them.[9] These scope conventions can in some reasonable sense be called 'grammatical'.

However, it is overwhelmingly clear that this sort of thing does not exhaust Wittgenstein's intentions. It is abundantly clear that by the use of an expression Wittgenstein also means its use in the context of, and as a tool for, certain nonlinguistic activities. Language-games are not games *in* language, they are typically games played *by means of* language. The first language-game of the *Philosophical Investigations* (I, 2, p. 3) ought to be enough to show this. Wittgenstein's central and deep idea is that words ultimately derive their meaning from their role in such complex activities. This is in keeping with my thesis.

13. THE IRRELEVANCE OF INTENTIONS

(ii) The opposite fallacy might indeed be more tempting. It consists in asking what conscious purpose might be served by uttering a sentence and by trying to use this purpose as a guide to the meaning of the sentence. For instance, in discussing Moore's defense of common sense, Norman Malcolm once asked what purpose could someone have in uttering 'I am a human being'.[10]

It is again clear that we are not far removed from genuinely Wittgensteinian ideas. I shall not try to argue that this kind of strategy is not to be found in Wittgenstein. In some sense it certainly is. However, this is likely to be a relatively superficial aspect of Wittgenstein's ideas. Uttering a sentence with a certain purpose normally presupposes already a connection between the utterance and the purpose. Purposeful uttering of sentences, we may perhaps say, already *is* a language-game, or at least presupposes one as its foundation. It does not clarify the meaning of the expressions Wittgenstein's builders use (see *Phil. Inv.* I, 2; p. 3) to ask for the *purpose* of the one who says 'Slab!' or 'Beam!' Is he perhaps intending to build a house for himself? Or is he just carrying out somebody else's orders? These questions are of course completely beside the point as clarifications of the use of the words (one-word sentences) 'Slab' and 'Beam' in the rudimentary language Wittgenstein envisages in any sense of 'use' which can be assimilated to meaning. Rather, the utterer can *intend* his utterance to help to have a house built only because of the already existing connection between the utterance and the other builder's bringing him something. In brief, the intention already presupposes the language-game and hence cannot serve to elucidate it.

Again we are pushed back to the realization that the primary function of language-games for Wittgenstein is to establish the connection between language and reality.

14. PERFORMATORY UTTERANCES OR UTTERABLE PERFORMANCES?

(iii) The same goes for theories of 'performatory utterances', 'speech acts', 'illocutionary forces', and suchlike. They are not incompatible with the language-game idea, but they presuppose it. In them, one concentrates on certain features of the meaning of an expression (such as illocutionary forces) or on certain aspects of the speech situation and its aftermath ('how to do things with words'). These are not self-explanatory, however. From the Wittgensteinian vantage point, they require as their explanation the description of more extensive 'games' (institutions) whose 'moves' are predominantly nonlinguistic (thinking, promising, etc.). These games are for Wittgenstein primary in relation to such phenomena as illocutionary forces and performatory utterances. To account for these 'forces' or 'things one can do with words' we have to resort to the description of the rule-governed activities in which the uttering of the expressions in question can play a role. Roderick Chisholm thus put his finger on the crucial spot when he asked pointedly in his review of J. L. Austin's *Philosophical Papers*[11] which is it that we are really dealing with here, performary utterances or utterable performances – performances, that is to say, which are not predominantly linguistic and which therefore are as it were only accidentally 'utterable'. As I have put the point elsewhere,[12] even if we did not use language (speech-acts) to thank or to promise, a mastery of the 'games' (institutions) of thanking or promising would be needed to understand the verbs 'to thank' and 'to promise'.

Nor does the speech-act idea exhaust the import of the language-game concept. Something very much like the claim that it does is nevertheless implied by the frequent assumption that those Wittgensteinian language-games that give an expression its meaning are always being played when we utter this expression, or that language-games are social games played always when we speak a language. Whatever confusion there may have been in Wittgenstein's own thinking concerning this point, such as interpretation of the language-game idea just is not viable. What is needed for the understanding of an expression is the mastery of a certain game in which the expression in question has a role. But from this it does not follow that one is playing this particular game every time one uses the expression to some purpose. I do not understand what 'to promise' means unless I have at least a rudimentary grasp of the custom of promising. But I am not playing the language-game of promising every time I utter this magic word. I am not playing it if I say 'John promised Sue to marry her' or 'I don't promise you anything'.

This kind of indirect meaning-giving function is not examined by Wittgenstein very much. Later, we shall find a paradigm case of how an utterance can derive its meaning from certain language-games without being a move in them.

15. LANGUAGE-GAMES NOT ONLY MODAL

(iv) What confuses the situation is that Wittgenstein is often including more in the idea of language-game than what is needed to bring language and reality somehow together. He is also emphasizing the nondescriptive purposes which language can serve and which serve to give some of its expressions their meanings. The famous list of different kinds of language-games in *Phil. Inv.* I, 23 (p. 11) illustrates this function of the language-game idea.

This has apparently encouraged some philosophers not only to emphasize the nondescriptive language-games but also to think that the descriptive function of sentences can be separated from their role in language-games. This line of interpretation is in conflict with my thesis in so far as it claims that the descriptive function is independent of language-games, for instance explicable by means of the picture idea. This interpretation may take the form of a theory of the modal character of language-games played by means of certain sentence-radicals.[13] These sentence-radicals (phrastic components of sentences)[14] can be understood independently of the games (according to this view), and they can occur in many different kinds of games. These games will in effect serve to define the meaning (use), not of sentence-radicals, but the modal (neustic) elements to be added to them in order to form different kinds of sentences (assertions, commands, questions, etc.). This connection between games and modality is why I proposed to dub this view the fallacy of mood and language-game.

There is one passage in the *Philosophical Investigations* which *prima facie* encourages this interpretation. "Imagine a picture representing a boxer in a particular stand. Now, this picture can be used to tell someone how he should stand, should hold himself; or how he should not hold himself; or how a particular man did stand in such-and-such place; and so on. One might (using the language of chemistry) call this picture a proposition-radical". (Page 11, added note; cf. *Notebooks*, pp. 27, 38.) However, a comparison with *Phil. Inv.* I, 22 (pp. 10–11) suggests that this quote does not represent Wittgenstein's own view at the time of the writing of the *Investigations*, but was inserted as material for criticism. Hence it has to be used with extreme caution.

Be this as it may, it is amply clear from other evidence that Wittgenstein did not think of language-games as being relevant only to the modal element in language, but related them also to the basic representative relationships between language and reality. The point is perhaps too obvious to need argument. Let us nevertheless recall what Wittgenstein says of his building game: "What is the relation between name and thing named? – Well, what *is* it? Look at [this] language-game . . . or at another one: there you see the sort of thing this relation consists in" (*Phil. Inv.* I, 37; p. 18).

The interpretation under criticism is thus so far off the mark that it is not interesting even as a rational reconstruction of Wittgenstein. In fact, the opposite question present a more urgent exegetical problem: Did Wittgenstein believe in any sort of separation of the descriptive and modal elements in language? Admitting that we need language-games to interpret both and not just the latter, can any theoretically interesting line of demarcation be drawn between the two? Is the purely descriptive function of language somehow primary? I shall not discuss these difficult questions here either as interpretational or as systematical problems.

16. LANGUAGE-GAMES OF SEEKING AND FINDING

Some light on the whole situation may nevertheless be thrown by new objects of comparison. I suspect that the prime reason why the fallacy of mood and language-game has come about at all is that in the *Philosophical Investigations* Wittgenstein never gives a clear-cut, fully worked-out example of a language-game, or a kind of language-game, which would unmistakebly serve to give an important logical concept of its main overall use (meaning). Concrete examples of language-games doing this for descriptive terms are likewise relative few and unconvincing. The reason for this again, I think, not that Wittgenstein did not believe in the existence of such language-games, but simply that he did not manage to formulate sufficiently important and convincing ones.

It is here that the language-games of seeking and finding which I have discussed elsewhere[15] and which I have argued to constitute the logical home of quantifiers are useful also for the purpose of evaluating Wittgenstein. They are the semantical games referred to in the title of this paper. They are made convincing by their success as tools for elucidating the semantics of both formal and natural languages.[16] They supply examples of language-games of precisely the sort we expect to find but do not in Wittgenstein. They illustrate the function of language-games as giving a meaning also to nonmodal words. They likewise show that the language-games which serve to give nonmodal words their meaning need not be inextricably involved with language-games of a practical sort, for these games are (to borrow a phrase used for a different purpose by Gilbert Ryle) "games of exploring the world" without any ulterior practical motive.

(v) My semantical games also help to discredit a subtler fallacy related to 'mood and language-game' fallacy. I shall label this the fallacy of utterances as moves in a game. According to this fallacy, the language-game which gives a word its meaning is always or at least typically such that each meaningful utterance of the word marks a move in this game.

The semantical games which give quantifiers their meaning provide counter-examples to this fallacy. As was said, an indicative sentence S is true if and only if the player I have called 'myself' has a winning strategy in the correlated game $G(S)$. Although a quantifier sentence S as it were received its meaning from these games (in that these language-games are the logical home of quantifiers), one is not playing such a game every time one utters a quantifier word. To borrow a phrase from Davidson, in uttering a sentence containing quantifiers, one is not representing oneself as making a move in one of the semantical games. Nor is one representing oneself as winning such a game if one utters an indicative sentence S in which a quantifier word occurs. In this jargon, one is merely representing oneself as having a winning strategy in $G(S)$. And to do this is not to make a move in $G(S)$. It is to make a claim about $G(S)$. The claim makes sense only to a hearer who understands $G(S)$, but it is not itself a part of $G(S)$.

This fallacy is closely related to the performatory fallacy, and can be illustrated by some of the same examples. If I say, 'Bill promised Sue to marry her', what I say can only be appreciated by a hearer who masters conceptually the institution ('language-game') of promising. However, I am not representing myself as making a move, much less a winning move in the language-game of promising. My utterance describes such a move, but is not itself one.

The general point which underlies these special observations is a corollary to the insight that it is only by means of language-games that we can link language with reality. It follows that language-games are needed already for the understanding of indicative sentences, for they of course require as much world-language connection as any other sentences. But equally obviously making indicative statements is a game different from most of these connection-establishing games. Hence an utterance of an indicative sentence is not in general itself a move in those language-games that serve to give a meaning to its several constituent words and thereby to the whole sentence.

17. PRAGMATICS NOT AN EMPIRICAL SCIENCE

(vi) Since the representative relationships between language and reality were left unanalyzed (as we saw) also in logical semantics, Wittgenstein's idea of language-games as establishing those relationships marks an at least potential advance over the customary logical semantics and not only over the picture theory. Unfortunately this relevance of Wittgenstein's later philosophy to contemporary logical and linguistic theorizing has been overlooked virtually completely until recently. One reason has been the unsystematic character of most of Wittgenstein's thought and of the thought of most of his followers. Another reason has been a misunderstanding concerning the kind of use of language exemplified by Wittgenstein's language-games. This misunderstanding is often embodied in definitions of the familiar trichotomy syntax–semantics–pragmatics.[17] Syntax is the study of language (and its logic) without reference to its representative function, while this function is studied in semantics. Pragmatics is defined as the study of the *use* of language. The misunderstanding I am speaking of consists in taking pragmatics, so defined, to be an empirical science, part of the psychology and sociology of the language-users. The fallaciousness of this idea is as surprising as is its prevalence. For of course we can study certain aspects of the rules governing the use of a language in abstraction from the idiosyncrasies of the people using it. This feat is no more remarkable, I am tempted to say, than studying syntax in isolation from the idiosyncrasies of handwriting and typeface. If pragmatics is a part of psychology and sociology of language, syntax ought to be by the same token a part of graphology.

Yet the idea of pragmatics as an empirical science was for a long time surprisingly prevalent. Applied to Wittgenstein's language-games, it of course had the effect of sweeping them right away into the 'pragmatical waste-basket'. Here the longtime aloofness of the two traditions, the Wittgensteinian and the model-theoretic one, was especially regrettable in my judgement. Even though in the last few years serious attempts have been made to develop explicit logical and philosophical pragmatics, little notice has been taken by most of the logicians working in this area. In this situation the language-games of seeking and finding mentioned above in Section 16 and the game-theoretic semantics studying them may be expected to be especially significant. They are at one and the same time designed as language-games in Wittgenstein's sense; they are games in the precise sense of mathematical game theory; they offer a handy tool for systematizing logical theory; and they give rise (in my judgement) to an extremely promising approach to the semantics of natural language. Here we seem to have an excellent chance of bringing Wittgensteinian and model-theoretic theoretizing as close as they were in the picture theory of the *Tractatus.*

18. THE INEFFABILITY OF WITTGENSTEIN'S LANGUAGE-GAMES

(vii) This analogy may turn out to be regrettably accurate also in a negative respect. We saw earlier that the Wittgenstein of the *Tractatus* did not admit of any court of semantical appeal higher than some one system of names for the different objects in the world. This system itself can only be shown, it cannot be discussed in the language nor consequently theorized about. We just cannot discuss, or even think of, alternatives to this representational system (Wittgenstein avers).

Later when the role of systems of names was for Wittgenstein taken over by language-games, an analogous question came up, and was given an analogous answer by Wittgenstein. One language-game may be more comprehensive than another, and can hence be used to elucidate the latter, not unlike Russell's earlier hierarchy-of-languages suggestion. But this cannot be done absolutely. Wittgenstein could have said *mutatis mutandis* of the rules of his language-games precisely the same he says in the *Tractatus* (3.263) of the meanings of primitive signs: The rules of language-games can be explained by means of elucidations. Elucidations are moves in games which obey these rules. So they can only be understood if the rules are already understood. For this reason, ultimately we cannot (according to Wittgenstein) disentangle ourselves from our complex of language-cum-associated-language-games. We cannot step outside it and as it were view it in abstraction from our own involvement in it. For this reason,

it cannot be analyzed theoretically, nor can there be a general theory
of language-games which would be applicable to our own in a large
scale. Our total language-game is the ultimate arbiter in semantics. In
the last analysis we can only say: "This language-game is being
played" (*Phil. Inv.* I, 654; p. 167). On, somewhat less cryptically,
"The common behavior of mankind is the system of reference by
means of which we interpret an unknown language" (I, 206, p. 82).
This point is also connected with Wittgenstein's insistence on a certain
communality in behavior as a precondition for understanding a foreign
tribe's tongue.

The analogous Wittgensteinian doctrine about the picture theory
was labelled by Stegmüller 'absolutism'. Here one is rather tempted to
speak of 'relativism'. In order to have a term which covers both, let us
speak in both cases of Wittgenstein's *holism.*

This holism is the partial analogue to the inexpressibility of reference in the *Tractatus.* The contrast between *saying* and *showing* in the
Tractatus is now taken over by a contrast between *saying* and *playing,*
I am tempted to say. (Perhaps the ultimate contrast should nevertheless be called *saying* versus *living.*)

Some philosophers have complained that the later Wittgenstein gave
up all attempts to explain how our language is related to the world. In
one respect, there can scarcely be a more unjustifiable criticism, for the
main function of Wittgensteinian language-games was to spell out
those very language-reality relations. What has probably prompted
such complaints is Wittgenstein's idea that we cannot have a real
theory about language-games, that is, a theory expressible in language.
But, then, the Wittgenstein of the *Tractatus* did not believe that there
can be such a theory that groundfloor connection between language
and reality which he called naming, either.

19. LANGUAGE-GAMES INTRODUCED BY
SPECIFYING THEIR RULES

I cannot but find Wittgenstein's holism rather dubious, at least as a
matter of concrete research strategy. In fact, Wittgenstein's own
language-game idea apparently provides us with a method of overcoming the limitations of our own language. In order to envisage a

language with a semantics different from our own, all we have to do is to specify a suitable language-game. Once its precise rules are given, and understood, we do not have to grasp any further mysteries.

Nor is this a merely speculative possibility. By defining suitable language-games of seeking and finding, we can in fact show by way of examples what it would mean in concrete practice to employ a nonclassical logic instead of the classical one. We can also ask whether the logic we use in our ordinary discourse is in certain specifiable respects a classical or nonclassical one, and we can discuss whether we prefer to employ a classical or a nonclassical language.[18] Can there be more convincing examples of transcending the limitations of one's own language and logic?

Such a concrete interpretation of applied nonclassical logic is indeed a greater feat than might first appear. For a long time, nonclassical logics were explained only syntactically, by specifying the logical axioms and the rules of inference of the nonclassical logics in question. This is a far cry from a satisfactory explanation of the semantics and pragmatics of nonclassical languages. At their best, they used to be explained by reference to extraneous epistemic concepts, intralinguistic dialogical games indeterminate truth-values due to empty singular terms, or other equally half-hearted devices, which do not really tell us much about what it would really mean to use an interesting nonclassical logic to gather, codify, or convey information about empirical (nonconceptual) matters. Nor are the particular nonclassical logics which we can easily interpret by means of my semantical games devoid of interest. The most important of them is the one resulting from Gödel's "extension of the finitistic viewpoint".[19]

Moreover, Wittgenstein himself shows how to avoid the difficulties that arise when the semantics of one language is explained in another one. Some of these difficulties are spelled out in Gödel's and Tarski's famous results which among other things show on certain assumptions that the semantics of a language can be specified only in a richer language.[20] Just because we are dealing with game rules, we do not have to write them down in any particular language. They can be conveyed to a learner, not by means of formal truth-definitions, but by example and by other forms of nonverbal inculcation. Thus the inscrutability assumption is much less plausible, if not outright self-defeating, as applied to language-games than it is when applied in the usual model theory.[21]

20. WITTGENSTEIN ON RULE-FOLLOWING

Wittgenstein has reasons for his holism, however. An opening for his arguments is created by the notion of a rule which has to be used in the explanation of language-games. When we introduce a fresh language-game, we have to specify its rules. Can this be done independently of antecedent familiarity with the corresponding games? Wittgenstein discusses at length the concepts of rule and of rule-following. We can now see how vitally important that discussion is for the overall structure of his philosophy.

Wittgenstein tries to show that the understanding of a rule is based on the understanding of a language-game, not *vice versa*. If so, it follows that we cannot introduce new language-games at will by presenting their rules, for these rules can only be grasped by mastering the underlying game. If he does not manage to show this, he will be open to the line criticism mentioned earlier.

Are Wittgenstein's arguments to this end really convincing? This is far too large a question to be discussed adequately here. The answer may also depend on the level on which it is discussed. On a working logician's level, we certainly have a vast supply of rules we can describe perfectly clearly even though we do not have slightest inclination to follow them and also all sorts of systematic theories of different kinds of rules (functions). (Good examples are recursive function theory and certain constructivistic theories of mathematics.) Nor does there seem to be any connection with our mastery of these different rules and their potential connection with our overall 'way of life'.

If Wittgenstein's doctrine is defensible, it is defensible only as a philosophical absolute. Even as such, I strongly suspect that it should rather be approached by way of the systematic logical problems which are connected with the concept of an arbitrary function (rule) rather than in the way Wittgenstein does. It seems to me that Wittgenstein's unfortunate way of arguing for his position led him to ultra-finitistic and ultra-constructivistic doctrines which do little justice to his own deeper ideas or to the actual work in logic and the foundations of mathematics. But even if this should be the case, we certainly ought not to dismiss Wittgenstein's discussion of rule-following too lightly.

21. WITTGENSTEIN VS. PLATONISM

We can in any case see who is Wittgenstein's most important antipode among contemporary logicians and philosophers of logic. He is Kurt

Gödel with his realistic (Platonistic) attitude to such concepts as function and rule.[22] It is also instructive to see what a central role is played in game-theoretical semantics by the notion of strategy (a sort of rule for playing some particular in sense of choosing one's moves). There we literally have to quantify over rules, and the modifications which result in nonclassical logic are restrictions on the strategy sets of the players of these games.[23] This is an indication of the depth of the realistic (Platonistic) attitude we have to adopt in game-theoretical semantics towards functions. Such an attitude is deeply antithetical to Wittgenstein's holism.

Even though Wittgenstein's thought thus appears as strongly original as ever, we have found a wealth of important connections between his problems and those of other contemporary philosophers and logicians.

Academy of Finland and Stanford University

NOTES

[1] G. H. von Wright, *Logik, filosofi och språk*, second ed., Aldus/Bonniers, Stockholm, 1965, p. 202.

[2] Wolfgang Stegmüller, 'Eine modelltheoretische Präzisierung der wittgensteinischen Bildtheorie', *Notre Dame Journal of Formal Logic* 7 (1966), pp. 181–195.

[3] Erik Stenius, *Wittgenstein's Tractatus: A Critical Exposition of Its Main Lines of Thought*, Blackwell, Oxford, 1960.

[4] G. H. von Wright's formulation in his *Logik, filosofi, och språk* (note 1 above).

[5] 'Quantification and the Picture Theory of Language', *The Monist* **55** (1969), pp. 204–230, reprinted in Hintikka, *Logic, Language-Games, and Information*, Clarendon Press, Oxford 1973, chapter 2. In this paper I also present some further evidence to show how closely related Wittgenstein's picture theory of language is to Russell's and Frege's logical formalism. This relationship is badly underestimated in most of the literature on the *Tractatus*.

[6] Cf. Alfred Tarski, *Logic, Semantics, Metamathematics*, Clarendon Press, Oxford, 1957.

[7] Jean van Heijenoort. 'Logic as Calculus and Logic as Language', *Synthese* **17** (1967), pp. 324–330. Cf. also Jean van Heijenoort, editor, *From Frege of Gödel*, Harvard University Press, Cambridge, Mass., 1967.

[8] On the difficulty of interpreting this passage, see section 15 below.

[9] See my paper 'Quantifiers in Natural Languages' in the present volume.

[10] Norman Malcolm, 'George Edward Moore' in *Knowledge and Certainty*, Prentice-Hall, Englewood Gliffs, N.J., 1963. see esp. p. 171.

[11] *Mind* **73** (1964), pp. 1–26; see here p. 9.

[12] 'Language-Games for Quantifiers', *American Philosophical Quarterly, Monograph Series*, vol. 2 (1968), pp. 46–72. (Blackwell's, Oxford.) Reprinted as chapter 3 of *Logic, Language-Games, and Information* (note 5 above).

[13] Cf. here Erik Stenius, 'Mood and Language-Game', *Synthese* **17** (1967), pp. 254–274.

[14] The terms 'phrastic' and 'neustic' are Richard Hare's. See his book, *The Language of Morals*, Clarendon Press, Oxford, 1952.

[15] For the first time in 'Language-Games for Quantifiers' (note 12 above), later in several of the other essays collected in *Logic, Language-Games, and Information*.

[16] See the various essays in the present volume.

[17] See e.g., C. Cherry, *On Human Communication*, second ed., Cambridge, Massachusetts, 1966; Arthur Pap, *Semantics and Necessary Truth*, New Haven, 1958.

[18] Cf. the last few paragraphs of 'Quantifiers vs. Quantification Theory' (note 16 above). The nonclassical interpretation I have in mind here is obtained simply by restricting the strategy sets of the players to recursive ones. This is a most natural restriction, perhaps even an inevitable one, from the vantage point of game-theoretical semantics. For how could anyone actually play a game in accordance with a nonrecursive strategy?

[19] See Kurt Gödel, 'Über eine bisher noch nicht benutzte Erweiterung des finiten Standpunktes', in *Logica: Studia Paul Bernays Dedicata*, Editions du Griffon, Neuchatel, 1959, pp. 76–83.

[20] Cf. Andrzej Mostowski, *Thirty Years of Foundational Studies*, (Acta Philosophica Fennica, vol. 17) Blackwell, Oxford, 1965, Chapter 3.

[21] Cf. my rejoinder to Timothy Potts, entitled 'Back to Frege?', pp. 260–270 in Stefan Körner (ed.), *Philosophy of Logic*, Basil Blackwell, Oxford, 1976.

[22] Cf. 'Russell's Mathematical Logic', in *The Philosophy of Bertrand Russell*, ed. by P. A. Schilpp, (The Library of Living Philosophers, vol. 5), Evanston, Ill., 1946.

[23] Cf. Note 18 above.

APPENDIX

The claim that Wittgenstein's objects (*Gegenstände*) in the *Tractatus* have all the logical type of an individual has been put forward by Irving Copi. Some reasons against it were already given in the bulk of my paper above. These reasons are easily multiplied.

Copi relies in effect on Wittgenstein's silence in the *Tractatus* where Wittgenstein never says in so many words that properties and relations are *bona fide* objects. This argument from silence does not carry much conviction, however, because the silence is easily accounted for. Wittgenstein's reluctance in the *Tractatus* to commit himself more explicitly to the role of properties and relations as *Gegenstände* in his extended sense of the word is merely an unfortunate corollary to his more general idea that "it would be completely arbitrary to give any specific form" characteristic of elementary sentences. (*Tractatus* 5.554.) For instance, we cannot legitimately ask whether "I need to sign for a 27-termed relating in order to signify something" (5.5541). What Wittgenstein is trying to bring home to us is that "we have some concept of elementary propositions quite apart from their particular logical forms" (5.555). It is this avoidance of the "particular logical forms" of elementary sentences which drove Wittgenstein to his misleading silence about the role of properties and relations in elementary sentences. (Cf. also Wittgenstein's 'Some Remarks on Logical Form', p. 163.)

If there is any *prima facie* evidence in the *Tractatus* for this Copi view, it is not the frankly metaphorical 2.03 but rather 5.526: "We can describe the world completely by mean of fully generalized propositions, i.e., without first correlating any name with a particular object". For it might seem the generality Wittgenstein speaks of here can only be generality with respect to individuals. Now if such generality is to be *complete* generality, as Wittgenstein presupposes, all his 'objects' must be individuals. However, the tables can be turned completely on the view under criticism. For conversely if complete generality *apud* Wittgenstein requires also generality with respect to properties and relations, they must be included in Wittgenstein's formulation which speaks of the correlation between names and *objects* (cf. above). Now in the very next proposition 5.5261 Wittgenstein in so many words speaks of quantification (generality) with respect to predicates, too. *Both* individual variables *and* predicate variables are said to "stand in signifying relations to the world". Hence taken together 5.526 and 5.5261 offer strong evidence to the effect that Wittgenstein's *Gegenstände* include (in the *Tractatus*) also properties and relations.

In 3.333, too, Wittgenstein countenances quantification with respect to predicates.

Further arguments against the Copi view are easily forthcoming. The most general one is the following. If all objects are individuals in the *Tractatus*, how can they form a state of affair? Such a state of affairs is a configuration of objects (2.0231). But being in such a configuration is a relation, not an additional individual. Where does this new relation come from? Copi denies that it can itself be an object. Wittgenstein emphatically rules out its being a logical relation. What remains? What remains are relations which are not logical but not ordinary descriptive relations, either, for the latter are ruled out by the alleged status of *Gegenstände* as individuals. The only reasonable candidates are spatial and temporal relations, and on the Copi view this is what the "links in a chain" expression in 2.03 must presumably amount to. However, these relations are ruled out by collateral evidence. In 'Some Remarks on Logical Form' Wittgenstein explicitly mentions as a step beyond the

Tractatus the view that spatio-temporal co-ordinates could enter into atomic propositions (pp. 165–167). Hence this cannot be the *Tractatus* view, which pretty much reduces the Copi interpretation *ad absurdum* by elimination.

JAAKKO HINTIKKA

QUANTIFIERS IN LOGIC AND
QUANTIFIERS IN NATURAL LANGUAGES

1. THE PROBLEM OF NATURAL-LANGUAGE QUANTIFIERS

Once upon a time most logicians believed that their quantifiers were obtained from the quantifiers of natural languages by abstraction or regimentation. (In this paper I shall restrict my attention to logicians' existential and universal quantifiers plus their counterparts in natural languages.) This belief was expressed in so many words time and again in textbooks and treatises of logic and in discussions of the philosophical problems of logic.[1] When the syntax and semantics of natural languages began to be taken seriously by contemporary linguists, it nevertheless soon became clear that there are all sorts of subtle problems about natural-language quantifiers which have no counterpart in logicians' so-called quantification theory. Nor were most of these problems touched, let alone solved, by ordinary-language philosophers.

This has by no means destroyed the belief that there is a close connection between the two kinds of quantifiers. However, in the last few years the traffic seems to have been moving mostly in the opposite direction. Generative semanticists like George Lakoff have proposed using formulas of formalized quantification theory not only as semantical representations of natural-language sentences but as the basis of their syntactical generation as well.[2] If this view were correct, a poor logician like myself would have no business poking his nose into the topic indicated by the title of my paper. In that eventuality, the relationship between the quantifiers of formal logic and the quantifiers occurring in the surface structures of natural languages would be determined by the syntactical transformations which are supposed to take us from the former to the latter. And the investigation of these transformations, prominently including the restraints they are subject to, is on this view a major task of linguists, not of logicians.

It is easy enough to pick holes in this Lakovian programme. Some indirect indications of its insufficiency will be given in this paper. It is

27

E. Saarinen (ed.), Game-Theoretical Semantics, 27–47. All Rights Reserved.

considerably harder, however, to propose a more satisfactory overall view of ordinary-language quantifiers. In another paper, I have in fact shown that first-order logic (lower predicate calculus), logicians' 'quantification theory', is insufficient as a semantical representation of English quantifier sentences.[3] In this sense, the received view of quantification theory as a regimentation of natural-language quantifiers is demonstrably false. Where, then, can we turn to for a better theory of natural-language quantification?

There exists one particularly natural way of looking at quantifiers which has never been put to use entirely satisfactorily before. It is to consider quantifiers as *singular terms*. It is plain even to a linguistically naked eye that quantifier phrases like 'some man', 'every woman', 'a girl', and even phrases like 'some boy who loves every girl' behave in many respects in the same way as terms denoting or referring to particular individuals. They can sometimes be used to report the same events as proper names. We can apply to them many such notions (e.g. the notion of coreference) as are primarily applicable to noun phrases which denote particular individuals. In fact, linguists have recently indulged in such applications to no end (and, according to some commentators, to no good purpose). Quantifier phrases can occur in most of the same grammatical constructions as noun phrases denoting particular individuals. One can also apply to certain quantifier phrases the same distinction between the referential and the attributive reading which Keith Donnellan and others have claimed to exist in the case of certain denoting phrases of a different sort, viz. definite descriptions.[4] (I can say 'I saw a pretty girl walking by' and refer either to some particular female in perambulatory motion, or just make an impersonal existential statement concerning what I witnessed.) In view of such obvious facts, it seems eminently desirable to try to treat quantifier phrases both syntactically and semantically in the same way as singular terms.

This is what the late Richard Montague tried to do in his treatment of quantification in English.[5] The idea was not original with him, however. Bertrand Russell had already in *The Principles of Mathematics* tried to treat quantifiers as denoting phrases.[6] Russell's theory is quite interesting in several respects, one of which is that he tries to describe the semantical differences between different quantifiers in English, such as 'all', 'every', 'any', 'some', and 'a'. (As Russell was aware, the differences between those quantifiers is a feature of natural languages which has no obvious counterpart in formal logic. Hence it is an interesting task to account for those differences in precise logical terms.) However, I shall not discuss Russell's theory here. In spite of its interest, this theory is not strong enough to capture many crucial facts about English quantifiers.

Montague's idea was to treat quantifier phrases on a par with singular denoting terms not only syntactically but also semantically. The usual explanation as to how he did this is to say that he reversed the usual interpretation of predication. Instead of reading 'John is clever' as expressing the membership of John in the class of clever people, he took it to express the membership of cleverness in the class of John's attributes. Then a quantifier sentence like 'every Welshman is clever' can be understood in the same way, as expressing the membership of cleverness in the class of attributes all Welshmen have. Thus the semantical entity correlated with 'every X' will be the class of attributes all X have, and analogously for 'some X'.

I cannot try to evaluate this treatment here.[7] A few remarks on Montague's theory are nevertheless in order. Obviously it cannot make great claims to pragmatic or psycholinguistic plausibility. What is more important, in the real development of Montague's semantics little use is made of the correlation of 'every X' with the class of attributes all X have. For instance, the semantic interpretation of 'every boy loves some girl' or 'the lover of every woman' will have to be obtained by a more complicated process into which 'every boy', 'some girl', and 'every woman' do not enter just through the semantical entities correlated by Montague with them. Thus Montague does not really treat of quantifier phrases like singular terms except in a Pickwickian sense.

Neither Russell's nor Montague's treatment of quantifiers is thus fully satisfactory. Although quantifier phrases are very much like ordinary singular terms there are important differences between the two, differences which perhaps explain why earlier treatments of quantifiers as singular terms have not been successful. Intuitively, one is tempted to say that quantifier phrases denote, but that they just do not denote any particular constant individuals in the way ordinary singular terms do. This is among other things reflected by the fact that quantifier phrases do not even obey the usual laws of identity, in the sense that different occurrences of the same unambiguous quantifier phrase have to be treated differently in one's semantics. What I mean is illustrated, e.g., by the fact that in the sentence

(1)   John saw a warbler yesterday, and Bill saw a warbler, too

the two occurrences of 'a warbler' cannot be understood as referring to the same bird.

The same puzzling phenomenon appears in connection with reflexivization and pronominalization. For instance,

(2)   every man hates every man

says something quite different from

(3)   every man hates himself.

Likewise,

(4)   Some boy believes that Mary loves him

differs in meaning from

(5)   Some boy believes that Mary loves some boy.

These examples are of particular interest in that they show that the most natural rules for reflexivization and pronominalization fail to preserve meaning in the presence of quantifiers. (Cf. Barbara Hall Partee's essay on the alleged meaning preservation of transformations, pp. 9–10.)[8] The same goes for equi-NP deletion, as shown by the non-synonymy of the following sentences.

(6)   Every contestant expected to come in first.

(7)   Every contestant expected every contestant to come in first.

This marks another contrast between quantifiers and singular terms, for the following sentences are synonymous.

(8)   John expected to come first.

(9)   John expected John to come first.

The same can be said of the most straightforward rules of relative clause formation, as illustrated by the fact that (10)–(11) are non-synonymous while (12)–(13) are synonymous.

(10)   Every Democrat who voted for a Republican was sorry.

(11)   Every Democrat voted for a Republican, and every Democrat was sorry.

(12)   John who voted for a Republican was sorry.

(13)   John voted for a Republican, and John was sorry.

As emphasized by Barbara Hall Partee, these phenomena present problems of more than casual interest for our ideas of linguistic semantics at large.

For any satisfactory semantics of quantifiers, these phenomena pose interesting problems. How can quantifier phrases be in some respect so like singular terms and in other respects so unlike? Traditionally, such discrepancies between quantifiers and singular terms are often dealt with by saying that quantifier phrases stand for 'arbitrarily chosen' or 'random' individuals. However, it is scarcely satisfactory just to say this. Who is supposed to make this arbitrary choice? When? Why has the 'arbitrary choice' to be repeated for each occurrence of one and the same phrase? Moreover, not all these 'arbitrary choices' are comparable. What is the difference between the choices associated with 'some man' and 'every man', respectively? Traditionally, this line of thought has also led to difficult philosophical problems about *ekthesis*, 'general triangles', etc.[9]

The 'arbitrary choice' suggestion is an attempt to keep what is good in the analogy between quantifier phrases and singular terms and reject what is bad. What is bad is (among other things) that the analogy easily commits us to treating quantifier phrases as if they referred to constant individuals. What we have seen is enough to show that the 'arbitrary choice' idea does not avoid this difficulty and that it gives rise to others as well.

Formal logic offers no instant solutions, either. There are important discrepancies between logicians' quantifiers and quantifiers in English. One of them is the presence of several existential and several universal quantifiers in English which nevertheless exhibit subtle differences in their behaviour, for instance 'every' and 'any'. As we saw, Russell already tried to spell out some of the differences between the members of such pairs of quantifiers, but without much success. It is also clear that the 'arbitrary choice' idea does not help us here at all.

Another peculiarity of English quantifiers is the use of the indefinite article 'a', which obviously is in its typical employment an existential quantifier, in an apparently different function in the construction '– is a(n) . . .' to express predication.

The main obstacle to applications of quantification theory to the study of natural-language quantifiers is nevertheless the difficulty of giving explicit translation on transformation rules to connect the two. Generative semanticists' claims notwithstanding, nothing remotely like a satisfactory set of such rules can be found in the literature.

Such discrepancies between the quantifiers of logic and the quantifiers of natural language require explanations. The task of supplying them is neither a problem in formal logic alone nor yet a merely linguistic problem, it seems to me.

2. GAME-THEORETICAL SEMANTICS AS A SOLUTION

The game-theoretical semantics of quantifiers I have recently developed can be viewed as a way of overcoming the problems of these very kinds.[10] In the game-theoretical approach, the semantical properties of a quantified sentence S are determined by a two-person game $G(S)$ correlated with it.[11] In any actual round of this game $G(S)$ (the usual game-theoretical term for my 'round' is of course 'play') the quantifier phrases of S are replaced by proper names of individuals chosen one by one by the one or the other of the two players. We might almost say that in such a round of the game, quantifier phrases are interpreted as standing for these chosen individuals. This explains the partial similarity of the semantical behaviour of quantifier phrases with that of singular terms, indeed with that of proper names. Quantifier phrases do indeed function precisely like proper names, although not absolutely but only in each particular play of a semantical game. Since these games determine the semantics of quantifiers (in my approach), small wonder that quantifiers are easily and naturally thought of as a curious kind of singular denoting phrases not unlike proper names.

My approach nevertheless does not commit us to treating quantifier phrases semantically as if they stood for constant individuals, for the semantical properties of S can be characterized in terms of the overall characteristics of the correlated game $G(S)$, for instance in terms of the existence of different kinds of strategies for the two players. Such characteristics of G(S) are independent of what happens during any particular play of G(S), while the quantifier phrases of S are related to specific individuals only in some particular round (play) of that abstract game. For this reason, quantifier phrases cannot absolutely speaking be understood as picking out definite individuals, however 'arbitrarily selected'.

Some of the precise rules for the games G(S) will be given below in Section 4. There the reader will also find detailed examples of what may happen in these games.

We can nevertheless see already at this stage of discussion, that is to say without knowing anything more of my semantical games, how the game-theoretical idea allows us to overcome several of the difficulties mentioned earlier.

The choices of individuals for which quantifier phrases stand which are made in the different rounds (plays) of the abstract game G(S) are indeed arbitrary in the sense that they are not determined by the general properties of the game G(S). (Of course they are *not* arbitrary if each of the two players is actually trying to win.) Since the choices of individuals whose names are to replace quantifier phrases are made one by one, different occurrences of the same phrase may be replaced by different proper names, thus explaining the failure of the usual identity principles and also the failure of the usual pronominalization and reflexivization rules. (The same goes *mutatis mutandis* for equi-NP deletion and relativization.) Choices associated with different kinds of quantifiers (existential vs. universal) can be separated from each other in that they are made by different players.

This suffices to explain some of the puzzles mentioned above. The others, for instance the precise semantical difference between 'every' and 'any' and the relation of the copulative phrase '– is a(n) –' to the uses of the indefinite article as a quantifier, can also be explained in the game-theoretical semantics, but only after it has been developed somewhat farther.

The general interest of these semantical games is shown by the fact that they are tantamount to the language-games of seeking and finding whose philosophical implications are studied in my book, *Logic, Language-Games, and Information* (Clarendon Press, Oxford, 1973). Their connection with the Wittgensteinian idea of language-game is obvious. Now we are beginning to see that they are also directly relevant to the semantics of natural languages.

3. GAME-THEORETICAL SEMANTICS FOR
FORMAL LANGUAGES

Game-theoretical semantics can nevertheless be applied also to formal quantificational (usually called 'first-order') languages and not only to natural languages. Indeed, they are probably appreciated more easily by first seeing how they can be set up for formal first-order languages.

These languages are of course to be thought of as *interpreted* languages, which means that we are given a domain of individuals D on which all the predicates of the language in question – call it L – are interpreted. (We also assume that the only free singular terms of L are proper names of members of D.) This in turn means that each atomic sentence built up of the predicates of L and of the names of the members of D has a definite truth-value, true of false. Since the crucial concept of all semantics is that of truth (on an interpretation), what our task is is essentially to extend the notion of truth from these atomic sentences to all the sentences of L, no matter how many quantifiers and sentential connectives they contain.

The games $G(S)$ that serve to accomplish these may be thought of as idealized processes of verification in which one of the two players, called 'Myself' or 'I', is trying to show that S is true, and his opponent, who is called 'Nature' and who is perhaps best thought of as a Cartesian *malin genie*, is trying to show that it is false. My purpose in the game $G(S)$ is in fact to produce a true atomic sentence. If that happens, I have won and Nature has lost. If the game ends with a false atomic sentence, I have lost and Nature has won. Since the verification of an existential statement requires the searching for and the finding of a suitable individual, these verificational games are essentially games of seeking and (hopefully) finding.

At each stage of the game, a sentence S' is being considered. (This S' will belong to L or to a slight extension of L obtained by adding to it a finite number of names of members of D.) From the basic idea on which the game $G(S)$ is based we can at once gather what the game rules must be. What happens at a certain stage of the game is determined by the form of S'. We can distinguish the following cases depending on what this form is.

(G.E) If S' is $(Ex)F(x)$, I choose a member of D, give it a proper name (if it does not have one already that can be used), say 'b'. The game is then continued with respect to $F(b)$.

(G.U) If S' is $(x)F(x)$, the same happens except that Nature chooses b.

(G.∨) If S' is $(F \vee G)$, I choose F or G, and the game is continued with respect to it.

(G.∧) If S' is $(F \wedge G)$, the same happens except that Nature makes the choice.

(G.∼) If S' is $\sim F$, the roles of the two players (as defined by the rules (G.E), (G.U), (G.∨), (G.∧), (G.∼), and (G.A)) are reversed and the game is continued with respect of F.

Although (G.∼) is formally unobjectionable, it is a somewhat unintuitive rule. For many purposes, it is more natural to replace this rule with a number of others dealing with the different kinds of negated sentences, or else to introduce obligatory rewriting rules which serve to push negationsigns deeper into our sentences. An example of the former kind of rule is the following.

(G.∼∨) If S' is $\sim(F \vee G)$, Nature chooses $\sim F$ or $\sim G$, and the game is continued with respect to it.

An example of the latter kind of rule is the following.

(N.E) If S' is of the form $\sim(Ex)F(x)$, it is to be rewritten as $(x) \sim F(x)$.

In a finite number of moves an atomic sentence A is reached containing solely predicates of L and names of members of D. Winning and losing are defined with respect to it.

(G.A) If A is true, I have won and Nature lost; if A is false, vice versa.

If each type of negated sentence is dealt with by means of a special rule instead of (G.∼), we also need the following rule.

(G.∼A) If the game has reached the sentence $\sim A$, A atomic, I have won and Nature has lost if A is false; if A is true, vice versa.

The crucial point here is of course to be able to define truth independently of what happens in any particular play of these semantical games. The intuitive idea is of course that if S is true, it can be verified. This idea is captured as follows:

(G.T) S is true if and only if I have a winning strategy in $G(S)$.

Here 'strategy' is to be understood in the precise sense of the mathematical theory of games.[12] The idea it embodies is nevertheless so natural that it can be understood without any familiarity of game-theoretical results or conceptualizations. A player has a winning strategy if he can choose his moves in such a way that, no matter what his opponent does, he in the end wins the game. (Of course his choices will in general depend on the opponent's earlier moves.)

It is most easily seen that if S is indeed true in the traditional sense, I can make my moves so that all the sentences S produced during the game are (apart from switches of roles induced by (G.~)) true in the traditional sense. Since this includes the outcome, I have a winning strategy. Conversely, if I have a winning strategy in $G(S)$, it is easily seen that S is true in the traditional sense. Hence what (G.T) defines is indeed equivalent with the traditional concept of truth.

In spite of this equivalence, game-theoretical semantics has interesting uses already as applied to formal languages. One of them is discussed elsewhere at some length. In showing the equivalence of what (G.T) defines with the traditional concept of truth, we have to assume that our semantical games are games with perfect information. (Intuitively speaking, either player always comes to know and never forgets what has happened at the earlier moves.) If this requirement is given up, we obtain semantics not only for ordinary quantificational logic but for the logic of what are known as finite partially ordered quantifiers as well. Although their theory is much more powerful than that of ordinary (linearly ordered) quantifiers, I have argued that it has to be resorted to in order to interpret English quantifiers. This line of thought will not be developed here, however. It is taken up in my paper, 'Quantifiers vs. Quantification Theory', *Linguistic Inquiry* **5** (1974), pp. 153–77 reprinted in the present volume, pp. 49–79.

4. GAME-THEORETICAL SEMANTICS FOR A
FRAGMENT OF ENGLISH

Game-theoretical semantics can be extended easily from formal languages to a fragment of English. The two players can be kept intact and so can the given domain D. (The fact that many English quantifiers range over some specifiable subclass of D, for instance the class consisting of persons, does not cause any difficulties in principle.) In English, there are admittedly no variables which could be replaced by the names of individuals. However, what we can do is to substitute such a name for the whole quantifier phrase. This phrase will then have to be taken care of somehow, in the sense that it imposes certain conditions on the individual chosen.

This motivates, for instance, the following special case of the game rule for the English quantifier 'some'.

(G.some) If the game has reached a sentence of the form

X – some Y who Z – W

then I may choose an individual and give it a name if it does not have one already, say 'b'. The game is then continued with respect to

X – b – W, b is a(n)Y, and b Z.

It is being assumed here that the 'who' in 'who Z' occupies the subject position and that the main verb in Z is singular. The context X – W is so far allowed to be an arbitrary one, except that 'who Z' must of course be an entire relative clause. Certain restrictions on the context will later be imposed by the principles that govern the order of application of our rules. They will not be studied in this paper, however.

For instance, when applied to the sentence

Some man who loves her promised Jane to marry her

(G.some) yields a sentence of the form

John promised Jane to marry her, John is a man, and John loves her.

Here we have X = empty, W = 'promised Jane to marry her', Y = 'man', and Z = 'loves her'. The special case of (G.some) just formulated is readily extended to all the other special cases in the singular and also to plural uses of 'some'. No general formulation is attempted in this paper, however. Its uses with mass terms are in any case disregarded here.

The only real difference between the special case of (G.some) just formulated and others is that in general we have (so to speak) to watch out to see where the wh-phrase comes from. For instance, in addition to the sentence of the form

$$X - \text{some } Y \text{ who } Z - W$$

we may want to consider also sentences of the form

$$X - \text{some } Y \text{ where } Z_1 - Z_2 - W$$

where

$$\text{where } Z_1 - Z_2$$

can be thought of as being formed from

$$Z_1 - \text{in } d - Z_2.$$

Applied to them, (G.some) yields, through my choice of a place b, the sentence

$$X - b - W, \ b \text{ is a(n)Y, and } Z_1 - \text{in } b - Z_2.$$

For instance, when applied to

Some town where Bill lived as a child is located in Holland

(G.some) might yield

Dubbeldam is located in Holland, Dubbeldam is a town, and Bill lived in Dubbeldam as a child.

Here $X = $ empty, $Y = $ 'town', $Z_1 - Z_2 = $ 'Bill lived – as a child'. and $W = $ 'is located in Holland'.

The other special cases of (G.some) are equally straightforward to formulate.

An analogous game rule for the English indefinite article will be called (G.an). Generic uses of the indefinite article may perhaps be excused from its purview. It might seem that another exception is needed here for the situation in which 'is a' expresses predication. However, no distinction is needed between the uses of 'is a' to express predication from the ones in which the 'is' expresses identity and 'a' is an existential quantifier. For instance, the sentence

John is a boy

can be parsed either as

> Boy (John)   (predication)

or as

> John = a boy   (identity).

In the latter case (G.an) applies, yielding a sentence of the form.

> John is Jack, and Jack is a boy

where again the 'a' may be given either interpretation without any embarrassment. Thus we need a special rule for the so-called predicative uses of 'is a' only as a stopping rule, to avoid regress. We can for instance stipulate that if the only rule that applies to

> a is a(n) X

(where X does not contain relative pronouns and where 'a' is a proper name) is (G.an), then here 'is a(n)' is treated as expressing predication.

This observation solves one of the problems posed earlier in Section 1 of this paper. It also goes a long way towards explaining how a natural language like English can use the same word 'is' both for identity and (in the combination 'is a') for predication without any ambiguity resulting therefrom.

A special case of the game rule for the English universal quantifier 'every' can likewise be formulated in my approach.

(G.every)   If the game has reached the sentence

> X – every Y who Z – W

then Nature may choose an individual and give it a proper name (if it did not have one already), say 'b'. The game is continued with respect to

> X – b – W if b is a(n)Y and (if) b Z.

It is assumed here that the 'who' in 'who Z' occupies the subject position. The second (bracketed) 'if' is clearly an idiomatic peculiarity which merely serves to make the punctuation of the sentence clear.

This rule is easily extended to other uses of 'every', and parallel rules for 'any' and 'each' (we shall call them (G.any) and (G.each)) are easily formulated. The rule (G.any) can also be extended to plural uses of 'any'. For 'no', occurring (say) in

$$X - no \ Y \ who \ Z - W,$$

a similar rule (G.no) can be formulated. Nature chooses now an individual, call it 'b', and the game is then continued with respect to

$$neg + (X - b - W) \text{ if } b \text{ is a(n)}Y \text{ and if } b \ Z$$

Here 'neg+' indicates the process of forming a (sentential) negation in English.

Our game rules for quantifiers are also readily extended so as to cover the 'absolute' quantifiers 'anyone', 'somebody', 'everyone', 'anybody', 'nobody', 'anything', 'everything', 'something', etc.

The extension of our earlier game rules for formalized sentential connectives to English connectives is straightforward. The earlier rules are easily transformed into rules for the English particles 'or', 'and', and 'not'.

The resulting game rules will be called, unsurprisingly, (G.or), (G.and) and (G.not). In addition to them, a special rule (G.if) for 'if' will be considered.

A few remarks are in order concerning these rules.

(i) The applicability of (G.and), (G.or) and (G.if) will be ruled out whenever there are pronominal cross-references between conjuncts, disjuncts, or the consequent and the antecedent, respectively. However, the rules do apply when the pronominal reference is to a proper name. Then (G.and), (G.or) and (G.if) must also have the effect of replacing the pronoun by this proper name (depronominalization).

(ii) The rule (G.if) applies (with the restriction just indicated) to sentences of the form

$$X \text{ if } Y$$

allowing me to choose either X or not + Y. The latter alternative means that suitable rules for forming sentence negations must be built into my game rules.

A further development of the game-theoretical semantics would show how such rules can be motivated and formulated. In this paper, we shall just take them for granted.

(iii) Phrasal 'and' must of course be excused from the scope of (G.and). For a sentential 'and' binding terms, we must have some rule of the following kind.

(G.conj) $a_1, a_2, \ldots,$ and a_k

X may be replaced by

$a_1 X', a_2 X', \ldots,$ and $a_k X'$

where X' is like X except that the main verb is in the singular. (In X it must of course be in the plural.)

It is assumed here that the conjunction in the original sentence occupies the subject position. The rule (G.conj) is easily extended to cover the other cases as well.

(iv) Instead of (G.not), it is much more natural to introduce a number of obligatory rewriting rules which serve to define the operation 'not+' of forming a sentential negation in English. What these rules will look like in the case of quantified English sentences can nevertheless be determined only by means of a further inquiry which will not be attempted here.

(v) Pronominalization will in fact occasion certain qualifications to our game rules for quantifiers, for the reshuffling of X, Y, Z, and W which takes place in these expressions can sometimes disturb pronominalization relations between them. In this paper, I shall nevertheless disregard this problem.

If we follow the crude first-approximation rules for English pronominalization which have been proposed by Langacker and others,[13] we can safeguard rules like (G.some) simply by requiring the pronominalization relations between Z and W to be reversed when (G.some) is applied. However, this does not yet amount to a satisfactory analysis of the situation. Such an analysis will not be attempted in this paper.

It is easy to extend game-theoretical semantics to epistemic, modal, and doxastic concepts, at least in some of their typical uses. The basic idea is a straightforward combination of possible-worlds semantics for these notions with our game-theoretical principles.[14] What is being defined then is the truth of a sentence S in a world ω. Since we are dealing with an interpreted language, a set of possible worlds (with the appropriate alternativeness relations defined on it) must be given. At each stage of the extended games, the two players are considering a sentence S' and a world ω', beginning with S and ω. The game rules for epistemic and other modal notions (in the wide sense of the term) can then be formulated as rules for stepping from one world to another. The following rules are cases in point. Others are easily formulated by anyone familiar with possible-worlds semantics.

(G.knows) If the game has reached a world ω' and a sentence of the form

$\qquad$ *a* knows that X,

where '*a*' is a proper name, Nature may choose an epistemic *a*-alternative ω'' to ω'. The game is continued with respect to ω'' and X', where X' results from X by replacing all pronominal cross-references to the initial '*a*' by '*a*'.

(G.knows not) If the game has reached the world ω' and the sentence

$\qquad$ *a* does not know that X

where '*a*' is a proper name, then I may choose an epistemic *a*-alternative ω'' to ω'. The game is continued with respect to ω'' and neg+X', where X' is like X except for the replacement of pronouns referring back to '*a*' by '*a*'.

Sentences of the form

$\qquad$ *a* does not know that X

will of course have to be exempted from the scope of (G.not), if it is being used.

Only the part of English which can be dealt with by means of these rules is what will be considered in this paper. This fragment of English could be delineated more clearly, but such an enterprise is not necessary for most of my observations. In any case, several of the results to be obtained I believe to obtain more widely than this fragment.

Selected examples may perhaps help to illustrate the game rules. It is for instance of interest to see how the validity of well-known logical principles of logic appears in the game-theoretical semantics. As an example, consider the self-contradictory sentence

(14)   John loves himself, but nobody loves him.

Here (G.and) applies ('but' here being but a stylistic variant of 'and'), enabling Nature to choose between

(15)   John loves himself

or

(16)   nobody loves John.

If the former is false, Nature can defeat me by choosing it. If it is true, Nature can choose the latter and have the opportunity of choosing an individual whose name is to be substituted for 'nobody' in (16) (in accordance with the absolute version of (G.no)). Among others, Nature can choose John, this choice resulting in the sentence

(17)   neg + (John loves John)

which obviously is synonymous with

(18)   John doesn't love himself.

But this is false by hypothesis, making Nature the winner and myself the loser.

In neither case can I defeat Nature, which means that I cannot have a winning strategy in any domain. In virtue of (G.T), this means that (14) is logically false.

As another example illustrating also the epistemic rules, consider the sentence

(19)   Some clever boy who loves every pretty girl believes that he
         is lucky.

Although we have not yet discussed the order in which the game rules are to be applied, in this particular case the order is easy to guess. An application of (G.some) to (19) yields a sentence of the form

(20)   John believes that he is lucky, John is a clever boy, and
         John loves every pretty girl.

Here Nature may choose any conjunct in virtue of (G.and), for there is no pronominalization between them. If Nature chooses the last one, then Nature's further application of (G.every) may yield

(21)   John loves Mary if Mary is a pretty girl.

If Nature chooses the first conjunct in (20), she may then select, in virtue of a doxastic analogue (G.believes) to (G.knows), a doxastic alternative ω' (with respect to John) to the world ω in which we are evaluating (20). The game then continues with respect to ω' and the sentence 'John is lucky'.

Such examples also illustrate a useful moral about our semantical games. First, from the set of all different sequences of applications of our game rules to a given English sentence S (in the fragment we are studying), we can obtain a representation of S in a suitable logical notation. How this is to be done is indicated here only informally. For instance, when (G.some) is applied to a sentence, the new name may be replaced by a variable bound to an existential quantifier which is invented immediately after the quantifiers which have likewise resulted from earlier applications of (G.some), (G.every), (G.an), (G.any) or (G.each). The bound variable is subsequently treated in the same way as the substituting name.

We shall use this translatability only unsystematically in this paper without studying its precise limits.

The solutions to our initial puzzles which were described earlier in informal terms in Section 2 above, can now be confirmed by means of our precise game-theoretical rules. For instance,

(2)   Every man hates every man

is correlated with a game in which Nature has two different choices by (G.every) which typically result in a sentence of the form

(21)   Tom hates Harry if Tom is a man and Harry is a man.

This means that the original sentence is of the form

(22) $(x) [x$ is a man $\supset (y)(y$ is a man $\supset x$ hates $y)]$.

In contrast, in

(3)   every man hates himself

Nature has only one choice by (G.every). It results in a sentence of the form

(23)   Tom hates himself if Tom is a man.

The correlated logical structure is clearly

(24) $(x)(x$ is a man $\supset x$ hates $x)$

Likewise one can deal with such sentences as

(4)   some boy believes that Mary loves him

and

(5)   some boy believes that Mary loves some boy

as well as with

(1)   John saw a warbler yesterday, and Bill saw a warbler, too.

as distinguished from

(25)   John saw a warbler yesterday, and Bill saw it, too.

For instance, when applied respectively to (4) and (5) (G.some) yields entirely different results, in the former case for instance (if John is my choice)

(26)   John believes that Mary loves him, and John is a boy

and in the latter

(27)   John believes that Mary loves some boy, and John is a boy.

Applied to the first conjuncts of (26)–(27) (G.believes) takes us to a doxastic alternative of the original world and yields respectively

(28)   Mary loves John

and

(29)   Mary loves some boy,

thus illustrating the difference in meaning between (4) and (5).

In a similar way, the failure of equi-NP deletion and of relative clause formation (in their customary formulations) to preserve meaning becomes easily explainable in our game-theoretical semantics.

This still leaves unexplained the differences between such apparently similar natural-language quantifiers as 'every', 'each', and 'any'. The precise differences between their respective meanings can nevertheless be explained in the game-theoretical approach, it seems to me. This requires a closer examination of the consequences of an important difference between the games associated with the sentences of a formalized first-order language and those associated with English quantifier sentences. In the former, the order in which the several game rules are brought to bear is completely determined by the form of the sentence which has been reached in the game. In the latter, the order has so far been left largely arbitrary. As was pointed out earlier, for instance in (G.some) $X - W$ can be any context in which the quantifier phrase 'some Y who Z' may occur.

Far from being a defect of our game-theoretical semantics for a fragment of English, this freedom is a tremendous asset. It allows certain important types of further conceptualization. It serves to explain certain ambiguities in English. What is even more important, it allows us to develop an account of the ways in which other ambiguities are avoided in English. For they must of course be avoided (if they are avoided) by imposing further restraints on the order in which the game rules are applied (over and above such trivial restraints as the *ceteris paribus* preference of the left-to-right order). It seems to me that a full account of the semantics of such special quantifiers as 'any' can be given in this way, that is to say, given in terms of the order of application of (G.any) with respect to other game rules.

Furthermore, the same ordering principles show how the negation-forming operation must function in English, thus giving us important insights into the semantics of English quantifiers as distinguished from logicians' formalized quantifiers and at the same time filling a gap in my presentation so far. For reasons of space, these ordering principles cannot be examined here, however.

In general, it seems to me that the game-theoretical approach gives us a powerful and flexible theory of the semantics of quantifiers in natural languages. A comparison between the games associated with formalized first-order sentences and those associated with English sentences will then show the difference between logicians' quantifiers and natural-language quantifiers.

Academy of Finland and Stanford University

NOTES

[1] Cf., e.g., W. V. Quine, *Mathematical Logic* (Harvard University Press, Cambridge, Mass., 1955), pp. 1–8; P. F. Strawson, *Introduction to Logical Theory* (Methuen, London, 1952), *passim*; G. H. von Wright, *Logical Studies* (Routledge and Kegan Paul, London, 1957), pp. 1–6.

[2] Cf. George Lakoff, 'Linguistics and Natural Logic', in Donald Davidson and Gilbert Harman, eds., *Semantics of Natural Language* (D. Reidel, Dordrecht, 1972), pp. 545–665; 'On Generative Semantics', in D. D. Steinberg and L. A. Jakobovits, eds., *Semantics: An Interdisciplinary Reader* (Cambridge University Press, Cambridge, 1971), pp. 232–95.

[3] 'Quantifiers vs. Quantification Theory', *Linguistic Inquiry* 5 (1974), pp. 153–77. Reprinted in the present volume pp. 49–79.

[4] Cf. Keith Donnellan, 'Reference and Definite Descriptions', in D. D. Steinberg and J. A. Jakobovits (Note 2 above), pp. 100–14 (appeared originally in *Philosophical Review* 75 (1966), pp. 281–304); 'Proper Names and Identifying Descriptions', in Davidson and Harman (note 2 above), pp. 356–79.

[5] See the papers collected in Richmond Thomason, ed., *Formal Philosophy: Selected Essays of Richard Montague* (Yale University Press, New Haven, 1974), especially 'The

Proper Treatment of Quantifiers in Ordinary English', first printed in Jaakko Hintikka, Julius M. E. Moravcsik, and Patrick Suppes, eds., *Approaches to Natural Language* (D. Reidel, Dordrecht, 1973), pp. 221–42.

[6] Bertrand Russell, *The Principles of Mathematics* (George Allen and Unwin, London, 1903), pp. 56–65.

[7] For a few critical remarks, see my paper 'On the Proper Treatment of Quantifiers in Montague Semantics', in Sören Stenlund, ed., *Logical Theory and Semantic Analysis* (D. Reidel, Dordrecht, 1974), pp. 45–60.

[8] Barbara Hall Partee, 'On the Requirement that Transformations Preserve Meaning', in C. J. Fillmore and D. T. Langendoen, eds., *Studies in Linguistic Semantics* (Holt, Rinehart and Winston, New York, 1971), pp. 1–21. I am relying heavily on this important paper in several respects.

[9] Cf. Jaakko Hintikka, *Logic, Language-Games, and Information* (Clarendon Press, Oxford, 1973), pp. 109–11.

[10] It was nevertheless foreshadowed by the informal uses several logicians made of game-theoretical ideas for their own purposes. Cf., e.g., A. Ehrenfeucht, 'An Application of Games to the Completeness Problem for Formalized Theories', *Fundamenta Mathematicae* **49** (1960), pp. 129–41; Leon Henkin, 'Some Remarks on Infinitely Long Formulas', in *Infinitistic Methods* (Pergamon Press and Państwowe Wydawnictwo Naukowe, Oxford and Warszawa, 1961), pp. 167–83. (This latter paper was accidentally omitted from the bibliography of my 'Quantifiers vs. Quantification Theory', see Note 3 above.)

[11] For the basic ideas of game theory, see for instance R. D. Luce and H. Raiffa, *Games and Decisions* (John Wiley, New York, 1957).

[12] Cf. Luce and Raiffa, op. cit., p. 43.

[13] See Ronald W. Langacker, 'On Pronominalization and the Chain of Command', in David A. Reibel and Sanford A. Schane, eds., *Modern Studies in English: Readings in Transformational Grammar* (Prentice-Hall, Englewood Cliffs, New Jersey, 1969), pp. 160–86; John Robert Ross, 'On the Cyclic Nature of English Pronominalization', in *To Honor Roman Jakobson* (Mouton, The Hague, 1967), vol. III, pp. 1669–82; reprinted in Reibel and Schane, pp. 187–200.

[14] For possible-worlds semantics, see for instance my book, *Models for Modalities* (D. Reidel, Dordrecht, 1969).

QUANTIFIERS VS. QUANTIFICATION THEORY

The syntax and semantics of quantifiers is of crucial significance in current linguistic theorizing for more than one reason. The last statement of his grammatical theories by the late Richard Montague (1973) is modestly entitled 'The Proper Treatment of Quantification in Ordinary English'. In the authoritative statement of his 'Generative Semantics', George Lakoff (1971, especially pp. 238–267) uses as his first and foremost testing-ground the grammar of certain English quantifiers. In particular, they serve to illustrate, and show need of, his use of global constraints governing the derivation of English sentences. Evidence from the behavior of quantifiers (including numerical expressions[1]) has likewise played a major role in recent discussions of such vital problems as the alleged meaning-preservation of transformations,[2] co-reference,[3] the role of surface structure in semantical interpretation,[4] and so on.

In all these problems, the behavior of natural-language quantifiers is one of the main issues. Quantifiers have nevertheless entered the *Methodenstreit* of contemporary linguistics in another major way, too. (These two groups of problems are of course interrelated.) This is the idea that the structures studied in the so-called quantification theory of symbolic logic – otherwise known as first-order logic, (lower) predicate calculus, or elementary logic – can serve and suffice[5] as semantical representations of English sentences. Views of this general type have been proposed by McCawley (1971)[6] and Lakoff (1972)[7] (among others). A related theory of 'Deep Structure as Logical Form' has been put forward and defended by G. Harman (1972). Theories of this general type may be compared with the traditional idea that quantification theory can be viewed as an abstraction from the behavior of natural-language quantifiers (as a representation of their 'logical form'[8]) and with W. V. Quine's (1960) view of quantification theory as the 'canonical notation' of all scientific discourse. It is not clear precisely how much is gained or lost linguistically according to these last two types of views in the transition from ordinary discourse to the language of first-order logic, but obviously some sufficiently loose 'congruence of meaning'[9] is being assumed.

E. Saarinen (ed.), Game-Theoretical Semantics, 49–79. All Rights Reserved.

It will be shown in this paper that these views are seriously inadequate as they are usually formulated. (I shall not examine whether, and if so how, they can perhaps be repaired.) For this purpose, I will first sketch a more satisfactory semantical theory of certain English quantifiers, viz. those corresponding most closely to logicians' familiar universal quantifier and existential quantifier.[10] I shall indicate the range of problems that can apparently be dealt with by means of this theory, and go on to show how it naturally leads us to consider certain English quantifier expressions whose semantical representations go beyond first-order logic and hence are beyond the purview of the competing theories just mentioned. Indeed, we obtain in this way interesting specific results concerning the logical strength of quantification in English as compared with various kinds of logical systems. Finally, these results will prompt certain conjectures concerning the methodological asymmetry of syntax and semantics.

The semantics of English quantifiers I am about to sketch is formulated in terms borrowed from the mathematical theory of games, and might be referred to as game-theoretical semantics. (For the basic ideas of game theory, see e.g. Luce and Raiffa, 1957 or Davis, 1970.) The concepts involved are so straightforward, however, that they can be appreciated without any knowledge of game theory. This theory is a direct analogue to a corresponding game-theoretical semantics for formal (but interpreted) first-order languages, sketched in Hintikka (1968a) and (1973, Ch. 3).[11] Its leading ideas can perhaps be best seen from this somewhat simpler case, which I will therefore first outline briefly.

Let's assume we are dealing with a language with a finite list of predicates (properties and relations). That we are dealing with an interpreted language means that some (non-empty) domain D of entities, logicians' 'individuals', has been given and that all our predicates have been interpreted on D. This interpretation means that the extentions of our predicates on D are specified. This specification in turn implies that each atomic sentence, i.e., sentence in which one of our n-place predicates is said to apply to an n-tuple (sequence) of individuals, has a determinate truth-value, true or false. In a sense, what we are doing here is to extend this definition of truth to all the other (first-order) sentences. They are obtained from atomic sentences by propositional operations, for instance, by applying '$\sim$' (negation), '$\wedge$' (conjunction), and '$\vee$' (disjunction),[12] and/or by applying existential or universal generalization, i.e., by replacing a number of occurrences of an individual name by an individual variable (taken from the list 'x', 'y',...) bound to an existential quantifier '$(\exists x)$', '$(\exists y)$',... or to a universal one '(x)', '(y)',..., prefaced to the sentence.[13]

The essential restriction here is that only individuals (members of D) are being quantified over. Intuitively speaking, 'every' thus means 'every *individual*' and 'some' means 'some *individual*'. Examples are offered by such expressions as (1), (29), and (33) below. (Note that all quantifiers in them range over individuals.) In contrast, as soon as we are binding predicates, predicates of predicates, or any other variables of a higher type,[14] for instance quantifying over all the subsets of D, or over all the subsets of some other (infinite) set, we are no longer dealing with first-order logic, and the situation is entirely different. Examples of second-order sentences are offered by (2), (32), and (34) below, with their quantifiers ranging over functions.

Just how different the situation is from first-order logic as soon as we let in any second-order quantifiers is shown by an earlier observation of mine (Hintikka, 1955, pp. 100–101) to the effect that even one single universal quantifier with a monadic (one-place) second-order predicate variable in a sense gives us all the power not only of second-order logic but of all of the other (finite) types as well. For any sentence S of the theory of (finite) types, a sentence $r(S)$ involving only one such quantifier (over and above constant predicates and first-order quantifiers) can be found effectively which is valid (logically true) if and only if S is.

The game-theoretical semantics serves to extend the concept of truth from atomic sentences to all others. This is accomplished by correlating with each sentence S of our interpreted first-order language a two-person game $G(S)$. It may be thought of as zero-sum game (i.e., what one player wins, the other one loses). The players will be called Myself and Nature. The former is trying to produce eventually a true atomic sentence, the latter a false one. At each stage of the game, a sentence S' of our language (or of a mild extension of it) is being considered, beginning with S. The next move depends on the form of S' according to the following rules.

(G.E) If S' is of the form $(\exists x)S''$, the next move is made by Myself: I go to the domain D, choose an individual, give it a name[15] (if it did not have one already), say 'b'. This name is plugged in for 'x' in S'', the result being called '$S''(b/x)$'. The game is continued with respect to $S''(b/x)$.

(G.U) If S' is of the form $(x)S''$, the same thing happens except that the individual is chosen by Nature.

(G.∨) If S' is of the form $(S'' \vee S''')$, I choose one of the disjuncts S'' and S''' and the game is continued with respect to it.

(G.∧) Likewise if S' is of the form $(S'' \wedge S''')$, except that the choice is made by Nature.

(G.~) If S' is of the form $\sim S''$, the roles of the two players (as defined by the game rules and by the rule for winning soon to be defined) are switched and the game continued with respect to S''.

In a finite number of moves, the game yields an atomic sentence. Winning and losing is defined by reference to it, as already indicated. If the outcome is a true sentence, the winner is Myself and the loser Nature; if false, *vice versa*.

In Hintikka (1973, p. 101), I have shown how the personification of Nature apparently involved in the games just explained can be dispensed with. Hence it does not cause any problems here.

The concept of truth for non-atomic sentences can now be defined. A sentence S is true (in the model constituted by D and by the interpretation of our predicates on D) if and only if I have a winning strategy in the correlated game $G(S)$, that is to say, if I can always choose my moves (depending on what has already happened in the game) so that I will win no matter what Nature does.

Clearly this definition of truth is equivalent to the usual formulations presented in the semantics (model theory) of first-order logic.[16] For if S is true, I can choose my moves so that all the sentences obtained during the game are true (and *mutatis mutandis* when a switch of roles takes place), and *vice versa*. In spite of this equivalence, even in pure first-order logic the game-theoretical approach may offer philosophical, linguistic, and heuristic advantages. For one thing, the games I have defined are the only explicitly defined games so called both in the sense of game theory and in the sense of Wittgenstein's language-games (see Wittgenstein, 1953, 1958; Hintikka, 1968b) to be found in the literature. (They are language-games because they are rule-governed activities serving to connect our language to the reality it speaks of.) Clearly the activities involved in my moves governed by (G.E) are not random choices of individuals from D, if I want to win the game. Rather, a realistically understood move normally involves careful searching for a suitable individual. Thus the semantical games connected with quantifiers are essentially games of searching and finding. In Hintikka (1973), Chapters 5 and 10, some of their philosophical implications are discussed.

Moreover, game-theoretical semantics is much more readily extended beyond first-order logic in certain directions than the usual one, as will be seen later in this paper.

My game-theoretical semantics can be further illustrated by noting that it naturally yields a translation of first-order logic into a fragment of second-order logic. For if the truth of S means the existence of a winning strategy of a certain sort, I can express this by a suitable explicit sentence asserting the existence of such strategy. Now my strategies are (for the quantificational moves in first-order logic) defined by those functions that tell me, as a function of Nature's earlier moves, which individual to choose when I make a move. Such functions are known to logicians as Skolem functions.[17]

The translation we obtain will simply assert the existence of suitable Skolem functions. For instance, I have a winning strategy in the game correlated with the sentence

(1) $(x)(\exists y)(z)(\exists w)F(x, y, z, w)$

(where F may contain propositional connectives but does not contain any quantifiers) if and only if the following second-order sentence is true.

(2) $(\exists f)(\exists g)(x)(z)F(x, f(x), z, g(x, z))$

Here the function f tells me how to choose the individual serving as the value of 'y' in (1), and g how to choose the individual whose name is to be substituted for 'w' in (1). The second-order sentence (2) as a whole says that there are functions (strategies) of this sort such that no matter what x and z are chosen by Nature, the outcome is true (i.e., such as to admit a winning strategy in the rest of the game). Hence (2) can serve as a translation (explication) of (1).

In general, the use of Skolem functions can usually be interpreted in terms of my game-theoretical semantics, and conversely this semantics can be viewed as a kind of systematization and generalization of the notion of Skolem function. The main ideas of this kind of game-theoretical treatment of first-order logic have already for some time belonged to the bag of tricks of all sophisticated logicians, although they have not always been formulated systematically. What has not been pointed out before is that this game-theoretical semantics can be extended to natural languages like English. There are of course no variables in English for which names can be substituted, but the basic idea is that a whole quantifier phrase beginning with 'some', 'every', 'any', etc. can be substituted for in the same way as a formal variable.[18] As a special case of the resulting game rules, consider an English sentence of the form[19]

(3)   X – some Y who Z – W

(where Y and Z are singular). A game rule (G.some) will now tell me to choose a member of D and give it a proper name (say 'b') just as in the case of formal first-order languages. The proper name is then plugged in for the quantifier phrase. Of course extra clauses are now needed to take care of the quantifier phrase itself. Thus the resulting sentence will be

(4)   X – b – W, b is a(n)Y, and b Z.

In fact, a general formulation of the rule (G.some) can be gathered from this example. I will not attempt an explicit formulation here, however. The syntactical part of the rule would involve (among other things) directions for taking a relative clause and a noun phrase of a suitable sort and for constructing from them a sentence from which the relative clause could be formed by the usual rules of relative clause formation in English. In brief, it would involve writing down explicit rules for relative clause formation in the reverse direction (i.e., in the form of rules unpacking a relative clause rather than forming one).[20] It is not my purpose to discuss the details of such rules here, and hence I will let a special case of game rules like (G.some) do duty for the whole rule. (Let me nevertheless point out the obvious fact that the explicit rule would of course restrict the above form of (3) to the cases in which 'who' in 'who Z' occupies the subject position.)

Likewise, the rule (G.every) would take us (via Nature's choice of a member d of the given domain D) from

(5)   X – every Y who X – W

to

(6)   X – d – W if d is a(n)Y and if d Z.

Likewise, (6) could be the result of applying (G.any) to the sentence

(7)   X – any Y who Z – W.

Since (4) and (6) are grammatical English sentences (if (3), (5), and (7) are), the game can be continued with respect to them.

A rule (G.an) similar to (G.some) may be formulated for the indefinite article,[21] and (G.some) extended to plural uses of 'some'. Numerous further extensions are also possible.

In applying rules for propositional connectives – we shall call them (G.and), (G.or), (G.if), and (G.not) – certain new aspects of the situation (as compared with formal first-order languages) have to be heeded.

(i) The fully explicit form of the rule for negation (G.not) and of the rule for conditionals (G.if) would have to involve directions for forming sentence negation in English, operating in a direction opposite to the usual one (i.e., as rules for going from a negated sentence to the corresponding unnegated one).[22] Again, I will not discuss the details here.

(ii) Sentential game rules for conjunctions, disjunctions, conditional sentences, etc. are normally inapplicable in the presence of pronominal cross-references between conjuncts, disjuncts, etc. They may be applied, however, in the special case in which the pronominalizing NP is a proper name. Then they must be combined with suitable directions for depronominalization.

(iii) It is easily seen that (ii) is not enough to handle all pronominalization problems. In some cases, changes of pronominalization may have to be built into my game rules. This problem will not be examined here, however. One particularly natural course might be to marry my game rules to the treatment of pronominalization which was tentatively proposed by R. Grandy and presented in G. Harman (1973). However, I am not ready yet to commit myself to one particular treatment.

The scope of game-theoretical semantics can be expanded by wedding it to a suitable possible-worlds semantics for epistemic and modal notions. (For the basic ideas of the latter, see Hintikka, 1969.) The extension is very simple. Instead of just one 'world' (D with predicates interpreted on it), we must consider a set of them with suitable alternativeness relations defined on it. At each stage we are considering a world ω and a sentence. The progress of a game is seen from an example. When we have reached 'John doesn't know that X' and a world ω_1, I may select an epistemic alternative ω_2 to ω_1 with respect to John, and the game is continued with respect to neg+X and ω_2.[23] When we have reached 'John knows that X', Nature may select a similar world ω_3 and the game is continued with respect to X and ω_3. (In each case, pronominal cross-references to 'John' in X must also be replaced by this name.)

Examples of what might happen (syntactically speaking) in specific games may help to understand my game-theoretical semantics. The following sentences may come about in the course of a play of the game correlated with the first one.

(8)   Some gentleman who loves every blonde married a brunette.

My move by (G.some) may yield here

(9)   John married a brunette, John is a gentleman, and John loves every blonde.

Nature's move by (G.and) may yield

(10)   John loves every blonde.

Nature's move by (G.every) may here yield

(11)   John loves Susan if Susan is a blonde.

Here (G.if) gives me (as you can guess from the truth-table of 'if') a further choice between

(12)   John loves Susan

and

(13)   Susan isn't a blonde.

Another example shows that crossing pronominalization does not cause any special problems here. A round of a game might take us successively to the following sentences.

(14)   Some boy who was fooling her kissed a girl who loved him.

(15)   John kissed a girl who loved him, John is a boy, and John was fooling her.

Here Nature cannot choose by (G.and) the last conjunct because it involves a pronominal reference to 'a girl' in the first one. (See point (ii) a few paragraphs back.) However, (G.an) can be applied to 'a girl', yielding something with the same form as the following.

(16)   John kissed Sally, John is a boy, John was fooling her, Sally is a girl, and Sally loved him.

Here we have utilized a simple convention of **omitting** 'and' between conjuncts other than the last two. In (16), pronominal references are all to proper names, and (G.and) therefore applies. The rest of the game is not of interest here.

Although work is still in progress on the game-theoretical semantics of English quantifiers, it is already clear that it gives us a method of dealing with several different kinds of problems. Some of these applications are immediately suggested by our general game-theoretical point of view.

As a by-product of my semantics, we obtain an approach to the syntax of English quantifier sentences.[24] The game rules involved as their syntactical part a kind of decomposition of sentences with quantifiers into simpler sentences. Turning around this syntactic part of our semantical rules, we can obtain a set of rules for building up English quantified sentences. (For the purposes of explicit syntax the proper names that will be introduced in the course of a round of a game may of course be replaced by variables serving as dummy names.) They differ from the types of rules fashionable in transformational grammar in these days, which are therefore useless for my purposes. One reason for this difference is that much recent syntax has been motivated by a desire to uphold the meaning-preservation of transformations. (Cf. Partee, 1971.) Our 'transformations' do not preserve meaning because they serve to introduce quantifiers. The example (14)–(16) above suggests that this need not be a drawback syntactically. Certain problems at least become easier to handle.

A major difference as compared with formal first-order languages is that our game rules so far formulated can often be applied in more than one order. This seems to me an advantage rather than a disadvantage. Natural languages clearly employ further principles (ordering principles) to govern this order, which in more familiar logical terminology often amounts to governing the scope of various logical operations.[25]

Such principles can easily be formulated (just because the order of game rules is otherwise left open), and they will (among other things) take over in game-theoretical semantics the role of Lakoff's global constraints for quantifiers. (See Lakoff, 1971, and cf. my comments on Jackendoff below.)

It turns out, however, that Lakoff's constraints are not quite adequate in their present form. For one thing, our principles can be applied more flexibly so as to explain certain multiple ambiguities (e.g., 'three hunters shot five tigers and four panthers') apparently in a more satisfying manner than Lakoff's account. (Cf. Partee, 1970, 1971, and Lakoff, 1970.) Moreover, Lakoff's constraints are not universally applicable. On the contrary, we have here an interesting possibility of characterizing the meaning of certain special quantifiers, especially that of 'any', by specifying the peculiar ordering principles the game rule (G.any) governing it obeys vis-à-vis other rules. I conjecture that a full characterization of the meaning of 'any' can be given in this way[26] and that we can in this way also explain its distribution in the sense that it can apparently occur only where the ordering principles create a semantical difference between 'any' and the 'normal' quantifiers 'every' and 'all'.[27] For instance, (G.any) has as a rule the right of way with respect to (G.if) and (G.not), whereas (G.every) does not.

Besides calling our attention to the possible underdeterminacy of meaning due to the vagaries of order of the game rules, the game-theoretical viewpoint suggests that another kind of underdeterminacy may be expected. It is the uncertainty as to which player is to make a move associated with a phrase in English. It turns out that this is in fact the case with the interrogative morpheme 'wh-'. An essential part of its semantical behavior, besides its operating as a kind of quantifier, is that either player may make a move connected with it. Thus our game rules may take us from a sentence like

(17)   John knows who is coming.

either (through a move by Myself) to[28]

(18)   John knows that Bill is coming, and Bill is coming.

or (through a move by Nature) to[29]

(19)   John knows that Arthur is coming, if Arthur is coming.

These two correspond to the two readings of (17) which may be represented respectively as

(20) $(\exists x)$[John knows that x is coming $\wedge x$ is coming]

and as

(21) (x)[x is coming $\supset$ John knows that x is coming].

This kind of underdeterminacy of meaning (due to an underdeterminacy of the player in question) is indispensable for understanding the semantics of English questions,[30] especially of multiple wh-questions.[31]

Other applications of game-theoretical semantics seem to be in the offing. For instance, the so-called problems of coreference do not cause any special difficulties in our approach.[32]

The most striking observations suggested by our game-theoretical semantics are nevertheless the most straightforward ones. Our whole discussion so far has been based on an assumption which is *a priori* completely arbitrary. We have been assuming that our semantical games are games with perfect information. (For this notion, cf. e.g. Luce and Raiffa, 1957, p. 43.) Intuitively speaking, this means that a player always comes to know, and never forgets, what has happened at earlier stages of the game. This is not always the case in real games, for a player may be prevented by the very rules of game from knowing what has happened at certain earlier moves. Then he has to make a move without knowing the outcome of these earlier moves, which of course affects the strategies he has available. These strategies are now defined by functions independent of the unknown earlier moves.

This possibility of the failure of perfect information affects in principle already the games connected with formal first-order languages. However, if the requirement of perfect information is relaxed, we are not dealing with first-order logic any longer, but with an essentially different kind of logic.

What it is can be seen from the idea that in first-order logic a quantifier which lies in the scope of another depends on the latter in the sense that the move connected with the former depends on that associated with the latter. This is reflected by the dependence of Skolem functions on all earlier universally quantified variables. (See, for instance, how the function g in (2) has both x and z as its arguments.) Hence linearly ordered quantifiers cannot express the failure of perfect information. Instead, we must allow branching quantifiers and, more generally, partially ordered (but still finite) quantifiers.[33] We must thus resort to sentences that may look like the following examples.

$$(22) \quad \left.\begin{array}{l}(\exists x) \\ (y)\end{array}\right\} F(x, y)$$

$$(23) \quad \left.\begin{array}{l}(x)(\exists y) \\ (z)(\exists w)\end{array}\right\} F(x, y, z, w)$$

$$(24) \quad (\exists x)\left\{\begin{array}{l}(y)(\exists u) \\ (z)(\exists w)\end{array}\right\} F(x, y, u, w)$$

$$(25) \quad \begin{array}{l}(x_1)(x_2)\ldots(x_i)(\exists y_1)(\exists y_2)\ldots(\exists y_j) \\ (z_1)(z_2)\ldots(z_i)(\exists w_1)(\exists w_2)\ldots(\exists w_j)\}F(x_1, x_2, \ldots, x_i, \\ \qquad\qquad y_1, y_2, \ldots, y_j, z_1, z_2, \ldots, z_i, w_1, w_2, \ldots, w_j)\end{array}$$

$$(26) \quad \left.\begin{array}{l}(x_1)(y_1)(\exists z_1) \\ (x_2)(y_2)(\exists z_2) \\ \quad \cdots \\ (x_k)(y_k)(\exists z_k)\end{array}\right\} F(x_1, x_2, \ldots, x_k, y_1, y_2, \ldots, y_k, z_1, z_2, \ldots, z_k)$$

Here F is assumed not to contain any quantifiers any longer, although it may of course contain sentential connectives. Notice that only the left-to-right order of quantifiers counts in (22)–(26). The up-and-down order of branches is of course irrelevant.

The totality of sentences obtainable in this way, with the obvious game-theoretical semantics associated with them, is known as the theory of finite partially-ordered (f.p.o.) quantification.[34] The game rules for f.p.o. quantified sentences are the same as of old, except that moves connected with quantifiers in one branch are made without knowledge of those connected with the quantifiers in another.

All f.p.o. quantifier sentences can be translated into the sentences of ordinary (linear) second-order sentences in the same way as first-order sentences. Precisely the same procedure as was used in going from (1) to (2) above is applicable here, too. The only difference is that the Skolem function associated with an existential quantifier (say '$(\exists x)$') depends on (i.e., has as its arguments) only variables bound to those universal quantifiers which occur earlier in the same branch (more generally, which bear the partial ordering relation to '$(\exists x)$'). (It is easily shown, as pointed out in Enderton (1970, p. 394), that other sorts of dependencies do not matter anyway.) For instance, in the same way as (1) becomes (2), (23) thus becomes

(27) $(\exists f)(\exists g)(x)(z)F(x, f(x), z, g(z))$

and (25) becomes

(28) $(\exists f_1) \ldots (\exists f_j)(\exists g_1) \ldots (\exists g_j)(x_1) \ldots (x_i)(z_1) \ldots (z_i)$

$F(x_1, \ldots, x_i, f_1(x_1, \ldots, x_i), \ldots, f_j(x_1, \ldots, x_i),$

$z_1, \ldots, z_i, g_1(z_1, \ldots, z_i), \ldots, g_j(z_1, \ldots, z_i)).$

These Skolem function reformulations of f.p.o. sentences also serve to show more fully how semantical games connected with these sentences are played, precisely in the same way as (2) brings out more explicitly the strategies available in the game associated with (1). Skolem functions again serve to define that part of my strategies which deals with the applications of (G.E).

Finite partially ordered quantifiers have not been studied very long yet by logicians. They were introduced in Henkin (1961), and are sometimes referred to as Henkin quantifiers. I have located only two other substantial studies of them in the literature. (See Enderton, 1970 and Walkoe, 1970.) A few facts are nevertheless known about f.p.o. quantification theory. Of course, not all branching quantifiers result in sentences which have no first-order equivalents. For instance, (22) is easily shown to be equivalent to

(29) $(\exists x)(y)F(x, y).$

It is known that most of them go beyond first-order logic, however. In fact, (23) represents the simplest kind of sentence which does not have any first-order equivalents,[35] and all the other kinds may be thought of as more complicated versions of (23).[36] For it is shown in Walkoe (1970, p. 542) that any f.p.o. quantifier sentence is equivalent to a sentence of form (25) and likewise to one of form (26).

The greater force of the f.p.o. quantification theory as compared with first-order logic prompts the question whether branching quantifiers (failures of perfect information) can be found among natural-language quantifiers. Quine has argued (1969, pp. 107–112; 1970, pp. 89–91) for a negative answer to this question, but his tentative negative conclusion is a mistaken one. It is in fact easy to find any number of examples of branching quantifiers in perfectly grammatical English, including quantifier sentences which do not have any first-order equivalents. The following example is not the best one intrinsically but nevertheless allows for a more intuitive insight into the semantical situation than many others.

(30)   Every writer likes a book of his almost as much as every critic dislikes some book he has reviewed.

I shall argue, if the point is not already obvious, that (30) can be considered an instance of branching quantification representable in the form (23) as follows.

(31) $\begin{matrix} (x)(\exists y) \\ (z)(\exists u) \end{matrix}$ $\begin{matrix} [(x \text{ is a writer} \land z \text{ is a critic}) \supset (y \text{ is a book} \land x \text{ has} \\ \text{authored } y \land u \text{ is a book} \land z \text{ has reviewed } u \land \\ x \text{ likes } y \text{ almost as much as } z \text{ dislikes } u)] \end{matrix}$

This admits of the second-order translation

(32) $(\exists f)(\exists g)(x)(z)$ $((x$ is a writer $\land z$ is a critic$) \supset (f(x)$ is a book $\land x$ has authored $f(x) \land g(z)$ is a book $\land z$ has reviewed $g(z) \land x$ likes $f(x)$ almost as much as z dislikes $g(z)))$

but not of any first-order translation. In a first-order translation the quantifiers will have to be linearly ordered, which creates the kind of dependence which is not being presupposed in (30). In order to see this, notice that since the left-to-right order would presumably be followed here, the prime candidate for a first-order translation of (30) is apparently

(33) (x) $[x$ is a writer $\supset (\exists y)$ $(y$ is a book $\land x$ has authored $y \land (z)$ $(z$ is a critic $\supset (\exists u)$ $(u$ is a book $\land z$ has reviewed $u \land x$ likes y almost as much as z dislikes $u)))]$.

which has a 'game-theoretical' second-order equivalent

(34) $(\exists f)(\exists g)(x)(z)$ $[x$ is a writer $\supset (f(x)$ is a book $\land x$ has authored $f(x) \land (x$ is a critic $\supset (g(x, z)$ is a book $\land z$ has reviewed $g(x, z) \land x$ likes $f(x)$ almost as much as z dislikes $g(x, z))))]$.

Here (32) is stronger than (34) in the relevant respect, for a function with fewer arguments can always be thought of as a degenerate case of a function with more arguments. This extra force of (32) is due to the requirement that the values of y and u in (31) are determined on the sole basis of x and z, respectively. Hence the situation in which (32) (and therefore also (34)) is true will be described by the following sentence.

(35)   Every writer likes his first book almost as much as every critic dislikes the latest book he reviewed.

Since (35) implies both (32) and (34), it does not yet serve to distinguish them. We can distinguish them intuitively, however, by considering the situation described by the following sentence.

(36)   Every writer likes his latest book almost as much as every critic dislikes the first book by that writer he had to review.

It is of course being assumed here that every critic has reviewed at least one book by each writer – a not unimaginable state of affairs.

In circumstances in which (36) is true, (33)–(34) are clearly true. Nevertheless (32) is not. For it may still be true that different writers like their most recent efforts to entirely different degrees, as long as for each separate writer there obtains a nearly uniform degree of disapprobation among critics towards the earliest effort of that particular writer they had to pronounce themselves on. This is not enough to make (32) true, for it requires that for all pairs of writers and critics books can be found towards which they *all* exhibit about the same intensity of feeling.

The remarkable thing here is that by pretty much the same token it can be seen that (36) does *not* imply (30), either, on the intended, natural reading of (30). This provides strong evidence that (30) can be expressed as (32) but not as (34). The same conclusion follows *a fortiori* if we try other linear orderings of quantifiers in interpreting (30). For instance, if we give the two universal quantifiers the widest scope in (30), we obtain the reading

(33)* $(x)(z)$ [x is a writer $\wedge z$ is a critic) $\supset (\exists y)$ (y is a book $\wedge x$ has authored $y \wedge (\exists u)$ (u is a book $\wedge z$ has reviewed $u \wedge x$ likes y almost as much as z dislikes u))]

which has as its second-order counterpart the following sentence.

(34)* $(\exists f)(\exists g)(x)(z)$ $[(x$ is a writer $\wedge$ z is a critic) $\supset$ $(f(x, z)$ is a book $\wedge$ x has authored $f(x, z)$ $\wedge$ $g(x, z)$ is a book $\wedge$ z has reviewed $g(x, z)$ $\wedge$ x likes $f(x, z)$ almost as much as z dislikes $g(x, z))]$.

The same example (36) which showed that (32) and (34) differ in meaning and which showed that (30) cannot naturally be understood as (34) serves to demonstrate the same of (34)* vis-à-vis (32) and (30). For in the circumstances envisaged in (36) the sentences (33)*–(34)* are clearly true while (32) and (30) may be false by the same token as before. Hence we are again led to conclude that (30) must have the force of (32).

It follows from what has been said earlier that (32) does not have any first-order synonyms. Hence if what we just found is right and (30) and (32) have the same force, we have in (30) an example of an English sentence which is essentially quantificational but which cannot be translated into the first-order notation.

Once this is seen, similar examples can be constructed at will. They cannot be much simpler than (30), however, for (as was already stated) it takes four quantifiers to reach a sentence that cannot be translated into a first-order language.

It is nevertheless clear that we can find more natural examples of 'branching quantification' than the single one Quine (1969, p. 109) disparages and dismisses in his discussion of non-standard quantification. The following is about as simple (syntactically simple) an example as I have found.

(37)   Some relative of each villager and some relative of each townsman hate each other.

This may even offer a glimpse of the ways in which branched quantification is expressed in English. Quantifiers occurring in conjoint constituents frequently enjoy independence of each other, it seems, because a sentence is naturally thought of as being symmetrical semantically vis-à-vis such constituents.

Notice that in order for (37) to be true the relative of each townsman mentioned in it must not depend on the villager. In other words, (37) need not be true in a situation described as follows.

The eldest relative of each villager and that relative of each townsman who is closest in age to the villager hate each other.

Yet in such a state of affairs a suitable linear-quantifier sentence analogue to (33) would be true. This example therefore serves to indicate why the linear-quantifier reading of (37) will not quite do.

Other examples can be expressed in the vocabulary which was already studied by Russell (1903). The following is a case in point, assuming that a and b are sets of sets.

(38)   Some element of each a contains some element of each b.

In (38) and (37) the preposition 'of' is used, although no semantical rules are given for it. The reason is simple: in these examples no special rules for it are needed, except for an ordering principle which tells us to unpack iterated of-phrases from right to left. What ordering principles are perhaps needed in other cases and what supplementary rules have to be formulated in an exhaustive treatment of 'of' is not discussed here.

In order to avoid unnecessary misunderstanding, it is in order to point out that certain sentences not unlike (30) admit of a first-order translation after all. My discussion has been predicated on treating 'x likes y almost as much as z dislikes u' as expressing a relation whose analysis does not involve further quantifiers. Even if this assumption should fail in our particular case, the example still shows how others can be found in which the matrix 'F' of (23) does not contain any hidden quantifiers. The example (30) was chosen for expositional convenience only, and I am not putting forward any theses about its ultimate analysis.

In fact, someone might be tempted to analyze (30) as follows.

(30)* $(\exists d)$ (d is a degree of feeling $\wedge$ $(x)(\exists y)$ (x is a writer $\supset$ (y is a book $\wedge$ x has authored y $\wedge$ x likes y almost to the degree d)) $\wedge$ $(z)(\exists u)$ (z is a critic $\supset$ (u) is a book $\wedge$ z has reviewed u $\wedge$ z dislikes u to the degree d))].

It is important to realize that the kind of analysis represented by (30)* is not unproblematic but depends on a kind of reification of 'degrees of feeling'. Such a reification is possible only when the underlying relational structure satisfies suitable, rather strict conditions. Roughly speaking, these conditions are those that would suffice to establish a numerical representation theorem. Normally, these conditions are not satisfied. Whether they are satisfied in the case of (30) is not clear, and depends on the logic of 'almost'. In case you want (30) replaced by an example which is not subject to this mild uncertainty, the following will do.

(39)   Some book by every author is referred to in some essay by every critic.

A situation analogous to that described by (35) is one in which

(40)   The bestselling book by every author is referred to in the longest essay by every critic.

By this I mean a situation in which (39) is true (on its natural, f.p.o. reading). A state of affairs in which (39) is false on this reading but in which the most plausible of its putative linear-quantifier readings is true is described by

(41)   The bestselling book by every author is referred to in the obituary essay on him by every critic.

This is in other words analogous to (36). The point is that the essay in question is not chosen in (41) on the basis of the critic alone, but depends also on the author in question. Thus we can see that the need of a branching-quantifier interpretation does not depend on the use of comparatives or of the notion of sameness.

    The existence of quantificational sentences in English which cannot be translated into the language of first-order logic is not the only consequence of our observations, however, although it may be the most striking one. A no less interesting consequence concerns the overall situation even in the case of those failures of perfect information which do not lead to such breakdowns of translatability. When a breakdown of perfect information occurs, we have to translate an English sentence into the first-order notation in a way different from the one we would have followed if perfect information had prevailed. The possibility of imperfect information therefore affects our ideas of the semantic interpretation of many English sentences whose 'logical structure' can be exhibited in first-order terms.

    A case in point seems to be the following sentence.

(42)   John has not shown any of his paintings to some of his friends.

If translated into first-order notation on the assumption that the requirement of perfect information is satisfied, the preferred reading of (42) will presumably be (because 'any' and 'some' typically have priority over 'not')

(43)   (y) [y is a painting of John's ⊃ (∃x)(x is a friend of John's ∧ John has not shown y to x)].

Yet the reading of (42) that in fact is the most natural one by far assigns to it the force of

(44)   (∃x)[x is a friend of John's ∧ (y)(y is a painting of John's ⊃ John has not shown y to x)].

One might suspect that this exception to the general ordering principles of English has something to do with negation. However, the following example exhibits the same peculiarity as (42).

(45)   John has shown all his paintings to some of his friends.

One might also try to account for the switch from (43) to (44) by some further complication in our rules and principles. However, no natural revision of our ordering principles that would explain the reading (44) of (42) is in the offing.

The most natural explanation of the actually preferred reading (44) of (42) is to assume that the two quantifiers in (42) are independent. On this assumption, (42) will be (on its most natural reading) of the following 'logical from'.

(46) $\left.\begin{array}{c} (∃x) \\ (y) \end{array}\right\}$ [x is a friend of John's ∧ (y is a painting of John's ⊃ John has not shown y to x)].

This is easily seen to be logically equivalent to a first-order sentence, viz. (44), just in the same way (22) is logically equivalent to (29).

Thus we often have to take into account branching quantifiers even when they do not lead us beyond first-order logic, viz. for the purpose of explaining which first-order semantical representation a given English sentence has.

Although I do not propose to treat nonstandard quantifiers in this paper, it may be worth pointing out in the passing that the phenomenon of branching quantifiers is highly relevant to well-known examples of the type

I told three of the stories to many of the men.

The reading of such sentences which Jackendoff (1972, pp. 307–308) finds impossible to represent in a logical notation results precisely from making the nonstandard quantifiers 'three' and 'many' independent.

It is indeed easy to ascertain that the 'unaccountable' reading is simply an instance of branching quantification. In fact, examples of the kind Jackendoff uses can be employed to show that differences in meaning are often created more readily by branching nonstandard quantifiers than by standard ones.

Thus the realization that formal quantifiers may be unordered thus removes the whole basis of Jackendoff's criticism of attempts to account for the ambiguities which are due to multiple nonstandard quantifiers in terms of different underlying quantifier structures.

What we have seen shows conclusively that all attempts to base the semantical interpretation of natural languages like English on first-order logic alone are bound to be inadequate, and inadequate in a particularly interesting way.

Several logicians and linguists[37] have argued that the semantics of natural languages has to go beyond first-order logic in order to account for the semantics of such expressions as 'knows', 'believes', 'necessarily', 'may', etc. However, the extensions of first-order logic (quantification theory) needed to cope with these epistemic and modal notions are entirely different from the ones involved here, and relatively unsurprising. For it has been generally thought of that, whatever else quantification theory perhaps fails to capture, the one thing it does accomplish is to represent the logical form of the basic English quantifiers. This illusion has now been shattered.

It also turns out that our step away from first-order logic is in a sense much longer than those involved, e.g., in ordinary modal or epistemic logic. This point will be argued later in this paper.

Another consequence of our results is that the concept of scope is not alone sufficient to unravel the interplay of quantifiers in English. What we can do by means of the notion of scope is to describe the order of applications of the different rules. However, questions of informational independence of the different applications cannot be formulated by speaking just of the scopes of quantifiers.

We can also push our observations further. Not only do we have some of the irreducible logical forms of f.p.o. quantification theory represented by grammatical English sentences. A plausible (although not completely binding) argument can be put forward to the effect that every formula of f.p.o. quantification theory is reproducible as the semantical structure of some grammatical English sentence.

In order to obtain such an argument let us note that certain grammatical constructions of English either force or at least frequently give a preference to a reading of certain quantifiers which makes them independent. It was already noted that this is the case with quantifiers occurring in conjoint structures. Frequently this also applies to quantifiers occurring in different nested of-phrases. The following example, modified from an example by Julius M. E. Moravcsik (personal communication), is a case in point

(47)   Some family member of some customer of each branch office of every bank likes some product of some subdivision of each subsidiary of every conglomerate.

This sentence has the form

(48) $\left.\begin{array}{l}(x_1)(x_2)(\exists y_1)(\exists y_2) \\ (z_1)(z_2)(\exists w_1)(\exists w_2)\end{array}\right\}F(x_1, x_2, y_1, y_2, z_1, z_2, w_1, w_2)$

It is also obvious that arbitrarily long branches of quantifiers can be built up in the same way. In fact, any quantifier prefix exemplified by (25) can easily be obtained in this way.

Since any f.p.o. quantifier sentence has an equivalent sentence of the form (25), this seems to imply that the structure of every f.p.o. quantifier sentence is reproducible in English. This conclusion is in fact most likely true, but it does not follow quite strictly from what has been said. For one thing, the special form of nested of-phrases may induce restrictions as to what may occur as the formula F of sentence (25). Further arguments can be given to show that this does not spoil the possibility of finding English sentences of any form (25), but they will not be attempted here.[38]

Moreover, we ought to rule out also the possibility that analytical connections between English substitution-instances may likewise restrict the kinds of F in (25) reproducible in English. Although this objection is clearly less serious than the preceding one, for reasons of space it will not be met in detail here.

Instead, further supporting evidence will be given for the thesis that the logical form of every sentence of f.p.o. quantification theory can be matched by an English sentence. Another grammatical device that induces independence between English quantifiers is the construction known as relative clause with several antecedents. Although the status of this construction is not entirely clear (cf. Perlmutter and Ross, 1970), it seems to me impossible to deny that it yields grammatical English sentences. A case in point is the following.

(49)   Every villager envies a relative and every townsman admires a friend who hate each other.[39]

An argument similar to the one we conducted in connection with (30) shows that the two pairs of quantifiers in (49), and likewise in the different antecedents of one and the same relative clause in general, are naturally understood as being independent. (Intuitive symmetry considerations have again a valuable heuristic use here in convincing one of this independence.) Moreover, in so far as the grammatical device of split antecedents is acceptable at all, it can obviously be used so as to assign to a relative clause more than two antecedents. Equally obviously, there cannot be any definite limit to the number of antecedents. Moreover, the antecedents can contain three quantifiers instead of two. For instance, the following sentence appears perfectly grammatical, although it is rather complicated.

(50)   Each player of every baseball team has a fan, each actress in every musical has an admirer, and each aide of every senator has a friend, who are cousins.

Clearly, (50) is of the form (26) with $k = 3$. It is also easily seen that similar examples can be constructed at will. Since the number of antecedent clauses apparently cannot be restricted, we can in this way see that all prefixes of form (26) are exemplified in English. Since all f.p.o. sentences have equivalents of form (26), we can again conclude, with the same qualifications as before, that the semantics of English quantifiers comprises all of f.p.o. quantification theory.

Nor is this conclusion tied to the particular construction (relative clauses with several antecedents) just used. Although a strict argument would be somewhat messy here, examples can be given which suggest that each quantifier prefix of form (26) can be captured in English even apart from this particular construction. The following example may serve to convey some flavor of the situation.

(51)   Some reviewer of every magazine of each newspaper chain admires some book by every author of each publisher although this book is disliked by some proof-reader of each printer in every city.

All these observations lead us toward the conclusion that the logic of idiomatic English quantifiers is at least as strong as f.p.o. quantification theory. If so, striking results follow. For f.p.o. quantification theory is an enormously powerful theory, immensely more powerful than first-order logic ('quantification theory'). Henkin (1961, pp. 182–183) already reported Ehrenfeucht's important result that the set of valid (logically true) sentences of f.p.o. quantification theory is not recursively enumerable. Furthermore, Enderton (1970, pp. 395–396) has shown that every $\bigvee_1^1$ (second order existential) and every $\bigwedge_1^1$ (second order universal) formula[40] admits of an equivalent formula in f.p.o. quantification theory. The argument which Enderton (1970, proof of Theorem 2) and Walkoe (1970, proof of Theorem 4.3) sketch for this result can be carried out in the presence of ordinary free (second-order) predicate variables or similar predicate constants. Hence it may be combined with the result of mine mentioned earlier[41] to the effect that the validity problem for all second order sentences (and for all sentences of any finite type) can be effectively reduced to that for sentences with just one second-order quantifier, over and above first-order quantifiers and free (second-order) predicate variables. Putting these results together yields the conclusion that the set of valid sentences of pure second-order logic (and of the whole of finite type theory) is recursively isomorphic with the set of valid sentences of f.p.o. quantification theory.[42] In this special but important sense, the whole of second-order logic reduces to f.p.o. quantification theory. In plain English, f.p.o. quantification theory is (semantically speaking) an incredibly powerful and rich logic.

Since our results suggest that the whole of f.p.o. quantification theory is built into the semantics of English quantifiers, it follows that the semantics of a relatively small fragment of English, viz. of English quantifiers plus a few supporting constructions, is a much subtler and much more complicated subject than anyone seems to have suspected.

In the eyes of a logician, it seems to be powerful beyond the wildest dreams of linguists and of philosophers of language.

This tentative result is not belied by the fact that only a small part of these riches is actually capitalized in ordinary discourse and that there also seem to exist systematic devices in natural languages like English which often serve to spare us the trouble of going beyond first-order structures. A study of these devices looks extremely interesting, but cannot be attempted here.

Instead, certain methodological speculations are suggested by the great logical power of natural-language semantics. The typical, and in many cases the only kind of evidence actually employed in linguistic discussion in these days is in terms of the classification of sentences or other expressions in certain important categories. In the case of syntax, these categories include prominently grammaticality, and in the case of semantics they include, according to one important type of view, such concepts as analyticity, sameness in meaning, ambiguity, and entailment. (Cf. Katz, 1972, pp. 3–7.) The distribution of sentences into these categories is said to be among the most important phenomena to be explained by a semantical theory. Although this kind of program does not necessarily imply that the rock bottom data of semantics are a competent speaker's intuitions about such notions, the cash value of the program indicated often is precisely such a view of the data of semantics.

Now one implication of our results seems to be that in this methodological respect there is an enormous difference between syntax and semantics. In order for the tacit methodology just adumbrated to be theoretically justifiable, one apparently has to assume that there is in principle some sort of procedure backing up a competent speaker's intuitions about the grammatical concept in question. Otherwise, there is no reason to expect that his direct intuitions can serve to characterize the extension of this concept.

In the case of syntax, this does not create any problems, for all the relevant sets of sentences seem to be safely recursive.[43] What we have seen shows, however, that the same presupposition is not satisfied in semantics. There is no effective procedure or anything distantly resembling an effective procedure which a speaker, however competent and well-informed, could in the last analysis rely on in classifying sentences as being analytical or non-analytical, synonyms or non-synonyms, etc. Hence no set of competent speaker's intuitions can constitute a fully sufficient basis for the explication of such concepts as analyticity, synonymy, or other basic concepts of natural-language semantics. Therefore the methodology on which much recent work has been based is bound to be inadequate in principle, however useful it may be in the short run.[44] Syntax, it seems, is a dubious methodological paradigm for semantics.

I am aware of the many pitfalls that lurk in this area, and hence offer these remarks as tentative speculations only. They seem to pose in any case serious problems for the methodology of linguistic semantics.[45]

One particular pitfall is interesting enough to be mentioned here.[46] It is connected with the basic ideas of game-theoretical semantics, and more specifically with the definition of truth for quantified sentences as the existence of a winning strategy in the associated game. If we want to think of our semantical games realistically, it may be suggested, we must restrict the strategy sets available to Myself drastically. For surely it makes no sense for me to try to play a game in accordance with a strategy represented by a function which is not recursive and perhaps not even remotely like a recursive function, it is perhaps thought. In a realistic game-theoretical semantics, the strategies available to Myself – possibly the strategies available to Nature also – must according to this view be restricted to recursive strategies or at least to strategies defined by some 'almost recursive' functions and functionals.[47]

It seems to me that this line of thought has to be taken very seriously. It will lead very quickly away from classical logic, however, for already in the classical first-order logic non-recursive strategies must be relied on if the game-theoretical interpretation is to yield the usual semantics.[48] It therefore marks an even more radical departure from traditional ideas than the earlier suggestions explored in this paper. The task of investigating the new perspectives cannot be undertaken here.[49]

Academy of Finland and Stanford University

REFERENCES

Addison, J. W. (1962) 'The Theory of Hierarchies', in E. Nagel, P. Suppes, and A. Tarski, eds., *Logic, Methodology, and Philosophy of Science: Proceedings of the 1960 International Congress*, Stanford University Press, Stanford, California, pp. 26–37.

Chomsky, N. (1971) 'Deep Structure, Surface Structure, and Semantic Interpretation', in Danny D. Steinberg and Leon A. Jakobovits, eds., *Semantics: An Interdisciplinary Reader*, Cambridge University Press, Cambridge, pp. 183–216.

Davis, M. D. (1970) *Game Theory*, Basic Books, New York.

Ehrenfeucht, A. (1960) 'An Application of Games to the Completeness Problem for Formalized Theories', *Fundamenta Mathematicae* **49**, 129–141.

Enderton, H. B. (1970) 'Finite Partially-Ordered Quantifiers', *Zeitschrift für mathematische Logik und Grundlagen der Mathematik* **16**, 393–397.

Gödel, K. (1959) 'Über eine bisher noch nicht benützte Erweiterung des finiten Standpunktes', in *Logica: Studia Paul Bernays Dedicata*, Editions du Griffon, Neuchâtel, pp. 76–82.

Harman, G. (1972) 'Deep Structure as Logical Form', in D. Davidson and G. Harman, eds., *Semantics of Natural Language*, D. Reidel, Dordrecht and Boston, pp. 25–47.

Harman, G. (1973) 'Noun Phrases Derived from Variable Binding Operations and Grandy's Theory of Pronominalization', preprint.

Henkin, L. (1950) 'Completeness in the Theory of Types', *Journal of Symbolic Logic* **15**, 81–91. Reprinted in K. J. J. Hintikka, ed., *The Philosophy of Mathematics*, Oxford University Press, London, 1969, pp. 51–63.

Henkin, L. (1961) 'Some Remarks on Infinitely Long Formulas', in *Infinitistic Methods*, Pergamon Press, Oxford, pp. 167–183.

Hintikka, K. J. J. (1955) 'Reductions in the Theory of Types', *Acta Philosophica Fennica* **8**, 61–115.

Hintikka, K. J. J. (1968a) 'Language-Games for Quantifiers', in *American Philosophical Quarterly Monograph Series 2: Studies in Logical Theory*, Basil Blackwell, Oxford, pp. 46–72.

Hintikka, K. J. J. (1968b) 'Logic and Philosophy', in R. Klibansky, ed., *Contemporary Philosophy*, La Nuova Italia Editrice, Florence, Vol. I, pp. 3–30.

Hintikka, K. J. J. (1969) *Models for Modalities*, D. Reidel, Dordrecht.

Hintikka, K. J. J. (1973) *Logic, Language-Games, and Information*, Clarendon Press, Oxford.

Hintikka, K. J. J. (1976) *The Semantics of Questions and the Questions of Semantics* (Acta Philosophica Fennica, Vol. 28, no. 4), North-Holland, Amsterdam.

Jackendoff, R. S. (1968) 'Quantifiers in English', *Foundations of Language* **4**, 422–442.

Jackendoff, R. S. (1972) *Semantic Interpretation in Generative Grammar*, MIT Press, Cambridge, Mass.

Katz, J. J. (1972) *Semantic Theory*, Harper and Row, New York.

Klima, E. S. (1964) 'Negation in English', in J. A. Fodor and J. J. Katz, eds., *The Structure of Language*, Prentice-Hall, Englewood Cliffs, N.J.

Kuno, S., and Robinson, J. J. (1972) 'Multiple *Wh* Questions', *Linguistic Inquiry* **3**, 413–462.

Lakoff, George (1970) 'Repartee, or a Reply to Negation, Conjunction, and Quantifiers', *Foundations of Language* **6**, 398–422.

Lakoff, George (1971) 'On Generative Semantics', in Danny D. Steinberg and Leon A. Jakobovits, eds. *Semantics: An Interdisciplinary Reader*, Cambridge University Press, Cambridge.

Lakoff, George (1972) 'Linguistics and Natural Logic', in D. Davidson and G. Harman, eds., *Semantics of Natural Language*, D. Reidel, Dordrecht and Boston, pp. 545–665.

Lasnick, H. (1972) *Analyses of Negation in English*, unpublished Doctoral dissertation MIT, Cambridge, Mass.

Luce, R. D., and Raiffa, H. (1957) *Games and Decisions*, John Wiley, New York.

McCawley, J. D. (1971) 'Where Do Noun Phrases Come From?' in Danny D. Steinberg and Leon A. Jakobovits, eds., *Semantics: An Interdisciplinary Reader*, Cambridge University Press, Cambridge, pp. 217–231.

Montague, R. (1965) 'Reductions in Higher-Order Logic' in J. W. Addison, L. Henkin, and A. Tarski, eds., *The Theory of Models*, North-Holland, Amsterdam, pp. 251–264.

Montague, R. (1973) 'The Proper Treatment of Quantification in Ordinary English', in K. J. J. Hintikka, J. Moravcsik, and P. Suppes, eds., *Approaches to Natural Language: Proceedings of the 1970 Stanford Workshop*, D. Reidel, Dordrecht and Boston, pp. 221–242.

Mostowski, A. (1965) *Thirty Years of Foundational Studies*, Basil Blackwell, Oxford.

Mycielski, J. (1964) 'On the Axiom of Determinateness', *Fundamenta Mathematicae* **53**, 205–224.

Partee, B. H. (1970) 'Negation, Conjunction and Quantifiers: Syntax vs. Semantics', *Foundations of Language* **6**, 153–165.

Partee, B. H. (1971) 'On the Requirement that Transformations Preserve Meaning', in Charles J. Fillmore and D. T. Langendoen, eds., *Studies in Linguistic Semantics*, Holt, Reinhart, and Winston, New York, pp. 1–21.

Partee, B. H. (1972) 'Opacity, Coreference, and Pronouns', in D. Davidson and G. Harman, eds., *Semantics of Natural Language*, D. Reidel, Dordrecht pp. 415–441.

Perlmutter, D., and Ross, J. R. (1970) 'Relative Clauses with Split Antecedents', *Linguistic Inquiry* **1**, 350.

Quine, W. V. (1951) *Mathematical Logic*, rev. ed., Harvard University Press. Cambridge, Mass.

Quine, W. V. (1960) *Word and Object*, MIT Press, Cambridge, Mass.

Quine, W. V. (1969) *Ontological Relativity and Other Essays*, Columbia University Press, New York.

Quine, W. V. (1970) *Philosophy of Logic*, Prentice-Hall, Englewood Cliffs, N.J.

Russell, B. (1903) *Principles of Mathematics*, George Allen and Unwin, London.

Walkoe, W. J., Jr. (1970) 'Finite Partially-Ordered Quantification', *Journal of Symbolic Logic* **35**, 535–555.

Wall, R. (1972) *Introduction to Mathematical Linguistics*, Prentice-Hall, Englewood Cliffs, N.J.

Wittgenstein, L. (1953) *Philosophical Investigations*, Basil Blackwell, Oxford.

Wittgenstein, L. (1958) *The Blue and Brown Books*, Basil Blackwell, Oxford.

Wright, G. H. von (1957) *Logical Studies*, Routledge and Kegan Paul, London.

NOTES

[1] Numerical expressions can for many purposes be dealt with in the same way as quantifiers. For instance, they exhibit most of the same ambiguities. This is not surprising in view of the fact that the usual existential quantifier can be read 'for at least one' and that it therefore is but a special case of the 'numerical quantifier' 'for at least α', where α is any cardinal number.

[2] Cf. Partee (1971).

[3] Cf. Partee (1972).

[4] Cf. Chomsky (1971).

[5] Nobody claims that any ordinary formulation of first-order logic is all we need. For instance, it is clear that ordinary language typically uses relativized quantifiers or many-sorted quantification (i.e., logic where different quantifiers may range over different domains) rather than logicians' absolute quantifiers which range over the members of some fixed domain, sometimes called 'the universe of discourse'. Such discrepancies do not matter for the purposes at hand, however. Where the essential departures from the purview of first-order logic lie will be indicated later. In fact, even ordinary modal logic is not what entails the most striking violations of first-order characteristics.

[6] McCawley writes (p. 219): "I will in fact argue symbolic logic, subject to certain modifications, provides an adequate system for semantic representation within the framework of transformational grammar". I am nevertheless oversimplifying the situation somewhat in that there are all sorts of minor differences ("certain modifications") between McCawley's logic and typical formulations of first-order logic.

[7] Qualifications resembling those mentioned in the preceding two notes are needed here, too. In particular, we should not forget departures from first-order logic in the direction of modal logic.

[8] Views of this type are frequent in expositions and discussions of elementary logic. See e.g. Quine (1951, pp. 2–3) or von Wright (1957, pp. 1–6).

[9] I borrow this apt term from Patrick Suppes' Presidential Address, APA Pacific Division Meeting, Seattle, March 30, 1973. ('Congruence of Meaning', *Proceedings and Addresses of the APA* **46** (1972–3), 21–38.

[10] Much of what will be said in this paper applies to other types of English quantifiers, too. Most of their peculiarities are disregarded here, however.

[11] There is no good exhaustive survey of the increasingly important uses of game-theoretical ideas in logic. Interesting glimpses are nevertheless offered e.g. by Ehrenfeucht (1960) and Mycielski (1964). In first-order logic, game-theoretical concepts have been employed earlier by Paul Lorenzen. The philosophical perspective from which he looks at the situation is different from mine, however. His 'dialogical games' are interpretationally quite unlike my language-games of seeking and finding. The former are indoor games, played by successive verbal 'challenges' and 'responses'. They cannot therefore be put to use in semantics, i.e., to discuss the relation of language to the reality it can convey information about. In contrast, my semantical games are 'outdoor' games, played among the entities our first-order language speaks of.

[12] The precise formulation of the formation rules involved here might be the following:

(F.A)   An n-place predicate followed by a sequence of n names of individuals (not necessarily different) is a sentence.

(F.&)–(F.v)   If S and S' are sentences, then so are $(S \wedge S')$ and $(S \vee S')$

(F.~)   If S is a sentence then so is $\sim S$.

Further rules may be introduced for other sentential connectives, although they can all be defined in terms of (say) '$\sim$' and '$\vee$'.

[13] The rule involved here may be formulated as follows:

(F.E)–(F.U)   If S is a sentence containing a name 'b' but not containing an individual variable 'x', then $(\exists x)S(x/b)$ and $(x)S(x/b)$ are sentences.

Here $S(x/b)$ is the result of replacing 'b' everywhere by 'x' in S.

[14] For the notion of type, see e.g. Henkin (1950).

[15] Of course, this proper name must not have been used earlier. – It is clear that the mild extension of our original language which is involved here is not problematic. For instance, in each round of a game only a finite number of new individuals are needed.

[16] Cf. Mostowski (1965), Chapters 3, 6, and 13.

[17] Of course together with the function that tells me how to choose a disjunct when it comes to that. However, in this paper I shall look away from the strategic problems connected with sentential connectives.

[18] In this respect, my approach is not unlike Montague's who treats quantifier phrases like 'every man' on a par with other name phrases. See e.g. Montague (1973).

[19] Here I am using an informal linguistic notation, not a logical one. For instance, in (3) 'X–W' marks any context in which a quantifier phrase of the form 'some Y who Z' can occur (subject to the restrictions to be indicated later).

[20] The problem of formulating such rules seems to be a syntactical, not a semantical one. I shall not try to treat it here.

[21] This rule does not handle generic uses of the indefinite article, which must be treated separately. Furthermore, allowance must be made for the fact that in unanalyzable sentences of the form

$$(*) \qquad b \text{ is a(n) } X$$

'is a(n)' may be thought of as expressing predication rather than identity *cum* existential quantification. Nothing untoward will happen, however, even if the latter interpretation is attempted. What we obtain by applying the rule (G.an) to (*) is a redundancy but not any mistake. In other words, in (*) 'is' may be thought to express either predication or identity, which goes some way towards explained why English can use the same word to express both. Hence the only caution needed here is not to apply (G.an) needlessly to (*) when it is grammatically unanalyzable further.

[22] Again, the details do not matter for my purposes at hand. Cf. Klima (1964).

[23] Thus in a negated 'knows that' statement there may in effect be a tacit negation *inside* the epistemic operator. This observation is important for the purpose of understanding the interplay of epistemic operators and quantifiers.

[24] I realize that this approach touches only some of the gross overall features of English quantifiers and leaves much of their finer features unaccounted for. Some idea of their actual complexity can be gathered from Jackendoff (1968).

[25] The limits of the applicability of the usual concept of scope will be examined later.

[26] A related suggestion is made in Lasnik (1972). It is not clear yet, however, what all the rules are with respect to which (G.any) behaves differently from (G.every). Further work is thus needed here.

[27] Reference to (G.all) is needed because 'any' can be plural, unlike 'every'. In its plural uses, (G.any) therefore has to be compared with (G.all) rather than (G.every).

[28] In (18) the second conjunct is of course semantically redundant, and is therefore naturally omitted in natural discourse. I am inserting it to bring out the parallelism between (18) and (19). – Certain additional restrictions are also needed when a proper name (like 'Bill' in (18)) is substituted for a quantifier phrase which involves 'quantifying into' an epistemic or modal context. These 'uniqueness conditions' will not be discussed in this paper, however. They would be analogous to their namesakes in formal languages, discussed in Hintikka (1969).

[29] More idiomatically, we would of course say instead of (19), 'If Arthur is coming, John knows that he is'.

[30] It also supplements in an important way my own earlier accounts of the construction *an epistemic verb + an interrogative clause*. Cf. Hintikka (1969).

[31] See e.g. Kuno and Robinson (1972), which gives references to earlier literature. See also Hintikka (1976).

[32] The reader may check that the semantical interpretation any games assign to such pairs of sentences as the following is precisely the right one.

> John saw a warbler yesterday, and Bill saw a warbler, too.
> John saw a warbler yesterday, and Bill saw it, too.

A great deal of further discussion is of course needed to show how all the different kinds of problems can be handled.

[33] A partially ordering relation is one which is (i) transitive, (ii) reflexive, and (iii) antisymmetric.

[34] Strictly speaking, we obtain here two slightly different generalizations of first-order logic. One is obtained by allowing the replacement of the quantifier prefix of a first-order sentence in the prenex normal form to be replaced by a partially ordered quantifier prefix in one full swoop. The other allows for the introduction of a partially ordered quantifier prefix as a rule of formation which can be used repeatedly, like the other formation rules. Cf. Walkoe (1970), p. 538, definitions of H and H'.

In this paper it suffices to restrict our attention to the former, narrower concept of a f.p.o. sentence.

[35] Henkin (1961), p. 183 (Ehrenfeucht's result). Cf. Walkoe (1970), Theorem 4.1 (p. 540).

[36] In the sense that their quantifier orderings are extensions of that of (23).

[37] Anyone who for instance takes possible-worlds semantics seriously as an essential tool for explicating the semantics of natural languages is committed to this type of a position.

[38] The conceptual situation here is illustrated by Enderton's reduction (pp. 396–397) of all f.p.o. prefixes of elementary number theory to the form (23). This shows that the essential question here is whether natural language is subtle enough to reproduce those combinatorial operations on which this further reduction depends – or to accomplish something equivalent. Although the details are messy, it seems to me quite unreasonable to doubt that this can be done.

[39] In order to spare the reader the trouble of restoring an innocuous ellipsis, I perhaps ought to write here '. . . a relative of his . . .' and '. . . a friend of his . . . .'

[40] For this notation, see Addison (1962).

[41] See Hintikka (1955). The result is generalized in Montague (1965).

[42] The term 'a language of order $1\frac{1}{2}$', which has sometimes been used for f.p.o. quantification theory, is thus profoundly misleading, even though my results do not preclude other sorts of differences in power between f.p.o. quantification theory and second-order logic.

[43] This is illustrated by the well known fact that even type 1 or context-sensitive grammars (constituent structure grammars) admit a decision procedure for membership. See Wall (1972), pp. 212, 234–235.

[44] This still leaves largely open the question of its empirical adequacy. I hope to be able to return to this question on another occasion.

[45] The whole question as to how a finite language user can as much as form the concept of nonrecursive entities is in need of further analysis.

[46] This line of thought is the analogue in formal semantics to constructivistic views on the foundations of logic and mathematics. For them, cf. Mostowski (1965), Chapters 1 and 10–11.

[47] What possibilities there are in this direction is indicated by Gödel's (1959) "extention of the finitistic viewpoint" which can be construed in game-theoretical spirit.

[48] Cf. e.g. Mostowski (1965), pp. 58–59.

[49] Much of the material in this paper was first presented in seminars and lectures at the University of Helsinki, Stanford University, NYU, and the Third Scandinavian Logic Symposium in Uppsala, Sweden. It has also appeared, with the appropriate permission, in *Linguistic Inquiry* 5 (1974). In working on it, I have profited from contacts with more people than I can name here. Two of them must nevertheless be mentioned. They are Erik Stenius, whose criticism first prompted me to explore the sufficiency of first-order logic for the representation of English quantifiers, and Joan Bresnan, whose expertise has proved invaluable in several ways. Neither is responsible for my shortcomings, however, nor are the anonymous referees of *Linguistic Inquiry* whose comments have proved extremely useful.

JAAKKO HINTIKKA

QUANTIFIERS IN NATURAL LANGUAGES:
SOME LOGICAL PROBLEMS

1. THE PROBLEM OF NATURAL-LANGUAGE QUANTIFIERS

Quantifiers are by common consent among the most important ingredients in the logical structure of both formalized and natural languages. As we all know, formalized quantifiers and their generalizations have been studied extensively by logicians. In contrast, relatively little close attention has been paid to the peculiarities of the logical behavior of quantifiers in natural languages, in spite of the fact that quantifiers have figured conspicuously in some of the most important recent methodological controversies in linguistics.[1] It is the purpose of this paper to help to change this situation by surveying some of the non-trivial logical phenomena that we find in examining natural-language quantifiers. In doing so, I am largely restricting my attention to the natural-language counterparts of logicians' existential quantifier and universal quantifier, neglecting such 'nonstandard' quantifier words as 'many' and 'most'. I shall cover in the survey a number earlier observations of mine which have already been partly published,[2] but I shall also try to concentrate on certain new insights which serve to extend and to consolidate the old results.

2. SCOPE PROBLEMS AND THE DIRECTION OF SEMANTICAL RULES

A heuristically useful place to begin to study the logic of natural languages are the differences between formal systems and natural languages with respect to the overt behavior of quantifiers. One of the most revealing differences lies in the behavior of what logicians would call the *scope* of quantifiers in natural languages. The way in which scope is handled in ordinary discourse is almost paradoxical. On the one hand, scope does not seem to be particularly important. It is not indicated by brackets, parentheses, dots, or by any comparable devices. Moreover, in some important sense absolute scope does not even seem to matter. The scope of a quantifier word can apparently extend arbitrarily far in a sentence and

81

E. Saarinen (ed.), Game-Theoretical Semantics, 81–117. All Rights Reserved.
Copyright © 1977 and 1978 by D. Reidel Publishing Company, Dordrecht, Holland.

even in a text or discourse. For instance, one can introduce an individual by a quantifier phrase like 'an X' or 'some Y' and keep on referring to that 'randomly chosen' individual virtually indefinitely long by using repeatedly pronouns ('he', 'she', 'it', etc.) or anaphoric the-phrases 'the X' or 'the Y', respectively. In this respect, natural-language quantifier phrases look more like Hilbert's 'scopeless' ε-terms than formalized quantifiers. An example of a grammatical device which can be used to extend the scope of an existential-quantifier phrase arbitrarily far in a given sentence is found in Section 5 below in the form of the construction (*).

But although the absolute scopes of quantifier phrases thus seem to be irrelevant (or arbitrarily large), the *relative* scopes of quantifier phrases are vitally important for the proper understanding of many natural-language sentences. To find an example of this, one only has to consider the preferred readings of such sentences as the following:

(1)   Every man loves some woman;

(2)   Some woman is loved by every man.

The difference between the two lies precisely in a difference between the relative scopes of the two quantifier phrases 'every man' and 'some woman'.

This difference between absolute scope indications and relative scope indications has no obvious counterpart in formalized languages.

How, then, are the relative scopes of quantifiers (quantifier phrases) marked in ordinary discourse? A full answer to this question will of necessity be quite complicated. (Several of the sample sentences to be given later illustrate this complexity; see especially Sections 7–8 below.)

What is not equally complicated is to see what an appropriate framework might look like for studying the principles governing those relative scopes of natural-language quantifiers. Usually, the semantics of a formalized language is constructed in terms of recursive truth-clauses which show how the semantical interpretation of a complex expression is obtained step by step from the semantical interpretations of its component expressions.[3] However, the underdeterminacy of quantifier scopes tends to spoil the corresponding strategy in natural languages. The reason is that the underdeterminacy makes it impossible – or at least very hard – to decide what the appropriate component expressions of complex sentences are. Any component expression containing a quantifier has to take in all of the scope of this quantifier. But if the scope is in principle unrestricted (cf. above), we can scarcely find any component expression in the relevant sense of the word at all.

What a better semantical treatment of natural-language quantifiers might be like is not very hard to see, either, in the light of such observations. Instead of trying to build up the semantical interpretation of a sentence from the inside out, we can formulate our semantical rules so as to operate from the outside in. The reverse direction of the two procedures makes a difference because a step of analysis may involve changes in the remaining expression.

It is interesting to see what this possibility implies for the familiar principle that the meaning (semantical interpretation) of a complex expression must be a function of the meanings (semantical interpretations) of its components. What remains true in the kind of theory I am envisaging is that the meaning of a complex expression S is a function of the meanings of certain simpler expressions. They are no longer always components of S, however, in any syntactically relevant sense, even though they may perhaps be recovered from S by means a rule-governed procedure.

3. GAME-THEORETICAL SEMANTICS: QUANTIFIER RULES

My game-theoretical semantics for English quantifiers[4] and for a number of related expressions can be thought of as a system of rules of semantical analysis of the kind just indicated. It covers a fragment of English which for our present purposes needs to be delineated only approximately. The leading idea is to define the truth of each sentence S of this fragment by reference to an associated semantical game $G(S)$. This game is a two-person, zero-sum game. The truth of S means that one of the players, called myself, has a winning strategy in $G(S)$. The falsity of S means that the other player, called Nature, has a winning strategy in $G(S)$. Certain sentences of our fragment – or of a mild extension of it – will have to be thought of as unanalyzable (atomic) ones, and their truth-values are assumed to be determined unproblematically. At each stage of the game an English sentence is being considered, beginning with S. I win a play of $G(S)$ if it ends with a true atomic sentence, lose if it ends with a false one. In a sense, $G(S)$ may thus be considered as an attempt to verify S, as far as my moves are concerned, against the schemes of a recalcitrant Nature. This helps to understand the intuitive motivation of the rules of my games. They will be presented by means of special cases which are readily generalizable. Here are some special cases of certain especially important rules.

(G.some) When the game has reached a sentence of the form

$$X - \text{some } Y \text{ who } Z - W,$$

a person may be chosen by myself. Let the proper name of that person be 'b'. Then the game is continued with respect to the sentence

$$X - b - W, b \text{ is a } Y, \text{ and } b \ Z.$$

An analogous rule can be set up for 'a(n)'.

(G.every) When the game has reached a sentence of the form

$$X - \text{every } Y \text{ who } Z - W$$

a person may be chosen by Nature. Let the proper name of this person be 'd'. Then the game is continued with respect to the sentence

$$X - d - W \text{ if } d \text{ is a } Y \text{ and if } d \ Z.$$

Analogous rules can be set up for 'any' and 'each'.

Several comments are needed here. What has been formulated are special cases of certain much more general rules. The generalization does not present any essential problems, however, once we realize what the relevant directions of the different extensions are.

(i) Each wh-word of English comes with a range of individuals (in a logician's sense of the word) associated with it. In the case of 'who' they are persons, in the case of 'where' they are places, in the case of 'when' they are times, etc. For each wh-word, the choices envisaged in (G.some) and (G.every) are made from the associated domain.

(ii) It was assumed above that 'who' occupies the subject position in 'who Z'. If not, a slightly more complicated rule is needed. Essentially, the proper name 'b' or 'd' in the above rules goes into that place in Z where the initial wh-word was moved away from in generating the relative clause in question. (This transformation is often called wh-fronting.)

(iii) If the individual chosen has a proper name, this proper name can be used. If it does not have one, the players must give it a proper name which is used throughout the play of the game in question. Hence the final unanalyzable sentence of a game G(S) may belong to a mild extension of the original language in which S was expressed. Each such extension comprises as its new symbols only a finite number of proper names of individuals, however.

(iv) The rules (G.some) and (G.any) for 'some' and 'any', respectively, must be extended so as to cover also the plural uses of these quantifier words.

(v) Relations of pronominalization between words in X, Y, Z, and W may cause extra complications which will not be discussed in this paper.

(vi) The rule (G.a(n)) does not cover certain 'generic' (universal-quantifier) uses of the indefinite article.

4. GAME-THEORETICAL SEMANTICS: PROPOSITIONAL RULES

The rules for the particles 'and' and 'or' in their clause-binding uses are obvious.

(G.and)   When the game has reached a sentence of the form

X and Y

where X and Y are clauses, Nature may choose X or Y, and the game is continued with respect to it.

(G.or)   Likewise for (X or Y) except that the choice is made by myself.

Similar rules may be set up for 'if', 'but', etc.

In all such propositional rules depronominalization instructions must be built into the rule, that is, each pronoun in the chosen clause must be replaced by its antecedent (in the appropriate case) when this antecedent occurs in the other conjunct or disjunct. Typically, these rules must also be restricted to situations in which all such pronominal antecedents are proper names. There are interesting exceptions to this, studied in the paper 'Pronouns of Laziness in Game-theoretical Semantics' by Hintikka and Carlson.

Further rules can be set up to deal with the uses of 'and' and 'or' to form conjunctive and disjunctive noun phrases, respectively.

There are many ways of treating negation. One of them is the following.

(G.neg)   When the game has reached a sentence of the form

neg⁺[X]

the two players switch their roles, as defined by the game rules (including the rules for winning and losing), and the game is continued with respect to X.

Here neg⁺[⁻] denotes the operation of forming the (semantical) negation in English. It will not be studied in this paper, even though it will have to be presupposed in some of our game rules. For instance, when confronted by

Y if X

or

If X, then Y,

I have a choice according to a rule called (G.if) between Y and neg⁺[X].

The ways in which this rule will have to be developed further are studied in Hintikka and Carlson, 'Conditionals, Generic Quantifiers, and Other Applications of Subgames'.

An appropriate choice of the negation rule helps us to appreciate also the fact that all personification of Nature can in principle be dispensed with. All that is needed is a temporary switch by myself into the role of Devil's – or, rather, Nature's – advocate.[5]

5. GAME-THEORETICAL SEMANTICS: SUNDRY ADDITIONAL RULES

The appropriate rule or rules for the definite article 'the' can be fully understood only after the further development of (G.if) just mentioned. For the purposes of this paper, it suffices to register the interesting 'pronominal' uses of a phrase like 'the Y' to recover a reference to the individual which we are invited to consider by a quantifier phrase of the form 'some Y who Z' or 'a Y who Z'. The way to deal with such phrases is to require them to be replaced by a proper name as soon as their antecedent is replaced by this proper name.

One particular construction employing such pronominal the-phrases is the following.

(*)   An X_1 who Y_1,
           an X_2 who Y_2,
           --- ---, and
           an X_i who Y_i are such that Z

where in Z we may have phrases like 'the X_1', 'the X_2', ..., 'the X_i'. (Instead of 'an' we may here have 'some'. Some of the quantifier phrases in (*) may also be replaced by proper names.)

The construction (*) can be dealt with semantically by substituting a proper name 'b' for the phrase 'the X_i' as soon as 'b' is substituted for the corresponding initial phrase 'an X_j who Y_j'. After the rule (G.a(n)) has been applied to all the initial quantifier phrases, we can simply drop the preface down to and including the words 'such that'.

By relying on suitable version of possible-worlds semantics, additional game rules can be formulated which apply to modal and epistemic concepts. (In this paper we shall use the term 'modal concept' in a narrow sense which excludes epistemic concepts, such as knowledge, belief, memory, perception, etc.).

6. GAME-THEORETICAL SEMANTICS: GENERAL REMARKS

It is easily seen how these game rules help to define a method for the semantical treatment of a class of English sentences. This method is of the kind sketched earlier as a *desideratum* for natural-language semantics. It begins with the given sentence G(S) in this class and proceeds to increasingly simpler sentences. By considering all the different things that might happen in applying the game rules (G.and) and (G.or) and by treating freshly introduced proper names as if they were variables bound to clause-initial quantifiers we can even obtain a partial translation of English quantifier sentences into a logical notation. (The translation is only a partial one because the atomic sentences cannot be translated in this way.)

Since there is another, slightly different translation from English to a logical notation obtainable from our game rules, we shall not comment on this first method of logical formalization in any detail here.

It is more important to note how game-theoretical semantics reflects the difference between absolute scope and relative scope mentioned earlier.

The quantifier phrase which in rules like (G.some) is replaced by a proper name can pronominalize pronouns arbitrarily far away, and an application of (G.some) can thus have arbitrarily distant repercussions. In this sense, absolute scopes are indefinite. However, the relative scopes of quantifier phrases are indicated by the order in which game rules are applied to them.

Two main questions are left open by our game rules. They are

(i)   the informational status of the different moves,

and

(ii)   the order in which the different rules are to be applied (whenever more than one of them is applicable).

7. INFORMATIONAL INDEPENDENCE AND SKOLEM FUNCTIONS

The question (i) really means: Which of the earlier moves are assumed to be known to the players at a given stage of the game? The only plausible answer might at first sight seem to be: all of them. Yet it can be argued that in certain natural-language sentences this will not be the case but that we must countenance the possibility of informally independent moves.

It is important to see precisely what this failure of perfect information means. In general, our game rules will yield a partial translation of English into logical notation. First, we have to realize that the part of a player's strategy which governs the choice of the individual mentioned in the quantificational rules is expressible by a function that specifies the choice, given those earlier moves the player in question is aware of (i.e., has in his information set). These functions are known to logicians as *Skolem functions*. Then we can simply assert the existence of such Skolem functions as codify a winning strategy for myself in $G(S)$ in order to find a translation of S. It is easily seen that Nature may be allowed to choose her moves arbitrarily.

For instance, (1) clearly translates as

(3) $(\exists f)(x)(x$ is a man $\supset$
       $(f(x)$ is a woman $\wedge$ x loves $f(x)))$

while (2) translates as

(4) $(\exists y)(x)(y$ is a woman $\wedge$
       $(x$ is a man $\supset y$ is loved by $x))$.

In (1)–(2), perfect information can clearly be assumed, and has been assumed in (3).

More interestingly, I have argued[6] that a sentence like

(5)   Some novel by every novelist is mentioned in some survey by every critic

exhibits informational independence as far as the two pairs of quantifiers are concerned. If so, it translates as

(6) $(\exists f)(\exists g)(x)(y)[(x$ is a novelist $\wedge$ y is a critic) $\supset$
       $(f(x)$ is a novel by $x \wedge g(y)$ is a survey by $y \wedge$
       $f(x)$ is mentioned in $g(y))]$

Likewise,

(7)   Every townsman admires a friend and every villager envies a cousin who have met each other

translates (if we take 'a friend' to be an ellipsis of 'a friend of his' and 'a cousin' an ellipsis of 'a cousin of his')

(8) $(\exists f)(\exists g)(x)(y)[(x$ is a townsman $\wedge y$ is a villager) $\supset$
       $(f(x)$ is a friend of $x \wedge x$ admires $f(x) \wedge$
       $g(y)$ is a cousin of $y \wedge y$ envies $g(y) \wedge$
       $f(x)$ and $g(y)$ have met each other)]$

8. PUTATIVE OBJECTIONS CONFOUNDED

Since these translations are still claimed in the literature to be controversial,[7] a brief defense is perhaps in order. The main competing translations[8] of (5) and (7) are like (6) and (8), respectively, except for containing the two-argument function variables $f(x, y)$ and $g(x, y)$ instead of the one-variable function variables $f(x)$ and $g(y)$, respectively. We shall call these translations (9) and (10), respectively. They are obtained by giving the two universal quantifiers in (5) and (7) a maximal scope. They are to be distinguished from the 'mixed' readings in which one and only one of the two function variables f and g has two arguments. (Cf. (6) and (8) above.)

These mixed readings of sentences like (5) and (7) are ruled out by their obvious semantical asymmetry with respect to the two pairs of quantifiers. For it seems to me quite obvious that (5) and (7) are semantically symmetrical with respect to these two pairs of quantifiers. (In (5) each pair contains 'every' and 'some', in (7) 'every' and 'a'.) Additional arguments against these mixed readings are given in my paper, 'Quantifiers vs. Quantification Theory'. This leaves only the interpretation exemplified by (9) and (10) to be considered.

There is no need for me to deny that many speakers of English might be tempted to interpret (5) and (7) as (9) and (10), respectively, instead of (6) and (8). The difference between (6) and (9) or between (8) and (10) is a very subtle one, as is the precise force of (6) and (8). It is therefore entirely natural that people should be confused enough to prefer (9) and (10) as readings of (5) and (7), respectively, even though this is not what a truly competent speaker would do.

There is even a good general reason why (6) and (8) are normally avoided as interpretations of what a speaker of English is likely to have in mind in uttering (5) or (7), respectively. This principle is that of charity. It tells us to give the words of a speaker the interpretation which is most likely to make the intended meaning of his utterance true, even if what he says is apt to be literally speaking false. This principle is applicable here because (6) and (8) are so strong as to be unlikely to be true in most normal circumstances.

In order to see how this extra force comes about, we may note that the Skolem functions which embody parts of my winning strategies contain in (6) and (8) fewer arguments than on any of the competing interpretations. For this reason, (6) and (8) are stronger than all the comparable linear-quantifier readings of (5) and (7), respectively. (The less information I need to employ a winning strategy, the less likely the existence of such a strategy is, and the stronger is the claim that such a strategy exists.) In fact, (6) and (8) are so strong as to be somewhat unlikely to be true. Much of Fauconnier's argumentation amounts in fact to pointing out this greater logical force of the reading instantiated by (6) and (8) as compared with the interpretation illustrated by (9) and (10). From this it only follows that people are likely to mean (9) and (10) when they utter (5) of (7), respectively, if one assumes the principle of charity, and absolutely nothing follows from Fauconnier's observations concerning the basic semantical force of (5) or (7). Hence his observations do not tell against my theory in the least.

A somewhat parallel case may illustrate my point. Suppose someone tells me, 'This is a dangerous street. Someone is hit by a car every week in it.' For obvious reasons, in interpreting his meaning I am apt to assign in the second sentence the widest scope to 'every'. In so doing, I am not uncovering an exception to the left-to-right ordering principle of English quantifiers. I am merely applying the principle of charity. Fauconnier's arguments are not any more conclusive against my theory. All that follows from them is that competent speakers of English are unlikely to assert sentences of the type (5) or (7) with their literal meaning.

What is decisive here are not different speakers' more or less confused uneducated intuitions but the systematical questions which one can ask and answer here. They include the question as to which semantical representation preserves the entailments we all intuitively accept as well as the question which translation is based on a consistent, general set of rules of semantical interpretation. I shall deal with these two questions in the opposite order.

There does not seem to be any natural set of rules of semantical interpretation that yields (9) and (10) rather than (6) and (8).[9] The translations (9) and (10) are obtained by giving the two universal quantifiers in (5) and (7) maximal (linear) scope, a scope that includes both existential quantifiers. If this were the way to understand (5) and (7), then there does not seem to be any way to avoid similarly giving both universal quantifiers a maximal scope also in the following sentences.

(11)   Some novel by every novelist is mentioned by every critic.

(12)   Every townsman admires a friend who has met every villager.

Yet the preferred readings of (11) and (12) are clearly different from these maximal-scope interpretations. For instance, (11) obviously means

(13) $(x)[x$ is a novelist $\supset$
        $(\exists y)(y$ is a novel by $x \land$
        $(z)(z$ is a critic $\supset$ y is mentioned by $z))]$

which is equivalent with

(14)   (∃f)(x)(z)[z is a novelist ⊃
        (f(x) is a novel by x ∧
        (z is a critic ⊃ f(x) is mentioned by z))]

Clearly (13) is different from what we obtain by giving the two universal quantifiers a maximal scope in (11). Analogous remarks apply to (12). This suggests strongly that (9) and (10) are not viable readings of (5) and (7), respectively. This observation in turn provides support for the translations (6) and (8) of the same sentences.

This observation is, moreover, just what is to be expected on my theory. Using an obvious 'branching-quantifier' notation (to be discussed in the sequel) we can say that on my theory (7) has the form

(7)*   (x)(∃z)
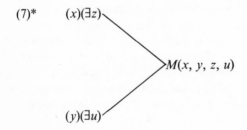
                            M(x, y, z, u)

        (y)(∃u)

while by the same token (11) has the form

(11)*   (x)(∃z)
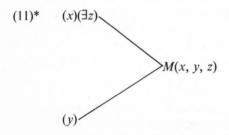
                            M(x, y, z)

        (y)

However, while (7)* does not reduce in general to a linear-quantifier form, (11)* can easily be seen to do so, and in fact to be equivalent with

(11)**   (x)(∃z)(y)M(x, y, z)

(which is equivalent with (14)). Thus my theory, unlike the views of my critics, predicts precisely the right reading for both (7) and (11).

A small qualification is needed at this point. The dropping of a quantifier from (5) and (7) so as to obtain (11) and (12), respectively, may have consequences other than the step from the form (7)* to (11)*. One of them is that the branching quantifier interpretation becomes somewhat less likely as compared with the linear quantifier reading. For instance, the sentence

(15)   Every writer is mentioned in some survey by every critic

has as its preferred reading (because of a left-to-right preference)

(16) $(x)(x$ is a writer $\wedge$
$(z)(z$ is a critic $\supset$
$(\exists u)(u$ is an essay by z $\wedge$
x is mentioned in $u)))$

The reason for this is that in (15) the quantifier pair 'some survey by every critic' is no longer taken to be informationally independent of 'every writer'. Why? Even though I have not discussed the conditions on which English quantifiers can be independent on each other, the behaviour of (15) is to be expected. The informational independence of quantifiers of each other goes hand in hand with their syntactical isolation from one another. Now in some clear sense the isolation is more marked in (5) and (7) than in (15). Hence a dependence and consequently a linear reading is only natural in (15). The logical form of (15) is therefore (cf. (7)* and (11)*).

(15)* $(y)(x)(\exists z)M(x, y, z)$

No counterevidence to my theory is hence forthcoming from examples like (15).

The most decisive refutation of (9) and (10) as semantical representations of (5) and (7), respectively, nevertheless turns on the obvious entailments between (5) and (7) on the one hand and certain other sentences on the other hand. If there is anything clear about (5), it is that (5) implies, together with the premise 'John is a writer', the sentence

(17)   Some novel by John is mentioned in some survey by every critic.

On the reading (6) I am defending, this entailment is valid. However, on the interpretation (9) which Fauconnier and Stenius defend, (17) is *not* implied by (6). As you can easily see, (9) does not imply logically

(18) $(\exists z)(y)(\exists u)$[John is a novelist $\supset$
        (y is a critic $\supset$
        (z is a novel by John $\wedge$
        u is a survey by y $\wedge$
        z is mentioned in u))]

which obviously has the force of (17).

In other words, on the Fauconnier-Stenius view, (6) could be true while there is no single novel by John the writer which is mentioned in some survey by every critic. This consequence of their view is patently counter-intuitive, indeed so clearly as to belie the whole maximal-scope interpretation (9) which my critics have tried to substitute for the branching-quantifier interpretation (6) of (5). The maximal-scope interpretation simply does not preserve obviously valid entailments. The same applies immediately to other similar sentences, e.g., to the attempted interpretation of (7) as having the force (10). Even though the preservation of intuitively valid entailments is often overestimated as a criterion of correct semantical representation of natural-language sentences, here this criterion works extremely well.

In contrast, (6) obviously implies the desired consequence (17). Thus a simple test in terms of logical entailments is enough to show the superiority of my branching-quantifier reading of English sentences like (5) and (7).

9. PARTIALLY ORDERED QUANTIFIERS IN NATURAL LANGUAGES

One major reason why these observations are interesting is that while (9) and (10) are linear first-order sentences and while (13) admits of a translation into a linear first-order notation, sentences of the form (6) or (8) do not automatically do so. Rather, instead of a linear first-order translation they admit of a formulation in terms of branching (partially ordered) quantifiers, for instance as follows.

(19) $(x)(\exists z)$

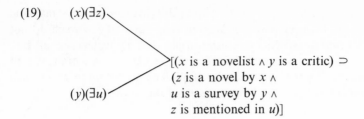

$[(x$ is a novelist $\wedge y$ is a critic$) \supset$
(z is a novel by $x \wedge$
u is a survey by $y \wedge$
z is mentioned in $u)]$

$(y)(\exists u)$

The general form of this type of sentence is

(20) $(x)(\exists z)$

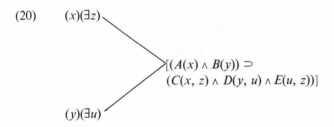

$[(A(x) \wedge B(y)) \supset$
$(C(x, z) \wedge D(y, u) \wedge E(u, z))]$

$(y)(\exists u)$

Can all sentences of this form be translated into linear first-order notation? It is known[10] that not all sentences of the general form

(21) $(x)(\exists z)$

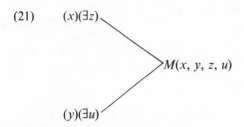

$M(x, y, z, u)$

$(y)(\exists u)$

can be translated into a linear first-order form. Now we can so enlarge the domain of individuals presupposed in (21) as to allow also ordered pairs of original individuals into it.[11] By allowing our quantifiers to range over the enlarged domain and by re-interpreting its unanalyzable predicates (21) can be converted into the form (20) *salva* satisfiability. (The main step is of course to re-interpret each primitive predicate $P(x, y, z, u)$ in (17) involving x, y, and one or both of z and u as a predicate $P(\langle x, z \rangle, \langle y, u \rangle)$ of the two ordered pairs $\langle x, z \rangle$, $\langle y, u \rangle$.) Since there is in general no linear first-order translation for (21), there cannot always be one for (20), either.

Thus there seems to be plenty of English sentences whose semantical representation involves partially ordered (p.o.) quantifiers which do not reduce to linear ones. One can even argue that equivalents to all p.o. quantifier formulas are needed in English semantics. An argument to this effect is facilitated by the results of Walkoe according to which each p.o. quantifier sentence has an equivalent of the form

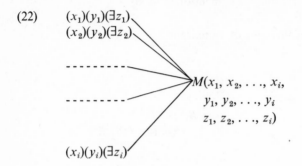

(22) $(x_1)(y_1)(\exists z_1)$
         $(x_2)(y_2)(\exists z_2)$

         $M(x_1, x_2, \ldots, x_i,$
         $y_1, y_2, \ldots, y_i$
         $z_1, z_2, \ldots, z_i)$

         $(x_i)(y_i)(\exists z_i)$

and an equivalent of the form

(23) $(x_1)(x_2) \ldots (x_j)(\exists z_1)(\exists z_2) \ldots (\exists z_k)$

                                              $M(x_1, y_1,$

         $(y_1)(y_2) \ldots (y_j)(\exists u_1)(\exists u_2) \ldots (\exists u_k)$

         $x_2, y_2, \ldots, x_j, y_j, z_1, u_1, z_2, y_2, \ldots, z_k, u_k).$

Now using the construction exemplified by (7), viz. a relative clause with several antecedents, we can easily construct English sentences of the form (22) with the matrix having the following structure.

(24) $A_1(x_1) \wedge A_2(x_2) \wedge \ldots$ $\wedge$
         $B_1(x_1, y_1) \wedge B_2(x_2, y_2) \wedge \ldots$ $) \supset$
         $(C_1(y_1, z_1) \wedge C_2(y_2, z_2) \wedge \ldots$ $\wedge$
         $D_1(z_1, z_2) \wedge D_2(z_1, z_3) \wedge \ldots$ $\wedge$
         $D_i(z_{i-1}, z_i))$

A case in point – illustrating the principles involved in constructing sentences of the form (24) – is the following:

(25)   Every actor of each theatre envies a film star, every review of each critic mentions a novelist, and every book by each chess writer describes a grand master, of whom the star admires the grand master and hates the novelist while the novelist looks down on the grand master.

By an argument which is an extension of our earlier argument concerning (20) and (21) it can be shown that every sentence (22) can be re-interpreted so as to be of the form (24). First, the domain of individuals is enlarged by allowing ordered pairs and ordered triples of earlier individuals. The primitive predicates are reinterpreted as before. Finally, the sentence is reformulated (as in first-order reduction theory) so as to involve only dyadic relations.

This shows – or at least suggests very strongly – that the special form of the matrix of those p.o. quantifier formulas which are obtained as translations of suitable English quantifier sentences does not essentially restrict their generality. This in turn suggests that not only are there more complicated p.o. quantifier structures present in the semantics of English quantifier sentences. Literally *all* such structures are needed there.

A similar argument can be carried out in terms of the 'normal form' (23) instead of (22). Since in this case we are dealing with only two branches of quantifiers, the situation is simpler in that the reduction to dyadic predicates is dispensable in the argument.

One English construction that can be used to build sentences whose semantical representation has the form (23) is the repeated use of the particle 'of'. The following is a case in point.

(26)   Some product of some subdivision of every company of every conglomerate is advertised in some page of some number of every magazine of every newspaper chain.

One reason why this is an interesting result is the observation – made in my earlier paper 'Quantifiers vs. Quantification Theory' – that the theory of p.o. quantifiers is as complicated as second-order logic (with standard interpretation) as far as its decision problem (degrees of unsolvability of the set of all valid sentences) is concerned. The two decision problems can be effectively (recursively) reduced to each other. An argument to this effect is given in 'Quantifiers vs. Quantification Theory'. Thus structures of enormous logical complexity must in effect be presupposed in the semantics of the English language.

10. ORDERING PRINCIPLES

The other main question concerning our game rules (cf. the end of Section 6 above) is about the order in which they are to be applied. In rules like (G.some), X, Z, and W may contain other quantifier phrases or other kinds of phrases to which game rules can be applied. What determines between all these possible applications?

Even though I cannot here present adequate evidence for it, an answer seems to be forthcoming. There are two kinds of ordering principles governing the order of application of the game rules, general principles and special ones. Of these, the general principles can be overruled by the special ones. The most important general principles are the following.[12]

(O.comm)   A game rule must not be applied to a phrase in a lower clause if some rule can be applied to a higher one (i.e., to a phrase in a clause dominating the former).

(O.LR)   When two phrases occur in the same clause a rule must not be applied to the one on the right if a rule can be applied to the one on the left.

The ordering principle (O.LR) obviously explains why (1)–(2) above have the preferred readings they in fact have. In (1), (G.every) is to be applied before (G.some), for the relevant occurrence of 'every' is to the left of the relevant occurrence of 'some' in (1). In (2), the relationship is the inverse one. Consequently, in (1) the choice of a woman depends on the choice of the man, as (27) (see below) spells out. In contrast, no such dependence obtains in (2), as one can see also from (28).

(27) $(\exists f)\,(x)\,(x$ is a man $\supset$
          $(f(x)$ is a woman $\wedge\ x$ loves $f(x)))$.

(28) $(\exists y)\,(x)\,(y$ is a woman $\wedge$
          $(x$ is a man $\supset\ y$ is loved by $x))$.

The most important special principles are perhaps the following.

(O.any)   (G.any) has priority over (G.not), (G.if), and over the modal rules.

(O.some)   (G.some) has priority over (G.not).

(O.each)   (G.each) has priority over other quantifier rules and over the propositional rules (G.and) and (G.or).

These principles have also a negative aspect: (G.any), (G.some), and

(G.each) do *not* have priority over the other rules in my fragment of English semantics.

It is important to realize that special ordering principles like (O.any) and (O.each) overrule general principles like (O.comm). For this reason, Robert May is entirely wrong in bracketing my approach with theories "of the relative scope of quantifiers involving the notion of 'command' ". I am immune to May's criticisms, as they are presented in his 'Logical Form and Conditions on Rules', *Proceedings of the Seventh Conference of the NELS*.

It would take me far too long to present adequate evidence for these principles. They seem to stand up fairly well to examples, provided that we keep in mind that not all of them are strict principles but only preferential ones.

For instance, the force of (O.each) is seen from such pairs of examples as the following.

(29)   Somebody is occupying each phone booth.
(30)   Somebody is occupying every phone booth.
(31)   A rifle or a submachine gun was given to each soldier.
(32)   A rifle or a submachine gun was given to every soldier.

It is clear that most of the every-sentences of this type admit of more than one reading. Hence our ordering principles are here preferential only.

11. THE ANY-THESIS

These ordering principles allow us to capture quite remarkable further regularities that hold in English, at least in the fragment of English we are here interested in. The most interesting further regularity is perhaps the following one.

Any-thesis: The word 'any' is acceptable (grammatical) in a given context X – any Y – Z if and only if an exchange of 'any' for 'every' results in a grammatical expression which is not identical in meaning with X – any Y – Z.

Again, the relevant evidence for the any-thesis – and against it – is too extensive to be reviewed here. A few characteristic examples will nevertheless be given in order to convey to the reader a sense of the power of the any-thesis. It is easy to work out the explanation of these examples of one's own. (Following the practice of linguists, ungrammatical expressions are marked by an asterisk.)

(33)   If any member contributes, I'll be happy.

(34)   If every member contributes, I'll be happy.

(35)   *If Jane wins, anybody is happy.

(36)   If Jane wins, everybody is happy.

(37)   Jane can win any match.

(38)   Jane can win every match.

(39)   *Jane has won any match.

(40)   Jane has won every match.

(41)   Jane hasn't won any match.

(42)   Jane hasn't won every match.

(43)   *If Jane has won any match, she has won any match.

(44)   If Jane has won any match, she has won every match.

You will easily see that no any-sentence without an asterisk is logically equivalent with its immediate successor, while those with an asterisk are. It is also readily seen how this follows from our game rules and ordering principles.[13]

The examples given above show that 'any' is acceptable in the antecedent of a conditional, but not in its consequent, other things being equal. The qualification 'other things being equal' is occasioned by the fact that the presence of some modal notion (or negation) in the consequent will make a difference, as illustrated by the following examples.

(45)   If Jane has been training hard, she can win any match.

(46)   If Jane has been training hard, she can win every match.

(47)   If Jane did not train hard, she has not won any match.

(48)   If Jane did not train hard, she has not won every match.

(49)   If Jane can win any match, she can win any match.

(50)   If Jane can win any match, she can win every match.

It is of interest to see how my rules and principles predict for each of the sentences (33)–(50) precisely the force it in fact has.

Likewise, 'any' is typically acceptable in connection with a negation, but not if the scope of 'every' is automatically as wide as that of 'any', i.e., if its scope includes the negation-operator. The following examples illustrate this:

(51)   John has not dated any girl.
(52)   John has not dated every girl.
(53)   *Any girl has not been dated by John.
(54)   Every girl has not been dated by John.

In (53) and (54), the same scope is predicted for 'any' and 'every', respectively, by (O.LR). Hence the asterisk.

The following pair of sentences illustrates the fact that a mere change in the order of our different game rules does not create the kind of asymmetry which justifies the presence of 'any'. It is required that the change of order affects the logical force of the sentences in question.

(55)   *John must pick any apple.
(56)   John must pick every apple.

Since 'must' and 'every' (or 'any') are both of the nature of universal quantifiers, their relative order does not always affect logical force. This explains the asterisk in (55).

All this adds grist to the mill of the any-thesis. Thus the any-thesis seems to hold up extremely well in a sufficiently small fragment of English. How much that fragment can be extended without violating the any-thesis remains to be examined. Certain extensions are in any case possible, for instance an extension that takes in the English future tense. It suffices for my present purposes, however, if the any-thesis holds in a relatively small fragment of English, as it indeed seems to do.

In fact, even if the any-thesis should turn out to need modifications when extended to sentences containing comparatives or to still other types of sentences not considered here, it seems to hold quite well indeed within a fragment which contains quantifier phrases, propositional connectives, the phrase 'such that', modal and epistemic operators, backward-looking (i.e., pronominal) the-phrases, the passive transformation, plus maybe a few other constructions. It was already mentioned that from its validity within this limited fragment certain important implications for the methodology of contemporary linguistics will ensue.

An interesting general qualification to my any-thesis has recently emerged from the work summarized in Hintikka and Carlson, 'Conditionals, Generic Quantifiers, and Other Applications of Subgames'. It turns out that in some cases a string of the form

X — every Y who Z — W

is unacceptable merely because of a failure by the every-phrase to serve as the right kind of antecedent for a pronoun or for some other kind of anaphoric expression. In such cases, the corresponding any-sentence, i.e.,

$$X - \text{any } Y \text{ who } Z - W$$

is acceptable.

This observation implies changes both in the formulation of the any-thesis and in the arguments based on it. (See especially Section 16 below.) These qualifications, which we shall not try to make here, do not affect my total argument, however.

12. SYNTAX VS. SEMANTICS. ANY-THESIS VS. GENERATIVE GRAMMAR

One of them is centered around the interplay of syntax and semantics in the any-thesis. In the any-thesis, the syntactic acceptability or unacceptability of certain (putative) sentences is explained by reference to their semantical properties. This is in sharp contrast to all approaches to grammar in which the syntactical component is independent of the semantical one. What is even more striking, the (partial) explanation of the distribution of 'any' obtained from the any-thesis is not even generative. Not only do we utilize certain semantical representations in the criterion of grammatically embodied in the any-thesis. This criterion is itself not couched in the generative terms at all. The grammaticality of a sentence is not specified by means of rules that may or may not generate it, nor in terms of syntactically formulated restrictions on such rules. The criterion turns on a comparison of the semantical properties of the outcome of a generation with those of another sentence. This is an even more radical departure from the early theories of generative grammar than what can e.g. be found in the so-called generative semantics. (See Lakoff 1971 for an exposition of this approach.) Not only is our game-theoretical *semantics* not generative. It leads us to formulate certain *syntactical* regularities that are not dealt with in generative terms at all.

It seems to me that we have here a pertinent reminder of the fact that there is no deep methodological reason why all linguistic regularities, even syntactical ones, should be explained in generative terms. Indeed, we have here a clear example to the contrary.

Its relevance might seem to depend on how representative the syntactical explanation will turn out to be that we obtain from the any-thesis, in other words, to depend on whether there are other syntactical phenomena whose most natural explanations are nonsyntactical or nongenerative. I have in fact been led to think that there are certain highly important linguistic phenomena which can only be accounted for in terms other than generative ones. (See here my monograph on *The Semantics of Questions and the Questions of Semantics*.) However, I also believe that the question of the generalizability of the any-thesis is not the crux of the matter here. For as long as the any-thesis holds within an interesting fragment of English, and as long as it proves to be in some realistic sense the right explanation of certain aspects of the distribution of 'any' in that fragment, we have a clear-cut counter-example in our hands to the alleged power of generative methods to explain *all* interesting grammatical phenomena. This suffices for most of the important philosophical and methodological suggestions that can be teased out of our observations. It is thus the correctness of the any-thesis as the best explanation of the distribution of 'any' in our fragment of English that is the crucial claim here, not the generalizability of the any-thesis or even the generalizability of the type of explanation it exemplifies.

13. GRAMMATICALITY NOT A RECURSIVE CONCEPT ?

This brings us to the question whether, and if so in what sense, the explanation which the any-thesis offers to us is preferable to possible alternative explanations in generative terms. It is *prima facie* not very clear how this question could be answered.

However, an interesting argument is forthcoming for the impossibility of any generative account of the usual sort for the distribution of 'any'. (By 'distribution' we mean, following the usage of linguists, the set of contexts in which an expression can occur.) This argument has a certain interest as an application of well-known logical concepts and results. In virtually every type of formal grammar that has been seriously proposed for natural languages, the set of grammatical (acceptable) sentences is recursive. This is not only true of all context-free grammars, it is likewise true for instance of the so-called type one context-sensitive grammars. Now the criterion of grammaticality embodied in the any-thesis is semantical: it turns on the synonymy (identity in meaning) of two expressions. Being semantical, it is *prima facie* less likely to yield a recursive set of grammatical (acceptable) sentences than any generative grammar of the usual sort.

In fact we can present an argument which on certain assumptions proves that the specific criterion of grammaticality expressed by the any-thesis does not yield recursive set of acceptable sentences.

The most important, and the most questionable, of these assumptions is an identification of the synonymy (identity in meaning) of two English sentences on the basis of our game-theoretical semantics with the logical equivalence of the semantical representations this semantics assigns to the two sentences in the case of sentences whose non-logical vocabulary does not exhibit any logical (analytical) dependencies between its several items. (Alternatively we could consider the question whether the equivalence is logically implied by the conjunction of the meaning postulates for this vocabulary.) Essentially, this means assuming that logical equivalence preserves meaning.

I find this identification of sameness in meaning with logical equivalence questionable.[14] Hence the rest of the argument in this paper has to some extent the character of a thought-experiment rather than the nature of a series of definite theses. The experiment is so interesting, however, as to be worth being considered in some detail.

Other requisite assumptions will be registered in the course of our attempt to establish the nonrecursivity of the class of grammatical English sentences.

14. AN ARGUMENT FOR NONRECURSIVITY

The obvious way of proving a result of the kind indicated is to reduce some well-known unsolvable decision problem to the problem of testing whether the interchange of 'any' and 'every' affects meaning. The difficulty in this enterprise is that we have not studied in any real detail the relation-ship (intertranslatability) of first-order formalism and English quantifier sentences. However, if we can assume fairly straightforward translatability we can prove the desired result.

It has been established in the literature that the class of sentences of the following form is a reduction class for satisfiability. (See Suranyi and cf. Rogers.)

$$(57) \qquad (x)(y)(z)M_1(x, y, z) \wedge (x)(y)(Ez)M_2(x, y, z)$$

Here M_1, M_2 do not contain any quantifiers. It is likewise known from the literature that various other restrictions can be imposed on M_1 and M_2. For instance, they can be chosen so as to contain only one two-place predicate (relation), over and above one-place predicates.

By a reduction class for satisfiability in first-order logic, logicians mean a class of sentences such that the problem of deciding the satisfiability of any first-order formula can be reduced to the problem of deciding the satisfiability of members of this class. A reduction class for logical truth (validity) is defined analogously.

Now (57) can be rewritten

(58) $(x)(y) \sim [(Ez)M_2(x, y, z) \supset (Ez) \sim M_1(x, y, z)]$

which is the negation of

(59) $(Ex)(Ey)[(Ez)M_2(x, y, z) \supset (Ez) \sim M_1(x, y, z)]$.

Formulas of this form (with the same freedom of choice for M_1 and M_2 as in (58) constitute a reduction class for logical truth (provability).

Here we shall assume that (59) can be translated effectively into an English quantifier sentence which has an internal conditional like (59) and where this internal conditional has the form

(60)   if any X, then Y.

The plausibility of this translation is enhanced, over and above any general belief in the expressive power of natural languages, by the heavy restrictions which can be imposed on M_1 and M_2 and which were mentioned earlier. Furthermore, it suffices for our purposes to have, for each formula of the form (59), one sentence of this form (with logically independent atomic predicates) translated into English.

Examples can easily be produced which strongly suggest that this is possible. Remembering that M_1 and M_2 need only contain one two-place relation (transitive verb), over and above one-place predicates, we can for instance formulate in English the following instance of (59).

(61)   Some A_1 which is also an A_2 but neither a B_1 nor a B_2 and some A_2 which is also a B_1 but neither an A_1 nor a B_2 and which R's the A_1 are such that if any B_2 which is not an A_2 R's the A_1 and is R'ed by the A_2, then some B_1 either R's the A_1 and is R'ed by the A_1, or else R's both the A_1 and the A_2.

This example is chosen at random. However, it illustrates clearly the principles which can be used in finding effectively an English translation for a suitable sentence exemplifying any given logical formula of the form (59).

Hence the translatability required here is an extremely plausible assumption.

Now the exchange of 'any' for 'every' changes (60) into

(62)   if every X, then Y.

The whole sentence resulting from this interchange will be the translation of

(63) $(Ex)(Ey)[(z)M_2(x, y, z) \supset (Ez) \sim M_1(x, y, z)]$

which can be rewritten as

(64) $(Ex)(Ey)(Ez)(\sim M_1(x, y, z) \vee \sim M_2(x, y, z))$

From the theory of first-order logic it is known that there exists a decision method for formulas of the form (64) = (63). This gives us a method of testing (59) for validity on the assumption that the equivalence of (59) and (63) can be effectively (recursively) tested. If this test yields a positive result, (59) and (63) are equivalent, and we can test the former for satisfiability by testing the latter. If the test yields a negative result, we observe that (59) logically implies (63). Hence the failure of their equivalence must mean that (63) does not imply logically (59). But if so, (59) cannot be valid, for then it would be implied by any sentence.

Hence we could decide the logical truth of (59) and hence the satisfiability of its negation (58) (or (57)) if we could test recursively the equivalence of (59) and (63). Since the decision problem for the whole first-order logic is unsolvable, we cannot decide the latter. But on the assumptions made, we could decide this if we could decide whether the interchange or 'any' and 'every' affects meaning. Hence the latter decision problem is also unsolvable. But if the any-thesis holds, this means that the class of acceptable English quantifier sentences is not recursive: we cannot have an effective test for membership in this class.

This result is tentative in that it depends on assumptions of translatability which we have not explicitly justified. In fact, the whole question of translatability between natural languages like English and first-order formalism needs much closer scrutiny. However, it seems to me that such a closer examination will confirm our hypotheses rather than disconfirm them.

15. AN ALTERNATIVE ARGUMENT

It is of some interest to see that essentially the same argument can be carried out in terms of negation instead of the conditional. We do not have to consider the formula (57). In its stead, we can focus on

(65) $(Ex)(Ey)[(z) \sim M_2(x, y, z) \vee (Ez) \sim M_1(x, y, z)]$.

Let us assume that an instance of each formula of this kind can be translated into English in such a way that the clause corresponding to

(66) $(z) \sim M_2(x, y, z)$

contains an any-phrase which in virtue of (O.any) has a wider scope than the negation in the same clause. In order to see if this translation is grammatical, we will have to compare it with the sentence which contains a corresponding every-clause (assuming the any-thesis). Let us assume that this corresponding sentence is in turn a translation of

(67) $(Ex)(Ey)[\sim(z)M_2(x, y, z) \vee (Ez) \sim M_1(x, y, z)]$

Then to test the grammaticality of the any-sentence will be to test the equivalence of (65) and (67). But for the same reasons as in the earlier version of the same argument, (67) can be effectively tested for validity. In the same way as before the equivalence test thus yields a test of the logical truth of (65). Such an effective test is known to be impossible, however. Hence the equivalence test is impossible, too. On the translatability assumptions just made, there cannot exist an effective test of grammaticality, either.

There does not seem to be any reason to doubt the translatability assumptions, either, although I shall not discuss them in any detail here.

What this parallel argument shows is that my result does not depend on any peculiarities of either 'if' or 'not'. The second version of the argument may even be more natural than the first one in that conditionals do not seem to occur often in the scope of quantifiers in natural language.

16. CONSEQUENCES OF NONRECURSIVITY

In so far as our assumptions concerning translatability can be justified, we therefore have a counterexample to the recursivity of the class of acceptable strings (grammatical sentences). Moreover, the counterexample, if valid, is stronger than this. If there is a recursive test of well-formedness (which *ipso facto* is a similar test of non-well-formedness) except for the effects of the any-thesis (and there certainly seems to be such a test for English quantifier sentences), then there is a recursive enumeration of the non-sentences in this fragment of English. (For in the recursive enumeration of all valid equivalences each any-every equivalence which causes a putative any-sentence to be ungrammatical will eventually make its appearance.) If so, and if the complement class of grammatical sentences is not recursive, the latter class cannot of course be recursively enumerable, either. (A recursive class can be characterized as one which is recursively enumerable and whose complement is likewise recursively enumerable.)

Hence, given all the qualifications made in the course of the argument above, we have here a clear-cut counter-example to generative grammar. We have, in an interesting fragment of English, a situation in which the class of all grammatical sentences just cannot be generated by *any* algorithm, not just by the kinds of generation processes generative grammarians favor in these days. And of course an explanation of grammaticality through an algorithmic generation process is the very essence of generative grammar.

As a by-product, we obtain an answer to the obvious objection which is likely to be raised against my point above that the explanation of grammaticality and ungrammaticality through the any-thesis is essentially semantical and not syntactical. For what is there to rule out an alternative syntactical account? What we have seen shows (given the assumptions made in the course of our argument) that there just cannot be any syntactic account whatever, if this account is to be generative. And what a non-generative purely syntactical account might be is hard even to imagine.

I have all along spoken of a fragment of English and of showing that the set of all grammatical sentences of this fragment is not recursively enumerable. This is unnecessary modesty, however. A simple supplementary argument shows that if the result we have obtained holds true, the set of all grammatical English sentences cannot be recursively enumerable, either. The diagram on the next page shows how the land lies.

In it A = all grammatical English sentences, B = all grammatical sentences of our fragment, C = sentences ruled out by the any-thesis but not by any other grammatical principle.

Now B + C can be seen to be recursive. If A were recursively enumerable, we could obtain a recursive enumeration of B, too, by omitting from the former enumeration all the sentences that do not belong to B + C. since B+C is recursive, this can be done effectively.

The recursivity of B + C is perhaps not quite obvious, especially since we have not given explicit formation rules for its members. However, the constructions contained in it are syntactically quite straightforward, and it can easily be argued that the other special restrictions on membership in B + C (other than the any-thesis) are likely to be recursive. Hence B + C is recursive, and hence a recursive enumeration of A would yield a

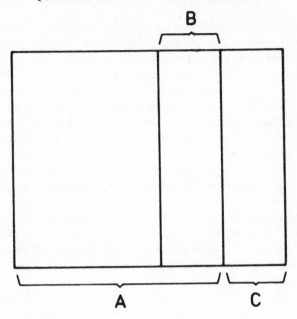

similar enumeration of B. But it was shown that B is not recursively enumerable. Hence A cannot be recursively enumerable, either, which was to be proved.

Hence what my argument shows, to the extent it is valid, is that the set of all (grammatically correct) sentences of English is not recursively enumerable. There just cannot exist an exhaustive and purely generative grammar of the English language. This observation, even though it is a tentative one, is striking indication of the limitations of generative methods in theoretical linguistics.

17. AN OBJECTION MET

Even without rehearsing the full evidence for the any-thesis, we can disprove one potential objection to it. This objection can be illustrated by pairs of sentences of the following kind.

(68)   If everyone is hurt, someone is hurt.
(69)   If anyone is hurt, someone is hurt.

These are both logically true, and hence logically equivalent. Hence the exchange of 'any' and 'every' in them does not make any difference to their logical force – nor therefore to their meaning, on the tentative assumption we have been operating on. By the any-thesis, 'any' thus would have to be unacceptable in (69). Yet (69) seems to be acceptable enough.

The answer to this objection is that logically true and logically false sentences are in ordinary discourse frequently given a spontaneously non-standard interpretation. For instance, the natural conversational force of (68) is certainly different from its basic logical force as a tautology (logical truth). Such conversational force is a pragmatic 'surface' pheno-menon, however, which is not to be incorporated in one's basic semantical theory. For this reason, it is disregarded here. (For the methodological distinctions evoked here, see the first chapter of my *Models for Modalities*, D. Reidel, 1969.)

The same obviously holds for (69). The undeniable fact that it can have a nontrivial conversational force therefore does not tell against the any-thesis, for such a force is habitually assigned to logically true sentences anyway. Such a force can be present in (69) even if this sentence is basically ungrammatical.

When such a force cannot – for pragmatical reasons which we shall not discuss here – be assigned to a logically true any-sentence, the sentence is sometimes unacceptable. This is illustrated by the following pair of sentences (strings).

(70)   If everyone loses, everyone loses.
(71)   *If everyone loses, anyone loses.

Here the second expression seems to be ungrammatical. (If it is not, in a suitable context, I will have to maintain that it has a nonstandard force in that context.)

All told, the putative objection mentioned above thus does not seem to hold water.

18. ON THE LIMITS OF THE ANY-THESIS

It is not my purpose in this paper to examine the scope and limits of the any-thesis. A few remarks on the subject are nevertheless in order in order to avoid misunderstanding.

The main point is that it suffices for my argument if the any-thesis holds in a suitable fragment of English. Hence the question whether any-thesis holds in larger fragments of English or perhaps even in the whole language does not concern me here.

However, certain constructions which are hard to avoid seem to introduce exceptions to the thesis. One of them is the future tense. For instance, even though (15) is not acceptable, the following is.

(72)   Jane will win any match.

This is not very disconcerting if we are merely thinking of the letter of the any-thesis. For clearly (72) says something different from

(73)   Jane will win every match.

Rather, the problem is to explain the difference in meaning between (72) and (73) in terms of game-theoretic semantics.

This is not an occasion to develop or even outline a game-theoretical treatment of tenses, even though I believe that it is possible to do so. However, the main observations needed here are clear enough. In using the future tense, we are semantically speaking contemplating in effect several different courses of events of which one is selected for consideration. This selection operation is closely comparable with those associated with modal operators. This similarity in behavior extends to the ordering principles (O.any). Hence the order of the moves associated with the future-tense operator and (G.any) or (G.every), respectively, is a different one. Even if the choice associated with the future-tense operator is made by Nature, this ordering difference has consequences in that the domain of individuals is different on the two orderings. If an individual is chosen before the future tense is dealt with, all individuals existing under the different future courses of events are eligible. If a particular future is chosen first, an application of (G.any) or (G.every) pertains only to individuals in that particular future.

This accounts well for the relevant evidence. For instance, consider the following Vendlerian pair of examples.

(74)   Any doctor at the convention will tell you that Stopsneeze helps.
(75)   Every doctor at the convention will tell you that Stopsneeze helps.

In (75), only those doctors are considered who will actually come to the convention, whereas in (74) all doctors who might show up are within the range of the universal quantifier 'any'. Similar remarks apply to (72) and (73).

This analysis is continued in an interesting fashion by considering cases where an intensional operator with respect to which (unlike modal operators in the narrow sense) (G.every) and (G.any) behave in the same way governs a future-tense that-clause. Then the choice of the 'world' (typically a course of events) is absorbed to the intensional operator and hence precedes the choice of an individual involved either in (G.every) or (G.any). In brief, no difference in meaning between 'any' and 'every' results, and 'any' is consequently unacceptable. Thus even though (72) is acceptable,

(76)   *Mary hopes that Jane will win any match

is unacceptable. So are the following.

(77)   *Mary believes that Jane will win any match.
(78)   *Ralph hopes that any doctor at the convention will tell him that Stopsneeze helps.

Examples can easily be multiplied, and they yield strong (although indirect) evidence for my theory.

The same account as was used in dealing with 'any' in future-tense sentences applies *mutatis mutandis* to those uses of present-tense verbs which express habitual action, non-momentary states or anything else that does not pertain exclusively to the present movement. For instance, while (11) is unacceptable, the following is acceptable.

(79)   If Jane wins, anybody who appreciates good tennis is happy.

What distinguishes (79) from

(80)   If Jane wins, everybody who appreciates good tennis is happy

is that in the former the speaker is not sure who all the *cognoscenti* are while in the latter they are assured to constitute a known class. Clearly there is a difference in meaning between (79) and (80), as any-thesis requires for the acceptability of (79).

There can be a similar difference between sentences of the form 'necessarily $X - any - Z$' and 'necessarily $X - every - Z$', respectively. Even though 'every', 'any', and 'necessarily' are all universal quantifiers (of sorts), the order makes a difference here because of the possible dependence of the range of 'every' on the choice associated with 'necessarily'.

Sometimes the relevant differences in meaning are *prima facie* not very easy to account for in terms of game-theoretical semantics. More specifically, in some contexts any relative clause appended to any + NP seems to make 'any' acceptable even though no reference to the future and no other sort of reference to several alternative courses of events is involved. A case in point might be

(81)   If Jane wins, anyone who has bet on her is happy.

Adjectives following 'any' sometimes seem to have the same effect, as can be predicted on the basis of the syntactical generation of the sentences where they occur.

Such examples present a challenge, not so much to any-thesis as to the general framework of semantical analysis I have been proposing. It seems to me that the key to the situation is that 'if' has typically a modal force, however weak. Essentially, a choice of a possible world of a certain kind by Nature is involved in the processing of 'if'. Since rules like (G.any) introduce an 'if', this opens the door for the kind of dependence of the choice of an individual in (G.every) or (G.any) on the possible world chosen in connection with 'if'. More precisely, the dependence obtains for (G.every) but not for (G.any).

This distinction does not make a difference in the simplest situations. However, in more complicated cases we have the kind of semantical difference which according to the any-thesis justifies their presence of 'any'.

This account seems to suffer from a fatal weakness in that no 'if' is present when an individual is chosen in accordance with (G.any) or (G.every). Hence Nature seems unable to make the selection on which the former choice may depend in time.

This objection does not hold water, however. The kind of dependence we need can easily be built into the strategies of the two players. Even though the matter deserves a great deal of further investigation, I do not see any serious objections to the any-thesis emerging from such investigations. In order to get a feeling for the situation, we may for instance observe that there is a difference in meaning between (81) and

(82)   If Jane wins, everyone who has bet on her is happy

similar to the difference between (74) and (75).

Let me illustrate this in terms of an informal discussion of the game connected with (81).

An application of the game rule for 'if' will yield (through a choice by Myself) either

(83)   Jane doesn't win

or else

(84)   Anyone who has bet on Jane is happy.

An application of (G.any) to (84) yields a sentence of the form

(85)   Mary is happy if Mary has bet on Jane.

Now let us assume that 'if' here gives rise to a choice of a world by Nature. In that world, a choice must be made by Myself between

(86)   Mary hasn't bet on Jane
(87)   Mary is happy.

Now there is nothing in the game rules which necessitate making Nature's choice of an individual (our 'Mary') in the step from (84) to (85) dependent or independent of the world chosen because of the presence of 'if' in (85). The ordering principles governing (G.any) and (G.every) may thus create a semantical asymmetry between the two, thereby explaining the possibility of 'any' in (81).

Actually, what normally happens is slightly different. Since the admissibility of 'any' in (81) depends on there being a modal force to 'if' in (85), there is a similar modal force present in (81). Hence the semantics of (81) I have expounded.

However, there is no need for 'if' to have any modal force in order to make (82) acceptable. Hence the normal economic way of understanding (82) is to take 'every' to range over actual individuals only. This explains very well the contrast between (81) and (82), and by the same token the force of many similar occurrences of 'any'. Typically, 'every' ranges over actual individuals only while 'any' as it were ranges over possible ones. This is well in accord with the facts.

19. A MORAL OF THE STORY

The application of game-theoretical semantics sketched above is calculated to illustrate a rather general thesis. Sight unseen, the logical and semantical behavior of natural-language quantifiers might perhaps be expected to be rather trivial from the vantage point of a logician. In reality, there are problems of considerable complexity concerning natural-language quantifiers. The problems about branching quantifiers and the problems about the distribution of 'any' in English serve to exemplify such problems. It is to be hoped that more logicians will follow Richard Montague's example and become interested in the fascinating logical problems of natural-language semantics.[15]

This hope is enhanced by the striking consequences of our tentative findings for the methodology of theoretical linguistics. On the one hand, the logical strength of ordinary English is seen – at least tentatively – to come close to that of second-order logic. On the other hand, even the grammaticality of English quantifier sentences apparently is beyond the power of generative methods. Whatever the definitive status of these preliminary observations will turn out to be, there is no doubt about their tremendous potential interest and importance.

NOTES

[1] See, for instance, Partee (1970), (1971) and Lakoff (1970), (1971).

[2] See Hintikka (1974), (1975a).

[3] See Davidson (1967), (1968), (1969), (1970), (1973), and cf. Hintikka (1975b), (1976b).

[4] See Hintikka (1974), (1975a), (1976a).

[5] Almost all that we need to do for the purpose of this depersonalization is to eliminate universal quantifiers and conjunctions in favor of existential quantifiers, disjunctions, and negations.

[6] See Hintikka (1974), and cf. Hintikka (1976c).

[7] See Fauconnier (1975) and Stenius (1976).

[8] See especially Fauconnier (1975).

[9] This is in fact a general methodological point of considerable importance both in semantics and in syntax. I have been amazed time and again by linguists who claim that they are dealing with competence and not performance and then go on to base their theories on people's uneducated and unanalysed reactions to complicated sentences.

[10] See Walkoe (1970).

[11] With the immediately following argument and with others like it in the sequel, please compare the procedures employed in the reduction theory of first-order logic, as e.g., in Suranyi (1959).

[12] With the following, cf. Hintikka (1975a).

[13] Examples of the type (44) were apparently introduced to the literature by Peter Geach. But aren't they artificial philosophers' examples? No, they are not. Here is a quote from Walter Cronkite being interviewed by Morley Safer on 'Who's Who', March 15, 1977, about the undesirability of self-censorship of the media in connection with terrorist activities:

> "If we cover up under any circumstances, the public has the right to believe
> that we cover up under any circumstances."

[14] For the steps needed to dispense with this assumption, see Hintikka (1975c).

[15] Cf. Thomason (1974).

BIBLIOGRAPHY

Davidson, Donald, 'Truth and Meaning', *Synthese* **17** (1967), pp. 304–323.

Davidson, Donald, 'On Saying That', *Synthese* **19** (1968), pp. 130–146.

Davidson, Donald, 'True to the Facts', *Journal of Philosophy* **66** (1969), pp. 748–764.

Davidson, Donald, 'Semantics for Natural Languages', in *Linguaggi nella società e nelle tecnica*, edizioni di Comunità, Milan, 1970, pp. 177–188.

Davidson, Donald, 'In Defense of Convention T', in H. Leblanc (ed.), *Truth, Syntax, and Modality*, North-Holland, Amsterdam, 1973, pp. 76–86.

Fauconnier, Giles, 'Do Quantifiers Branch?' *Linguistic Inquiry* **6** (1975), pp. 555–567.

Hintikka, Jaakko, 'Quantifiers vs. Quantification Theory', *Linguistic Inquiry* **5** (1974), pp. 153–177. Reprinted in the present volume, pp. 49–79.

Hintikka, Jaakko, 'On the Limitations of Generative Grammar', in the *Proceedings of the Scandinavian Seminar on Philosophy of Language*, Filosofiska förening & Filosofiska Institutionen vid Uppsala Universitet, Uppsala (1975a), vol. 1, pp. 1–92.

Hintikka, Jaakko, 'A Counterexample to Tarski-type Truth-Definitions as Applied to Natural Languages', in Asa Kasher (ed.), *Language in Focus: Foundations, Methods and Systems. Essays in Memory of Yehoshua Bar-Hillel*, D. Reidel, Dordrecht (1975b), pp. 107–112.

Hintikka, Jaakko, 'Impossible Possible Worlds Vindicated', *Journal of Philosophical Logic* **4** (1975c), pp. 475–484. Reprinted in the present volume, pp. 367–379.

Hintikka, Jaakko, 'Quantifiers in Logic and Quantifiers in Natural Languages', in S. Körner (ed.), *Philosophy of Logic*, Oxford, Basil Blackwell (1976a), pp. 208–232. Reprinted in the present volume, pp. 27–47.

Hintikka, Jaakko, 'The Prospects of Convention T', *Dialectica* **30** (1976b), pp. 61–66.

Hintikka, Jaakko, 'Partially Ordered Quantifiers vs. Partially Ordered Ideas', *Dialectica* **30** (1976c), pp. 89–99.

Hintikka, Jaakko, *The Semantics of Questions and the Questions of Semantics* (*Acta Philosophica Fennica*, Vol. 28, No. 4), North-Holland Publishing Company, Amsterdam, 1977.

Hintikka, Jaakko and Lauri Carlson, 'Pronouns of Laziness in Game-Theoretical Semantics', *Theoretical Linguistics* **4** (1977), 1–29.

Hintikka, Jaakko and Lauri Carlson, 'Conditionals, Generic Quantifiers, and Other Applications of Subgames', in A. Margalit (ed.), *Meaning and Use*, D. Reidel, Dordrecht, 1978. Reprinted in the present volume pp. 179–214.

Hintikka, Jaakko and Esa Saarinen, 'Semantical Games and the Bach-Peters Paradox'. *Theoretical Linguistics* **2** (1975), pp. 1–20. Reprinted in the present volume, pp. 153–178,

Lakoff, George, 'Repartee, or a Reply to "Negation Conjunction, and Quantifiers," ' *Foundations of Language* **6** (1970), pp. 398–422.

Lakoff, George, 'On Generative Semantics', in Danny D. Steinberg and Leon A. Jakobovits (eds.), *Semantics: An Interdisciplinary Reader*, Cambridge, Cambridge University Press, 1971, pp. 232–296.

Partee, Barbara Hall, 'Negation, Conjunction, and Quantifiers: Syntax vs. Semantics', *Foundations of Language* **6** (1970), pp. 153–165.

Partee, Barbara Hall, 'On the Requirement that Transformations Preserve Meaning', in Charles J. Fillmore and D. Terence Langendoen (eds.), *Studies in Linguistic Semantics*, Holt, Rinehart and Winston, New York, 1971, pp. 1–21.

Rogers, Hartley, Jr., 'Certain Logical Reduction and Decision Problems', *Annals of Mathematics* **64** (1956), pp. 264–284.

Stenius, Erik, 'Comments on Jaakko Hintikka's Paper', *Dialectica* **30** (1976).

Suranyi, Janos, *Reduktionstheorie des Entscheidungsproblems im Prädikatenkalkül der ersten Stufe*, Verlag der ungarischen Akademie der Wissenschaften, Budapest, 1959.

Thomason, Richmond, editor, *Formal Philosophy: Selected Essays of Richard Montague*, Yale University Press, New Haven and London, 1974.

Walkoe, W. J., Jr., 'Finite Partially-Ordered Quantification', *Journal of Symbolic Logic* **35** (1970), pp. 535–555.

CHRISTOPHER PEACOCKE

GAME-THEORETIC SEMANTICS, QUANTIFIERS AND TRUTH: COMMENTS ON PROFESSOR HINTIKKA'S PAPER*

Professor Hintikka's sophisticated and ingenious paper consists of a statement of his game theoretic semantics as applied to a natural language, a claim about the quantifier 'any' that he calls the '*any-thesis*', and some more general conclusions about grammaticality. I find myself with some queries about what he says in each one of these areas, and I shall take them in turn before returning to consider briefly some more general motivations for game-theoretic semantics.

I

In Professor Hintikka's game-theoretic semantics, a sentence S is said to be true just in case there is a winning strategy for a player who may be labelled 'Myself' in the game $G(S)$ correlated with S. The correlated game $G(S)$ is fixed by a set of rules which specify for any sentence whether a move is to be made by Myself or my opponent Nature and which kind of move is to be made; in each non-terminal move, a sentence is picked in accordance with these rules with respect to which the game is then continued. The sentences chosen are progressively reduced in complexity; after a finite number of moves an atomic sentence results, and no further move is possible. If that sentence is true, the winner of this play of the game is Myself; if it is false, Nature wins. A typical rule is that for the quantifier 'some':

(G.some) When the game has reached a sentence of the form

$$X - \text{some } Y \text{ who } Z - W$$

a person is chosen by Myself, and that person either has already in English or is given a proper name 'b'; the game continues with the sentence

$$X - b - W, b \text{ is a } Y \text{ and } b \text{ is } Z.$$

(This is subject to restrictions of the kind Professor Hintikka notes.)

119

E. Saarinen (ed.), Game-Theoretical Semantics, 119–134. All Rights Reserved.
Copyright © 1978 by D. Reidel Publishing Company, Dordrecht, Holland.

Two points should be immediately noted. Given an appropriately defined concept of truth for the atomic sentences, Professor Hintikka's rules, unlike some other game theoretic constructions, succeed in defining the absolute concept of truth which any semantical theory must either define or explain its reasons for ignoring: for whether the player labelled 'Myself' has a winning strategy depends on the way things actually are. Second, the truth conditions (TC's) Professor Hintikka's rules give for sentences containing the phrase 'some Y who Z' are clearly, as they should be, objectual and not substitutional (in Quine's sense).

Nevertheless, although they agree on the TC's attributed to whole sentences, it would not be incorrect to say that there is a *more* intimate relation between the truth of quantified sentences and the truth of singular sentences on Professor Hintikka's account than there is in the classical account of Tarski. This unspecific remark can be given a sharp formulation as follows. If we were to transform Professor Hintikka's game theoretic clauses into the natural finitely axiomatixed corresponding theory of absolute truth what we would initially obtain would be *not* a theory containing Tarski's notion of satisfaction but rather something along the following lines. We consider languages that *finitely extend* English in the sense that they contain at most finitely many new proper names, of objects already quantified over in English (intuitively), and we consider *every* such language. Then we would say that a sentence of the form

$$X - \text{some Y who Z} - W$$

is true in English iff some such language L finitely extending English and some proper name b in it are such that

$$X - b - W, \; b \text{ is a Y, and } b \text{ is Z}$$

is true in L.

It is important in what follows to keep such a theory in mind. Such a theory is not just an abstract possibility. It can actually be written out if Professor Hintikka's theory can be written out: the clauses of the theory will be obtained by transforming Professor Hintikka's clauses in the way in which the truth-theoretic rule for 'some Y who Z' is obtained from the game rule (G.some). Naturally the theory will appeal to a concept of truth for the atomic sentences (including atomic sentences containing newly-introduced names): in this it resembles Professor Hintikka's theory, and we know in any case how to analyze further the application of truth to the structured atomic sentences.

My first query concerns the generalizability of Professor Hintikka's construction to other quantifiers of English; he explicitly restricts his attention to a certain fragment of English, but a theory even of a fragment may be unattractive if it is of a kind that cannot be applied to cover quite analogous phenomena outside that fragment. There is a sense in which the existential and universal quantifiers, for which a single two-person form of game is appropriate, are extremely special cases. There are many quantificational phrases such as 'many', 'few', 'several' which are substitutable *salva congruitate* for 'some', and conversely. So *prima facie* given this similarity together with their common extensionality, one would expect that two semantical clauses stating the contribution of 'some' and 'several' respectively would differ only that in the *meta*language, one of the clauses would use 'some' where the other used 'several' (if our metalanguage is English): for any other difference would certainly not be one that could be reflected in the practice of speaking English.

But when we try to meet this condition in a theory along Professor Hintikka's lines, we do not quite succeed: we could say

(G.several) When the game has reached a sentence of the form

   X–several Y who are Z–W

several persons with names b_i (in finite extensions of English) are chosen by Myself, and then several games continue each with respect to one of the sentences

   $X - b_i - W$, and b_i is Y, and b_i is W.

But this now involves the consideration of several games, and truth must now be defined by the existence of a winning strategy in *all* of them; similarly other quantifiers will force us to consider *many* games of a certain kind, *few* games, and so forth. So one of my first and more minor queries for Professor Hintikka is whether this is the kind of extension he envisages, and, if so, whether he ought not to treat the universal quantifier in similar fashion. Why is there this special case at one end of the spectrum

none, some, several, many, most, almost all . . . ?

One proposal that might be made on Professor Hintikka's behalf to allow him to treat the nonstandard quantifiers within a single game is this. Consider the sentence

(α)   Nearly all men love many women

which a logician using restricted quantification might represent

(β) $N_{[Fx]}xM_{[Gy]}yLxy$

This is equivalent to the condition (γ):

(γ) $N(\{x : Fx\}, \{x : M(\{y : Gy\}, \{y : Lxy\})\})$

i.e., nearly all members of the set of men are members of the set of objects x such that many members of the set of women are members of set of objects loved by x. In this formulation, binary predicates of sets replace the nonstandard quantifiers 'nearly all' and 'many'. Professor Hintikka's game-theoretic construction can then be applied to this sentence (γ), in a way dependent upon the treatment of the terms formed by a set-abstraction. If these terms, which are a particular kind of definite description, are expanded in accordance with Russell's theory, then (γ) will unfold into a sentence containing existential and universal quantifiers over sets. The game theoretic construction can cope with the resulting sentence, provided we allow that at moves made at subformulae starting with quantifiers over sets, the domain of choice, for Myself or Nature is the domain of all subsets of the range of the individual variables. (Actually, the predicative subsets will suffice.) Alternatively, set-abstraction may be taken as a primitive operation; then (γ) is from the point of view of Professor Hintikka's constructions an atomic sentence, whose truth conditions are taken as already defined. Any problems raised by (γ) will then not be distinct from problems raised by the treatment of primitive functors generally. The method of replacement by binary predicates of sets is quite general: let us briefly look at one more case:

(δ)   Few men give nearly all they own to charities

i.e.,

(ϵ) $W_{[Fx]}xN_{[Oxy]}y\exists_{[Cz]}zGxyz$

becomes

(μ) $W(\{x:Fx\}, \{x:N(\{y:Oxy\}, \{y:\exists z(Cz \& Gxyz)\})\})$.

Does this solve the problem? Surely it just highlights the original objection. The (ineliminable) ontology of sets has been read into this fragment of English solely to preserve the game-theoretic treatment: no new fact about English has been cited to justify the remaining sharp asymmetry of treatment of 'some' and 'any' on the one hand and 'few', 'many', 'nearly all' &c. on the other. This asymmetry is vividly shown by the fact that the same treatment as binary predicates of sets can be applied to the standard quantifiers too. If '$A(\xi, \zeta)$' is used to express the relation that holds between sets ξ and ζ just in case all members of ξ are members of ζ, and '$S(\xi, \zeta)$' holds just in case some members of ξ are members of ζ, then for instance

(ν)   All men love some woman

can be expressed

(ρ) $A(\{x:Fx\}, \{x:S(\{y:Gy\}, \{y:Lxy\})\})$.

So both standard and non-standard quantifiers *can* be treated as predicates of sets; and from the point of view of the construction of a theory of truth, neither kind *needs* to be.[1] The set-theoretic proposal cannot meet the needs of the game theoretic view unless this asymmetry of treatment can be independently motivated.

That first question about quantifiers other than the universal and existential leads, however answered, to another. What are the advantages of the specifically game-theoretical features of Professor Hintikka's rules, that is, what is lost if we gave a theory similar in structure to his but omitting the game-theoretical formulation?

The answer cannot lie in the TC's attributed to whole sentences, for as Professor Hintikka says, these are the *same* as those given by a classical truth theory or definition of truth once we eliminate by successive deductive steps semantical or game theoretic predicates from the statement of the TC for a sentence, provided that the same TC's are given for the atomic sentences in both cases. Nor would it be correct to appeal to the knowledge that a speaker who understands English must have: it is even less plausible to say that speakers know what is expressed by Professor Hintikka's clauses and the definition of truth in terms of the existence of a winning strategy than it is to say that they know what is expressed by the clauses of a Tarskian recursion. No doubt anyone who understands English (and is of a certain level of intellectual competence) can work out that the Hintikka clauses yield the correct TC's: but of course this is equally true of the corresponding theory of absolute truth that we noted above can be obtained from the Hintikka clauses.

A more interesting answer to the question would be that the game theoretic clauses have certain linguistic advantages not shared by a Tarskian account. We noted for instance the specially intimate relation between singular and quantified sentences in Professor Hintikka's treatment; and indeed each of the clauses contains in effect a transformation of one sentence into another, which read in reverse and combined with one another give a means of generating each sentence of the fragment that concerns him. This involves forming quantified sentences *via* singular ones, and various facts about reflexivation and pronominalization might be explained by these connexions. Thus, given a good account of pronominalization and reflexivization for proper names, the nonequivalence of 'Someone loves someone' with 'Someone loves himself' may be explained by the absence of any requirement in the game rules that in the former sentence one of the *same* individual's names be used in both applications of the 'someone' with it. This may well be a sound thought, but it would be a confusion to advance it on behalf of the game-theoretic construction: the advantage accrues to *any* account that thus closely links quantified and singular sentences, and in particular to a recursion on truth that employs the finite extensions of English that I said earlier we ought to keep in mind.

A more philosophical motivation for the game theory would be provided by the thought that one who understands a sentence S must at least have a certain grasp of verification and refutation procedures for S: and this idea, of what procedures one knows must or may or must not have a certain outcome if S is to be true, receives a quite specific reflection in the successive moves of a correlated game. This motivation, which is (unlike the others) of the right kind to motivate the features in question, may operate at one of two levels. At a conservative level, it just invokes the idea that a truth condition limits or demands certain outcomes of certain procedures. This conservative position regards a sometimes transcendent TC for a sentence as a conception determining these limits or requirements: so on such a position, the game theory fixes nothing not already fixed by the TC. At the more radical level, the possession of a TC by a sentence consists in nothing more than the limits or requirements on genuinely possible procedures that correspond with the moves of a game, where these procedures do not use a heavily idealized notion of findability. This is the motivation to which I shall return later. Since it can hardly fail to differ at some points from the classical TC's, we can though already note that we have still failed to find a compelling motivation that *both* makes essential use of the game theory *and*, as Professor Hintikka says, gives TC's indentical with those of the classical account. So my second request on this first area of his paper is for a motivation for the use of game theory that avoids appeal to attractions with which it is only inessentially connected.

II

I turn now to Professor Hintikka's *any*-thesis. We should consider this closely partly because of the powerful conclusion Professor Hintikka claims follows from its truth, viz. that the set of grammatical English sentences is neither recursive nor recursively ennumerable. If we *can* in a finite time tell of any string whether it is a grammatical English sentence however complex, we would then have a decisive argument that human abilities at a formal level quite outstrip those of any Turing machine however complex.

I am myself not convinced of the *any*-thesis, and will try briefly to offer an alternative account of the examples Professor Hintikka supplies which covers, as his does not, a number of other cases.

The ordering principle he gives for *any* is that the game rule for *any* has priority over, is to be applied before, those for *not, if* and the modal operators: it does not have priority over the others. The *any*-thesis is then stated as:

> The word *any* is grammatical in a given context X – any Y – Z iff an exchange of *any* for *every* results in a grammatical expression which is not identical in meaning with X – any Y – Z.

Professor Hintikka is here not of course in the absurd position of a man asking us to compare the TC's of sentences containing *every* with the TC's the *any*-sentences might have had had things been different, without any further information: the game rule for *any* together with the ordering principles determine quite definite TC's for putative sentences of English containing *any*, which may thereby be predicted as grammatical or not by the *any*-thesis.

The aspect of the ordering principle for *any* that I question is that (G.any) always takes priority over (G.if): this aspect of the principle plays a major part in the defence of the *any*-thesis and the consequences Professor Hintikka draws from it.

He does not initially consider occurrences of *any* not preceded by other operators that are quite grammatical. Consider the pair

(a)   Any candidate will be considered on his merits.

(b)   Every candidate will be considered on his merits.

Is there, as (a generalization of) the *any*-thesis suggest, a failure of equivalence between these two? It is in fact quite plausible to say that there is (though not for the reason Professor Hintikka gives), *viz.* that the utterer of the *any*-sentence is not presupposing that there will *be* any candidates, whereas the utterer of the *every*-sentence is presupposing that there will be some. We can use this later to explain some of the cases Professor Hintikka cites.[2]

There are cases where (G.any) does not take priority over (G.if); there is surely one reading of the sentence (c) on which it does not:

(c)   If John believes that and any man who believes that is mistaken, then John is mistaken.

I do not deny that Professor Hintikka's reading for this exists, as in the most natural reading for 'If any man can prove that, Kreisel can', but it does seem that it is certainly not preferred: if anything, the reading on which (c) must be true (if John is a man) is preferred. Yet the *any*-thesis would make (c) ungrammatical for the reading on which *any* has narrow scope. What this example suggests is that (G.any) and (G.if) are not mutually ordered, and neither does the left-to-right principle apply to them.[3]

But if that suggestion is correct, how are we to explain some of the other examples Professor Hintikka cites? What of his (35) and (36)?

(d, 35) If Jane wins, anybody is happy.

(e, 36) If Jane wins, everybody is happy.

Professor Hintikka's explanation here cannot be the whole, if any part of, the truth, for there is nothing wrong with the following sentence:

(f)   If Jane wins, anybody who likes her is happy.

Again, this seems to differ from the corresponding *every*-sentence in not presupposing that these are people who like Jane. The extreme oddity of (d, 35) is to be explained not by the *any*-thesis, but by the very great difficulty (approaching impossibility) of not being in a position to presuppose that there are any persons *tout court*, and this in the context of use if a sentence containing 'Jane' that seems to commit one to the existence of at least one person.

I take it that similar arguments, with a careful choice of contexts, may be applied to the sentences Professor Hintikka marks as ungrammatical, 'Jane has won any match' and 'If Jane has won any match, she has won any match'. In many of the other examples Professor Hintikka cites the differences are explained by the priority of (G.any) over (G.not) and the modal rules; that priority is being granted, as it must be in the face of such examples as

(g)   John can solve any problem in this paper in three hours.

(h)   John can solve every problem in this paper in three hours.

But this still leaves us with a few of Professor Hintikka's examples to explain. The pair that seems most strongly to support his case is Quine's pair,[4]

(i, 33)   If any member contributes, I'll be happy.

(j, 34)   If every member contributes, I'll be happy.

But again our confidence is shaken by our ability to hear the sentence

(k)   If Smith is a member and any member contributes, Smith
          contributes

in one way as a logical truth; and I at least can hear (i, 9) with (G.if)
applied first, though this reading is strongly not preferred.

There is indeed a reason why on the account suggested here the
reading Professor Hintikka says does not exist is strongly not preferred
if we remember Grice's conversational principles. Since the left-to-right
ordering principles applies to *if* and *every*, an *every*-sentence will (in
simple cases) have only one reading whereas the *any*-sentence has two.
Conversational efficiency requires us strongly to prefer the reading of
the *any*-sentence that differs from that for the *every*-sentence, for
otherwise the hearer might reason "The speaker hasn't used the
every-sentence that would have made his meaning unambiguous, so he
probably doesn't mean something that could be expressed by the
every-sentence".

The remaining kind of example Professor Hintikka offers for the any
thesis is one in which *any* has as wide a scope as *every* in the
corresponding *every*-sentence, a scope that includes a negation: this is
meant to explain the oddity of

(l, 53)   Any girl has not been dated by John.

But the now familiar alternative accounts of its oddity apply once
more; and the explanation offered by the *any*-thesis again seems not to
be sufficient since the sentence

(m)   Any socialist will not grant that point.

is not ungrammatical. (See Note 2 for more on the use of *any* in such
sentences.) In his Section 'On the limits of the *any*-thesis', Professor
Hintikka admits examples like (m) as grammatical, but holds that
it is crucial to their possession of that status that they contain the
future tense, or other operators with respect to which *any* and *every*
may be differently ordered in the game-theoretical semantics for
this fragment of English. But there are examples which, in Professor
Hintikka's words, "pertain exclusively to the present moment":
for instance

(n)   Any delegates from Rome are landing at the airport at this very moment

(or more vividly: '. . . are landing precisely *now*'.) Professor Hintikka also holds, whilst agreeing that the matter needs a great deal of further investigation, that it is consistent with the truth of the *any*-thesis for his fragment of English that the sentence

(o, 81)   If Jane wins, anyone who has bet on her is happy

is acceptable. His explanation of this phenomenon is that *if* typically has a modal force, however weak, and

Since rules like (G.any) introduce an *if*, this opens the door for the kind of dependence of the choice of an individual in (G.every) or (G.any) on the possible world chosen in connection with *if*.

It is not, however, plausible that the English 'either . . . or − ' has modal force, and yet the sentence

(p)   Either Jane loses or anyone who has bet on her is happy

is not ungrammatical.

III

Professor Hintikka draws his tentative general conclusion about grammaticality from the *any*-thesis and certain other premises that he made clear. It seems to me that even if we reject these premises, his suggestion is still an important contribution to the subject: for it shows how relatively simple rules can yield a set of sentences that is not r.e., and no one can rule out in advance of linguistic investigation that the principles take the form he suggests.

Nevertheless the principles governing (G.any) that I have suggested use purely syntactic restrictions plus their notion of presupposition and do not, unlike the *any*-thesis, employ the recursively undecidable relation of logical equivalence. And as Professor Hintikka himself notes at one point, even if the examples had fitted the *any*-thesis, it has not been shown that logical equivalence, rather than some tighter and possibly decidable relation is the relevant one: for one relation can be a subrelation of a second, and the first be recursive while the second is not. At first blush it may seem surprising that Professor Hintikka does not appeal to the stronger (and decidable[5]) notion of intensional isomorphism, since that would solve the problem which he notes that the pair

(q, 68)   If everyone is hurt, someone is hurt

(r, 69)   If anyone is hurt, someone is hurt

presents for him; but on reflection it is clear that such a move would then leave him with no explanation of the oddity of 'If Jane wins, anybody is happy', since that is not, by his lights, intensionally isomorphic with 'If Jane wins, everybody is happy'.

Professor Hintikka's attitude to the examples (q, 68) and (r, 69) seems to be heroic. His answer to the objection that they are counterexamples to the *any*-thesis is that (I quote)

logically true and logically false sentences are spontaneously give a non-standard interpretation in any case. For instance, the natural conversational force of (68) is certainly different from its basic logical force as a . . . logical truth . . .

The obvious answer to this is that systematic syntax and semantics must be concerned not with 'natural conversational force' but with what is strictly and literally said by an utterance of the sentence in a given context, if we are not to be faced with hoardes of irrelevant counterexamples. (The fact that the 'spontaneous' interpretation amongst philosophers and linguists of the sentence 'George Lakoff is George Lakoff' is unlikely to be presented as an instance of the law of the reflexivity of identity cannot be used to defend a view according to which that sentence construed as an instance of that law is not strictly speaking a grammatical sentence of English.)[6] In any case it is clear that one's means of *getting across* what one may naturally intend to get across to one's audience by an utterance of (v, 69) may well make essential use of the fact that (r, 69) is a logical truth. It really is a consequence of Professor Hintikka's theory that 'If anyone is hurt, someone is hurt' is not a grammatical sentence of English; on the alternative view I offered it presents no difficulties.

We left consideration of possible motivations for specifically game-theoretic semantics with the thought that these could be provided only if the account of sentence senses they yield differs at some point from those given by classical truth theories or definitions. I turn finally to consider the large topic of such stronger motivations, at only such length as is required to raise a few questions.

One *prima facie* plausible doctrine which would in this way ground Professor Hintikka's semantics might go:

> To understand a sentence is to know what one must possess in order to meet arbitrarily skilful challenges to the effect that certain cited objects stand in relations the sentence excludes.

Contrary to appearances, this conception need not involve two distinct stages, first a fixing of what the sentence excludes and *then* a determination of appropriate moves to meet the challenges: in specifying what meets the challenges we thereby simultaneously specify what is excluded. Thus on this view one who understands an $\forall\exists\,\forall\exists\ldots$, i.e., in logicians' terms a Π_4^0 sentence, knows to meet such a challenger he will need somehow to know of two functions, in effect Skolem functions corresponding to the two existential quantifiers, of one and two arguments respectively, which applied to the first and to the first and second objects of any pair the challenger may cite yield two objects verifying the quantified predicate, and so meeting the challenge. Here knowledge of the conditions imposed on the functions stands to understanding of the sentence as knowledge of the conditions imposed on legitimate proofs of it stand to understanding of a sentence on intuitionistic views.

Let us fix for simplicity on an $\forall\exists$ sentence, so only one function is involved. Let us consider what further restrictions must be imposed upon it. Could all the challenge-meeting functions be nonrecursive? It seems clear that for finite beings like ourselves, any assertion of the sentence in those circumstances would be at best a *guess*. In the case in which for instance the quantifiers range over the natural numbers, we might accidentally keep meeting the challenges correctly, but we would have no assurance that we would continue to do so. Obviously it is of no help to appeal to the possibility of an assurance from a nonconstructive proof of the $\forall\exists$ sentence since such a proof would use logic that would be questioned by this stronger motivation. In short, unlike some at least of the recursive cases (perhaps only the primitive recursive ones), nothing involved in the mastery exhibited in cases where the assertion of a quantified sentence is conclusively justified determines that the sentence is to be asserted (or denied) in this kind of case. That formulation makes it clear that one form of anti-realist doctrine could strongly motivate the game-theoretic construction (in the sense of 'strongly motivate' we used above, which does not require any endorsement of the doctrine).

This gives us enough to raise a number of questions for Professor Hintikka. It is well known that when we restrict the strategy set for the player Myself to those containing only recursive Skolem functions, a nonclassical logic results: and in fact the motivation suggested would require a more severe restriction than to general recursive functions, but would plausibly allow in some recursive functionals. So a first query is: is Professor Hintikka prepared to admit such a stronger motivation, and if so what nonclassical logic does he think is determined by a proper semantics for a natural language? And does he think this is the *only* strong motivation for game-theoretic semantics?

A final remark upon which it would be interesting to know Professor Hintikka's comments is this. If a strong constructive motivation were accepted for the game-theoretical construction, that motivation immediately carries over to quantifications in natural language over unsurveyable domains of concrete objects, say over all galaxies. Now in the arithmetical case there was no difficulty in seeing even under the constraints of the strong motivation how a language user could be equipped with some functions that would put him in the position of knowing he could meet the challenges of the skilful challenger: for he has available the conclusions of proofs by induction. But in the empirical case there is nothing analogous, and appeals to the *evidence* for, say, a sentence of the form 'All galaxies are ... ' would be quite inadequate to justify the rôle of deduction in a strict sense from such quantified English sentences. From this point of view, on one if not the only motivation for the game-theoretical account, about the semantics of natural language quantifiers it seems to me we know very little indeed.

All Souls College, Oxford

NOTES

* 'Quantifiers in Natural Languages: Some Logical Problems', pp. 81–117 above, Professor Hintikka read this paper at a meeting of the Oxford Philosophical Society on 4 November 1976, and the present 'Comments' consist of a slightly revised version of the text of the reply read at that meeting. I should say that I have not explicitly registered all

my points of disagreement – nor all my points of agreement – with Professor Hintikka's paper. The paper read at Oxford did not contain the sections on partially-ordered quantifiers, which I do not discuss here.
[1] The general treatment that shows that neither kind needs to be construed as a predicate of sets is this. We will consider first a theory using a Tarskian relation of satisfaction. 'σ' ranges over countable sequences, 'i' over natural numbers, '$\sigma(i/x)$' abbreviates 'the sequence that differs from σ (if at all) only by having x in its ith place' and 'x_i' abbreviates 'ith variable'. Then when quantifiers are regarded as operating on a pair of predicates, the following form of axiom will suffice whether '\$' is construed as 'some', 'any', 'few', 'many', 'most', 'several', &c:

$$\forall\sigma\forall i\forall A\forall B(A, B \text{ contain at least } x_i \text{ free \& are open sentences. } \supset$$
$$\text{sats}(\sigma, \ulcorner\$x_i(A, B)\urcorner) \equiv \$x(\text{sats}(\sigma(i/x), A), \text{sats}(\sigma(i/x), B))).$$

(David Wiggins originally proposed such a clause for 'most'.) One need not insist on binary quantifiers to make this point: consider

$$\text{sats}(\sigma, \ulcorner\$x_i(A)\urcorner) \equiv \$x(\text{sats}(\sigma(i/x), A)).$$

(Note that we have here a general model for the treatment of second-level extensional operators on predicates. 'Widespread' is such an example: the axiom

$$\text{sats}(\sigma, \ulcorner\text{widespread } x_i(A)\urcorner) \equiv \text{widespread } x(\text{sats}(\sigma(i/x), A))$$

is true, and suffices for the derivation of T-sentences provided we have, as we need with 'few' and the rest, rules permitting substitution of coextensive predicates in the position of 'A' in 'widespread $x_i(A)$'.) In a truth theory extracted from Professor Hintikka's game theoretic clauses, which as we saw would use a recursion on truth, the analogue of the last-but-one cited axiom in this footnote would be

$$\text{True }(\ulcorner\$x_i(A)\urcorner, L) \equiv \$x\exists L'\exists\alpha \text{ (α denotes x in L' and L' finitely extends L}$$
& and the result of substituting α for all free occurrences of x_i in A is true in L').

'L' and 'L'', variables over languages, will of course be universally quantified in the axiom of such a theory, and the theory will entail truth conditions for all sentences of languages that are or extend the given language for which we wish to define truth.
[2] We can also use it to explain an observation by Vendler, to the effect that one who is prepared to assert that any F is G is much more commonly (I do not say always) prepared to accept for particular objects x that if x were F, x would be G, than is the person who is prepared to assert that *every* F is G. The explanation runs thus. When the strongest assertion we are prepared to make is that any F is G, then given the difference between *any* and *every* suggested in the text the assertion cannot be made on the basis of belief of a particular instance that it is both F and G. So one's grounds for one's assertion must be some general principles that lead one to expect this connexion between F and G. But such general grounds will commonly sustain the counterfactual. This argument shows that we do not need to postulate a *further* difference in meaning between *any* and *every*

in order to account for Vendler's observation. This difference in likely grounds that is consequent upon the presuppositional difference between *any* and *every* I would also use to explain the difference between Professor Hintikka's (74),

>Any doctor at the convention will tell you that Stopsneeze helps

and his (75),

>Every doctor at the convention will tell you that Stopsneeze helps.

We may note also that rational, efficient speakers may utter (74) instead of (75) even when it is common knowledge (in David Lewis's sense) between them and their interlocutor that there are doctors at the convention, precisely in order to emphasize they are possessed of grounds for their assertion that would be strong enough to justify the *any*-assertion, if they did not in fact know there to be any doctors at the convention. (Here we have an example of a linguistic thesis that can be used, in conjunction with considerations about rational agents engaged in communication, to account for apparent counterexamples to the thesis itself.)

I would also explain the admitted oddness of Professor Hintikka's (71):

>*If everyone loses, anyone loses.

by the fact that if a speaker is in a position to make the presupposition that there are people in the range in question in the discourse, and has no other reason for not using *everyone* to indicate this then it makes no sense for him to use *everyone* in the first clause and the presupposition-free *anyone* in the second clause. (Why then it may be asked is 'If anyone loses, everyone loses' not deviant? The answer is that sometimes *any* has wider scope than *if*: to repeat, I am not denying that.)

[3] We do not need conjunction in the antecedent of the conditional to make this point: the sentence 'If any man who saves in a period of inflation is irrational, then I am irrational' has a reading on which *any* has narrow scope.

[4] Approximately. See *Word and Object*, (MIT Press, Cambridge, 1960) p. 138.

[5] Provided the translation into regimented notation the game will indirectly supply is effective.

[6] Professor Hintikka is of course really well aware of this familiar point: see his paper 'Language-Games', Section 13(ii), p. 13 above.

JAAKKO HINTIKKA

REJOINDER TO PEACOCKE

Christopher Peacocke raises in his perceptive and lucid comments several issues which are vital to the evaluation of game-theoretical semantics as a general approach to logical and linguistic semantics and also to the evaluation of some of its specific applications to logico-linguistic problems. I am greatly indebted to him for this chance to clarify what I have said earlier of game-theoretical semantics and of its uses. Both his critical comments and his alternative suggestions serve to illuminate my semantical theory indirectly, through the reflected light of the replies that can be made to them.

Mr. Peacocke's main comments pertain to several different matters. I shall therefore try to deal with them separately one by one, beginning with the most general one.

(i) Mr. Peacocke says that in game-theoretical semantics "there is a *more* intimate relation between the truth of quantified sentences and the truth of singular sentences . . . than there is in the classical account of Tarski" (p. 120). He seems to think that this is at least a partial explanation for the success of game-theoretical semantics. In reality, he intimates, more than one apparent advantage of game-theoretical semantics "accrues to *any* account that thus closely links quantified and singular sentences" (p. 124). Accordingly, Peacocke is led to ask for a motivation for game-theoretical semantics which would not be shared by all approaches which, like the game-theoretical one, link quantified sentences closely with their substitution-instances, or perhaps by all and sundry approaches which operate with recursive truth-clauses but otherwise have the same structure as my theory.

In particular, Peacocke considers as a close alternative to my game rule (G.some) for the English quantifier word 'some' the following clause in a recursive truth-definition.

A sentence of the form

$$X - \text{some } Y \text{ who } Z - W$$

is true in English iff some finite extension E and a proper name 'b' in this extension E are such that

$$X - b - W, \quad \text{is a Y, and } b Z$$

is true in E.

E. Saarinen (ed.), Game-Theoretical Semantics, 135–151. All Rights Reserved.
Copyright © 1978 by D. Reidel Publishing Company, Dordrecht, Holland.

'Finite extension' means here a finite extension obtained by adding a finite number of proper names of individuals "already quantified over in English" (p. 120).

This last phrase of Peacocke's shows one source of trouble in his suggested truth-conditional alternative to my approach. What *is* the class of entities "already quantified over in English"? How can we ascertain what it is, at least in principle? The rules of my semantical games are set up in such a way that the class of individuals quantified over is shown by the behavior of the players of these games. It is the class of all those individuals among which the games of seeking and finding are played. If we turn my game theoretical truth-definition into a recursive one along the lines of (T.some), this observability disappears. How the class of individuals quantified over is to be gathered (in principle) in understanding a foreign language will then be a problem which would delight Professor Quine. It is not quite enough to try to explain, as Mr. Peacocke does, the class of objects quantified over in English by writing "(intuitively)".

Some of the ramifications of this problem of observability are discussed in my essay 'Behavioral Criteria for Radical Translation', in *Logic, Language-Games, and Information* (Clarendon Press, Oxford, 1973, pp. 83–97). This advantage of game-theoretical semantics is also connected with the role of semantical games as examples of Wittgenstein's language-games. On this relationship, the reader is invited to see my essay 'Languages-Games' in *Essays on Wittgenstein in Honour of G. H. von Wright*, (Acta Philosophica Fennica, Vol. 28, nos. 1–3, pp. 105–125) reprinted above in the present volume, pp. 1–26. The most important kinship between game-theoretical semantics and Wittgenstein's ideas is a subtle one, and might easily be overlooked. In both, the precise force (meaning) of our words is to be seen from the more or less institutionalized activities of the people that use them in their primary context (in the language-game which is their 'logical home').

In addition to these philosophical advantages game-theoretical semantics offers over recursive truth-definitions, it incorporates several technical novelties which promise linguistic, logical, and philosophical advantages. These novelties imply, as it happens, that the kind of simple translation of game-theoretical semantics into a semantics which operates with recursive truth-definitions is sometimes bound to fail. Admittedly, in their totality game-theoretical rules do the same job as the (properly) recursive clauses of a truth-definition. (In both approaches, atomic sentences are treated separately.) But in game-theoretical semantics the rules operate in a direction opposite to the recursive clauses of a conventional truth-definition. They operate from outside in, not from inside out, as the usual truth-definitions.

This is a distinction with a difference. For instance, it means that game-theoretical semantics can capture context-dependencies which cannot be naturally handled by means of recursive truth-definitions. Indeed, the behavior of 'any' offers us a small but instructive case in point. Why the apparent difference in the force of 'any' in the following sentences?

(1)   Any corporal can become a general

(2)   If any corporal can become a general, it shows the opportunities of a military career.

The difference between (1) and (2) is due to the fact that in (2) 'any' as it were jumps out of its context, i.e., from the clause (1) in which it occurs, and semantically speaking precedes the whole sentence (2). Such context-dependencies are much more numerous in natural languages than first meets the eye. They are much more easily dealt with in game-theoretical semantics than in its recursive-definitional rivals. They may even be impossible to deal with in a theoretically satisfactory manner in the latter.

For instance, I have argued elsewhere that one of the contexts in which the context-dependence of certain English words manifest itself is one half of Tarski's T-schema. For instance, the following instance of one half of it is false.

(3)   'Any corporal can become a general' is true if any corporal can become a general.

(For further discussion of this phenomenon, see my notes 'A Counter-Example to Tarski-type Truth-Definitions as Applied to Natural Languages', *Philosophia* **5** (1975), pp. 207–212, and 'The Prospects of Convention T', *Dialectica* **30** (1976), pp. 61–66.

This illustrates the difficulties which confront a conventional 'inside out' semantics when applied to context-dependencies rather than proves that they are unsurmountable. But they are in any case serious reminders of important general theoretical problems. I am planning to discuss the limitations and the occasional failures of the 'inside out' principle (also known as Frege's principle or the principle of compositionality) in a separate essay. Suffice it to say here that all the exceptions to this principle can be dealt easily and naturally in game-theoretical semantics.

Perhaps the most important phenomenon on which game-theoretical semantics has shed new light through its rules operating from outside in is the behavior of multiple questions in English. Such questions are discussed in my monograph *The Semantics of Questions and the Questions of Semantics* (North-Holland, Amsterdam, 1976), especially in Chapters 6 and 8. There I argue that certain combinatorially possible readings of multiple questions are not acceptable in English because in processing them game-theoretically we would be led to consider ill-formed strings of English words. This explanation depends crucially on the 'outside in' direction of game-theoretical rules. It cannot be reproduced in any semantical theory whose rules proceed from inside out.

There is sometimes an even sharper reason why game-theoretical truth-definitions cannot be replaced by step-by-step recursive ones. Game rules like (G.some) do not tell the whole story of my semantical games. They do not themselves tell which earlier moves are known to a player when he makes his choice. That such differences can make a tremendous difference in the semantics of natural language is shown in my essay 'Quantifiers vs. Quantification Theory', reprinted in the present volume, and in the first half of the essay on whose second half Mr. Peacocke is commenting. Ignorance of earlier game moves will lead to sentences with branching quantifiers. Their semantics is immediately clear from a game-theoretical vantage point, but cannot be dealt with satisfactorily in a recursive-clause semantics which operates from inside out. For how can one even say in an 'inside out' semantics that in an open sentence of the form $M(x, y, z, u)$ the values of 'y' and 'u' will depend on those of 'x' and 'z', respectively, but on none of the other values? Yet this is the partial dependence which is exhibited by the branching quantifier sentence

$$(4) \qquad \begin{matrix} (x)(\exists y) \\ \\ (z)(\exists u) \end{matrix} \Big\rangle M(x, y, z, u).$$

Similar remarks can be made, if I am right, of branching quantifiers in natural languages. There does not seem to be any remotest hope to handle their semantics by means of recursive truth-definitions.

These examples should satisfy Mr. Peacocke's second request, which is to supply "a motivation for the use of game theory that avoids appeal to attractions with which it is only inessentially connected" As Mr. Peacocke notes, game-theoretical semantics yields in the simplest case (linear first-order quantifiers, classically interpreted) the same results as Tarski-type truth-definitions. However, the examples just given show that game-theoretical semantics can be extended to deal with phenomena which conventional semantics cannot handle with its recursive clauses and inside out procedures.

The dynamization of the language-world relationships which game-theoretical semantics involves makes it also an excellent tool in the theory of the urn models of Veikko Rantala (see his essay in the present volume). Here we have an additional example of the advantages of game-theoretical methods over recursive inside out procedures. It remains to be investigated what precisely is essential to game-theoretical methods. The idea of dynamic, stage-by-stage comparisons of language with reality is certainly essential, however, and so is the direction of the procedure from outside in. Neither of these essential features is preserved in a transition to truth-conditions along the lines Mr. Peacocke suggests.

(ii) Another question Mr. Peacocke raises is the treatment of nonstandard quantifiers in game-theoretical semantics. It is indeed eminently reasonable to use the treatment of nonstandard quantifiers as a test problem which game-theoretical semantics has to be able to solve in order to prove its mettle.

One 'nonstandard' quantifier has already been given a partial game-theoretical analysis. It is the English definite article 'the', which is discussed in my joint paper with Esa Saarinen, 'Semantical Games and the Bach-Peters Paradox' (reprinted in the present volume; pp. 153–178). The remarks made there must be supplemented by the hints dropped towards the end of Lauri Carlson's and Jaakko Hintikka's joint paper which is likewise reprinted here. The details do not matter. Even though more has to be said of this 'quantifier', the success of the game-theoretical treatment is unmistakeable.

But what about other nonstandard quantifiers in English, such as 'several', 'many', 'few', 'almost all', 'most', 'some' (in its plural uses), etc.? I do not see any obstacles to treating them in game-theoretical semantics. For instance, for 'several' we can set up a game rule a special case of which is the following.

(G.several) When the game has reached a sentence of the form

X – several Y who Z – W

a number k of persons with the proper names 'b_1', 'b_2', ..., 'b_k' is selected by myself, where k is at least about n_0. Then the game is continued with respect to

X–b_1, b_2, ... and b_k –W, b_1, b_2, ..., and b_k are Y, and b_1, b_2, ... b_k Z.

Several comments are needed here, apart from those usually required in comparable quantifier rules. The number n_0 represents the approximate minimal number of individuals counting as 'several'. If this varies from one speaker to another, the meaning of 'several' varies accordingly. This is surely as things should be, and it is reflected by corresponding changes in (G.several).

Notice how actual plays of a semantical game in accordance with (G.several) will yield information concerning the value of n_0. This number is the minimal number used by the players as the value of k in applying (G.several). This is in keeping with our basic Wittgensteinian idea that the meaning of our words is to be seen from the relevant language-games.

In order for (G.several) to serve a useful purpose, we must of course have game rules for handling such conjunctive phrases as occur in the output sentence of (G.several). Such rules are not hard to formulate, however, and they are needed in any case in any adequate treatment of English. In fact, one is tentatively formulated in my essay on the Ross paradox reprinted in the present volume, pp. 329–345. Even though such rules will need further study and refinements, there does not seem to be any major problems associated with them.

A special case of another rule for nonstandard quantifier might be the following.

(G.many) When the game has reached a sentence of the form

X – many Y who Z – W,

a number of individuals b_1, b_2, ..., are chosen by Myself, and the game is continued with respect to the sentence

$X - b_1, b_2, \ldots - W,$

$b_1, b_2, \ldots$ are Y, and

$b_1, b_2, \ldots Z$

Here (i) the number of individuals chosen must be larger than a certain natural number n_0, and (ii) the relative frequency of b_1, $b_2, \ldots$ among the individuals satisfying 'x is a Y' and x Z' (where Y' and Z' are like Y and Z, respectively, except in being singular) must be larger than some constant c, $0 < c < 1$.

When (G.many) is applied in a situation in which there are an infinite number of Y who Z, we have to operate with infinitely long conjunctive phrases. This is not a deterrent to logicians who have for several years studied languages with infinitely long conjunctions and disjunctions.

A comparison with (G.several) shows how game-theoretical rules serve to bring out differences in meaning. With 'several', only the *absolute* number of individuals counts; with 'many' also the *relative frequency* of individuals matters. (We would not say, 'Many Chinese ride a bike to work' if 5, 500 or 50000 do so.) This semantical difference is forced on us as soon as we try to formulate game rules for 'several' and 'many'.

Similar game rules can be set up for many other nonstandard quantifiers. They can be used in the same way as other game rules for quantifiers. For instance, we can study the ordering principles governing them in relations to other rules in the same way as in the case of other rules. This seems to lead to an explanation of many phenomena, for instance to an account why we can say 'not many cars last long in arctic driving conditions' but not e.g. 'not several' or 'not few' instead of 'not many'.

Ordering principles likewise enable us to explain several types of ambiguity involving expressions with nonstandard quantifiers and related linguistic phenomena. For instance, the left-to-right preference explains the difference in meaning between the following sentences.

(5)   Few women love many men.

(6)   Many men are loved by few women.

Furthermore, the possibility of informational independence (branching quantification) serves to explain one of the readings of such sentences as the following.

(7)   Some detectives have solved many crimes.

This can either mean that there are some detectives each of whom has solved many crimes, or that there is a small set of detectives who have jointly solved many crimes. The latter reading, which has sometimes been claimed to be impossible to capture by means of logical representations, is obtained in a most straightforward manner by making the two quantifiers parallel instead of successively applicable. Indeed, the phenomenon of branching quantifiers seems to be more conspicuous among nonstandard quantifiers than among standard ones, whose nonlinear combinations often turn out to be reducible back to linear sequences.

Several of these hints must be elaborated before their full significance is obvious. However, they should be enough to answer Mr. Peacocke's question whether my game-theoretical semantics can be generalized to nonstandard quantifiers in an interesting way.

(iii) As an alternative to my theory of 'any', Peacocke proposes that at least some of the crucial differences between 'any' and 'every' be explained by reference to the fact "the utterer of the *any*-sentence is not presupposing that there will *be* any candidates, whereas the utterer of the *every*-sentence is presupposing that there will be some" (p. 126).

This rival suggestion seems to me demonstrably wrong, in the sense of insufficient. If it were a correct and exhaustive account of the any–every contrast, all we have to do to eliminate all differences between corresponding 'any' and 'every' sentences is to provide a context which guarantees that there are some individuals to fill the bill. But this disappearance of the difference simply does not take place in most cases. Consider, for instance, Peacocke's own pair of examples:

(8)   Any candidate will be considered on his merits.

(9)   Every candidate will be considered on his merits.

There can be an unmistakable difference in meaning between (8) and (9) even when the speaker and the hearer know perfectly well that there will be some candidates. In (8) the speaker might be committing himself or herself to fairness, no matter what dark horses might crop up among the candidates. In (9), in contrast, the speaker might for instance be thinking to himself: "Well, we have managed to scare away all the real undesirables. With the rest, we can afford to be objective; every candidate will therefore be considered on his merits after all."

To put the same point in terms of another example, surely one need not suspect that the convention will be cancelled to hear the difference between the old pair of sentences:

> Any doctor at the convention will tell you that Stopsneeze helps.

> Every doctor at the convention will tell you that Stopsneeze helps.

In 'Quantifiers in Natural Languages: Some Logical Problems' I have indicated briefly how the difference between contrastive 'any' and 'every' sentences in the future tense comes about. The future tense is in effect a modal operator, tacitly introducing several possible courses of future events. In (8) we are quantifying over individuals which might crop up in any of them. In (9), we are quantifying over individuals in one of these worlds, which is usually taken (for reasons I am not completely clear of) the actual one. Hence in the absence of all actual candidates (9) becomes vacuous, whereas (8) can still convey a nontrivial meaning. Thus the difference Peacocke uses as the basis of his allegedly competing explanation is really only a special case of my theory, a point that can be generalized to all its uses.

It follows that the explanation he offers on the basis of his alternative hypothesis do not tell against my theory. For instance, Peacocke's remarks on the following sentence can be so assimilated to my treatment.

(10)   Any delegates from Rome are landing at the airport at this moment.

In so far as I can deal with quantifier phrases of the form

(11)   Any X who Y

in general, I can deal with the phrase

(12)   any delegates who are coming from Rome

occurring in (10). I shall return to this general problem in section (vi) below.

The same is also the case with Peacocke's explanation of Zeno Vendler's observations.

At one point Mr. Peacocke suggests in effect that the sentence

(13)   If Jane wins, anybody is happy

is strange because the stronger presupposition of the corresponding 'every' sentence

(14)   If Jane wins, everybody is happy

is trivially true, viz. that there are people. But at worst this would make (13) awkward to utter, in the same way as sentences which violate pragmatic principles. It would not, and could not, make (13) ungrammatical, as it clearly seems to do.

(iv) This may be a natural opportunity to mention a correction that is needed in my earlier formulations of the any-thesis, even though Peacocke does not mention it. The thesis says that 'any' is acceptable in a given context

(*)   X – any Y – W

iff the result of replacing 'any' by 'every', i.e.

(**)   X – every – Y – W

is grammatical but not identical in meaning with (*).

In formulating the any-thesis in this way I overlooked that (**) could be ungrammatical for reasons that have nothing to do with the any–every contrast. They are due to the fact that 'every Y' cannot always function as the antecedent of a pronoun when 'any Y' can. The following pair of strings illustrates this difference.

(15)   If Bill owns any donkey, he beats it.

(16)   *If Bill owns every donkey, he beats it.

There is some fuzziness here, but in the main 'any' appears acceptable in these contexts. This is explainable in terms of a hidden modal force of 'if' (cf. below, Section v). However, (15)–(16) show that we cannot require that the sentence (**) is grammatical when (*) is acceptable.

What we have to do here is to assure that there is a process of generating strings of the respective forms (*) and (**) in parallel with each other. Our semantical game rules will assign truth-conditions to both strings. Then we on the one hand use the equivalence of (*) and

(**) as a criterion for weeding out a number of strings as being ungrammatical, and on the other hand also use the failure of pronominalization as an independent further criterion to rule out other strings, especially those with 'every', as in (18). This seems to account for all the evidence we have, and preserve all the theoretical implications of the any-thesis.

(v) As to Peacocke's specific putative counter-examples to my theory, I cannot quite follow his comments on the following example.

(17)   If John believes that and any man who believes that is mistaken, then John is mistaken.[1]

He points out, quite correctly, that (17) has a reading on which the clause 'any man who believes that is mistaken' has the same interpretation as it would have in isolation. All that this probably shows, however, is only that the ordering principle (O.any) is not absolute but only preferential, at least in so far as the priority of (G.any) over (G.if) is concerned. (Peacocke notwithstanding, an ordering principle may be less than one hundred per cent binding without thereby leaving the rules in question unordered.) Such merely preferential interpretation of (O.any) is not incompatible with my theory.

The resulting ambiguity of (17) is no objection to the any-thesis, either. Just because (17) is ambiguous, it is not identical in meaning, let alone identical in meaning on its preferred reading, with the corresponding 'every' sentence which does not exhibit the same ambiguity.

I am also puzzled by Peacocke's phrase "ungrammatical for a reading" (p.127). A string is grammatical or ungrammatical *simpliciter*.

Another factor which makes (17) hard to evaluate is the relative clause. As I already noted in 'Quantifiers in Natural Languages', Section 15, relative clauses appended to 'any' + NP tend to make 'any' acceptable even in contexts in which it apparently ought not to be according to the any-thesis. This interplay of 'any' with a relative clause apparently discourages it somewhat from jumping out of its context in the way (O.any) says.

This may be connected with another qualification (O.any) (and consequently the any-thesis) needs. The ordering principle (O.any) says that (G.any) has a priority *vis-à-vis* any one application of certain rules, such as (G.if), (G.not), and modal rules.

This does not say anything yet as to whether (G.any) has the priority over any sequence of these rules. Whether it does, and in what circumstances, remains to be investigated. Clearly (G.any) does not jump over any combination of rules over each of which it has priority considered singly. This is shown by examples like the following conditional.

(18)   If John has not dated any girl, his mother is worried.

Sometimes (G.any) does have priority over two successive rules, as witnessed by the following:

(19)   You must not tell any lies.

Where precisely the boundary between the two kinds of examples goes would require a separate examination.

(vi) The most numerous and most plausible-looking putative counter-examples to the any-thesis which Mr. Peacocke offers are in terms of phrases of the form

(20)   any X + relative clause,

for instance,

(11)   any X who Y.

I realize that I did not make it clear in the original paper to what extent these require additional comments, thus tempting both Mr. Peacocke and undoubtedly many other readers to put forward too easy putative counter-examples.

Consider, for instance, the following pair of examples.

(21)   Any candidate who can hope to be elected is catholic.

(22)   Every candidate who can hope to be elected is catholic.

Prima facie, there is no problem about (21) *vis-à-vis* any-thesis. Plainly, they are not equivalent in meaning, thus squaring well with the any-thesis which correctly predicts (21) to be acceptable. (If you don't see this, think of (21) as being said of the selection of the next president of Notre Dame and (22) as being said of a mayoralty race in New York City in which the three front runners happen to be Irish.) The same holds in general of the pair of sentences

(23)   X – any Y who Z – W

(24)   X – every Y who Z – W

with a non-empty Z. Often, the situation is less clear, but in principle we always seem to be able to hear a difference.

The trouble, if there is any here, does not lie so much with the any-thesis as with the question as to how the difference in meaning between (23) and (24) is to be explained in terms of my rules and principles.

Here, too, the beginnings of an explanation are clear. By any token, there is a conditional hidden in the 'logical form' of (11) and of

(25)   every X who Y.

A conditional typically has modal force, and modal force creates a semantical asymmetry between 'any' and 'every', just as was required.

Unfortunately, the details of this outline argument are not quite clear to me yet. Its force should not be under-estimated, however. It explains for instance why the difference between (23) and (24) often is as small as it is. This difference is, as I indicated in Section 18 of the paper Peacocke is commenting on, due to a difference in the domain of values of the quantifiers 'any' and 'every' in (23) and (24), respectively. Often this difference does not matter very much, making the difference between the respective surface forces of (23) and (24) minimal.

This account also explains why the effect of the added relative clause is independent of the context. The explanation turns on the interaction of 'any' or 'every' with the tacit 'if' which as it were is hidden inside (11) and (25). Hence it is independent of the context. This seems to be in good agreement with the available data.

Some further evidence for the same explanation is presented in my original paper.

The apparent problem with the account I am proposing is that it involves a difference in the ordering of (G.any) (and of (G.every)) with respect to the rule (G.if). Now (G.if) applies to an element (the word 'if') which is only introduced by the application of one of the former rules. How can (G.if), with or without an added modal component, possibly precede (G.every)?

I am not sure what the best answer to this question is. I am sure, however, that it is not unanswerable in game-theoretical semantics. The best hypothesis I can think of is to do something that can be independently motivated, viz. to formulate a rule for restrictive relative clauses, which so far have been dealt with only as a part of the operation of the quantifier rules. The simplest procedure is probably a rule which deals with restrictive and nonrestrictive relative clauses (with antecedents).

(G.rel) When a game has reached a sentence of the form

$$X - Y \text{ who } Z - W$$

where 'who Z' is a restrictive (nonrestrictive) relative clause, the game may be continued with respect to the following sentences

$$X - Y - W \text{ if } \begin{Bmatrix} he \\ she \\ it \end{Bmatrix} Z$$

$$\text{If } Y Z, \; X - \begin{Bmatrix} he \\ she \\ it \end{Bmatrix} - W$$

if these are acceptable English sentences. (In the case of a nonrestrictive relative clause, the output has 'and' instead of 'if'.) The choice of the pronoun $\begin{Bmatrix} he \\ she \\ it \end{Bmatrix}$ is determinated by the antecedent of the relative clause in the obvious way.

This rewriting rule is of course optional. The same qualifications are of course needed in it as in the other rules I have formulated. The rule (G.rel) is motivated among other things by the naturalness of having a rough one-to-one correlation between the different ingredients of sentences of our fragment of English and the semantical game rules.

The ordering principles governing (G.rel) remain to be investigated. They are complicated by the fact that the pronominalization involved in the output of (G.rel) is not always possible. Furthermore, typically the order of (G.rel) with respect to (G.any) or (G.every) does not matter for any other purposes than the any-thesis. However, it appears that sometimes (G.rel) can be applied before (G.any), introducing the modal 'if' which makes the any-thesis applicable.

Further study is needed to see whether this is the best diagnosis of what happens to any 'X + relative clause' *vis-à-vis* the any-thesis. It suffices to show that a treatment of these expressions in game-theoretical semantics is very likely to be possible in a way that is in agreement with the any-thesis.

Grammarians have recently presented evidence for a close relationship between expressions such as the following.

> a man who is stupid
> a stupid man

Hence it is to be expected that the latter will behave somewhat in the same way as the former. This expectation seems to be satisfied, and serves to explain a number of apparent difficulties in connection with the any-thesis.

(vii) Among the most important problems Peacocke raises there are his last two questions. They are: Do I accept a motivation for game-theoretical semantics which turns on the necessity of restricting the set of my strategies in semantical games to recursive ones, or to some other humanly manipulable ones? Do I think that this is the only motivation for game-theoretical semantics?

The latter question has already been amply answered. There is a plethora of other reasons for using, and studying, game-theoretical semantics, for the purposes of the theory of both natural languages and of symbolic ones. There are plenty of important phenomena that are amenable to a game-theoretical analysis but not to a traditional one.

My answer to the first question is an affirmative one, qualified by two major *caveats*. I do not have much to add to what I have said earlier about the kind of motivation for game-theoretical semantics Peacocke mentions, viz. a motivation which is based on the possibility of restricting strategy sets to recursive strategies or to some other narrower class of strategies. Much work simply remains to be done to see what precisely happens if we restrict my strategy sets in semantical games in different ways. Nor do I have much to add to what Peacocke says of the subject, except perhaps to demur and take exception to his initial formulation of "one *prima facie* plausible doctrine which would. . .ground Professor Hintikka's semantics". I do not believe that "to understand a sentence is to know what one must possess in order to meet arbitrarily skillful challenges to the effect that certain cited objects stand in relations the sentence excludes" (p. 131). Even though it often is tempting to describe semantical games by speaking what has to be 'defended' by Myself, these formulations are not indicative of the philosophically most relevant nature of the games. These games are games of exploring the world, of verifying and falsifying sentences, rather than dialogical games in which verbal 'challenges' are met by putting forward new sentences. The latter is perhaps not what Peacocke means, but even so his formulation seems to me to miss the gist of the matter.

Apart from this difference in emphasis, there is a substantial observation to be made here. The kind of motivation we are here discussing becomes much more interesting – and turns out to have all sorts of connections with other conceptualizations in logic and foundational studies – when combined with still another extension of the basic game-theoretical apparatus. This extension is even more closely bound up with the game idea than the other ones I have mentioned. It turns on the concept of a *subgame*. As indicated in my joint paper with Lauri Carlson (the present volume, pp. 179–214), we sometimes have to think of a semantical game as being split up into successive subgames each of which is played 'to the bitter end', whereupon one of the players uncovers his or her strategy in that subgame.

Since the players' later moves in a game will now depend on this strategy and since it is this very dependence that a player's strategy codifies, strategies can now be functionals (functions of functions). The result is a kind of *functional interpretation* of first-order logic and of certain parts of natural languages.

This functional interpretation can be compared with earlier functional interpretations familiar to logicians. The best known is Kurt Gödel's interpretation of elementary arithmetic. As Dana Scott has pointed out (in an unpublished note), Gödel's functional interpretation admits an extremely simple game-theoretical formulation. In my judgement, this game-theoretical formulation also shows the motivation of Gödel's proposal much more clearly than his original argument.

Gödel's interpretation involves precisely the same restriction on the strategies of one of the players to recursive ones (i.e., to strategies codified by recursive functions and functionals) as I have mentioned. Here we therefore have an interesting connection with between game-theoretical semantics and other foundational ideas.

Gödel's interpretation turns out to differ from the ones which Carlson and Hintikka argue to be most apt to match the semantics of English conditional sentences. It is not clear how this discrepancy is to be understood, but even in the presence of this discrepancy the same basic idea of combining the use of subgames with the restriction of my strategies to computable ones is seen to underlie both functional interpretations. This helps to show how suggestive this basic idea is logically, linguistically, and philosophically.

How is this approach to be evaluated? I shall not venture an answer here. Instead, I shall merely refer the reader to another paper of mine where I show that the step from unlimited strategy sets to restricted sets (e.g. to the set of all recursive strategies) is parallel with, and can be considered as a special case of, the step of standard to suitable nonstandard interpretations, in a sense that generalizes Henkin's distinction between standard and nonstandard interpretations of higher-order logics. (This paper 'Standard vs. Nonstandard Modal (and First-Order) Logics' is forthcoming in the proceedings of the 1977 Rome Conference on Modern Logic, to be published by Istituto della Enciclopedia Italiana, Rome.) What this observation implies is in my judgement that the question Peacocke raises must be considered in a wide context, as a special case of the general problem whether we should prefer nonstandard models (interpretation) to standard ones, and if so, what kinds of nonstandard models we should use. This 'what kinds' question is of course a straight generalization of the question as to how my strategy sets in semantical games are to be restricted. The wider problem is too large, however, to be discussed here. Even so, it serves to illustrate the interesting connections that there are between game-theoretical semantics and important logical and philosophical problems.

Mr. Peacocke tries to consider game-theoretical semantics as a relatively small variant of ordinary semantics which operates with recursive truth-definitions. The differences between the two are greater than he realizes, however, and the range of phenomena that can be handled by the former but not by the latter much more wider than he assumes. This is not to say, however, that a great deal of work is not needed to tighten many of the details of game-theoretical semantics.

Academy of Finland and Stanford University

SEMANTICAL GAMES AND THE
BACH–PETERS PARADOX*

This paper is mainly addressed to the question: What is the semantics of a sentence with crossing pronominalization between two different the-phrases? In terms of a representative example we might as well ask: What is the semantics of the following sample sentence (1)?

(1)   The boy who was fooling her kissed the girl who loved him.

This sentence is an instance of the so-called Bach–Peters paradox which has been claimed to arise because (1) does not seem to be obtainable from any finite deep structure. In Karttunen (1971) it is shown how on certain assumptions (1) be generated after all from such a deep structure. (His main assumption is that pronominalization is *not* a cyclic rule.) In his approach (1) is declared to be ambiguous between three readings two of which can also be expressed by the surface forms (2) and (3). (Karttunen does not present an alternative surface form for the third reading.)

(2)   The boy who was fooling the girl who loved him kissed her.

(3)   The girl who loved the boy who was fooling her was kissed by him.

Karttunen's proposals have subsequently been discussed among others by Kuroda (1971) and by Wasow (1973), who agree with Karttunen that (1) is ambiguous between (2) and (3). We shall argue here that this view is incorrect and that there is only one semantical representation underlying (1). Our results do not contradict the general idea of Dik (1973) but will rather extend and deepen his arguments.

Our approach to the problems at hand will be in terms of Hintikka's game-theoretical semantics. For a more complete exposition of the basic ideas on this approach the reader is referred to Hintikka (1974) and to Hintikka (1976), both of which are reprinted in the present volume. In the former paper it is pointed out that when Hintikka's game-rules are applied to the sentence

(4)   A boy who was fooling her kissed a girl who loved him

E. Saarinen (ed.), Game-Theoretical Semantics, 153–178. All Rights Reserved.
Copyright © 1975 by Verlag Walter de Gruyter & Co.

with indefinite articles in the place of the definite ones, they automatically yield the expected natural semantical representation of (4). It is clear, however, that there are more semantical problems about (1) than about (4).

In order to resolve them, let us extend Hintikka's game-theoretical semantics so as to apply to the English definite article in the kind of use exemplified by (1). This can be accomplished by means of a game rule of which the following is a special case:

(G. singular the) Assume that the game reached a sentence of the form

(5)   Z – the Y who Z – W

where Y and Z are singular and where the 'who' in 'who Z' occupies the subject position. Then I may choose an individual, say a, from the domain of discourse, whereupon Nature also chooses an individual, say b, different from a. The game is continued with respect to b, different from a. The game is continued with respect to

(6)   X – a – W, a is a(n)Y, a Z, and b is not a(n)Y who Z.

Although we shall in this paper confine our attention to this use of the definite article, it is to be noted that there are several others, including the following:

(a)   the corresponding plural one;

(b)   the anaphoric use;

(c)   the generic use(s).

For (a) we can formulate the following game-rule:

(G. plural the) Assume that the game has reached a sentence of the form

(7)   X – the Y who Z – W

where Y and Z are in the plural and where the 'who' in 'who Z' occupies the subject position. Then I may choose an individual, say a, from the domain of discourse, whereupon Nature also chooses an individual, say b. The game is continued with respect to the following sentence (8).

(8)   X' – a – W', a is a(n)Y', a Z', and X' – b – W' if b is a(n)Y' and b Z'.

Here $X' - W'$ is like X—W except that pronouns pronominalized by the quantifier phrase 'the Y who Z' in (7) are changed from the plural to the corresponding singular. Moreover, if this quantifier phrase (or one of the pronous just mentioned) occupies the subject position in some clause in (7), this clause is likewise changed from the plural to the singular. Y' and Z' are like Y and Z except for being in the singular and not in the plural.

As they were just formulated, both (G.singular the) and (G.plural the) is a special case of a more general rule. What this general rule is in each case is easily seen from our special cases.

The intuitive idea on which our game rule (G.singular the) is based is clear. I must be able to choose an individual to serve as the reference of 'the Y who Z'. However, there must not be more than one such individual, and hence any other individual that Nature may choose must not be a(n)Y who Z.

The uses of 'the' covered automatically by (G.singular the) and (G.plural the) are such that the the-phase that they are applied to does not refer back to an earlier noun phrase. When it does, we have to do with anaphoric use (b) of a the-phrase. These uses of the-phrases can be handled in game-theoretical semantics by allowing a semantical game to restrict the choice of a and b in (G.singular the) to individuals which are considered in the course of a game. This suggestion, which is due to Lauri Carlson, is based on the observation that in many anaphoric uses a the-phrase can be understood only when the part of the domain is specified which is taken to be 'known'. We are in effect suggesting that this 'known' part consists of those members of the underlying domain which have been chosen or otherwise considered in the course of a game by the time it reaches the anaphoric the-phrase. (Even further restrictions may occasionally be needed, especially a restriction to individuals chosen by Myself.) This implies that we must resort to semantical considerations in determining the coreference relations between anaphoric the-phrases (in context) and their antecedents, for no straightforward syntactical account of these relations seems to be adequate. In order to see the point, consider the following example:

> Two girls were walking on the street. The girl with dark hair was beautiful.

When the the-phrase present here is evaluated, we have to assume some knowledge of the model. For instance, the individual who is referred to by the anaphoric the-phrase is the one of the two girls who has dark hair. That the two players' choice is restricted in this way cannot be determined on the basis of syntactical considerations alone pertaining to the sentence in which the the-phrase occurs. Even if the truth value of the first sentence has been determined, purely syntactical considerations will not be sufficient to determine the reference of the the-phrase.

It is easily seen that this example of the anaphoric uses of a the-phrase can naturally be treated in game-theoretical framework if this approach is extended in the way suggested. Thus immediately after the game connected with the first sentence, players' domain of choice will be restricted to the two girls. In evaluating the second sentence we apply normally (G.singular the) with respect to this restricted domain of discourse.

We will not discuss in this paper the details of this way of treating anaphoric uses of the-phrases. Enough has been said, we hope, to indicate what can be done in this respect and to suggest that in game-theoretical framework it is possible to put forward a unified treatment which applies both to the (usual) the-phrases (thought of along the lines indicated by (G.singular the)) and to their anaphoric uses. Even though many details still cry out for further discussion, we hope to have kindled in the reader some optimism *vis-à-vis* a game-theoretical account of these phenomena.

We shall not study generic uses (c) of the-phrases in this paper.

In the game rules X – W is allowed to be any context whatsoever. However, it should be noted that (G.singular the) as well as (G.plural the) is subject to restriction of the same kind as the rules for some other English quantifiers presented in Hintikka (1974) or in Hintikka (1977).

In order to preclude criticism which may be well taken in itself but irrelevant to the concerns of this paper, a comment may be in order. As it stands, (G.singular the) is not quite all right. This is because the step from (5) to (6) may upset intended relations of pronominalization. Indeed, (6) may even be ungrammatical.

Something can be done to rectify the situation. For instance, if the Langacker-Ross criterion of acceptable pronominalization in English is accepted, we can guarantee the grammaticality of (6) simply by reversing in (6) the pronominalization relations between Z and W (as compared to (5)). However, this does not guarantee that the pronouns in (6) are pronominalized by the same word or phrase as in (5).

The exact rules which determine which noun phrase pronominalizes which pronoun will not be studied here. As long as we have not found them out and formulated them, our game-rules are admittedly defective. This defect can be corrected for a large number of cases by requiring – or perhaps merely allowing – each pronoun pronominalized by a quantifier phrase (including a the-phrase) to be replaced by a proper name as soon as this proper name is substituted for the quantifier phrase. More explicitly stated, when a quantifier phrase occurs in a context X – W, the pronouns occuring in X or W are replaced by a proper name, say 'a', as soon as this name is substituted for the quantifier phrase. (Genitive pronous will have to be replaced by the genitive form of the name, of course.) In what follows, we shall make use of this depronominalization possibility.

In applying (G.singular the) and (G.plural the) we face the same problem of rule-ordering as arises elsewhere in game-theoretical semantics. (See e.g. Hintikka, 1977.) However, in the special cases we are here studying the situation is clear enough without extensive analysis. If we restrict our attention for a while to (1), we note that there are two the-phrases in the same main clause of (1) but no other quantifier structures. Hence the presumption is that the usual left-to-right order applies. If so, then the game rule yields sentences of the following form when applied to (1):

(9)   John kissed the girl who loved John, John is a boy, John was fooling her, and Bill is not a boy who was fooling her.

Because of the pronominalization we cannot use (G.and) (except to detach 'John is a boy', which does not matter here). Hence we have to apply (G.singular the) again, which yields

(10)   John kissed Jane, John is a boy, John was fooling Jane, Bill is not a boy who was fooling Jane, Jane is a girl, Jane loved John, and Jill is not a girl who loved John.

From (10) it is immediately seen that the semantical representation we obtain in this was for (1) is (in the usual quantificational notation)

(11) $(\exists x)(y)(\exists z)(u)(x$ kissed $z \wedge x$ is a boy $\wedge x$ was fooling z
$\wedge (y \neq x \supset \sim(y$ is a boy $\wedge y$ was fooling $z))$
$\wedge z$ is a girl $\wedge z$ loved x
$\wedge (u \neq z \supset \sim(u$ is a girl $\wedge u$ loved $x)))$.

Let us abbreviate this by

(12) $(\exists x)(y)(\exists z)(u)M(x, y, z, u)$.

Now because of the uniqueness clauses in (11) a situation somewhat unusual in quantification theory arises in that the order of the quantifiers in the prefix does not matter very much. (For a formal proof and a generalization of this observation, see the appendix below.) E.g., (11) is logically equivalent with (13) and (14).

(13) $(\exists z)(u)(\exists x)(y)M(x, y, z, u)$.

(14) $(\exists x)(\exists z)(y)(u)M(x, y, z, u)$.

Here (14) in turn is logically equivalent with the following formula containing partially ordered quantifiers.

$$\begin{matrix} (\exists x)(y) \\ \\ (\exists z)(u) \end{matrix} \Big\rangle M(x, y, z, u)$$

Now (12) was the semantical representation we obtained when (G.singular the) was applied to (1) in the natural left-to-right order. Similarly (13) is the translation of the sentence we obtain when the rule is applied to (1) in the opposite, right-to-left order, as the reader can easily verify. Finally, (15) can similarly be taken to be the representation we obtain when the two quantifier moves are made independently of each other.

It is tempting to surmise that this indifference to quantifier switches is one of the main tacit rationales for the ubiquity of the definite article in many natural languages. It has been pointed out repeatedly that quantifier nesting and quantifier ordering are among the most difficult things for us humans to master in our native information processing. Any grammatical device which facilitates the handling of these two complications will therefore be an especially useful tool in ordinary discourse.

The partial irrelevance of quantifier order means that the order of the applications of (G.singular the) to (1) does not matter. We always obtain the same semantical representation no matter which game tactics (order of applications) we choose. It is the characteristic feature of (1) that the references of the the-phases are picked up independently of each other, or, more precisely, that the reference of each of the the-phrases is *not* picked up with the essential help of the other – contrary to what will turn out to be the case with (2) and (3). This result of ours can be seen as an explication of Dik's statement that "it is clear that in (1) the two definite descriptions are not explicitly given in a hierarchical relation to each other". (1973, p. 321.)

On the other hand there is only one semantical representation underlying (1) – a fact that squares well with one's intuitions but which is not reflected faithfully in most of the existing discussions of the Bach-Peters paradox.

The models of (11)–(15) and hence those of (1) are of the following

(16)

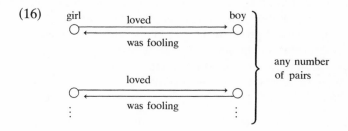

form (16). Thus the models of (1) are perhaps *prima facie* a little surprising in that more than one pair of boys and girls may in each of them satisfy the uniqueness clauses. Notwithstanding the initial surprise, this is how things ought to be. For clearly the only kind of uniqueness required in (1) is that the boy in question was the only one to fool the girl in question, and that she in turn was the only one to love him. Certainly this kind of uniqueness does not exclude other similar couples. In fact, if one considers the noun phrase

the boy who was fooling her

it becomes quite obvious that more than one boy can be referred to by it, *depending on* who 'her' is. What this means is that this NP presupposes there to be one and only one boy relative to 'her', *not* in any absolute sense. That there is nothing awkward in this conclusion is witnessed for instance by the following sentence where the NP 'the girl who is married to him' clearly can refer to more than one individual, depending on who 'him' is:

Every boy is loved by the girl who is married to him.

By the same token, the presupposition associated with the sentence (1) cannot require that there is one and only one boy (and one and only one girl) in some absolute sense, but only relative to certain individuals. There has to be one and only one boy with respect to a certain girl, viz. that girl who is the one and only one to love that boy. There is nothing in (1) to prevent there being another similar boy if that boy is the one and only one fooling some other girl, viz. the girl who is the one and only one to love that boy. Hence the models of (1) are indeed of the form (16). (More arguments for the same conclusion will be given below.) The fact that the models of (1) are of this kind seems to have been unnoticed in all the discussions of the Bach-Peters paradox mentioned above, including Dik's (cf. Dik, 1973, pp. 321–322).

One might also expect *prima facie* that (1) is synonymous with (2) and (3). This expectation, however, is not fulfilled. Applied for instance to (2), (G.singular the) yields a sentence of the following form. (Note that we have reversal pronominalization between Z and W for reasons indicated above.)

(17)   John kissed the girl who loved him, John is a boy, John was fooling her, and Bill is not a boy who was fooling the girl who loved him.

In (17) there is nothing to prevent us from using (G.and) and detaching from the main clause the sentence (18).

(18)   Bill is not a boy who was fooling the girl who loved him.

What this shows is that the quantifiers there tacitly are in (18) have as their scope (18) only. It follows also that the existential quantifier tacitly involved in (18) is *not* independent of the first universal quantifier of (2). This fact is faithfully reflected in (18) by the fact that the individual referred to by the clause 'the girl who loved him' depends explicitly on the individual Nature has happened to choose. If Nature had chosen some other individual instead of Bill, say Jack, the reference of 'the girl who loved him' might have changed. If the two the-phrases are now played off with this fact in mind (similar considerations apply to the first conjunct in (17), too) (17) yields a sentence of the following form.

(19)   John kissed Jane, John is a boy, John was fooling Jane, Bill is not a boy who was fooling Ann, Jane is a girl, Jane loved

John, Jill is not a girl who loved John, Ann is a girl, Ann loved Bill, and Barbara is not a girl who loved Bill.

From (19) we immediately see that the overall semantical representation underlying (2) is, in the usual quantificational notation, (20).

(20) $(\exists x)(\exists z)$ [x kissed z $\wedge$ x is a boy $\wedge$ x was fooling z
$\wedge$ z is a girl $\wedge$ z loved x
$\wedge$ $(u)(u \neq z \supset \sim(u$ is a girl $\wedge$ u loved $x))$
$\wedge$ $(y)(y \neq x \supset \sim(y$ is a boy
$\wedge$ $(\exists v)(v$ is a girl $\wedge$ v loved y $\wedge$ y was fooling v
$\wedge$ $(w)(w \neq v \supset \sim(w$ is a girl $\wedge$ w loved $y)))))]$.

This *not* logically equivalent with (11)–(15). Nor is the semantical representation (21) we likewise obtain for (3) logically equivalent with (11)–(15).

(21) $(\exists z)(\exists x)$ [z was kissed by x $\wedge$ z is a girl $\wedge$ z loved x
$\wedge$ x is a boy $\wedge$ x was fooling z
$\wedge$ $(y)(y \neq x \supset \sim(y$ is a boy $\wedge$ y was fooling $z))$
$\wedge$ $(u)(u \neq z \supset \sim(u$ is a girl
$\wedge$ $(\exists s)(s$ is a boy $\wedge$ s was fooling u $\wedge$ u loved s
$\wedge$ $(t)(t \neq s \supset \sim(t$ is a boy $\wedge$ t was fooling $s)))))]$.

This shows that the properties of (1) must be distinguished sharply from those of (2) and (3).

The models of (20) – and hence those of (2) – are of the following form (22).

(22)

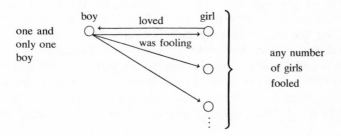

The models of (21) and (3) are likewise of the form (23).

(23)

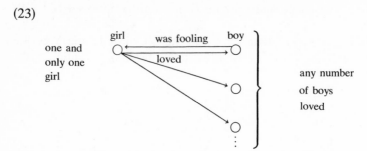

A striking constrast to the models of (1) (cf. (16)) is that (2) and (3) do not allow more than one pair of individuals to satisfy the uniqueness clauses. What this means is that though the conjunction of (2) and (3) logically implies (1), (1) does not imply the conjunction of (2) and (3), not even their disjunction. For instance, the model depicted by (24) is a model of (1) but not one of (2) or (3).

(24)

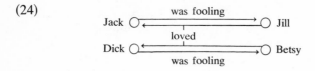

where Jack kissed Jill and Dick Betsy.

This fact has not been taken into account in any of the discussions of the Bach-Peters paradox mentioned above. It also destroys completely the idea that (1) is ambiguous between (2) and (3).

By hindsight, it is in fact easy to see that the uniqueness presuppositions associated with (2) are different from those of (1), and that the two hence cannot be synonymous. For in (2) it must make sense to speak of '*the* boy who was fooling *the* girl who loved him', which implies that (2) can be true only if there is precisely one boy who was fooling the one and only one girl who loved him. This kind of uniqueness is quite foreign to (1). The same of course holds of (3), too.

It is instructive to compare our results with the problems that arise about (1) in linguistics. As we noted earlier, Karttunen argues that (1) is ambiguous between two readings whose surface forms are (2) and (3). In the end Karttunen nevertheless comes to the conclusion that (1)

(25)

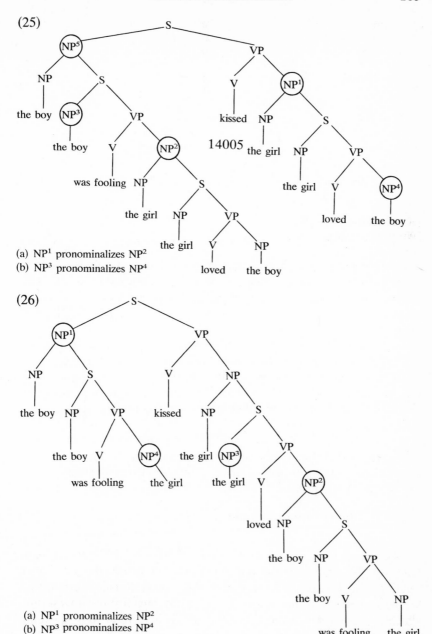

(a) NP¹ pronominalizes NP²
(b) NP³ pronominalizes NP⁴

(26)

(a) NP¹ pronominalizes NP²
(b) NP³ pronominalizes NP⁴

(27)

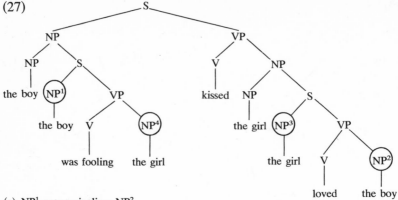

(a) NP¹ pronominalizes NP²
(b) NP³ pronominalizes NP⁴

is not ambiguous in two ways but in three, though he finds only two surface structures to go together with the different readings. This conclusion is due to the fact that in the generation process Karttunen finds for (1), (1) is generated from the three seemingly different deep structures (25)–(27).

The crucial point is that if pronominalization is not a cyclic rule we can generate (1) from a finite deep structure while preserving all the usual requirements on the pronominalizing NP and the NP replaced by the correlated pronoun. In particular, the two NP's can – and must – be required to be coreferential (whatever that means in the last analysis).

Now in (25) we can let NP¹ pronominalize NP² and NP³ pronominalize NP⁴. If we reverse the former pronominalization and let the highest NP in the first branch pronominalize the lowest one, we are supposed to obtain (2) instead of (1). Thus intuitively speaking NP² is the source of the phrase

(28)   the girl who loved him

in (2).

Likewise, in (26) we can on this view either let NP¹ pronominalize NP² and NP³ pronominalize NP⁴, obtaining (1), or reverse the former relation (which is possible only after the passive transformation) and let the highest NP in the second branch pronominalize the lowest one, which is supposed to yield (3). Thus NP² is here intuitively speaking the source of

(29)   the boy who was fooling her

in (2).

The following intuitive line of though may be helpful here. If Karttunen's deep structures are to have any down-to-earth significance, then what can it mean that in (25) the reference of 'her' is obtained from 'the girl who loved him' but 'him' in turn from 'the boy'? The former fact seems to mean that 'the boy who was fooling her' is in fact 'the boy who was fooling the girl who loved him'. Hence in finding out the reference of the first the-phrase in (1) we have to make essential use of the other the-phrase. Now if 'him' in turn is taken from 'the boy' this just seems to mean that we are somehow supposed to pick out the reference of 'him' without considering the other the-phrase. There clearly is no such back reference to another the-phrase in the phrase 'the boy'. In fact, this is in effect just how the infinite regress or an infinite deep structure was avoided by Karttunen.

The crucial effect of the deep structure (26) can be understood similarly, the only difference being that we in this case fix the reference of 'the boy who was fooling her' by taking 'her' from 'the girl', the reference of which can be settled without recouse to the other the-phrase. It is then possible to fix the reference of 'the girl who loved him' by letting this to be the reference of 'the girl who loved the boy who was fooling her'.

It now becomes clear why (25) and (26) have as their surface interpretations (2) and (3), respectively. These semantical representations simply amount to assuming the 'hierarchical relations' between the different the-phrases there explicitly is in (2) and (3). (It is to be noted that this hierarchical order is something quite different from the order of applications of the game-rules.)

There is a further sentence that naturally suggests itself to our attention. This is (30), a sentence that has to a large extent been disregarded in the connection of the Bach–Peters paradox:

(30)   The boy who was fooling the girl who loved him kissed the girl who loved the boy who was fooling her.

(Wasow, 1973, discusses a parallel example but rules it out as "anomalous". This does not seem to concord with one's intuitions, however.) By means of game-theoretical semantics it is easy to find the semantical representation underlying (30) and to note that its models are of the following form (31). (Another method to find the representation of (30) is to compare it directly with (2) and (3) and their models.)

(31)
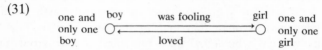

Now (30) is the missing structure that serves as the surface interpretation of Karttunen's deep structure (27). Karttunen himself, as well as the other authors, have not put forward (30) or any other acceptable surface interpretation of (27). The closest they have to come to (30) is the following barely acceptable sentence (32).

(32)   The boy who was fooling the girl kissed the girl who loved the boy,

where 'the boy' is supposed to be coreferential with 'the boy who was fooling the girl' and 'the girl' coreferential with 'the girl who loved the boy' (whatever that means). It is not clear, however, why these supposed coreference relations should obtain here. The only possible explanation seems to be that the the-phrases 'the boy' and 'the girl' were used anaphorically. But if so, then the models of (32) are *not* of the form (31) but of the form (16). In other words, the only possible way to make sense of (32) renders it synonymous with (1).

It is now easier to see why the models of (1) have to be of the form (16) and not of the form (31). Were the models of (1) of the latter form – as most of the discussions of the Bach–Peters paradox have indeed assumed – we ought to explain why (1) and (30) are synonymous with each other but not with (2) and (3). (The models of (30) certainly have the form (31).) But no such arguments are forthcoming. Moreover, it is plain that what is required in order for the NP

the X who Z

to make sense is that there is one and only one X who Z, and nothing else. If this idea is consistently followed one cannot avoid the conclusion that the presuppositions of (1) are quite different from those of (30), as we indicated above.

It is now easy to state explicitly what the difficulty is with Karttunen's deep structures. The fact is that his deep structures presuppose a kind of uniqueness that is quite foreign to (1), to wit, presuppose that there is only *one* suitable individual in the model. In (25) only one boy of the relevant kind is admitted into a model, in (26) one girl is admitted and in (27) one boy and girl are admitted. Although this kind of presupposition is characteristic of (2), (3), and (30), it is quite foreign to (1), as we pointed out earlier. It is worth noting how well this unjustified presupposition matches the intuitive interpretation of Karttunen's pronominalization trick sketched above. In order for it to make sense to speak of 'the boy' or 'the girl' there clearly has to be only one such individual. That is how 'the' works in such cases. (Any attempt to interpret 'the boy' and 'the girl' in Karttunen's structures anaphorically seems to fail, and it would in any case beg the question.)

Some linguists would probably claim that the kind of stronger uniqueness which is imposed by (30) on (31) but not by (1) on (16) is part and parcel of the force of the English definite article 'the'. Some aspects of the operation of the anaphoric 'the' seem to support this idea, for sometimes the only reason for understanding a the-phrase anaphorically is that otherwise it does not make any sense. In other words, we look for contextual uniqueness when we cannot find absolute uniqueness. It is this quest of uniqueness that seems to rule out (16) as a model of (1).

In view of what has been said, this idea is not very credible one, even though some of our unedited intuitions seem to accord with it. Pushed to a conclusion, however, it pretty much reduces to absurdity. For the ultimate suggestion is not so much that (16) is not a model of (1) but that (1) is unacceptable, because it does not guarantee the uniqueness which is endemic in the definite article. This removes the syntactic Bach–Peters paradox rather than solves it, and goes against most linguists' intuitions which apparently vouchsafe the well-formedness of (1).

These observations may nevertheless help to understand the temptation to take (1) to say what in reality it takes (30) to say, and by so doing help to understand Karttunen's position, if not to justify it.

It is to be noted that (1) does not imply the disjunction of (2), (3), and (30). The model (24) above is a model of (1), but not one of (2), (3), or (30).

Hence our conclusion is that Karttunen has not been able to find a satisfactory generation of (1) in the traditional framework. Hence the Bach–Peters paradox is paradoxical after all. It remains as an open problem whether one can find a satisfactory generation of (1) within the traditional framework. This renewed difficulty will undoubtedly be construed by some linguists as an argument against any pronominalization transformation or rule.

In one important sense the paradox has nevertheless disappeared. There are no problems left open by our results concerning the *semantics* of any of the allegedly paradoxical sentences. There is no Bach–Peters paradox on the semantical level.

What counts as a satisfactory generation of (1) depends of course on the requirements imposed on generation rules in general. We shall not examine here the pros and cons for the different restraints that are usually presupposed. Suffice it to emphasize the basic difficulty which is reasserting itself here. It is a difficulty in generating (1) while maintaining some residual form of the principle that transformations preserve meaning. One corollary of this principle is the requirement that the NP which is replaced by a pronoun and the NP which pronominalizes it are coreferential. Even if we do not believe in the meaning preservation principle in general, it is hard to see what can be done by way of pronominalization rules if the principle is not maintained in this special case.

The difficulty of generating (1) in a satisfactory manner can also be illustrated by pointing out that it presents a problem also for the conventional logical notation. Admittedly, we have presented a semantical representation for (1) and not only for (2), (3), and (30) in terms of ordinary first-order logic. However, we have not required that English the-phrases be expressed by the definite descriptions of logic. When this requirement is imposed on the translations of the relevant English sentences into logical notation, we can still translate (2), (3) and (30) without any difficulty. For instance, (2) and (3) can be expressed by the following formal sentences.

(33) $(\imath x)B(x)$ kissed $(\imath z)(z$ is a girl $\wedge z$ loved $(\imath x)B(x))$

and

(34) $(\imath x)G(x)$ was kissed by $(\imath z)(z$ is a boy $\wedge z$ was fooling $(\imath x)G(x))$

where

$B(x) = (x$ is a boy $\wedge x$ was fooling $(\imath y)(y$ is a girl $\wedge y$ loved $x))$

and

$G(x) = (x$ is a girl $\wedge$ x loved $(\imath y)(y$ is a boy $\wedge$ y was fooling $x))$.

It is of interest to see how very closely the structure of (33)–(34) matches that of (25)–(26), respectively.

However, there exists no similar translation of (1) into conventional logical notation in which definite descriptions would match the the-phrases of English. If we try to translate (1) along the same lines as (2) and (3), we shall stumble on precisely the same difficulty as in the conventional syntactical derivations of (1). We need a definite description to replace 'her'. But this definite description contains 'him' which needs a definite description to replace it. This definite description in turn contains 'her', and so on *ad infinitum*. Thus the Bach–Peters paradox is essentially the same puzzle as the problem of translating English the-phrases consistently into logical notation in terms of definite descriptions (i.e., by means of the iota-operator). (The same point is made implicitly in Harman, 1972, cf. pp. 41–43.)

The usual logical notation can nevertheless be amplified so as to allow for a desired kind of translation of (1). One possibility is to think of the definite description $(\imath x)(F(x))$ as a quantifier which has as its scope a formula $G(x)$ in which x may still occur. Then

(35) $(\imath x)F(x)[G(x)]$

will be a well-formed formula for which a semantical interpretation can readily be given. The same interpretation can be extended without any difficulty to doubly 'quantified' formulas of the form

(36) $(\imath x)(\imath y)(F_1(x,y) \wedge F_2(y, x))[G(x,y)]$.

We can even extend Russell's theory of definite descriptions without any difficulty to such expressions.

Then we can also translate (1) as follows.

(37) $(\imath x)(\imath y)((x$ is a boy $\wedge$ x was fooling $y) \wedge$
(y$ is a girl $\wedge$ y loved $x))[x$ kissed $y]$.

We shall not examine here whether there is any parallel to this solution to 'logicians' Bach–Peters paradox' on the linguistic side of the fence. It seems, however, that McCawley's proposals as modified by

Dik (1973) are closely related to this line of thought. What this relation is precisely will not be studied here.

Notice, incidentally, that the novelty is logical notation just put forward will also solve a problem which lurks in (33) and (34) as formalizations of (2) and (31). For, as the reader probably feels like saying, (33) actually is *not* the most natural semantical representation of (2): the two are equivalent only if we analyze the pronoun 'her' occurring in (2) as a pronoun of laziness rather than as an anaphoric pronoun. (This is seen from the fact that 'her' of (2) is mirrored in (33) by the clause '$(\imath z)(z$ is a girl $\wedge z$ loved $(\imath x)B(x))$'.) With the new type of definite description operator, one can easily rectify the situation, however. Instead of (33) we can now write

(33)' $(\imath x)$ $(x$ is a boy $\wedge x$ was fooling $(\imath y)$ $(y$ is a girl $\wedge y$ loved $x))$ $[x$ kissed $y]$.

These problems of representing (1), (2), and (3), in a satisfactory logical notation suggest a more general moral. For they suggest that we should not try to interpret natural language sentences by translating them into a customary logical notation. Rather, what we ought to do is to develop interpretational rules for the natural language directly. This is precisely what we are doing in game-theoretical semantics. Semantical games are defined for natural language sentences directly. It may be that these semantical games can often be 'translated' into a conventional logical notation. However, in general there is no guarantee that this can be done. But should we care here about this failure? The best semantical representations for the natural language sentences are given to us by the semantical games themselves. They are the link between language and reality. Thus the problems involved in expressing the import of (1)–(3) in a customary logical notation can be interpreted as indirect evidence for game-theoretical semantics in general.

If we look at the semantical representations underlying (1), (2), (3), and (30), we note that the essential difference between them is a difference in the structure of the *uniqueness clauses* involved. In the case of (1) these uniqueness clauses are such as to allow different game tactics (different ways of applying the semantical rules which all yield the same representation (the equivalence of (12)–(15)). What happens in applying these different game tactics is that the order in which the reference of 'the boy who was fooling her' and 'the girl who loved him' are picked up is different. But the same seems to be the case with

(25)–(27), i.e., with Karttunen's three semantical representations. From this we immediately see what the source of Karttunen's difficulties is. The fact is that the uniqueness clauses characteristic of 'the' are *not* taken into account at all in Karttunen's deep structures. But what the difference between the semantical representations of (1), (2) (3), and (30) amounts to is precisely a difference in the structure of the uniqueness clauses they involve. In the type of analysis adopted by Karttunen one just cannot disentangle different types of game tactics from different uniqueness clauses. Hence in spite of his awareness (as it seems to us) of the different types of game tactics associated with (1) Karttunen fails to distinguish these two different types of orderings from each other. But this is all that is needed to obscure the semantics of (1) as compared to (2), (3), and (30). It is worth noting how naturally the kind of semantical analysis employed here takes this difference into account.

This shortcoming of the kind of semantical analysis adopted by Karttunen reflects another, deeper shortcoming. This shortcoming lies in the fact that such semantical representations as (25)–(27) yield no criterion as to when two or more apparently (notationally) different deep structures are semantically equivalent. Such a situation does not arise in the game-theoretical semantics where the concept of logical equivalence can be used.

This criticism of Karttunen affects all generative approaches which treat quantifier structures like 'the X' as unanalysed wholes. Hence it seems to us that a satisfactory treatment of (1) in the traditional framework would require considerable modifications of the framework.

There is one more sentence which has been discussed in connection of the Bach–Peters paradox.

(38)   The girl who loved him was kissed by the boy who was fooling her.

In our semantical approach this sentence is straightforward to handle. It turns out to be exactly like (1) as far as the uniqueness clauses of the semantical representation are concerned. The only difference in the semantical representation of (38) as compared to that of (1) is that instead of 'x kissed z' we have 'z was kissed by x'. This is of course just as it should be intuitively.

There is a constructive approach to the generation of (1) which is naturally suggested by our game-theoretical approach. Why cannot we simply turn our game-rules or, rather, their syntactical components, around and use the result as a set of rules for generating complex sentences from simpler ones? Of course, in principle we can try to do so. But what happens then? In this approach to the syntax of the Bach–Peters paradox we obtain for instance (4) from something like the following.

(39) x kissed a girl who loved x
        x is a boy
        x was fooling her.

(It is of course more natural to use here variables rather than particular proper names.) Moreover, the first conjunct of (39) would likewise be obtained from

(40) x kissed y
        y is a girl
        y loved x

Without entering the details of the syntactical theory that would have to be presuppoed here, we can note that this appoach would yield precisely the right treatment of the definite article version of the (syntactical) Bach–Peters paradox. For on certain natural assumptions (1) would have to be generated in this approach from a set of simpler sentences different from that underlying (2), (3), or (30). The formation rule that we would need here will be something like the following

(F. singular the) From the strings

        $X - a - W$
        a is a(n)Y
        a Z
        b is not a(n)Y who Z

    derive

        $X -$ the Y who $Z - W$.

The principal assumption which we have to make here corresponds to the semantical ordering principle (O. comm) of Hintikka (1975). This is the following:

> When
> applying (F. singular the) to $X - a - W$, we must apply it to
> the least embedded occurrence of 'a' in $X - W$.

It is now easy to see that (1) arises of

(41) x kissed y
  x is a boy
  x was fooling y
  z is not a boy who was fooling y
  y is a girl
  y loved x
  u is not a girl who loved x.

On the other hand (2) is derived from a different set of sentences, viz. from

(42) x kissed y
  y is a girl
  y loved x
  u is not a girl who loved x
  x is a boy
  x was fooling y
  z was not fooling w
  w is a girl
  w loved z
  t is not a girl who loved z.

Likewise, (3) and (30) can only be derived from still other sets of simpler sentences. Even though our inverted game-theoretical approach to syntax fails to preserve meaning in the course of generation, it discriminates between (1), (2), (3), and (30) in a way the transformational generation proposed by Karttunen does not. Note that in our approach we *per definitionem* do not leave the problematic quantifier phrases unanalysed in the simpler elements we start the generation from. Hence we of course avoid the kind of criticism we levelled above at Karttunen's approach.

Even if we shall not here examine the new type of syntax further, it thus exhibits unmistakable promise. It has certain similarity in its general spirit with Jackendoff's proposals concerning the Bach–Peters paradox, even though its details will obviously be rather different from Jackendoff's treatment.

APPENDIX

We noted above that because of the uniqueness clauses in (1) the dependence of the existential quantifier on the universal one does not matter. This is of course an unusual situation in quantification theory. It is not difficult to see that our observation can be generalized even further, however. In fact the existential quantifier which there tacitly is in a the-phrase is independent of the universal quantifiers which there may likewise be tucked into other the-phrases. For instance, in the following sentence it does not matter whether or not each of the existential quantifiers depends on the universal quantifiers in the other the-phrase:

(43)   The mother of each villager envies the father of each townsman.

Hence any of the following formulas (44)–(46) can serve equally well as the semantical representation underlying (43), because they all are logically equivalent:

(44) $(x)(\exists y)(z)(v)(\exists u)(w)(x$ is a villager $\land$ y is mother of x
         $\land$ $(z \neq y \supset \sim(z$ is mother of $x)) \land z$ is townsman
         $\land$ u is father of $z \land (w \neq u \supset \sim(w$ is father of $z))$
         $\land$ y envies $u)$
         $= (x)(\exists y)(z)(v)(\exists u)(w)M(x, y, z, v, u, w)$

(45) $(v)(\exists u)(w)(x)(\exists y)(z)M(x, y, z, v, u, w)$

(46) $\begin{matrix} (x)(\exists y)(z) \\ \\ (v)(\exists u)(w) \end{matrix} \Big\rangle M(x,y,z,v,u,w).$

This observation might be worth giving a proof of. We shall show it by proving a more general theorem. We shall show that the following formulas (47)–(49) are logically equivalent if in M there are uniqueness clauses for x and y with respect to Q_1 and Q_2, respectively, where Q_1 and Q_2 are any finite sequences of universal quantifiers.

(47) $\begin{matrix} Q_1(\exists x)(t) \\ \\ Q_2(\exists y)(v) \end{matrix} \Big\rangle M(x_0, \ldots, x_n, y_0, \ldots, y_k, x, t, y, v)$

(48) $Q_1(\exists x)(t)Q_2(\exists y)(v)M$

(49) $Q_2(\exists y)(v)Q_1(\exists x)(t)M.$

(Here Q_1 and Q_2 bind the variables $x_0, \ldots, x_n$ and $y_0, \ldots, y_k$ respectively.)

It is clear that (47) implies both (48) and (49). For a proof in the other direction we first establish that (48) implies (47). We may do this by translating both the formulas to second order predicate logic (see Hintikka, 1974). In this translation we obtain from (47)

(50) $(\exists f)(\exists g)(x_0), \ldots, (x_n)(y_0), \ldots, (y_k)(t)(v)M(x_0, \ldots, x_n,$
       $y_0, \ldots, y_k, f(x_0, \ldots, x_n), t, g(y_0, \ldots, y_k), v).$

Likewise (48) yields

(51) $(\exists f)(\exists g)(x_0), \ldots, (x_n)(y_0), \ldots, (y_k)(t)(v)M(x_0, \ldots, x_n,$
       $y_0, \ldots, y_k, f(x_0, \ldots, x_n), t, g(x_0, \ldots, x_n, t, y_0, \ldots, y_k), v).$

It is now easy to see from (50) and (51) what the essential difference is between partially ordered quantifiers like (47) and linearly ordered quantifiers like (48). The Skolem functions that give us the values of the existential quantifiers depend only on variables bound by universal quantifiers occurring earlier in the same branch of the quantifier prefix. Now in the linear case there is only one such branch, hence in this case the Skolem functions depend not only on variables bound to Q_2 but also those variables bound to Q_1 and to (t). This is not so in the partially ordered prefix where the Skolem functions are functions of variables bound to Q_2 only.

To prove that (51) logically implies (50) (on the assumptions we made about the structure of M) we have to show that the Skolem function g in (51) does not after all depend on the values of $x_0, \ldots x_n$ and t, i.e.,

(52) $g(x_0, \ldots, x_n, t, y_0, \ldots, y_k) = g(y_0, \ldots, y_k),$

for any values of the variables. Assuming the antithesis we obtain that for some $x_0', \ldots, x_n', t'$ and $x_n'', \ldots, x_n'', t'', y_0, \ldots, y_k$ such that $(x_0', \ldots, x_n', t') \neq (x_0'', \ldots, x'', t'')$

(53) $g(x_0', \ldots, x_n', t', y_0, \ldots, y_k) \neq g(x_0', \ldots, x_n'', t'', y_0, \ldots, y_k).$

Due to the assumed structure of (51) we know that for any values of $y_0, \ldots, y_k$ there is an u such that

(54) $P(u, y_0, \ldots, y_k) \;\&\; (w)(w \neq u \supset \sim P(w, y_0, \ldots, y_k)).$

(P is here the relation which says that u is unique with respect to the other individuals mentioned.) Now by (51) such an u is given by the function g. In particular, we can take $u = g(x'_0, \ldots, x', t', y_0, \ldots, y_k)$. Hence (54) yields

(55) $(w)(w \neq g(x'_0, \ldots, x'_n, t', y_0, \ldots, y_k) \supset \sim P(w, y_0, \ldots, y_k))$.

But by assumption

$$g(x'_0, \ldots, x'_n, t', y_0, \ldots, y_k) \neq g(x''_0, \ldots, x''_n, t'', y_0, \ldots, y_k)$$

which yields

(56) $\sim P(g(x''_0, \ldots, x''_n, t'', y_0, \ldots, y_k), y_0, \ldots, y_k)$.

But this is a contradiction, because by assumption there is for any $y_0, \ldots, y_k$ an u such that (54) and because such an u is according to (51) obtained as the value of the function g for any $x_0, \ldots, x_n$ and t.

It is straightforward to apply a similar argument to show that (49) implies (47). Hence our claim is established.

It is unusual for an existential quantifier of natural language that its dependence on an earlier universal quantifier does not matter. One might argue that it is a characteristic feature of the quantifier 'the'. In Hintikka (1974) it is pointed out that it *does* make a difference if the following sentence (57) is formalized using linear as compared to partially ordered quantifiers:

(57)   Some book by every author is referred to in some essay by every critic.

As pointed out by Hintikka, such a sentence simply cannot be expressed without loss of meaning in first order logic (with linearly ordered quantifiers). But we argued that an apparently analogous sentence like (58) *can* be expressed in first order logic, because the dependence of the latter existential quantifier on the universal ones does not matter anyhow:

(58)   The first book by every author is referred to in the longest essay of every critic.

Note, however, that in some cases there are universal quantifiers that both of the the-phrases depend on. In such cases the dependence of course counts as far this quantifier is concerned, though the dependence on other universal quantifiers there possibly are in the other the-phrase does not matter. A case in point is the following:

(59)   The first book by every author is referred to in the obituary essay on him by every critic.

As the semantical representation for this sentence any of the following formulas can serve equally well, because they all are logically equivalent with each other.

(60) $(x)(\exists y)(z)(u)(\exists v)(w)$ (x is author $\wedge$ y is first book of x
$\wedge (z \neq y \supset \sim(z$ is first book of $x))$
$\wedge u$ is critic $\wedge$ v is obituary essay by u on x
$\wedge (w \neq v \supset \sim(w$ is obituary essay by u on $x)))$
$= (x)(\exists y)(z)(u)(\exists v)(w)M(x, y, z, u, v, w)$

(61)
$$(x) \underset{\textstyle (u)(\exists v)(w)}{\overset{\textstyle (\exists y)(z)}{<\qquad>}} M(x, y, z, u, v, w)$$

(62) $(x)(u)(\exists v)(w)(\exists y)(z)M(x, y, z, u, v, w).$

But note that it is essential that both the existential quantifiers depend on the value of the variable x.

Academy of Finland and Stanford University (J.H.)
Academy of Finland (E.S.)

NOTE

* Most of this paper represents independent work by the junior author, based on the suggestions of the senior author.

REFERENCES

Dik, Simon (1973) 'Crossing Coreference Again', *Foundations of Language* **9**, 306–326.
Harman, Gilbert (1972) 'Deep Structure as Logical Form', in D. Davidson and G. Harman (eds.) *Semantics of Natural Language*, D. Reidel Publishing Company, Dordrecht-Holland, 25–47.
Hintikka, Jaakko (1974) 'Quantifiers vs. Quantification Theory', *Linguistic Inquiry* **5**, 153–177, reprinted in the present volume, pp. 49–79.
Hintikka, Jaakko (1976) 'Quantifiers in Logic and Quantifiers in Natural Languages', in S. Körner (ed.) *Philosophy of Logic*, Basil Blackwell, Oxford. Reprinted in the present volume, pp. 27–47.
Hintikka, Jaakko (1977) 'Quantifiers in Natural Languages: Some Logical Problems', *Linguistics and Philosophy* **1**, 153–172, reprinted (with additions) in the present volume, pp. 81–117.

Karttunen, Lauri (1971) 'Definite Descriptions With Crossing Coreference; A Study of the Bach-Peters Paradox', *Foundations of Language* **7**, 157–182.

Kuroda, S.-Y. (1971) 'Two Remarks on Pronominalization', *Foundations of Language* **7**, 183–198.

Wasow, Thomas (1973) 'More Migs and Pilots', *Foundations of Language* **9**, 297–305.

JAAKKO HINTIKKA AND LAURI CARLSON

CONDITIONALS, GENERIC QUANTIFIERS, AND OTHER APPLICATIONS OF SUBGAMES

In examining the interrelations of use and meaning, one of the most promising testing grounds is constituted by the theory of conditional sentences in natural languages. On this ground the differences between different approaches to meaning and those between the several uses of "use" have clashed dramatically, and yet left many of the principal problems unresolved. The truth-functional analysis of "if–then" sentences is as interesting an example of an approach to meaning by means of recursive truth-characterizations as one can hope to find. Yet it has run into a sharp criticism from those philosophers of language whose paradigm of meaning-giving use is usage, i.e., intralinguistic use. These philosophers are sometimes misleadingly called ordinary-language philosophers. However, they have likewise failed to solve many of the most interesting questions concerning the actual behavior of conditionals in natural languages. The initial problems we shall be dealing with in this work are cases in point. Hence the field is wide open for new approaches.

In order to avoid misunderstandings, it is important to realize that there are reasons of two different kinds why the truth-functional treatment of natural-language conditionals is inadequate. Here we shall confine our attention to those problems that are caused by the conditional character of if–then sentences. This is not what has primarily occupied most philosophers of language, however, when they have been considering conditionals. What has caught their fancy is usually the stronger logical tie that binds the antecedent and the consequent of a natural-language conditional as compared with purely truth-functional conditionals. This extra force is seen in problems about counterfactuals, paradoxes of "material" implication, and so on.

This extra force of natural-language conditionals is a much less subtle problem than the conditional character of if–then sentences in, say, English. A suitable modal analysis of conditionals goes a long way toward solving the problems of extra force. Furthermore, these problems are also amenable to a treatment in terms of conversational forces. However, they will not be treated

179

in the present essay, which focuses exclusively on the conditional nature of conditionals. The phenomena caused by this nature are quite different from the problems of extra (non-truth-functional) force of natural-language conditionals. They are considerably subtler than these, and cannot be treated in the same way.

How can they be treated, then? One promising approach — not necessarily a completely new one, though — can be reached by taking the use that figures in the famous identification of meaning and use to be, not usage or intra-linguistic use (use in language) but use in the sense of those rule-governed activities ("language-games") which link a language, or a part of it, to the world it enables us to describe or to interact with. Some such language-games happily turn out to be games also in the strict sense of the mathematical theory of games. Some of these have been studied by the authors of this essay and by their associates in what they have called "game-theoretical semantics." In this work, game-theoretical semantics is brought to bear on a number of apparently unrelated semantical (linguistic, logical) phenomena. They include certain "generic" (i.e., universal-quantifier) uses of words like "a(n)" and "some," certain difficult types of pronominalization, and the semantics of conditionals. They all turn out to be closely related to each other and to admit of very natural explanations which all involve the same basic idea. The most prominent one of these problems is precisely the semantics of conditionals just mentioned.

For the fundamentals of game-theoretical semantics, the reader is referred to Hintikka (1974), (1975) and (1976). The main idea underlying our se-mantical games may be said to be to consider each such game as an attempted verification of a sentence S against the schemes of a malevolent Nature who is trying to defeat me. These games are thus games against Nature. Their two players will be called "myself" and "Nature." The former wins if the game ends with a true atomic sentence; the latter wins if it ends with a false one. The rules of these games can be gathered without much difficulty from what has been said. For instance, to verify a sentence of the form

$$X \ - \ \text{some Y who Z} \ - \ W$$

(where the "who" in "who Z" is for simplicity assumed to occupy the subject position and to be singular) I clearly will have to choose a person, say b, such that in the rest of the game I can verify

$$X \ - \ b \ - \ W, \ b \text{ is a(n) Y, and } b \text{ Z.}$$

The game rule for "some" whose special case this recipe is will be called (G. some).

In order to verify the sentence

$$X — \text{every } Y \text{ who } Z — W$$

(with the same proviso concerning "who Z") I will have to verify

$$X — d — W \text{ if } d \text{ is a(n) } Y \text{ and } d \, Z$$

for any individual d Nature might choose. This can be generalized into a game rule (G. every) for the English quantifier word "every."

To verify "S_1 or S_2" I will have to verify S_1 or verify S_2, i.e., choose one of them for the rest of the game to deal with, and to verify "S_1 and S_2" I will have to verify which ever conjunct Nature chooses. (Special attention will have to be paid here to anaphoric relations between S_1 and S_2.)

These examples will suffice to illustrate how our games are played. The rule for truth and falsity embodies an improved version of the old idea that a sentece S is true if it can, in principle, be verified. This is now taken to mean that S is true iff I have a winning strategy in the correlated game $G(S)$, false iff Nature has a winning strategy in $G(S)$. If $G(S)$ is indeterminate (if neither player has a winning strategy), S is neither true nor false.

As a starting-point, let us recall the obvious simple-minded game-theoretic treatment of if-conditionals. In earlier game-theoretical treatments, they were handled by means of the following rule:

(G. if)   When the game has reached a sentence of one of the forms

      If X, Y

      or

      Y if X

then I may choose either neg+[X] or Y, and the game is continued with respect to it.

Here 'neg+' refers to the process of forming the (semantical) negation (contradictory) of a given sentence. Its analysis presents a separate problem. This problem is not the reason why (G. if) is not wholly satisfactory. The rules for negation will have to be discussed in game-theoretic semantics anyway (cf. Hintikka, forthcoming). Indeed, the rule (G. if) is in many respects a good first approximation. For instance, it enables us to discuss the important principles that govern the order in which the game rules are applied (cf. Hintikka, 1975).

The problem with (G. if) is connected with its purely truth-functional character. As was already indicated, ordinary-language philosophers have time and again claimed that a conditional like

(1)   If X, Y

is not equivalent with the disjunction

(2)   neg+[X] or Y.

In asserting the conditional (1) one does not assert the disjunction (2). One somewhat makes, rather, a purely conditional assertion whose force does not come to the play at all until its antecedent clause X is verified or otherwise asserted. However, these ordinary-language philosophers also have totally failed to spell out the precise logical and semantical difference between (1) and (2).

If anything, the game-theoretic approach encourages an emphasis on the differences between (1) and (2). One reason for what happens in the case is that a semantical game G(X) connected with X turns out to be indeterminate. (It is trivially true that both players cannot have a winning strategy in one of our semantical games. However, there is no general guarantee that either of them must have one.) If the game is indeterminate, the associated logic is a non-classical three-valued one. It is well known that in such a three-valued logic it is unnatural to define (1) as (2). Hence the possibility of indeterminacy makes the putative game rule (G. if) unnatural, for it has precisely the force of assimilating (1) to (2).

The purely truth-functional character of (G. if) is also seen from the fact that this rule is virtually identical with the game rule (G.⊃) for material implication in the semantical games connected with formal first-order languages. In fact, in the sequel we shall treat (G. if) and (G.⊃) as being essentially identical. The inadequacies of (G. if) as an explication of the semantics of natural-language conditionals are to some extent paralleled by the criticism presented by certain philosophers of mathematics and of logic who prefer non-classical logic to the classical one.

It is also clear that rules like (G. if) do not do justice to the way in which speakers process a conditional sentence like (1) semantically. In some sense, we process (1) by first processing X and only then — depending on the outcome of the first stage — processing Y. In so far as our rules of semantical games are supposed to approximate the way in which we actually deal with ordinary-language sentences semantically — in so far as they capture the *dynamics* of natural-language semantics, we might say — in so far they fail to deal with (1) in a realistic fashion.

How can our game rule for "if" be improved on? In order to answer this question, let us go back to the idea of (1) as a genuine conditional which only becomes operative if and when its antecedent X is found to be true. Then, and only then, must I be able to show that Y is true, too.

Now the different attempted ways of verifying X can be understood as the different strategies available to me in the associated game G(X), and the attempted ways of verifying Y are my strategies in G(Y). For, as it was already indicated above, the basic crude but useful intuitive interpretation of our semantical games G(Z) is that they are my attempts to verify Z against the schemes of a malicious Nature. What I undertake to do in defending (1) is therefore naturally understood to be to correlate to each winning strategy of mine in G (X) a winning strategy Φ of mine in G(Y). The force of (1) itself is to assert the existence of a functional Φ which carries out this correlation. This simple idea captures very well the notion of conditionaliza-tion, and we shall argue that it leads us to an eminently natural game rule for if-sentences.

First, however, we have to develop it a little further. One trouble is that the concept of a *winning* strategy is not an absolute one, but relative to an opponent's strategy set. This makes it awkward to speak of a mapping of my *winning* strategies in G(X) on my *winning* strategies in G(Y). The natural thing is to consider mappings of *all* my strategies in G(X) into *all* my strategies in G(Y).

The natural way to realize this idea through actual game rules is to have the two players carry out a play of the game G(X) first, fought to the bitter end. For it is part and parcel of the basic ideas of game theory that to play a game is to choose a strategy. To play a game to the end is thus naturally interpreted as divulging one's strategy in it. Since these strategies are (or are represented by) functions, the strategies of the two players at the later stages of the game will have functions as their arguments and hence be higher-order functions (functionals). For their moves at these later stages will depend on their already divulged strategies in a completed subgame. Thus it is the idea of a concluded *subgame* that leads us to consider strategies representable by *functionals* rather than (first-order) *functions*.

In order to force myself to consider all of my strategies in G(X), as re-quired for the purpose of speaking of a function on the set of all such strategies, the two players must exchange roles in G(X): Nature chooses one of the strategies that would ordinarily be mine, and *vice versa*. If I win in G(X), I have in effect falsified X, and no need to consider Y arises. Hence we might declare myself a winner in this case.

However, if Nature wins, she has verified X and hence forced myself to consider Y. In this case, the players must move on to carry out a play of G(Y). The fact that the game is continued only if one of "my" strategies, as chosen by Nature, wins in G(X) is the precise technical counterpart of the earlier crude and inaccurate idea that in a conditional "If X, Y" we are dealing with a mapping of my *winning* strategies in G(X) into my *winning* strategies in G(Y).

My strategy in G(Y) will now depend on the way in which X was verified, i.e., on Nature's choice of "my" strategy in G(X). Nature, in contrast, clearly does not enjoy any comparable privilege. The outcome of this play will decide the outcome of the overall game G(If X, Y).

Thus the game rule for G(If X, Y) can be represented by means of the following "flow chart."

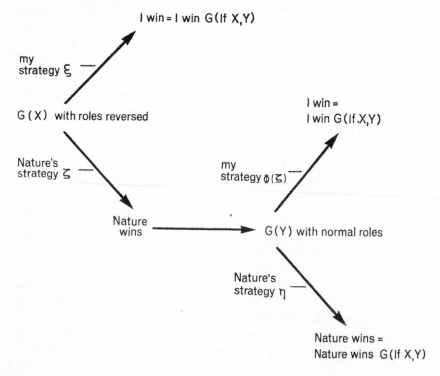

Hence "If X, Y" is true iff there is a functional Φ and a function ξ such that they win against any strategy of Nature's represented by the functions ζ and η.

We shall call a game rule defined by the flow chart (G. cond$_1$). If this game rule strikes the reader as being rather complicated, we would like to counter by asking whether he really feels entitled to expect a simple rule in view of all the complicated problems ("ifficulties") about natural-language conditionals. Moreover, we doubt that (G.cond$_1$) is felt to be very complicated when its precise import is appreciated.

But why are not both players asked to divulge their strategies in G(X)? In other words, why does not Nature's strategy η in G(Y) depend on my strategy ξ in G(X)? Why is ξ as it were forgotten in G(Y)? The answer is implicit in the intuitive motivation given above for the game rule (G.cond$_1$). It was intimated there that Y comes into play only when and after X has been verified, and its role will hence naturally depend on the way in which X turned out to be true. Now this way of turning out to be true is what ζ codifies. In contrast, ξ represents merely a hypothetical attempt to falsify X. Intuitively, we must therefore require that G(Y) should be played so as to disregard ξ. It may be recalled here that initially we tried to establish only a mapping of *my* winning strategies in G(X) into my winning strategies in G(Y).

Thus the point of the game rule (G.cond$_1$) is not really to add much to the intuitive ideas it is based on. Rather, what (G.cond$_1$) does is to show how the precise dependencies such as the roles of η and ξ in G(Y) serve as objective counterparts to our intuitive ideas of conditionality. An even more explicit way of spelling out the same basic idea would be to say that G(Y) is played with full knowledge of ζ but in ignorance of ξ.

The formulation of (G.cond$_1$) in terms of subgames implies that in an important respect the new rule does not change the character of our semantical games. Before replacing (G.$\supset$) by (G.cond$_1$), our game-theoretical semantics could have been said to effect a translation of each first-order sentence into a second-order sentence of the form

$$(3) \qquad (\exists f_1)\ (\exists f_2) \ldots\ (\exists f_m)\ (x_1)\ (x_2) \ldots\ (x_n)F(f_1, f_2, \ldots, f_m, x_1, x_2, \ldots, x_n)$$

where $f_1, f_2, \ldots, f_m$ are such Skolem functions as serve to define my strategies in so far as quantifier rules are concerned, and $(x_1), \ldots, (x_n)$ are all the universal quantifiers of the original sentence (assuming that all negation-signs were first driven in so as to precede immediately atomic formulas). Furthermore, in (3) F is the original sentence with quantifiers omitted and with each existentially quantified variable y replaced by a different term of the form $f(x_i, x_j, \ldots, x_k)$ where (x_i), (x_j), $\ldots$, (x_k) are all the universal quantifiers within the scope of which $(\exists y)$ occurs in the original sentence. The universal quantifiers (x_1), (x_2), $\ldots$, (x_n) in effect embody Nature's strategies as far as her quantificational moves are concerned. The import of (3) thus comes very close to saying just that I have a winning strategy in the game correlated with the original sentence.

The replacement of $(G.\supset)$ by $(G.\text{cond}_1)$ has the effect of replacing some of the function and individual variables $f_1, f_2, \ldots, x_1, x_2, \ldots$ by variables for functionals, i.e., higher-type functions (or for functions in the case of universal quantifiers), plus adding to their number. Since nested occurrences of "$\supset$" serve to push the types of these functionals higher and higher, we must in principle be prepared to use functionals of any finite type.

We can in fact obtain a kind of formalized expression of $(G.\text{cond}_1)$ by hanging on each subordinate clause X and Y two argument places, indicating respectively my strategy and Nature's in the correlated games. Then the game rule $(G.\text{cond}_1)$ corresponds to a translation rule which takes us from "If X, Y" to

$$(4) \qquad (\exists \Phi) \, (\exists \xi) \, (\zeta) \, (\eta) \, (X(\zeta, \, \xi) \supset Y(\Phi(\zeta), \eta) \,)$$

Our new game rule $(G.\text{cond}_1)$ calls for a few comments. First, the idea it incorporates is obviously related very closely to the ideas of the intuitionists. According to them, a conditional asserts that there is a way of obtaining a "proof" (verification) of the consequent from any given "proof" (verification) of the antecedent. This is very closely related to what (4) says. For basically what it asserts is just the existence of a functional Φ which takes us from a successful strategy in verifying X to a successful strategy in verifying Y.

Secondly, it is worth noting how the subgame idea which led us to $(G.\text{cond}_1)$ helps us to capture some of the dynamics of one's natural semantical processing of a conditional sentence which was mentioned above. Intuitively speaking, we first process the antecedent. This corresponds to the complete playing off of the game G(X) correlated with the antecedent. (This is what brings in subgames or, as we really ought to call them, *completed* or *closed* subgames.) Only after we have made clear to ourselves what the world would be like if the antecedent is true do we move on to consider what the consequent says on this assumption. This second stage corresponds to playing the game $G(Y)$, and its conditionality is reflected by the dependence of my strategy $\Phi(\zeta)$ in $G(Y)$ on Nature's strategy ζ in $G(X)$, played with reversed roles.

This insight into the dynamics of first-order semantics will be put to use later by considering the behavior of pronominalization in a context involving subgames. Conversely, what we shall find about those types of pronominalization will support the diagnosis we have built into the rule $(G.cond_1)$.

At this point, a skeptical reader may very well wonder how much real difference the replacement of $(G.if)$ (or $(G.\supset)$) by $(G.cond_1)$ really makes. There are in fact some *prima facie* reasons for skepticism here. It can easily be seen that on purely classical assumptions, including prominently the stipulation that all function variables (of any type) range over *all* functions of the appropriate type, the interchange of $(G.\supset)$ and $(G.cond_1)$ does not in fact make any difference to the truth of the sentences of formal first-order languages. For purely classically (i.e., if myself is declared the winner if I win in $G(X)$ with roles reversed) $X \supset Y$ is true iff $\sim X$ or Y is true, i.e., iff I have a winning strategy either in $G(Y)$ (call it ξ_o) or else in $G(\sim X)$ (call it ζ_o). Then I can respectively put either $\xi = \xi_o$ or (identically) $\Phi(\zeta) = \zeta_o$ in (4). Conversely, suppose that there are ξ and Φ in (4) such as to guarantee my win. Then either I have a winning strategy in $G(\sim X)$ or else for each winning strategy ζ in $G(X)$ there is λ such that I win in $G(Y)$ by playing λ against any strategy η of Nature's. But I can have as much as one such strategy classically only if Y is true.

However, even though formally and classically speaking there is little to choose between $(G.if)$ (or $(G.\supset)$) and $(G.cond_1)$, there are further possibilities that might seem to serve to drive a wedge between the two. In fact there are two entirely different openings for a distinction here.

(a)   The game-theoretical viewpoint strongly suggests that we restrict the strategy sets of the two players to *computable* functions and functionals. More accurately, we can restrict the strategies represented in (4) by functions and functionals to computable ones.

This modification immediately changes the whole situation. It does so already in the otherwise classical first-order case. The set of true sentences will be affected by the change.

More generally, we might be inclined to admit suitable nonstandard models in the sense of Henkin (1950) (see also the correction by Peter Andrews), that is to say, allow function quantifiers to range over suitable subsets of all arbitrary functions of the appropriate type. The most liberal policy here is to require merely that these subsets be closed with respect to Boolean operations and projective operations.

It turns out, however, as Laurence Nemirow first pointed out to us, that after a restriction to computable functions and functionals has been carried out, the distinction between $(G. \supset)$ and $(G.cond_1)$ does not make any difference. By modifying slightly the argument for the classical case, on this restriction $(G. \supset)$ and $(G.cond_1)$ can be shown to be equivalent. This equivalence may perhaps be considered a partial reason for the relative success of a purely truth-functional analysis of conditionals — and for the absence of any viable alternative in the earlier literature.

It also shows that the main reasons for the greater naturalness of $(G.cond_1)$ as compared with $(G. \supset)$ have to be sought for elsewhere.

There is a major change, however, that can result from restrictions imposed on strategy sets. Such a restriction may imply that neither player has a winning strategy in some of the semantical games. Then there will be a difference between asserting that a sentence is true, i.e., that I have a winning strategy in the correlated game, and asserting that it is not false, i.e., that Nature does not have a winning strategy in it. This in turn generates a certain ambiguity, as the sentence can be thought of as asserting either.

If a conditional like "If X, Y" is given the latter of these two interpretations, its force will be that of

$$(\zeta)(\eta)(\exists \Phi)(\exists \xi)(X(\zeta, \xi) \supset Y(\Phi(\zeta), \eta))$$

which is the same as that of

$$(\zeta)(\eta)(\exists \varphi)(\exists \xi)(X(\zeta, \xi) \supset Y(\varphi, \eta)).$$

This is related very closely to the so-called no-counter-example interpretation. (For it, see Mostowski, 1966, Ch. 5; Per Martin-Löf, 1970, p. 12.)

(b) In natural language, there are certain phenomena which become explainable as soon as the rule $(G.cond_1)$ (or some other rule which likewise involves subgames) is adopted. In order to see what they are, let us consider an example. What kind of anaphoric relation do we have in the following simple conditional?

(5)   If Bill owns a donkey, he beats it.

Here "it" cannot refer to any particular donkey referred to earlier, for taken as a whole (5) does not speak any more of one of Bill's donkeys than of another one of them. Hence we do not have here an instance of the usual function of pronouns (pronominal anaphora), viz. to recover an earlier reference to a particular individual. Nor does the "it" in (5) serve as a so-called "pronoun of laziness," that is, merely as a placeholder for its grammatical antecedent "a donkey," for (5) is not synonymous with

(6)   If Bill owns a donkey, he beats a donkey.

Sometimes it is said, in view of these facts and of the intended meaning of (4), that in (5) "a" has a "generic" function, i.e., serves as a universal quantifier rather than as an existential one. (We shall not try to criticize here this use of the term "generic," even though it is in certain respects a misleading one.) Why "a" should be generic in sentences like (5) has not been explained, however, even though such an explanation is made highly desirable by the fact that in many contexts the indefinite article "a(n)" must be construed as a genuinely existential quantifier.

Moreover, the explanatory force of a mere postulation of a new sense of "a(n)" with a "generic" force is greatly reduced by the fact that the truly universal quantifier "every" is not admissible in the same context, for we cannot say

(7)   *If Bill owns every donkey, he beats it.

The inadmissibility of (7) may have a partial explanation in terms of the relative order of the game rules for "every" and "if." However, that this explanation is not completely satisfactory is seen by turning (5) around. For we can say

(8)   Bill beats every donkey if he owns it.

Moreover,

(9)   Bill beats a donkey if he owns it,

is perhaps a little less natural than (5). Moreover, in so far as (9) is acceptable, it seems ambiguous between an existential-quantifier and a universal-quantifier reading, again unlike (5). In fact, a slight change in the example makes the existential-quantifier reading almost mandatory as, e.g., in

Bill will beat a donkey if he finds it.

Hence we have in our hands a problem both about the behavior of "a" in (5) and (9) and about the behavior of "every" in (7) and (8), over and above the question of the nature and conditions of pronominalization in all these different sentences.

The more general problem we are facing here concerns the conditions on which a quantifier phrase can be the antecedent of a singular pronoun. What we have just seen suggests that a satisfactory answer cannot be given, e.g., in terms of definiteness, for presumably "every" is more definite than "a," and is equally definite in (7) and (8). (Here we have one more indication of the unsystematic and frequently misleading character of linguists' concept of definiteness.)

It is not surprising that more complicated versions of these examples, such as

(10)   If Bill owns a donkey that he likes, he beats it,

have caused not inconsiderable difficulties in Montague-type grammars.

Further examples similar to (5), (7)–(9) are easily found. Here is one bunch:

(11)   If a member contributes, he will be praised.
(12)   *If every member contributes, he will be praised.
(13)   A member will be praised if he contributes.
(14)   Every member will be praised if he contributes.

Notice also that the conversion which takes us from (5) to (9) and from (7) to (8) might very well be expected to preserve not only meaning but acceptability. After all, all that happens in this conversion is the replacement of a sentence of the form "If X, Y" by "Y if X," together with a reversal of the relations of pronominalization between X and Y. It is hard to think of an operation which *prima facie* would seem likelier to preserve meaning and acceptability (including degree of acceptability). Yet we have seen that the latter sometimes changes in the operation, and later we shall find an example in which the preferred reading of the sentence in question is also affected. All this requires an explanation.

In order to begin to solve these problems, let us consider first (5). How do we get hold of the individual donkey that is supposed to be picked out in some sense by "it"? This question is well-nigh impossible to answer as long as we think of conditionals along the lines of semantically indivisible wholes as in (G.if). However, the basic idea underlying (G.cond$_1$) at once throws new light on the situation. This basic idea is that in the game connected with the conditional (1) I have to correlate with each of my strategies in G(X), say ζ, a similar strategy of mine in G(Y). This correlation is needed in the game iff ζ wins in the subgame G(X) (cf. our flowchart for G(If X, Y)). What does such a strategy look like in (5)? Here X = "Bill owns a donkey." Understanding "a" in the most straightforward way as an *existential* quantifier, my winning strategies in

(15)   G(Bill owns a donkey)

are simply the different choices of a donkey owned by Bill. Thus in the antecedent of the conditional (5) we are as it were considering Bill's donkeys one by one. And this is obviously just what semantically speaking gives us the foothold for pronominalization in (5). After we have chosen to consider some one winning strategy of mine in (15), i.e., to consider a donkey owned by Bill, we can in the consequent (5) refer pronominally to that very donkey and say something about *it*. And *this is just what happens in* (5). It is precisely the consideration of my several strategies in (15) that leads us to consider a particular beast which in the consequent of (5) can be recovered by a pronominal reference.

Thus we see how it is that the subgame idea serves to explain why certain quantifier phrases can serve as pronominal antecedents. They represent choices made in an earlier, already concluded subgame.

Several further observations can be made here which support our diagnosis. First, let us note that what we just saw is in effect *an explanation why the indefinite article "a(n)" comes to have a "generic" (universal-quantifier) sense in conditionals like* (5). This explanation has the merit of turning on the assumption that the basic force of "a" in (5) is that of an *existential* quantifier (in the precise game-theoretical sense marking *my* move in our semantical games). It thus dispenses with all assumptions of irreducibly different senses or uses of the indefinite article in English.

We must hasten to add that there are other generic uses of the indefinite article "a" which are also explainable in this way — but not without a great deal of further argument. A case in point is, e.g.,

(16)   A cat loves comfort.

However, there is further evidence to support our diagnosis of cases like (5). The only thing we assumed of "a" in (15) was that it expresses existential quantification (i.e., marks my move). But so does "some." Hence, by the same token, there ought to be a kind of generic sense to the sentence with "some" instead of "a" otherwise analogous with (5), i.e., to

(17)   If Bill owns some donkey, he beats it.

The acceptability of this sentence is not obvious, but in so far as it is acceptable, "some" in it clearly has a "generic" (*prima facie* universal) force, just like (5). The acceptability of (17) may in fact be improved greatly by changing it into

(18)   If Bill owns some donkey or other, he beats it.

Here we have an interesting indication of the strength of our explanation why "a" has a generic force in (5). If it is replaced there by "some," which normally does not exhibit any predilection for a generic sense, it is likewise forced to the role of a generic quantifier, albeit a little awkwardly.

The same point is strikingly confirmed by the fact that even the blatantly *existential* "there is" assumes the force of a *universal* quantifier in the antecedents of conditionals. In order to see this, witness examples like the following.

If there is a donkey that Bill owns, he beats it.

(Whether this is completely grammatical does not affect our present point, which pertains to the existential–universal contrast.)

Although we have not yet uncovered the mechanics of the conversion from (5) to (9) or from (7) to (8), it is of interest to see that "some" follows here roughly the same pattern as "a(n)." Applied to (17) the conversion yields

(19)   Bill beats some donkey if he owns it.

It is not clear whether this is acceptable, but in so far as it is, its preferred reading is clearly different from that of (17). In so far as (19) is acceptable, it seems to allege Bill's animus against some particular beast. Hence in (19) "some" seems to have the force of an initial existential quantifier, not that of a universal quantifier. This point is even clearer if we change the example to read

Bill will beat some donkey if he finds it.

The explanation we gave above for the possibility of pronominalization in (5) serves to explain also why (7) is not acceptable. The idea was that (G.cond$_1$) invited the players to consider my different strategies in G(X). In so far as certain individuals are produced in a play of the game by such a strategy, they can be referred to again pronominally. Now the individuals so produced (selected for special attention) are the ones that an *existential* quantifier prompts me to select. In contrast, my strategy does not specify which individuals Nature perhaps chooses as the values of a universally quantified variable. Hence our theory yields the prediction that only an existential-quantifier phrase can serve as an antecedent of a singular pronoun in the kind of pronominalization (i.e., from the antecedent of a conditional to its consequent) we have in (5).

This prediction is confirmed on its negative side by the unacceptability of (7). The acceptability of the analogous sentence

(20)   If Bill owns any donkey, he beats it

causes no problems here in view of the well-established ordering principle (O.any) which among other things gives the game rule (G.any) a priority over the rule for "if" (see Hintikka, 1975).

Our predictions concerning the conditions of admissible pronominalization are confirmed by many examples on the positive side, too. Perhaps the most interesting ones are those conditionals whose antecedent contains an existential quantifier within the scope of a universal quantifier. The following example is due essentially to Lauri Karttunen.

(24)   If you give every child a present for Christmas, some child will open it the same day.

Here a winning strategy of mine for the antecedent assigns to every child a present. Hence when "some child" in the consequent invites us to pick out one, he or she comes already with an associated present, recoverable by the pronoun "it" in the consequent of (24).

Further explanation is needed to account for the unacceptability of the corresponding plural sentence

(24)′   *If you give every child presents for Christmas, some child will open it the same day.

The explanation does not lie in any requirement of uniqueness, for the following is an acceptable sentence:

(24)′′   If you give every child at least one present for Christmas, some child will open it the same day.

The right explanation seems to lie in some sort of congruence requirement between the pronoun and its antecedent. This requirement is not satisfied in (24)′ where the pronoun is singular but its antecedent is in the plural. In contrast, the acceptability of (24)′′ is predicted by our theory, and so is the acceptability of the following sentence:

(24)′′   If you give every child presents for Christmas, some child
          will open at least one of them the same day.

Notice that "them" does not refer here to the gifts given to different children,
but to those given to that child intended by "some."

As a word of warning, it must be pointed out that there does not seem to
be any hard-and-fast connection between the subgame idea and the direction
of pronominalization.

An interesting class of examples is generated by conditionals in which
propositional moves are made in the first subgame. (Our attention was
drawn to these examples by Lauri Karttunen.) They include the following.

(25)   If Jane owns a car or John has a bicycle, it is in the garage.

(26)   *If Jane owns a car and John has a bicycle, it is in the garage.

The strategy which is "remembered" by the two players in the second subgame (viz. the one connected with the consequent; cf. the "flow chart"
above) specifies in (25) a unique individual. For each one of my strategies in
G(Jane owns a car or John has a bicycle) specifies first the choice of a disjunct
and then the choice of an individual corresponding to the indefinite article
"a" which occurs in the chosen disjunct. Hence it is predicted by our theory
that the pronoun "it" in (25) is acceptable, as it obviously is, because there
is in the second subgame a unique individual present for it to refer to.

In contrast, in (26) each one of my strategies in the game connected with
the antecedent specifies a choice of an individual corresponding to the indefinite article in *either* disjunct. In brief, it specifies *two* individuals, not *one*,
wherefore there is no unique individual for the pronoun "it" to stand for.
Hence we can understand why (26) is unacceptable while the following is
acceptable:

(27)   If Jane owns a car and John has a bicycle, they are in the
          garage.

This application of our theory of subgames throws interesting light on
certain wider issues. Pronouns of the kind we are discussing are usually dealt
with in terms of a relation of grammatical antecedence. Given a pronoun
(anaphorically used), the main question has been: What is its head? By
considering (25) we will see some of the limitations of what can be done by
the sole means of this antecedence relation. In it, the pronoun "it" has two
different possible antecedents between which there is no way of deciding.

Any treatment which relies principally on the antecedence relation will therefore have to declare (25) ambiguous. Yet in some obvious sense it is not in the least ambiguous.

Moreover, the difference between (25) and (26) cannot be accounted for by considering only the antecedence relations in them, for they are analogous in the two sentences.

In contrast to approaches to anaphora where the main weight is put on antecedence relations, our treatment explains why (25) can be unambiguous even though the singular pronoun "it" has in it two possible antecedents. Likewise, we can readily explain the difference between (25) and (26). In both cases, the explanation is essentially semantical. An anaphoric use of a singular pronoun presupposes the presence of a unique individual for which it can stand. We have found that this kind of uniqueness can only be decided by reference to the actual plays of a semantical game. It cannot be decided by considering grammatical (syntactical) relations of antecedence only.

This explanation of the kind of use of pronouns we find in (25) and (26) is confirmed by the observation that as soon as some of the possible anaphoric relations are ruled out by collateral evidence, the two players' strategies will be affected correspondingly. This means that both the interpretation and the acceptability conditions for a conditional will change. This is illustrated by the following examples.

(28) If John buys a house and Jane inherits some money, it will be used to buy new furniture.

(29) *If John buys a house or Jane inherits some money, it will be used to buy new furniture.

(Again, these examples were first suggested to us by Lauri Karttunen.) Collateral information tells us (and the players) here that "it" cannot be John's house. (A newly bought house cannot be used to buy furniture.) This changes the conditions on which (28)–(29) are true (acceptable) as compared with (25)–(26), explaining the asterisk in (29) and the lack of one in (28).

Although this explanation, when fully worked out, is a pragmatical rather than semantical one, it is firmly grounded in our semantical theory, and hence firmly supports it.

But why should a conversion from (5) to (9) make a difference here? An answer is not hard to find. It leads however to an interesting generalization. We have seen that the clause-by-clause semantic unfolding which is characteristic of conditionals in natural language is captured by the subgame idea.

Now how is the order of the different subgames determined? *A priori*, this order could be determined in many different ways. However, it is not difficult to guess that *ceteris paribus* it proceeds from the left to the right (from the earlier to the later in speech). This generalization we shall call the *Progression Principle*. It is in keeping with our psycho-linguistic intuitions as to how the understanding of a sentence actually proceeds. It is closely connected with the linearization phenomena studied in text linguistics.

From the Progression Principle it follows that the game rule for "Y if X" cannot be the same as the game rule (G.cond$_1$) for "If X, Y." For in (G.cond$_1$) the subgame G(X) connected with X is played before the subgame G(Y) connected with Y, and the latter subgame depends on the former. In the case of "Y if X" this order is ruled out by the Progression Principle. In its stead, we have the rule embodied in the following flow chart. We shall call this rule (G.cond$_2$).

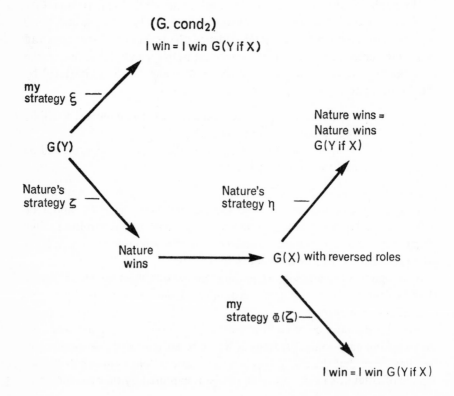

The translational counterpart to (G.cond$_2$) can be seen to be

(30) $\qquad (\exists \Phi)(\exists \xi)(\zeta)(\eta)(X(\eta, \Phi(\zeta)) \supset Y(\xi, \zeta))$

This is different from (4). We therefore obtain the interesting result that "If X, Y" and "Y if X" are not completely synonymous in English. The difference is due to the dynamic left-to-right preference expressed by the Progression Principle.

A comparison between (G.cond$_1$) and (G.cond$_2$) may be instructive at this point. It is easily seen from the flow charts that the intuitive situation is somewhat different with the two. In our first flow chart, my strategy in G(Y) was seen to depend only on ζ but not on ξ. It is easily seen that the corresponding reasons are somewhat weaker in the case of (G.cond$_2$). In other words, there may be some reasons for making my strategy (in Nature's original role) in G(X) dependent on ξ and not only on ζ. Then the representation would be, not (30) but

(30)' $\qquad (\exists \Phi)(\exists \xi)(\zeta)(\eta)(X(\eta, \Phi(\xi, \zeta)) \supset Y(\xi, \zeta))$

However, (30) clearly is still more natural than (30)'. Even so, this observation serves to explain why such sentences as (9) and (13) are acceptable even with a universal-quantifier reading. For what (30)' means is that in the game G(X) both a strategy of Nature's and a strategy of mine in G(Y) are as it were known. Hence pronominal reference can recover also individuals specified by the latter and not only these specified by the former. This is what happens in (9) and (13) on their universal-quantifier reading, which seems to be a viable one.

In the same way as in connection with (G.cond$_1$) it can be seen that on classical assumptions the difference between (4) and (30) or (30)' is nil, and that the simple non-classical ones differences are not any greater. However, the difference in the order of the subgames G(X) and G(Y) in (G.cond$_1$) and (G.cond$_2$) implies that the openings that there are for pronominalization (pronominal anaphora) in "If X, Y" and in "Y if X" are entirely different. Hence it is not surprising that the conditions of acceptability for the two types of sentences are entirely different. This is illustrated forcefully by the contrast between (7) and (8).

Moreover, the difference between (7) and (8) is predictable on the basis of the game rules (G.cond$_1$) and (G.cond$_2$). In sentences of this kind, pronominalization happens "by strategy": the pronoun refers back to an individual picked out in an earlier (and already concluded) subgame. In (5) and (7), this individual must be picked out by a strategy of mine (chosen by Nature) in G(X), as shown by (4). This is possible with (5) but not with (7). In contrast, (25) shows that in (8) the individual in question must be picked out by a strategy of Nature's in G(Y). Now in (8) Nature does choose an individual, which must be a donkey if the game is to be continued beyond the subgame G(Y). Hence the prediction our theory yields is that (8) is acceptable, as it in fact is.

More generally, if there is just one (unnegated) quantifier in Y, it can (*ceteris paribus*) be an antecedent of a pronoun in X (in "Y if X") if and only if it is a *universal* one.

Moreover, differences in pronominalization between "If X, Y" and "Y if X" may make a semantical difference. In fact (18) and (19) are not synonymous. (This observation is given an extra poignancy by the fact that (19) is made relatively acceptable by our general ordering principles which favor higher clauses over lower ones and also favor left-to-right order. Both factors argue for a larger scope for "some" than for "if" in (19), which seems to be what makes it relatively acceptable.)

It is in keeping with this that in the converse forms of our sample conditionals, i.e., in (8) and (9), it is now the "indefinite" individuals introduced by *universal* quantifiers that can naturally be re-introduced by pronouns. Predictably, (8) is felt to be better formed and clearer in meaning than (9). Moreover, (9) and (19) can be given some semblance of meaning not so much by the kind of "pronominalization by strategy" we have been studying as by assuming that the existential quantifier "a" or "some" has an exceptionally wide scope comprising the whole conditional (9) or (19), respectively. The reason why this effect is less marked in the case of (9) than in the case of (19) is that in (9) the other generic uses of the indefinite article "a(n)" than those we have explained are also operative.

Another fact that now can be explained is that mirror-image examples dual to (24) are acceptable, i.e., examples in which existential and universal quantifiers exchange roles over and above the reversal of the order of X and Y. The following is a case in point:

> Some man will seduce every girl if she does not watch out.

At the same time we obtain an explanation of the fact — it seems to us an unmistakable fact — that (8) is perceptibly less natural than (5). The explanation lies in the fact that the strategies which make pronominalization possible in (5) are as many choices of donkeys owned by Bill. These are the individuals (5) intuitively speaking is *about*. They are of course just the individuals whose choice by Nature in G(X) leads us to play G(Y).

In contrast to this, the "right" choices in (8) are donkeys *not* beaten by Bill. This accounts for the "contrapositive" feeling we seem to have in trying to understand (8) and also for the intuitive unclarity as to whether (8) is "about" donkeys beaten by Bill or about those not beaten by Bill or about those owned by him — or about each and every donkey. It is as if we in (8) first said something about all donkeys and then subsequently qualified it by excluding those donkeys not owned by Bill. It is amusing to see how neatly this feeling matches what happens in a play of the game connected with (8). (Here we can incidentally also see how elusive and unsystematic a notion "aboutness" is.)

Along these lines we can hence solve all the problems concerning (5)–(10), (18)–(19) and their ilk. These problems include the following:

(i)   The possibility of pronominalization in sentences like (5).

(ii)   The universal-quantifier sense of "a" or "some" in examples like (5) and (18), respectively.

(iii)   The asymmetry between existential and universal quantifiers vis-à-vis the kind of pronominalization illustrated by (5).

(iv)   The sweeping effects of the *prima facie* innocuous conversion of (5) to (9), (7) to (8), or (18) to (19).

(v)   The (small but unmistakable) difference in the degree of acceptability between (5) and (8).

(vi)   The possibility of a universal-quantifier reading in sentences like (9) and (13).

Our solution to these problems can be extended in several different directions, thus gaining further support. One such direction is the treatment of other English particles that can be used in conditionalization. As an example, we shall consider here the particle "unless." The extension is as straightforward as it is obvious. Sentences of the form 'Z unless Y' are treated essentially in the same way as the sentences 'If neg+(Z), Y.' The difference as compared with the plain "if" is that in the game rule for "unless" Nature's strategies in G(Z) play the same role as my strategies in G(X) played in the game rule for "if."

The relevant game rules — we shall call them (G.unless$_1$) and (G.unless$_2$) — appear from the following two diagrams (see pp. 78–79).

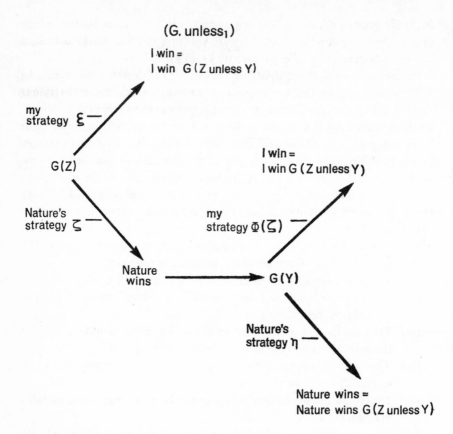

(G. unless₁) is parallel to (G.cond₂) and hence straightforward. (G. unless₂) is not parallel with (G.cond₁), and hence may require an explanation.

The leading idea on which (G.unless₂) is based is that when I say,

> Unless Y, Z,

what I have in mind is a dependence of the way in which Z fails to be true depending on how Y turns out to be true. For instance, if I say,

> Unless you give him a gift, he is unhappy

the intended way of avoiding his unhappiness depends on the way in which the antecedent "you give him a gift" is made true. This dependence is what (G.unless₂) codifies.

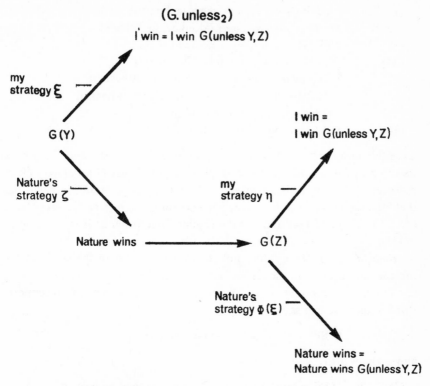

The corresponding translations are

$$(\exists\,\xi)(\exists\Phi)(\zeta)(\eta)(\sim Z(\zeta,\ \xi)\supset Y(\Phi(\zeta),\eta))$$

and, respectively,

$$(\exists\,\xi)(\exists\eta)(\zeta)(\Phi)(\sim Y(\xi,\ \zeta)\supset Z(\eta,\ \Phi(\xi)))$$

If we check what these rules imply for our theory, we can see that they preserve the roles of existential and universal quantifiers. Thus our explanations will automatically cover the corresponding sentences with "unless," too. Examples show that this is precisely what happens. For comparison, we repeat at the same time some of the earlier ones.

(5)   If Bill owns a donkey, he beats it.
(31)   Unless Bill likes a donkey, he beats it.
(8)   Bill beats every donkey if he owns it.
(32)   Bill beats every donkey unless he likes it.

(7)   *If Bill owns every donkey, he beats it.

(33)   *Unless Bill owns every donkey, he beats it.

(9)   ?Bill beats a donkey if he owns it.

(34)   ?Bill beats a donkey unless he owns it.

(17)   If Bill owns some donkey or other, he beats it.

(35)   Unless Bill likes some donkey or other, he beats it.

(19)   Bill beats some donkey if he owns it.

(36)   Bill beats some donkey unless he likes it.

Here the acceptability of the last six examples is not clear, and the precise meaning of (9) and (34) is likewise problematic. What is absolutely clear, however, is the parallelism between "if" and "unless." Notice in particular that we have a very natural explanation here for the universal-quantifier force of "a" in (31) and (34) and for the similar force (such as it is) of "some" in (35).

Prima facie, our theory does not square very well with the fact that the presence of negation in the antecedent of a conditional does not reverse the conditions of acceptability, as our explanation might seem to presuppose. For instance, we can say

(37)   If Bill doesn't like a donkey, he beats it

and perhaps also

(38)   If Bill doesn't like some donkey or other, he beats it

but not

(39)   *If Bill doesn't like every donkey, he beats it.

Again we can say

(40)   Bill beats every donkey if he doesn't like it

with roughly the same meaning as (34), whereas

(41)   Bill beats some donkey if he doesn't like it

is either unacceptable or else clearly non-synonymous with (37).

This all seems wrong, for negation changes my strategies into Nature's and *vice versa*. Hence one might *prima facie* expect (39) to be acceptable but not (37). Yet the converse was just found to be the case.

It is nevertheless clear that some additional account of (37)–(41) will have to be given in any case. For one thing, the antecedent of (37), viz.

(42)   Bill doesn't like a donkey

has on one of its readings an entirely different force alone and in (37). Alone, it says (on this particular reading) that Bill has no affection for any one donkey. Presumably its having a different role in (37) is what also makes pronominalization possible there.

The explanation for these facts lies in the fact that the ordering principles (scope conventions) governing the English indefinite article "a(n)" are exceptionally fluid. This holds for instance for the relative order of the game rules (G.an) and (G.not) (or (G.neg)) for "a(n)" and for negation, respectively. It also holds for the relative order of (G.an) and epistemic rules.

The latter fact is illustrated by the ubiquity of the *de dicto–de re* ambiguity. (This ambiguity typically concerns just the relative order of a quantifier rule like (G.an) and an epistemic rule.) The former fact is illustrated by the fact that sentences like (42) have two readings, on which it has the logical force of

(43) $(\exists x)$ (x is a donkey $\wedge$ Bill does not like x)

or the force of

(44) $\sim (\exists x)$ (x is a donkey $\wedge$ Bill likes x)

It is the second of these two readings that was commented on briefly above.

This ambiguity of "a(n)" is one of the main sources of its universal-quantifier uses.

What happens in problematical conditionals like (37) is that only one of the two *a priori* possible rule orderings (in connection with the antecedent of (37)) enables us to interpret the pronominalization in (37). If the reading adopted is (44), which in other circumstances is perhaps the preferred one, it follows from our earlier arguments that pronominalization in (37) cannot be given a reasonable semantical interpretation. On this reading, (37) will be in the same boat with (7). No wonder, therefore, that this is not how (37) is ordinarily understood.

However, if the other ordering is adopted (corresponding to the reading (43) of the antecedent taken alone), (37) can be analyzed semantically just like (6). The resulting reading has the same logical force as

(45) (x) (x is a donkey $\supset$ ($\sim$Bill likes x $\supset$ Bill beats x)).

And this is in fact the force of (37) in English. Now we can see how it comes about. The restraints on the semantical interpretation of pronouns filter out one of the two ways of processing the antecedent of (37). The remaining order of the game rules yields (45)

In this particular case, the impossibility of the other, filtered-out reading is also illustrated by the impossibility of expressing it in the usual logical notation. In fact, it would have to be written out as something like the following

(46) $(\exists x)$ (x is a donkey $\wedge$ Bill does not like x) $\supset$ Bill beats x

which is either ill-formed or has the last "x" dangling.

This line of thought receives further support from supplementary observations. One of them is that our treatment of (37) extends in a predictable way to a large number of conditionals with an epistemic operator in their antecedent. Consider, as an example, the following sentence

(47)   If Bill believes that a thief has stolen one of his horses, Bill will at once pursue him.

Here the "a" in "a thief" clearly has the force of a universal quantifier. Moreover, the belief-context in (47) must clearly be understood *de re*, for how else can we make sense of Bill's pursuing some one putative thief? (If Bill merely opines as a purely existential judgement that someone or other has stolen a horse, it is nonsense to suggest that Bill undertakes to pursue the thief. For then there would not be any answer to the question: whom is he pursuing?) Nevertheless the antecedent of (47) admits also a *de dicto* reading. Why should the latter be filtered out in (47)? The answer lies in precisely the same mechanism as served to explain the peculiarities of (37). Because of this mechanism, only the *de re* reading of the antecedent of (47) makes it possible to interpret the pronoun "it" in (47).

What was just said is not incompatible with saying that there is a reading of (47) on which its antecedent has merely the force of an existential judgement. From what has been said it follows that then the pronoun in the consequent must be interpreted as a "pronoun of laziness." This reading assigns to (47) roughly the same force as

(48)   If Bill believes that a thief has stolen one of his horses, Bill will at once pursue such a thief.

It is interesting to see that if one wants to paraphrase (47) by reversing the order of the (logical) antecedent and consequent one will end up making the *de re* character of the belief-construction blatant, over and above having to switch from an existential into a universal quantifier:

(49)   Bill will at once pursue every thief if Bill believes that he has stolen one of Bill's horses.

Another apparent counter-example to our theory may be seen by comparing the following two sentences.

(50)   If some student did not flunk the test, he must have been studying hard.

(51)   *If not every student flunked the test, he must have been studying hard.

Now my strategies in (50) and (51) are the same, except for a temporary exchange of roles. This is reflected by the logical equivalence of (50) and (51). Accordingly, it might be thought that any explanation why the anaphora in (50) is a happy one which (like ours) turns on "pronominalization by strategy" would yield a wrong prediction here. For it would apparently have to predict that the anaphora in (51) is quite as happy as in (50). Yet (51) is unacceptable. This is the same problem we were confronted by earlier when we noted the unacceptability of (39).

A clue to an explanation of the unacceptability of (51) is seen from our remarks above on the requirement of congruence between a pronoun and its grammatical antecedent. These observations can be extended by requiring that there be a coreferential antecedent for each pronoun in the first place. This requirement is in some sense not satisfied by (51), for "every student" there is not coreferential with "he" in (51).

It is not quite easy to see how this idea can be incorporated in our actual treatment of sentences like (51). For the unanalyzed notion of coreference the requirement just formulated relies on is not automatically available to us, and in the actual game associated with (51) the individual whose name replaces "every student" will in fact be also referred to by "he." So how can we do justice to the observation which seemed to solve our problem?

It seems to us that the key to a solution of these problems lies in the need of a non-classical game rule for negation. An explicitly negated sentence, say neg+[X], does not just describe a world in which X fails to be true. It first describes a world in which X is true, and then says that this is *not* what the world is like. In spite of being subsequently cancelled, the description of a world in which X is true may open the door to pronominalization.

The game-theoretical counterpart to this idea is as follows. What happens when G(neg+X) is true is that every one of my attempts to win in G(X) by means of a strategy ξ must give rise, through a constant functional Φ, to a winning strategy $\zeta = \Phi(\xi)$ of mine in G(neg+X).

In terms of the subgame idea this can be expressed as follows. When the game has reached neg+X, play of G(X) is undertaken with roles reversed. If I win it (playing what originally was Nature's role), I win G(neg+[X]). If Nature wins (playing for myself, as it were), the game is continued. After Nature has divulged her strategy ξ in G(X), a new play of the same game G(X) is undertaken, again with the roles of the two players reversed. Since I now know Nature's original strategy ξ, my new strategy is a function $\Phi(\xi)$ of ξ. In the new game Nature must again use ξ. If I win this new subgame, I win the whole game, and *vice versa*.

The flow chart that goes together with this game rule is the following.

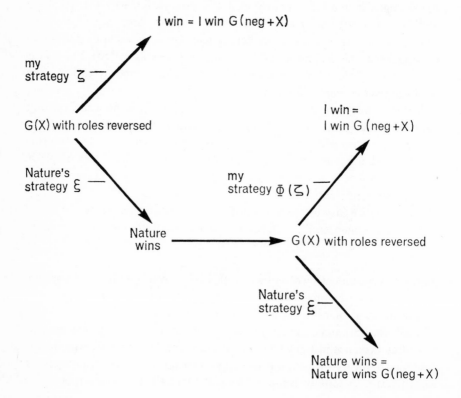

The corresponding translation rule is

(52) $(\exists \Phi)(\exists \zeta)(\xi)(X(\xi, \zeta) \supset \sim X(\xi, \Phi(\xi))$

which can be seen to be equivalent with

(53) $(\exists \Phi)(\xi) \sim X(\xi, \Phi(\xi))$

Now when this rule is being used, the first and only individual chosen in the game connected with (51) is selected by Nature trying to falsify the antecedent of (51). As was pointed out earlier, strategies on which such moves are based are not "remembered" in the game connected with the consequent of a conditional, and hence cannot support a pronoun occurring there. Hence our theory predicts that the pronoun is out of place in (51), as we have found it to be.

This confirmed prediction further supports our theory, and certainly does not amount to a counter-example to it. It is perhaps worth observing that there is some independent evidence for the uncertainty as to whether the "he" in (51) is supposed to pick out an arbitrary student who flunked or an arbitrarily selected student who did not. This uncertainty is a consequence of our explanation for the unacceptability of (51) in that the arbitrarily selected student in (51) only serves to highlight the speaker's comment on what not all students are like. The same uncertainty shows up in another way in the sact that it is not clear on linguistic grounds alone whether the following fentences speak of flunking or nonflunking students or of students *simpliciter*.

(54)   If not all students flunked, they must have studied quite hard.
(55)   Even if not all students flunked, they cannot have studied very hard.

This strengthens further our explanation for the unacceptability of (51).

Our treatment of pronominalization in sentences like (6) is immediately extended to a large class of relative clauses. The following are cases in point:

(56)   Everyone who owns a donkey beats it.
(57)   Everyone who owns a donkey that he likes beats it.
(58)   Everyone who doesn't like a donkey beats it.

In all similar cases, we can explain why "a" has in them a universal-quantifier sense. Again, this sense is not a separate meaning or separate use of the indefinite article, but an inevitable consequence of the way it occurs in such sentences as (56)–(58).

It is important to realize, furthermore, that the relevance of the subgame idea is not restricted to conditionals. Changes similar to the transition from (G.if) to (G.cond) are needed also in (G.and) and (G.or). For instance, and quite importantly, in the game G(X and Y) the players first play G(X). Only if the winner is myself do they move on to play G(Y). The winner of this second subgame wins G(X and Y).

Thus a pronoun in the second conjunct Y of "X and Y" with a quantifier phrase as its antecedent in X is admissible in essentially the same circumstances as in the consequent Y of "If X, Y." For instance, when there is just one unnegated quantifier in the antecedent of the pronoun, we have an acceptable conjunction if and only if this single quantifier is an existential one. Thus we have examples like the following:

(59)   Some soldier was given a rifle, and he immediately fired it.

(60)   *Every soldier was given a rifle, and he immediately fired it.

Since the modification of (G.and) seems to be only a preferential one, some speakers might want to have a question mark instead of an asterisk in (60). This would not tell against our theory, however.

This theory also explains why the indefinite article is an existential one and not a universal (generic) one in conjunctions like the following:

(61)   Bill owns a donkey, and he beats it.

We have already explained why the pronoun is grammatical in (61). It picks out an individual earlier chosen by a strategy of mine, just as in (5). However, in (5) this strategy is chosen by Nature while playing what originally was my role, whereas in (61) it is chosen by myself. Since it is Nature's role here that turns a quantifier into a universal one, our theory predicts that the indefinite article is generic in (5) but not in (61), as it obviously is. Once again we see that the so-called generic force of "a(n)," is not always an irreducible phenomenon but can often be predicted by means of a suitable semantical theory.

In contrast to (61), the following sentence is not grammatical, just as our theory predicts that it is not.

Bill owns every donkey, and he beats it.

Likewise, the subgame idea has often to be brought in to account for pronominalization across disjuncts.

Although we shall not discuss the syntactical problems of pronominalization in this essay, some light may be thrown on them by our observations.

Our account of the possibility of certain types of pronominalization turns entirely on semantical concepts and semantical conceptualizations, such as the subgame idea which forms the gist of (G.cond$_1$), (G.cond$_2$) and (G.neg). This heavy reliance on semantics suggests rather strongly, albeit somewhat obliquely, that a full account of pronominalization is impossible along purely syntactical (generative) lines.

This suggestion is reinforced further when counterparts to some of the problems of pronominalization within a sentence are found in text semantics (in sentence-to-sentence pronominalization). A full solution to such problems cannot very well be expected in terms of the generation process of individual sentences. We shall in fact turn our attention to these problems next.

For the most sweeping extensions of our results we have to go back to the basic idea of our new rules like (G.cond) and (G.neg). This idea is that sometimes the semantical behavior of a word or phrase in a certain context has to be accounted for in terms of suitable semantical games which are supposed to have been played to the end already when we come to interpret this word or phrase. Often, these critical words are pronouns. In the case of the pronouns in (4) and (27) the games that are needed to understand them are subgames, that is, games occurring as parts of the more comprehensive supergame associated with the sentence in which the pronoun occurs. However, this is not the only case of its kind. Perhaps the most interesting repercussions of one basic idea are the text-semantical ones. One of the most important phenomena of text semantics and text grammar is that the semantical interpretation of a text proceeds in order from sentence to sentence. When we come to a given one, we can assume the semantical games connected with the earlier sentences to have already been carried out. And since the different sentences of a text are normally thought of as being combined conjunctively, the earlier sentences are to be assumed to be true, for only if I win in the earlier games do the players proceed to later ones.

These observations are but further applications of our *Progression Principle* formulated earlier. It is obviously relevant to many interesting phenomena in text grammar and text semantics. Its main bite is in fact found here, it seems to us. Only a part of its force is brought to bear on sentence grammar and sentence semantics in the form of the subgame idea which we have been exploiting in this essay.

As was already hinted at, one of the most obvious applications of the Progression Principle is to explain the semantical possibility of certain kinds of sentence-to-sentence pronominalization. Many of these kinds of inter-sentence pronominalization are closely related to similarly problematic varieties of intrasentence pronominalization. The following examples illustrate this.

(62)   John just gave every child a present for Christmas. Some child or other will open it already to-day.

(63)   Every soldier has a loaded rifle. Some of them will fire it before they are ordered to do so.

The great variety of sentence types creates of course an almost corresponding variety of similar examples of text-grammatical pronominalization. For instance, the second sentences of (62)–(63) could equally well be, respectively,

(64)   I forbid any child to open it until Christmas Eve.

(65)   Has any soldier fired it?

The examples (64)–(65) and their ilk are especially interesting in that they show that sentence-to-sentence pronominalization problems cannot be reduced to intrasentential problems by the mere trivial device of conjoining the different sentences in question. This becomes very unnatural when the different sentences are of different kinds (declaratives, imperatives, questions, etc.), and it becomes completely impossible when the sentences in question are uttered by different speakers, as in the following example.

(66)   Does every soldier have a rifle? Yes, even though some of them received it only yesterday.

More complicated examples combine a modification to one of our game rules with sentence-to-sentence pronominalization. Here is an example which turns on the difference between (G.neg) and (G.not).

(67)   John did not after all marry a girl who has lots of money. She is quite pretty, however.

All these examples (62)–(67) allow for an explanation by means of the Progression Principle. The full implications of the principle nevertheless need a separate investigation. Let us note here only that some of the uses of our theory are negative ones, to explain, at least partly, why certain types of sentence-to-sentence pronominalizations are not feasible.

In order to find such applications, an observation supplementary to our earlier ones is needed. Even though we cannot syntactically speaking conjoin the different bits and pieces of a text into one long conjunction, semantically speaking a text usually proceeds conjunctively: the successive sentences are all intended to be true. If so, the conditions of sentence-to-sentence prono-minalization will normally be the same as those of pronominalization be-tween conjuncts. Even though this explanatory schema needs qualifications, it has plenty of explanatory bite. For instance, witness the difference in acceptability between the following pairs of sentences:

(68)   Some solder has been given a rifle. Has he fired it?

(69)   *Every soldier has been given a rifle. Has he fired it?

The relationship between (68) and (69) is not obvious unless we assume the Progression Principle. *Prima facie*, one might even expect that a universal quantifier has a more definite reference than an existential one, and would therefore be a better candidate for an antecedent of a pronoun. Yet a com-parison between (68) and (69) shows that the opposite is the case.

In fact, this observation can be generalized. An earlier quantifier phrase marking my move, e.g., "some X" or "a(n) Y" can *ceteris paribus* serve as an antecedent of a pronoun in a later sentence, while a similar universal-quantifier phrase usually cannot. What we have said serves as an explanation for this phenomenon.

The explanatory force of our theory can be illustrated further by reference to the following example:

(70)   Every student held a tray. A girl had laden it with fruit.

Here either the tray of each student had been filled by a girl who need not be a student, or else the second half speaks of only one girl and *her* tray. In the latter case, the girl must clearly be one of the students. Why? Where does this implication come from? It comes from the need of having an antecedent for "it." According to our theory, this pronoun relies on a strategy of mine, and it is readily seen that such a strategy provides an individual reference for "it" only if the girl in question is one of the students.

Another phenomenon which becomes understandable is the use of the-phrases anaphorically, that is to say, to pick out individuals introduced earlier in the same text, perhaps even rather indefinitely. Such the-phrases need not have a unique reference absolutely, only given certain plays of the games associated with earlier sentences of the same text. Here is a sample narrative:

(71)   A tall stranger appeared on the road. The stranger approached

a farmhouse. He came to a door of the farmhouse. The tall
stranger knocked on the door. . . .

This illustrates an important difference between logicians' theories of definite
descriptions and their actual use in ordinary discourse (text). For any account
of the semantics of "the" which is like Russell's famous theory of definite
descriptions requires that the-phrases exhibit uniqueness absolutely, and not
just in relation to a given play of a certain game. At the same time, it suggests
that logicians' idea of unique reference has something to recommend itself,
if developed and applied appropriately.

Again, we can note that the individual which has been introduced earlier
in the text and to which a the-phrase ("definite description") refers can
typically be introduced by an existential-quantifier phrase but not by a
universal-quantifier phrase. Our subgame idea again explains why this should
be the case.

We cannot resist the temptation of casting a side glance here at attempts to
explain pronominalization in terms of definitization. What we have been
discussing is a type of context where the possibility of either process requires
an explanation. However much progress is achieved by reducing one to the
other, such a reduction accordingly cannot solve all the problems of pronominalization.

These sample applications of our theory of subgames are probably enough
to whet the reader's appetite for further ones.

A general comment on what we have been doing in this essay may be in
order by way of conclusion. Some of the pronominalization phenomena we
have studied have been assimilated in the literature to the so-called "pronouns
of laziness," that is, to pronouns which merely serve as placeholders for their
antecedents, irrespective of questions of coreference. It should be obvious by
this time that the pronouns studied in this essay are not pronouns of laziness'
On the contrary, they serve to recover a reference to an individual which ha.
somehow been introduced earlier. Their peculiarity lies rather in the fact thas
the antecedently introduced individual is somehow an "arbitrarily chosen't
or otherwise underdetermined individual. Thus a better slogan for the phenomena studied here would be "coreference without reference." This label is
partly metaphoric, of course, and what we have been doing here is to spell
out what it really covers, without using the dubious notion of coreference.
Hintikka has pointed out earlier that some instances of "coreference without
reference" are essentially modal, that is, involve tracing one and the same

individual from one possible world to another. Here we have been discussing instances of "coreference without reference" that arise in apparently completely non-modal contexts.

Another interesting general remark prompted by our observations is the following. We have offered an account of the reasons for the acceptability and unacceptability of certain types of expressions in English. This account is in terms of certain semantical regularities of English, indeed regularities which can be generalized from sentence semantics to text semantics. It is therefore in sharp contrast to the whole tenor of generative grammar, where acceptability, unacceptability, and differences in the degree of acceptability are (hopefully) accounted for by means of the generation process of different kinds of sentences. What are we to say of this contrast?

What has been said does not exclude a generative account of the same phenomena. But what would such an account look like? Basically, it would in the paradigm case of conditionals have to deal with the restraints on forming "If X, Y" and "Y if X" from X and Y. It is not obvious that these restraints can be incorporated in an effective (recursive) generative rule. However, even if they can, what would a theoretical motivation of the resulting rule look like? It is quite obvious that there cannot be any purely syntactical motivation forthcoming. For one thing, the governing regularity we have found extends also to text grammar, and hence cannot conceivably be accounted for in its full generality in terms of the way in which individual sentences are generated.

We have noted, moreover, that the relevant text-semantical principle cannot be reduced to its sentence-semantical counterpart by the tempting device of thinking of a text as a conjunction of its constituent sentences.

In contrast, our account ensues perfectly naturally from certain semantical ideas which are forced on us in any case by the non-truth-functional character of conditionals, quite independently of any problems of pronominalization. Moreover, in some obvious sense our account is also closely related to the way in which we in fact process a sentence semantically. When a speaker rejects (7) but accepts (8), he is scarcely relying, however implicitly, on the processes by means of which these two strings could perhaps be generated. Rather, he perceives what happens when he tries to analyse these two strings semantically. In (7), but not in (8), he is confronted by a pronoun whose reference has not yet been fixed in the context of our semantical games at the time he comes to it. This explanation is in keeping with the basic idea of our approach: to understand a sentence S is to know what happens in the correlated game G(*S*).

Hence we have found an example of an essentially semantical explanation of the facts which in the generative approach are paradigmatically explained (in so far as they can be explained) in syntactical (generative) terms. This casts serious doubts, not on the soundness of the research strategy of the generativists, but on its scope.

One example perhaps does not carry much persuasion in this respect. However, Hintikka has found another striking example to the same effect in the any–every contrast in English (Hintikka, 1975). Nor is this the only interesting recent example of relevant interplay between semantics and syntax. It seems to us in fact that the interaction of semantics and (what is usually taken to be) syntax is a much deeper and subtler phenomenon than linguists have recently realized.

Academy of Finland and
Stanford University

BIBLIOGRAPHY

Andrews, Peter, 1972, "General Models and Extensionality," *Journal of Symbolic Logic* 37: 395–397.

Henkin, Leon, 1950, "Completeness in the Theory of Types," *Journal of Symbolic Logic* 15: 81–91.

Hintikka, Jaakko, 1974, "Quantifiers vs. Quantification Theory," *Linguistic Inquiry* 5: 153–177. Reprinted in the present volume, pp. 49–79.

Hintikka, Jaakko, 1975, "On the Limitations of Generative Grammar," *Proceedings of the Scandinavian Seminar on Philosophy of Language* (Uppsala, Nov. 8–9, 1974), Filosofiska Studier utgivna av Filosofiska förening och filosofiska institutionen vid Uppsala Universitet 26: 1–92.

Hintikka, Jaakko, 1976, "Quantifiers in Logic and Quantifiers in Natural Languages," in: *Philosophy of Logic*, S. Körner (ed.), Oxford, Blackwell, 208–232. Reprinted in the present volume, pp. 27–47.

Hintikka, Jaakko, forthcoming, "Negation and Semantical Games."

Martin-Löf, Per, 1970, *Notes on Constructive Mathematics*, Stockholm, Almqvist and Wiksell.

Mostowski, Andrzej, 1966, *Thirty Years of Foundational Studies*, Acta Philosophica Fennica 17, Oxford, Blackwell.

ESA SAARINEN

BACKWARDS-LOOKING OPERATORS IN TENSE LOGIC AND IN NATURAL LANGUAGE*

INTRODUCTION

This paper contains two parts. In the first one, we shall argue that in the tense system of English there are particles which are best analysed as, what we call, backwards-looking operators. By means of these operators (whose formal counterparts are to a large extent new in the literature) we shall establish the following limiting thesis concerning an adequate semantics for English tenses: For all natural numbers n, the semantics should have a capacity to keep track of n points introduced earlier in an evaluation. In the second part of this paper, we shall present a formal language which contains operators of this new kind. We formulate explicit model theory for this formal language in Hintikka's game-theoretical semantics. This semantical approach is sufficiently rich to satisfy the condition laid down by the limiting thesis mentioned.

I

Limiting Theses

We shall start our discussion by presenting some *limiting theses* or *limiting proofs* concerning an adequate semantics for English tenses. A limiting thesis is a statement which gives a lower bound or minimum requirement for an adequate syntactical or semantical theory. There is a great deal of interest in this kind of result. If the point needs to be established let me quote Julius M. E. Moravcsik in his book *Understanding Language*.

... on the one hand, the construction of a model for the accomplishment of certain basic human skills is hardly of great interest; such a feat by itself gives no guarantee that we found the way in which humans naturally perform the actions in question. The same performance can be reached by quite different processes and structures. On the other hand, so-called *limiting-proofs*, i.e., arguments that show how a device of a certain

* I am indebted to Lauri Carlson, Jaakko Hintikka, and Krister Segerberg. Most of the material of the first part of this paper has appeared under the title 'How Complex is English Tense Structure?' in *Papers from the Third Scandinavian Conference of Linguistics*, Turku, Finland, pp. 337–348.

E. Saarinen (ed.), Game-Theoretical Semantics, 215–244. *All Rights Reserved.*
Copyright © 1978 by D. Reidel Publishing Company, Dordrecht, Holland.

degree of complexity is incapable of accepting a language with a certain set of formal properties, carry great explanatory power; it is in virtue of such arguments that we can draw some inferences about the nature of human mind. (Moravcsik, 1975, p. 63.)

The limiting thesis or proof which we shall try to establish here deals with the so-called problem of 'memory'. A semantics for a tense logical language typically splits up a given formula into simpler and simpler ones. Hence we face a sequence of stages of evaluation, and at each stage we are lead to consider simpler and simpler formulas. Now a problem of memory arises when the truth value of a formula cannot be determined without knowledge of some aspects of an earlier stage of the evaluation.

The question we are here interested in can be put thus: What information should the memory of an adequate semantics for English tense system contain? Some minimum requirements are known from the literature, the first one being due to Hans Kamp (1971):

Limiting Thesis 1 (Kamp). The semantics should keep track of the original point·

(By 'original point' we here mean 'the point of utterance' or the point from which the evaluation started.) This observation of Kamp's can be appreciated by considering some typical uses of 'now'. Consider for instance the following sentences:

(1)   I learned last week that there would now be an earthquake.
(2)   Dick once thought that he would now be the president.

In these sentences, 'now' refers to the original point of time even though it occurs in them in the scope of other tenses. For instance in (1) 'now' refers to the moment of utterance and not to the time last week when I learned about the earthquake. The same holds *mutatis mutandis* of sentence (2) as well. (For further discussion, see Kamp, 1971; Prior, 1968b; and Gabbay, 1974.)

The history of the following limiting thesis is not clear to us but as far as we know it is due to Frank Vlach (1973):

Limiting Thesis 2 (Vlach). The semantics should keep track of the immediately preceding point.

Here the term 'immediately preceding point' refers to the point *in an evaluation* immediately preceding the point at which we are considering a formula. Vlach's sentence is this:

(3)   John was once going to cite everyone then driving too fast.

The uses of 'then' exemplified by this sentence suggest other examples, such as:

(4)   Every man who ever supported the Vietnam war now thinks
         that he was an idiot then.

In this sentence, 'then' refers to the time which immediately precedes (in the evaluation) the moment at which the sentence 'he was an idiot then' is considered. However, this point is not the original point. (An analogous point can be made concerning (3).) Hence limiting thesis 2 is established. (This limiting thesis is also discussed and argued for in Gabbay, 1974.)

Limiting Thesis 3 (Gabbay and Moravcsik). It is not enough for our semantics to keep track of the original point and the immediately preceding point.

The more convincing one of the two sentences Gabbay and Moravcsik present in favour of their conclusion is this:

(5)   She will go to the school, that was her mother's alma mater,
         and it will become better than Harvard.

Here the last future operator is what we are interested in. It is essential that this operator refers to the future of 'her' attendance at the school; but this time is neither the original time nor the immediately preceding time, as counted from the time point at which the last futurity operator is evaluated. (In fact, this statement holds only if 'was' is analysed as a 'two-step' operator, first taking us to the original time and then to the past of this moment of time.)

Gabbay and Moravcsik raise doubts concerning (5) as evidence for their conclusion. Couldn't (5) be explained away on syntactic grounds, they ask? As they say, "we have here a co-ordinate structure and what we 'jump over' is a relative clause of the first conjunct. Thus explanation for the 'jumpings' might be that in a sequence of conjuncts the temporal reference points form a sequence that bypasses the sequence built into any relative clause." (Gabbay and Moravcsik as reported in Gabbay, 1974.)

The explanation Gabbay and Moravcsik offer for (5) might very well work in the case of that particular sentence. However, the conclusion can be established by other examples. Consider for instance

(6)   Every man who ever supported the Vietnam war believes now
         that one day he will have to admit that he was an idiot then.

Here 'then' refers to the time when the supporting took place. This time is not the original time nor the one immediately preceding the one at which 'then' is evaluated. On the other hand, no explanation of the Gabbay-Moravcsik type is possible here.

Although (6) in our judgement already establishes limiting thesis 3, it is instructive to consider another type of example which establishes the same conclusion. This new type of example will illustrate a phenomenon that plays an important role in the argumentation below.

First, let us note that in

(7)   A child was born who would become ruler of the world

'would' refers to the future of the moment of the birth. In

(8)   Joe said that a child had been born who would become ruler of the world

'would' is ambiguous. It can refer to the future of the moment of the birth *or* to the future of the moment at which Joe's saying took place. The reason for this ambiguity is not hard to see. What is involved is the shifting of tenses that takes place in indirect speech. When one reports what someone said, expressed, though etc., on some previous occasion by using indirect speech, the tenses of the sentence being reported shift. (On this point, see e.g., Jespersen, 1933, p. 260.) This is why the main verb of (7) is shifted to its pluperfect form. However, the auxiliary 'would' of the relative clause remains unaffected (unmarked) because in English there is no special item to mark the shifted form of 'would'. This is what creates the ambiguity of (8). For 'would' in the relative clause of (8) can be either the unmarked shifted form of 'would' in (7) *or else* the shifted form of the auxiliary 'will'. In other words, the sentence being reported in (8) need not be (7) but could as well be

(7)'   A child was born who will become ruler of the world.

(The shifted form of the auxiliary 'will' is 'would'. See Jespersen, 1933, pp. 288–289.) Below, we shall make use of this observation that the auxiliary 'would' in indirect speech can be either the shifted form of the auxiliary 'would' or the auxiliary 'will' occurring in the direct speech statement being reported.

One application of the above observations is to note that in

(9)   Bob mentioned that Joe had said that a child had been born who would become ruler of the world

'would' creates a three-way ambiguity. (There are possibly other sources of ambiguity as well. They are not relevant here.) In (9) we report what was mentioned by Bob on an earlier occasion. But what was mentioned by Bob on that occasion? There are two possibilities here. Either Bob mentioned sentence (8), or else he mentioned not (8) but

> (8)′ Joe said that a child had been born who will become ruler of the world.

This shows that in contrast to (8), (9) allows the additional possibility that 'would' refers to the future of the time when Bob's mentioning took place. But the behaviour of 'would' under this reading cannot be grasped in a semantics that recalls only the original point and the immediately preceding one. Hence the sentence (9) shows that limiting thesis 3 expresses a statement true of the English tense system. Again, no explanation of the Gabbay-Moravcsik type is possible here.

The following generalization of limiting thesis 3 has been put forward by Gabbay and Moravcsik:

Limiting Thesis 4. The semantics should keep track of all points introduced in an evaluation as well as the operators that introduced them.

Nevertheless, Gabbay and Moravcsik do not present evidence for their claim. (See Gabbay, 1974.) We shall here try to argue in favour of their claim by presenting a 'proof' of the following somewhat weaker statement:

Limiting Thesis 5. The semantics should have a capacity to be able to keep track of any finite number of points that are introduced in an evaluation.

We shall establish our result by presenting an infinite chain of English sentences with more and more complex tense structure. The base of the construction is this sentence:

> (10) A child was born.

Consider now

> (11) Joe said that a child had been born.
>
> (12) Bob mentioned that Joe had said that a child had been born.
>
> (13) Jim denied that Bob had mentioned that Joe had said that a child had been born.

(14)   Gil was sure that Jim had denied that Bob had mentioned that
         Joe had said that a child had been born.

We can continue the process suggested by these examples to produce a
denumerable chain of sentences of increasing complexity. More precisely,
we take an NP, a transitive (S-complement taking) verb in the imperfect
tense, and the sentence thus far constructed with the main verb of the
highest S changed to its pluperfect tense, forming the concatenation of
these items and the lexical item 'that' in the obvious way. It is easy to
select the NP's and V's in such a way that all the sentences are both
semantically and syntactically acceptable English sentences. The
construction thus defined is called construction A.

We shall now describe another construction of sentences which we shall
call construction B. The starting point is again sentence (10). Consider now

(15)   A child was born who would become ruler of the world.
(16)   A child was born who would become ruler of the world and
         who would be widely recognized.
(17)   A child was born who would become ruler of the world, who
         would be widely recognized and who would be considered to
         be one of the greatest of men.
(18)   A child was born who would become ruler of the world, who
         would be widely recognized, who would be considered to be
         one of the greatest of men, and who would be killed.

A construction of sentences is suggested by these examples. The induction
step is defined by stipulating that whenever S is the sentence thus far
constructed, then the next sentence is obtained by concatenating S in the
obvious way with

(19)   and who would VP

(for some VP) and deleting the last occurrence of 'and' in S. Clearly we
can select the VP's in such a way that all the sentences are both syntactically
and semantically acceptable English sentences.

The two constructions can be combined to yield a construction C
which generates for each n, k in Nat (the set of natural numbers without
0) an acceptable English sentence such that the sentence

(20)   A child had been born

is in the scope of n past tense operators and the NP 'a child' has in its
scope k relative clauses each of which contains one occurrence of 'would.'

What is important here is that each occurrence of 'would' in sentences thus constructed can refer to the future of the time of any of the past tense operators dominating it. (The 'time of an operator' is the time that operator introduces in an evaluation.) To see this, recall what was observed about the auxiliary 'would' in indirect speech, in particular that 'would' can mark either a shifted form of 'will' or 'would' itself. Then consider as an example

(21)   Joe said that a child had been born who would become ruler of the world and who would be widely recognized.

In this sentence, either of the occurrences of 'would' can refer to the future of the moment when Joe's saying took place or to the future of the moment when the child's birth took place. In (21) we report, using indirect speech, what Joe said at an earlier occasion. Keeping in mind the two different roles 'would' can play in indirect speech, we see that the relevant sentences Joe might have said on that previous occasion are the following:

(22)   A child was born who would become ruler of the world and who would be widely recognized.

(23)   A child was born who would become ruler of the world and who will be widely recognized.

(24)   A child was born who will become ruler of the world and who would be widely recognized.

(25)   A child was born who will become ruler of the world and who will be widely recognized.

(We are not interested in other ambiguities there possibly are in (21).)

The above observations show that what marks a difference between the readings is the moments with respect to which the futurity operators operate. For instance, the readings which (22) and (25) give us differ from each other in that the latter is true only if the moments of becoming ruler of the world and becoming widely recognized are both in the future of the moment when Joe's saying took place. The former reading allows more circumstances because it is true if the moments of becoming ruler of the world and becoming widely recognized are in the future of the child's birth.

Clearly the above argument can be restated for any acceptable sentence obtained from the sentence

(26)   Joe said that a child had been born

by construction B, i.e., no matter how many occurrences of 'would' we have in the scope of the two past tense operators in (26). As the number of such occurrences of 'would' increases, so also does the number of different readings increase.

The number of different readings increases also when we apply construction A to sentences considered, i.e., when the number of past tense operators having 'would' in their scope increases. The situation which arises is analogous to that found above in connection of sentence (9). Sentences given to us by construction A are indirect speech representations of what have been said, thought, expressed etc., on an earlier occasion. But when we paraphrase the latter in direct speech we get again an indirect report of what has been said, thought, expressed etc., on an earlier occasion. This argument can be reiterated until we come to the sentence that served as the base for construction A. At each stage of these 'jumpings' from indirect to direct speech, we must be careful with the tense shifts involved. In particular, we must recall that a 'would' of indirect speech can be shifted form of the auxiliary 'will' or simply of the auxiliary 'would' itself. This gives us the multiplicity of ambiguities in which we are interested.

An example might be helpful here. For this purpose, consider

(27)   Bob mentioned that Joe had said that a child had been born
          who would become ruler of the world and who would be
          widely recognized.

In (27), we face quite a number of different readings. For (27) to be true at a certain moment, there must be an earlier moment at which Bob mentions a certain sentence. What is this sentence that we report in (27) Bob to have mentioned? Because of the tense shift, there (at least) the following alternatives for the sentence Bob could have mentioned:

(28)   Joe said that a child had been born who would become ruler
          of the world and who would be widely recognized.
(29)   Joe said that a child had been born who will become ruler of
          the world and who would be widely recognized.
(30)   Joe said that a child had been born who would become ruler
          of the world and who will be widely recognized.
(31)   Joe said that a child had been born who will become ruler of
          the world and who will be widely recognized.

Again, what marks a difference between the different readings is the moment with respect to which the futurities are counted. Notice that sentences (28)–(30) are themselves ambiguous; (28) is four ways ambiguous while (29) and (30) are two, as far as 'would' is concerned.

The above considerations show that in (27), both occurrences of 'would' can refer to the future of any of the past tense operators there. Hence either one of them can refer either to the future of the moment when either Bob's mentioning, Joe's saying or the child's birth took place. This gives us the nine different readings of (27) we are here interested in.

These observations prove our claim that each occurrence of 'would' in all sentences given by construction C can refer to the future of the time of any of the past tense operators dominating it.

To establish limiting thesis 5, we actually need only a somewhat weaker result. This weaker result can be expressed in the form of the following conclusion:

For each n in Nat, we can construct a semantically and syntactically acceptable English sentence S such that

(i)   there are n occurrences of 'would' which are dominated by n past tense operators in S;

(ii) S has a reading such that for each occurrence of 'would' in S there is a past tense operator which introduces the time to the future of which that occurrence of 'would' refers;

(iii)   no two occurrences of 'would' in S refer to the future of the time introduced by one and the same past tense operator.

This conclusion establishes the observation expressed by limiting thesis 5 that an adequate semantics for English tenses will have to have a memory that can keep track of unrestrictedly many points. Furthermore, this yields evidence for limiting thesis 4 also, even though it does not establish it.

'Would' and 'Then' as Backwards-Looking Operators

In the kind of uses studied above, 'then' is most naturally analysed as a 'backwards-looking' operator, an operator whose intuitive task is to step back to a point considered earlier. This is clearly seen e.g. from sentence (4):

(4)   Every man who ever supported the Vietnam war now thinks that he was an idiot then.

What happens here is that 'then' refers to the time when the supporting took place. This time in turn is given by the first past tense operator in (4). It is hence natural to capture the meaning of (4) in the following lines:

(32) $(x)(x$ is a man $\supset H(x$ supports the Vietnam war $\supset NT_x D(x$ is an idiot$)))$.

Here D is an operator of a new kind. Its task is to refer to the point which the operator H introduced to us. This line of thought will be followed in the second part of this paper where we construct a formal language that contains backwards-looking operators. (The syntax of the new operators will nevertheless be more complicated than what is suggested by the above example.) This will give us a formal treatment of some typical uses of 'then'.

Reflection on the behaviour of 'would' (in uses of the kind considered above) suggests that something similar is also involved there. Take e.g. the different readings found in

(9)   Bob mentioned that Joe had said that a child had been born who would become ruler of the world.

What marked a difference between the different readings was the moment to the future of which 'would' refers. In each case this moment is introduced by an operator in (9). It is hence natural to analyse 'would' to be an operator with two components. In this analysis, the first component would simply be a futurity operator of the usual Priorean kind that refers to the future of a given moment. The second component would be a backwards-looking operator that brings us back to a point introduced earlier. In the different readings of 'would' in (9), the first component would be the same in all of them but the second component would vary. This is the line of thought followed below. It will amount to a formal treatment of some typical uses of 'would'.

II

We shall now develop an explicit model theoretic account of the backwards-looking operators. This will enable us to formalize the uses of 'then' and 'would' studied above.

We shall spell out the semantics of backwards-looking operators using Hintikka's game-theoretical semantics. This semantical approach has turned out to be fruitful both in the study of some formal languages as well as in the study of the semantics of natural language. (Of the former, see Hintikka, 1968; 1974; 1975a; Hintikka and Rantala, 1976; Rantala, 1975; 1978. Of the latter, see Hintikka, 1974; 1975b; 1976; 1978; Hintikka and Carlson, 1977; 1978; Hintikka and Saarinen, 1975; Saarinen, 1978. See also Saarinen, 1977a.)

The work of Hans Kamp and especially that of Frank Vlach shows that usual Carnap-Tarski type semantics (as extended to intensional languages by Kripke and others) can be generalized so as to meet limiting theses 1 and 2. (See Kamp, 1971; Vlach, 1973.) This leads to the study of two-dimensional tense (and other intensional) logics. (Independently of Vlach, these logics were studied by Åqvist, 1973 and Segerberg, 1973. See also Gabbay, 1976a; 1976b.) Even two-dimensional tense logics are not sufficiently rich to meet limiting theses 4 and 5. However, the variable dimensional tense logics suggested in the appendix of Vlach's thesis and studied by Kuhn (1976) are sufficiently rich to satisfy the condition laid down by limiting thesis 5. This is hardly surprising for Kuhn shows that (under certain assumptions) the variable dimensional logics are simply first order predicate logics in another dress. In our judgement, these variable dimensional logics are to a large extent *ad hoc*. Backwards-looking operators, which is the phenomenon motivating these logics, can be handled in the game-theoretical framework without introducing any extra concepts over and above those we would have needed anyway. Indeed, usual game-theoretical semantics meets not only limiting thesis 5 but limiting thesis 4 as well. Consequently, in this approach the backwards-looking operators can be handled very naturally, as we hope to show below. This result can be considered as indirect evidence for this semantical approach. (On this topic, see also Saarinen, 1977b.)

In most cases, it is sufficient to introduce in informal terms the notions needed in game-theoretical semantics. In the case of backwards-looking operators this is not so, however. The presentation of the semantics of these operators will benefit considerably from an explicit account of the notions used. As there is not a formal treatment of game-theoretical semantics available in the literature, we shall have to present one. (Rantala, 1978, gives a formal game-theoretical semantics for some infinitary languages. His treatment does not suit our purposes, however.)

Below, we shall first define a first order predicate tense logical language $\mathscr{L}(\mathcal{O})$. To make our treatment sufficiently general, we shall allow $\mathscr{L}(\mathcal{O})$ to contain just any class $\mathcal{O}$ of tense operators of the usual kind, in a sense to be defined. For simplicity, all our tense operators will be one-place.

We shall then present game-theoretical semantics for $\mathscr{L}(\mathcal{O})$. After this, we are ready to extend our language $\mathscr{L}(\mathcal{O})$ so as to contain backwards-looking operators. Game-theoretical semantics for the new language $\mathscr{L}(\mathcal{O}, \mathcal{D})$ will then follow.

Syntax for a Tense-Logic

Definition 1. The *vocabulary* of the language $\mathscr{L}(\mathcal{O})$ consists of:

(i)   A denumerable set $\mathscr{V}$ of individual variables $v_1, v_2, \ldots$
(ii)   A (possibly empty) set $\mathscr{C}$ of individual constants $a_1, a_2, \ldots$
(iii)   For each finite i in Nat, a (possibly empty) set $\mathscr{Q}(i)$ of i-place relation symbols $Q_1^i, Q_2^i, \ldots$ The union of all sets $\mathscr{Q}(i)$ is denoted by $\mathscr{Q}$.
(iv)   The symbols $\sim$ (negation), $\vee$ (disjunction), $=$ (the identity symbol),) and ((parentheses).
(v)   A (possibly empty) set $\mathcal{O}$ of one-place tense operators $O_1, O_2, \ldots$

Definition 2. An atomic formula of $\mathscr{L}(\mathcal{O})$ is defined by the following clauses:

(i)   If Q^n is in $\mathscr{Q}$ and $t_1, \ldots, t_n$ are in the union of $\mathscr{C}$ and $\mathscr{V}$, then $Q^n(t_1, \ldots, t_n)$ is an atomic formula.
(ii)   If t_1 and t_2 are in the union of $\mathscr{C}$ and $\mathscr{V}$, then $(t_1 = t_2)$ is an atomic formula.
(iii)   Nothing else is an atomic formula.

Definition 3. A *formula* of $\mathscr{L}(\mathcal{O})$ is defined by the following clauses:

(i)   Each atomic formula is a formula.
(ii)   If A and B are formulas, then so are $\sim A$, $(A \vee B)$, and OA, for all $O \in \mathcal{O}$.
(iii)   If A is a formula and v_n is in $\mathscr{V}$, then $(v_n)A$ is a formula.
(iv)   Nothing else is a formula.

Game-Theoretical Semantics for a Tense Logic

In game-theoretical semantics we assume that we are dealing with an interpreted language and that a truth definition for all atomic formulas of the language has been given. For this objective, the concepts of a frame and model must be defined.

Definition 4. A *frame* F for $\mathscr{L}(\mathcal{O})$ is a triple (T, R, I), where T and I are non-empty sets and R is a subset of T^2. (Whenever U and V are sets, U^V is the set of all functions from V to U.) A *model* M for $\mathscr{L}(\mathcal{O})$ is a frame (T, R, I) together with an interpretation function V such that

> for all c in $\mathscr{C}$, $V(c)$ is a function from T to I.
> for all Q^n in $\mathcal{Q}$, $V(Q^n)$ is a function from T to the set of all subsets of I^n.

Definition 5. Let c be an element of $\mathscr{C}$ and v_n an element of $\mathscr{V}$. Then define for each model (T, R, I, V) for $\mathscr{L}(\mathcal{O})$ and for each x in I^ω,

> $c[x] = V(c)$,
> $v_n[x]$ is that function f from T to I such that for each $t \in T$,
> $f(t) =$ the nth element of the sequence x.

Definition 6. Let (T, R, I, V) be a model for $\mathscr{L}(\mathcal{O})$ and assume t is in T and x is in I^ω. Then *an atomic formula A of $\mathscr{L}(\mathcal{O})$ is true* at point t in model $M = (T, R, I, V)$ for $\mathscr{L}(\mathcal{O})$ with respect to sequence x in I^ω, in symbols $\overset{M}{\underset{t}{\vDash}} A[x]$ iff

(i)   if A is $Q^n(t_1, \ldots, t_n)$ for some $Q^n \in \mathcal{Q}(n)$, $t_1, \ldots, t_n \in \mathscr{C} \cup \mathscr{V}$, then $(t_1[x](t), \ldots, t_n[x](t)) \in V(Q^n)(t)$,

(ii)   if A is $(t_1 = t_2)$ for some $t_1, t_2 \in \mathscr{C} \cup \mathscr{V}$, then $t_1[x](t) = t_2[x](t)$.

Otherwise the atomic formula A is false at point t in model (T, R, I, V) with respect to sequence x, in symbols $\overset{M}{\underset{t}{\nvDash}} A[x]$.

Definition 7. If $F = (T, R, I)$ is a frame for $\mathscr{L}(\mathcal{O})$, then we say that T is the *universe* of F and I is the *domain* of it.

The treatment of individuals adopted above (and further developed in the quantifier-rule below) is not the only possible one. In the judgement of the present author, it is not even the best or most natural one. Because the problem of individuals and quantifiers in intensional contexts is not the main issue of this paper, we have nevertheless chosen to use this kind of treatment which is rather pleasant to work with. Something similar is also often found in the literature. (See e.g. Kamp, 1971.)

We shall now extend the concept of truth of a formula of $\mathscr{L}(\mathcal{O})$ from the atomic formulas to all formulas of the language. A fundamental concept of our semantics is that of a semantical game tree. This concept is given by the following inductive definition:

Definition 8. Let $\mathcal{T} = (\mathcal{N}, \mathcal{R})$ be a binary structure. Then $\mathcal{T}$ is *the semantical game tree* of a formula A of $\mathcal{L}(\mathcal{O})$ with respect to model $M = (T, R, I, V)$ for $\mathcal{L}(\mathcal{O})$, point t in T, and x in I^ω iff $\mathcal{T}$ satisfies the following conditions:

(1)   There is $r = (\mu_1, \ldots, \mu_4)$ in $\mathcal{N}$ such that $\mu_1 = A$, $\mu_2 = t$, $\mu_3 = x$, and $\mu_4 = (\phi, \phi)$. (Here ϕ is the empty set.)

(2)   Assume $n_1 = (\mu_1, \ldots, \mu_4)$ is in $\mathcal{N}$ and $r\mathcal{R}^k n_1$ for some k in Nat. Then $n_1 \mathcal{R} n_2$ for any $n_2 = (\zeta_1, \ldots, \zeta_4)$ in $\mathcal{N}$ iff μ_1 is a non-atomic formula of $\mathcal{L}(\mathcal{O})$ and the following conditions are fulfilled:

(C.$\sim$) If $\mu_1 = \sim B$ for some formula B of $\mathcal{L}(\mathcal{O})$, then $\zeta_1 = B$, $\zeta_i = \mu_i$ for $i = 2, 3$, and $\zeta_4 = (\mu_4, n_1)$.

(C.$\vee$) If $\mu_1 = (B_1 \vee B_2)$ for some formulas B_1 and B_2 of $L(\mathcal{O})$, then $\zeta_1 = B_1$ or $\zeta_1 = B_2$, $\zeta_i = \mu_i$ for $i = 2, 3$, and $\zeta_4 = (\mu_4, n_1)$.

(C.O) If $\mu_1 = OB$ for some formula B of $\mathcal{L}(\mathcal{O})$ and some O in $\mathcal{O}$, then $\zeta_1 = B$, ζ_2 is any element of T, $\zeta_3 = \mu_3$, and $\zeta_4 = (\mu_4, n_1)$.

(C.U) If $\mu_1 = (v_n)B$ for some formula B of $\mathcal{L}(\mathcal{O})$ and some v_n in $\mathcal{V}$, then $\zeta_1 = B$, $\zeta_2 = \mu_2$, ζ_3 is any element of I^ω otherwise identical with μ_3 but which differs from μ_3 in that the nth element of ζ_3 is allowed to be any element of $\mathcal{T}$, and $\zeta_4 = (\mu_4, n_1)$.

(3)   For each n in $\mathcal{N}$ other than r there is k in Nat such that $r\mathcal{R}^k n$, and for no n in $\mathcal{N}$, $n\mathcal{R}r$.

(4)   There is no binary structure $\mathcal{T}' = (\mathcal{N}', \mathcal{R}')$ such that $\mathcal{T}'$ satisfies (1)–(3) and $\mathcal{N}$ is a proper subset of $\mathcal{N}'$.

When a binary structure $\mathcal{T}$ is the semantical game tree of a formula A with respect to model $M = (T, R, I, V)$, point t in T, and sequence x in I^ω, we write $\mathcal{T} = (\mathcal{N}, \mathcal{R})_{A,x}^{M,t}$. We say that $\mathcal{T}$ is a semantical game tree for $\mathcal{L}(\mathcal{O})$ when there are A, M, t and x such that $\mathcal{T} = (\mathcal{N}, \mathcal{R})_{A,x}^{M,t}$.

We observe without proof that for each formula A of $\mathcal{L}(\mathcal{O})$, each model $M = (T, R, I, V)$, each t in T, and each x in I^ω, $(\mathcal{N}, \mathcal{R})_{A,x}^{M,t}$ is uniquely determined.

The fourth element of the nodes n in $\mathcal{N}$ of our semantical game trees $(\mathcal{N}, \mathcal{R})$ are there just to guarantee that our game trees are always trees in the topological sense of the word. The meaning of a tree we have in mind here is given by the following definition:

Definition 9. A binary structure $(\mathcal{N}, \mathcal{R})$ is a *tree* (in our sense) iff (i) there is a distinguished element r in $\mathcal{N}$ (called the *root* of the tree) such that for no n in $\mathcal{N}$, $n\mathcal{R}r$; (ii) for all n in $\mathcal{N}$ other than r there is k in Nat such that $r\mathcal{R}^k n$; for all n in $\mathcal{N}$ other than r there is precisely one n' in $\mathcal{N}$ such that $n'\mathcal{R}n$.

It can be easily checked that whenever $\mathcal{T}$ is a semantical game tree for $\mathcal{L}(\mathcal{O})$, then $\mathcal{T}$ is also a tree in the sense of the above definition.

Definition 10. Let $\mathcal{T} = (\mathcal{N}, \mathcal{R})$ be a semantical game tree for $\mathcal{L}(\mathcal{O})$. Each element in $\mathcal{N}$ is a *node*. If n is in $\mathcal{N}$ and there is no n' such that n' is in $\mathcal{N}$ and $n\mathcal{R}n'$, then n is *an end node*. A sequence $(n_1, \ldots, n_k)$ with n_i in $\mathcal{N}$ for each i ($1 \leq i \leq k$) is a *path* in $(\mathcal{N}, \mathcal{R})$ iff n_1 is the root of $(\mathcal{N}, \mathcal{R})$ and for each i ($1 \leq i \leq k$) $n_i\mathcal{R}n_{i+1}$. If $(n_1, \ldots, n_k)$ is a path in $(\mathcal{N}, \mathcal{R})$ and n_k is an end node, then the path is a *maximal path*.

As is generally the case in mathematical game theory, the intuitive meaning of the concept of a semantical game tree is not hard to see. A maximal path of a game tree $\mathcal{T}$ represents a play of the corresponding game. Each node in the game tree represents a position in the game, the root representing the initial position. The branches issuing from a given node represent all the different positions that are possible at the next stage of the game. In the definition of a semantical game tree, condition (4) ensures that all the relevant alternatives are present.

It would now be natural to proceed to define which player's move is marked by a given node in a semantical game tree. However, this will not be done here. The reason for this departure from the game-theoretical practice is the general treatment of the usual tense operators (members of $\mathcal{O}$) adopted by us.

Assume that $(\mathcal{N}, \mathcal{R})^{M,x}_{A,t}$ is a semantical game tree for $\mathcal{L}(\mathcal{O})$ with $M = (T, R, I, V)$, t in T, and x in I^ω. Then note that whenever $n = (\mu_1, \ldots, \mu_4)$ is in $\mathcal{N}$, the following statements hold:

(1)   If $\mu_1 = \sim B$ for some formula B of $\mathcal{L}(\mathcal{O})$, then there is precisely one node n' in $\mathcal{N}$ such that $n\mathcal{R}n'$.

(2)   If $\mu_1 = (B_1 \vee B_2)$ for some formulas B_1 and B_2 of $\mathcal{L}(\mathcal{O})$ (not

identical with each other), then there are precisely two nodes n' in $\mathcal{N}$ such that $n\mathcal{R}n'$.

(3)   If $\mu_1 = OB$ for some formula B of $\mathcal{L}(\mathcal{O})$ and some O in $\mathcal{O}$, then there are precisely card(T) many nodes n' in $\mathcal{N}$ such that $n\mathcal{R}n'$.

(4)   If $\mu_1 = (v_n)B$ for some formula B of $\mathcal{L}(\mathcal{O})$ and some v_n in $\mathcal{V}$, then there are precisely card(I) many nodes n' in $\mathcal{N}$ such that $n\mathcal{R}n'$.

(Whenever U is a set, then card(U) is the cardinality of U.)

To complete the definition of a semantical game, it is necessary to define the concept of a semantical pay-off function. As is generally the case in game theory, a pay-off function assigns an outcome to a play of a game. In our case the outcomes are simply the two truth values:

Definition 11. Let $\mathcal{T} = (\mathcal{N}, \mathcal{R})_{A,t}^{M,x}$ be a semantical game tree for $\mathcal{L}(\mathcal{O})$. *The semantical pay-off function* $\Phi(\mathcal{T})$ is a function such that whenever $n = (\mu_1, \ldots, \mu_4)$ is an end node in $\mathcal{T}$, $\Phi(\mathcal{T})(n) = 1$ if the atomic formula μ_1 is true at point μ_2 in model M with respect to sequence μ_3. $\Phi(\mathcal{T})(n) = 0$ otherwise. We now get our fundamental concept:

Definition 12. Let $\mathcal{T}$ be a semantical game tree for $\mathcal{L}(\mathcal{O})$. Then the pair $(\mathcal{T}, \Phi(\mathcal{T}))$ is a *semantical game* (for $\mathcal{L}(\mathcal{O})$).

Our semantical games (in the sense of the above definition) are not strictly speaking games in the sense of mathematical game theory. (See e.g. Gale and Stewart, 1953; Owen, 1968.) The reason is the departure of the game theoretical practice mentioned above, in that our semantical game trees do not tell which player's move a given node marks. Given this extra information, our semantical games would be games in the standard sense of mathematical game theory. (More precisely, they would be two person zero-sum games with perfect information. See Rantala, 1978.) Our reasons for not following the usual game theoretical line of thought were already mentioned. It can be pointed out, moreover, that while we gain in generality by this departure, there is nothing much we lose by it, at least as far as the purposes of the present paper are concerned. For it is the concept of truth of an arbitrary formula of our language that we want to define by reference to our semantical games. And for this purpose the extra information mentioned is not needed, as is shown below.

Even though we want to keep the treatment of the usual tense operators (members of $\mathcal{O}$) as general as possible, the interpretation of these logical symbols cannot of course be left completely arbitrary. Hans Kamp has suggested a general characterization of a tense. We shall adopt Kamp's suggestion here and will define a tense as follows:

Definition 13. (*Kamp*) A (one-place) *tense* is a function which for each binary structure (T, R) assigns a function in $\{0, 1\}^T \to \{0, 1\}^T$.

(See Kamp, 1968; 1971.) Even if this definition were not to be quite adequate, it is general enough for our present purposes. Therefore, we shall make the following assumption:

Assumption. With each O in $\mathcal{O}$, there is a tense f_O.

We can now proceed to extending the concept of truth from atomic formulas of $\mathcal{L}(\mathcal{O})$ to all formulas of it. This can be done by the following value function which for each semantical game for $\mathcal{L}(\mathcal{O})$ assigns a truth value:

Definition 14. Let $(\mathcal{T}, \Phi(\mathcal{T}))$ be a semantical game for $\mathcal{L}(\mathcal{O})$, where $\mathcal{T} = (\mathcal{N}, \mathcal{R})_{A,t}^{M,x}$ is a semantical game tree for $\mathcal{L}(\mathcal{O})$ with root r. Then *the value function* $W(\mathcal{T}, \Phi(\mathcal{T}))$ *for the semantical game* $(\mathcal{T}, \Phi(\mathcal{T}))$ *is* $g(r)$, where g is that function from $\mathcal{N}$ to $\{0, 1\}$ which for each $n = (\sigma_1, \ldots, \sigma_4) \in \mathcal{N}$ satisfies the following conditions:

(W.atom) Assume σ_1 is an atomic formula of $\mathcal{L}(\mathcal{O})$. Then $g(n) = \Phi(\mathcal{T})(n)$.

($W.\sim$) Assume σ_1 is $\sim B$ for some formula B of $\mathcal{L}(\mathcal{O})$. Then $g(n) = 1$ iff $g(n') = 0$ for that node n' in $\mathcal{N}$ such that $n\mathcal{R}n'$.

($W.\vee$) Assume σ_1 is $(B_1 \vee B_2)$ for some formulas B_1 and B_2 of $\mathcal{L}(\mathcal{O})$. Then $g(n) = 1$ iff $g(n_1) = 1$ or $g(n_2) = 1$, where n_1 and n_2 are those two nodes n' in $\mathcal{N}$ such that $n\mathcal{R}n'$.

($W.O$) Assume σ_1 is OB for some formula B of $\mathcal{L}(\mathcal{O})$ and some O in $\mathcal{O}$. Then $g(n) = f_O((T, R))(\bar{B})(\sigma_2)$, where f_O is the tense associated with O and $\bar{B} = \{t' \text{ in } T: \text{there is a node } n' = (\mu_1, \ldots, \mu_4) \text{ in } \mathcal{N} \text{ such that } n\mathcal{R}n', g(n') = 1 \text{ and } \mu_2 = t'\}$. (Here we assume that $M = (T, R, I, V)$.)

($W.U$) Assume σ_1 is $(v_n)B$ for some formula B of $\mathcal{L}(\mathcal{O})$ and some v_n in $\mathcal{V}$. Then $g(n) = 1$ iff for each n' in $\mathcal{N}$ such that $n\mathcal{R}n'$, $g(n') = 1$.

We now arrive at the usual semantical terminology by stipulating that a formula A of $\mathscr{L}(\mathcal{O})$ is *true at a point* t in the universe of a model $M = (T, R, I, V)$ for $\mathscr{L}(\mathcal{O})$ with respect to sequence x in I^ω iff $W(\mathscr{T}, \Phi(\mathscr{T})) = 1$, where $\mathscr{T} = (\mathcal{N}, \mathscr{R})_{A,x}^{M,t}$. In the same way we can define falsity as value 0 of the value function W. Other semantical concepts are defined as usually. A formula A of $\mathscr{L}(\mathcal{O})$ is *true* in model $M = (T, R, I, V)$ iff A is true at each point in the universe of M with respect to each sequence x in I^ω. A formula A is *valid in frame* $F = (T, R, I)$ iff A is true in the model (T, R, I, V) for each interpretation function V. A formula A is *valid* iff it is valid in each frame.

It is not difficult to show that the concept of tense logical validity defined above can be captured by using the more customary Carnap-Tarski type semantics (as developed for intensional languages by Kripke and others). Indeed, if we allow the vocabulary of our language $\mathscr{L}(\mathcal{O})$ to be the one presented by Kamp (1971, Section 4, p. 257) the set of valid formulas obtained is identical with Kamp's.

What is new here is indicated by the observation that game-theoretical semantics meets limiting thesis 4 while Carnap-Tarski type semantics as formulated e.g. by Kamp meets only limiting thesis 2. That game-theoretical semantics satisfies even the condition laid down by limiting thesis 4 suggests that in this framework it is not difficult to present semantics for backwards-looking operators. It is to this problem that we shall now turn.

Syntax for Backwards-Looking Operators

We shall now extend our tense logical language $\mathscr{L}(\mathcal{O})$ so that it contains backwards-looking operators. The extension of $\mathscr{L}(\mathcal{O})$ presented here is only one of several alternatives. Nevertheless, in our judgement it is intuitively the most natural one.

Definition 15. The *vocabulary* of our extended language $\mathscr{L}(\mathcal{O}, \mathscr{D})$ is that of $\mathscr{L}(\mathcal{O})$ together with the set $\mathscr{D}$ of backwards-looking operators defined by: For all O in $\mathcal{O}$, D_O is in $\mathscr{D}$; whenever d is in $\mathscr{D}$, then D_d is in $\mathscr{D}$.

Definition 16. The *formulas* of $\mathscr{L}(\mathcal{O}, \mathscr{D})$ are defined by clauses (i)–(iii) of Definition 3 together with the following extra clauses:

(iv)   If A is a formula, then DA is a formula, for all D in $\mathscr{D}$.

(v)   Nothing else is a formula.

In usual quantification theory, a sentence is defined to be a formula with no free variables. When defining sentences of $\mathscr{L}(\mathcal{O}, \mathscr{D})$ the situation is not quite as simple for now we have to take into account also 'free' occurrences of the new backwards-looking operators. What we mean by a free occurrence of a backwards-looking operator is not hard to see. For the very idea of these new operators is to 'look back' to a point introduced earlier in the same evaluation by an operator. Hence there typically must be such an operator in order for the backwards-looking operator to make clear sense. In case such an operator does exist, the occurrence of a backwards-looking operator considered is 'bound'.

In order for the above line of thought to be applicable, we must somehow correlate occurrences of backwards-looking operators in a formula with 'binding' operators in that formula. The kind of correlation we shall use below is intuitively the following. Given an occurrence of a backwards-looking operator in a formula, the correlated operator will be of the syntactic form given by the subscript of the backwards-looking operator. (The set $\mathscr{D}$ is defined in such a way that there always is such a subscript.) Not just any occurrence of an operator of the right syntactic form will do, however. Rather, the occurrence correlated with a D-operator, say D_d, in a given formula will be that occurrence of the operator d such that it has D_d in its scope and is not correlated with any other operator D_d with larger scope than the given one.

After thus syntactically correlating an occurrence of a D-operator with another operator having that D in its scope, we shall define a semantical requirement which demands that the former refers to the point where the latter was evaluated.

Semantics for Backwards-Looking Operators

In extending our game-theoretical semantics for $\mathscr{L}(\mathcal{O}, \mathscr{D})$ we shall first define the 'correlation' between D-operators and the operators 'binding' them in a precise way. For this purpose, the following concept will be needed:

Definition 17. Let S be any set of ordered pairs (k, O) with k in Nat and O in $\mathcal{O} \cup \mathscr{D}$ such that S is a function. Then S *determines the sequence* sq of operators in $\mathcal{O} \cup \mathscr{D}$ iff sq results from S by the following construction:

(i)   Assume n_1 is the smallest member of Nat in the domain of S. Then let S_1 be S with the pair $(n_1, S(n_1))$ deleted and let sq_1 be $S(n_1)$.

(ii)   Assume S_n and sq_n have been determined, for some n in Nat. Assume S_n is non-empty. Assume further that n_k is the smallest member of Nat in the domain of S_n. Then let S_{n+1} be S_n with the pair $(n_k, S_n(n_k))$ deleted and let sq_{n+1} be $sq_n S_n(n_k)$.

(iii)   Assume S_n and sq_n have been determined, for some n in Nat and S_n is empty. Then sq_n is the resulting sequence.

Note that any non-empty sequence is determined by infinitely many different sets.

Definition 18. Let S be any set that satisfies the conditions of the previous definition. We now define *the grammatical antecedent* of a pair (i, D_d) in S.

(i)   Assume k is the smallest i in Nat such that $(i, D_d) \in S$, for some $D_d \in \mathcal{D}$. Then $(j, d) \in S$ is the grammatical antecedent of (k, D_d) in S iff j is the largest member i of Nat such that $i < k$ and $(i, d) \in S$. If there is no i in Nat satisfying these conditions, then (k, D_d) doesn't have any grammatical antecedent in S.

(ii)   Assume n is the smallest i in Nat such that $(i, D_d) \in S$, for some $D_d \in \mathcal{D}$, there is at least one i' in Nat such that $(i', D_d) \in S$ and $i' < i$, and the grammatical antecedent of (i, D_d) in S is not yet determined. Then $(j, d) \in S$ is the grammatical antecedent of (n, D_d) iff j is the largest i in Nat such that $i < n$, $(i, d) \in S$, and (i, d) is not the grammatical antecedent of any $(n', D_d) \in S$ such that $n' < n$. If there is no i in Nat satisfying these conditions, then (n, D_d) has no grammatical antecedent in S.

It can be shown that whenever S and S' are two sets that determine one and the same sequence of operators, then the following holds. For all $j \in$ Nat and all $D_d \in \mathcal{D}$: If (j, d) is the grammatical antecedent of (i, D_d) in S then there are i' and j' in Nat such that (j', d) is the grammatical antecedent of (i', D_d) in S'; and if (j, d) is the grammatical antecedent of (i, D_d) in S', then there are i' and j' in Nat such that (j', d) is the grammatical antecedent of (i', D_d) in S.

This shows that we could consider grammatical antecedents of occurrences of D-operators directly in sequences of operators, without going through the sets that represent sequences. The condition $(C.D_d)$ on semantical game trees nevertheless can be more easily formulated by using the above defined concept of a grammatical antecedent.

We now turn to defining the concept of a *semantical game tree* of a formula A of $\mathscr{L}(\mathcal{O}, \mathscr{D})$. The definition is obtained from Definition 8 by modifying it as follows. First, we will have to consider formulas of $\mathscr{L}(\mathcal{O}, \mathscr{D})$ everywhere where Definition 8 considered those of $\mathscr{L}(\mathcal{O})$. (Frames and models for the two languages are of course identical.) Second, we will have to add the following extra clause to the construction conditions (2) of the definition:

$(C.D_d)$ Assume $\mu_1 = D_dB$ for some formula B of $\mathscr{L}(\mathcal{O}, \mathscr{D})$ and for some $D_d \in \mathscr{D}$. We have two cases:

(1) Assume there is a node $n = (\delta_1, \ldots, \delta_4)$ in $\mathscr{N}$ such that

  (i) $r\mathscr{R}^i n$ for some $i \in \text{Nat}_0$ (the set of natural numbers with 0) such that $i < k$;

  (ii) $n\mathscr{R}^l n_1$ for some $l \in \text{Nat}$;

  (iii) $\delta_1 = dB_1$ for some formula B_1 of $\mathscr{L}(\mathcal{O}, \mathscr{D})$ and $d \in \mathcal{O} \cup \mathscr{D}$; and

  (iv) (i, d) is the grammatical antecedent of (k, D_d) in the set $S = \{(n, O): n \in \text{Nat}_0 \: O \in \mathcal{O} \cup \mathscr{D}, \text{there is } n' = (\chi_1, \ldots, \chi_4) \in \mathscr{N}$ such that $r\mathscr{R}^n n', n'\mathscr{R}^m n_1$ for some m in Nat_0, and $\chi_1 = OB_2$ for some formula B_2 of $\mathscr{L}(\mathcal{O}, \mathscr{D})\}$.

  Then $\zeta_1 = B$, $\zeta_2 = \delta_2$, $\zeta_3 = \mu_3$, and $\zeta_4 = (\mu_4, n_1)$.

(2) Assume there is no node n satisfying the above conditions (i)–(iv). Then $\zeta_1 = B$, ζ_2 is any element of T, $\zeta_3 = \mu_3$, and (μ_4, n_1).

In $(C.D_d)$, case (1) is the one where we deal with a 'bound' occurrence of a backwards-looking operator. The condition laid down there is fulfilled precisely when there is an operator of the right syntactic sort correlated with the D-operator we are studying, i.e. when the D-operator has a grammatical antecedent in the sequence of operators dominating it. The moment of time to which the D-operator then refers is then the time of the correlated operator. This is precisely what is śtated in case (1) of $(C.D_d)$. It is not hard to see why we have chosen to handle D-operators as universal tense operators when there is no grammatical antecedent. For a formula of the form D_dA (say) does not make any clear statement when we are not told as to which point the backwards-looking operator there refers. Hence it is natural to consider such a formula true only if it is true no matter to which point the problematic D-operator there refers. This stipulation is also motivated by the semantical treatment of formulas with free variables in usual quantification theory. There such formulas are considered true when they are true for all values of the free variables.

The concepts of a semantical game tree for $\mathscr{L}(\mathcal{O}, \mathcal{D})$, and the semantical pay-off function $\Phi(\mathscr{T})$ for a semantical game tree $\mathscr{T}$ for $\mathscr{L}(\mathcal{O}, \mathcal{D})$ are defined analogously to what we did in the case of $\mathscr{L}(\mathcal{O})$. The same remark holds for the concept of a semantical game for $\mathscr{L}(\mathcal{O}, \mathcal{D})$ as well. The concept of the value function (for $\mathscr{L}(\mathcal{O}, \mathcal{D})$) is obtained from Definition 14 by requiring attention to semantical games, semantical game trees and formulas of $\mathscr{L}(\mathcal{O}, \mathcal{D})$ instead of those of $\mathscr{L}(\mathcal{O})$. Moreover, the following extra clause must be added to the conditions that the function g has to satisfy:

($W.D_d$) Assume σ_1 is D_dB for some formula B of $\mathscr{L}(\mathcal{O}, \mathcal{D})$ and some $D_d \in \mathcal{D}$. Then $g(n) = 1$ iff $g(n') = 1$ for all $n' \in \mathcal{N}$ such that $n\mathscr{R}n'$.

All the other semantical concepts are defined as above. This is all we have to do to complete our semantics for the tense logical language $\mathscr{L}(\mathcal{O}, \mathcal{D})$ with backwards-looking operators.

Formalizing 'Would' and 'Then'

We can now go on to formalizing the uses of 'would' and 'then' exemplified in the sentences of the first part of this paper. (It goes without saying that both these particles have uses semantically essentially different from the uses which are of interest for our present purposes.) For this purpose, let H be the usual past tense operator 'always in the past', P its dual operator 'sometime in the past', G the usual future operator 'always in the future' and F its dual operator 'sometime in the future'. The semantics of these operators can be easily spelled out within the above framework. (It can be easily seen what the one-place tenses corresponding to these operators are.) Let further N be Kamp's 'now' operator. Its semantics can also be formulated easily in the game-theoretical framework.

We shall not bother to formalize all the sentences considered in the first part of this paper but will formalize some of them as examples. The reader can then write the remaining formalizations himself or herself.

The sentence (4) can be formalized as follows:

(33) $(v_1)(v_1$ is a man $\supset$ $H(v_1$ supports the Vietnam war $\supset$
NThinks$_{v_1}D_N(v_1$ is an idiot))).

(We follow Hintikka's practice in symbolizing propositional attitudes, clauses such as 'a knows that', 'b believes that' etc. See e.g. Hintikka, 1962; 1969.)

Sentence (6) can be formalized as follows:

(34) $(v_1)(v_1$ is a man $\supset$ $H(v_1$ supports the Vietnam war $\supset$
NBelieves$_{v_1}F$Has-to-admit$_{v_1}D_N(v_1$ is an idiot))).

In (33) as well as in (34) the backwards-looking operator D_N refer to the time where the formula 'starting' with N was considered. This time, in turn, is the one that the past tense operator H introduced, i.e. the time when the supporting took place. This is of course precisely how things ought to be here.

The three readings of (9) can be formalized thus:

(35) PMentions$_{Bob}P$Says$_{Joe}P[(Ev_1)(v_1$ is a child $\wedge$ v_1 is born $\wedge$ $F(v_1$ becomes ruler of the world))].
(36) PMentions$_{Bob}P$Says$_{Joe}P[(Ev_1)(v_1$ is a child $\wedge$ v_1 is born $\wedge$ $D_PF(v_1$ becomes ruler of the world))].
(37) PMentions$_{Bob}P$Says$_{Joe}P[(Ev_1)(v_1$ is a child $\wedge$ v_1 is born $\wedge$ $D_PD_PF(v_1$ becomes ruler of the world))].

Here we have assumed that clauses like 'a mentions that' or 'b says that' are to be analysed as sentential operators. We hence follow Hintikka's practice in symbolizing these clauses. If the reader finds this assumption dubious, he is welcome to try the same sentences with the clearly operator-type locutions 'a knows that' and 'b believes that' substituted for our clauses. The sentences one thus obtains are perfectly acceptable but not quite as natural as our original ones.

What marks a difference between the three readings (35)–(37) of (9) is the moment the future of which the futurity operator F refers to. In (35), F refers to the future of the moment of birth; in (36) it refers to the future of the moment when Joe's saying took place; and finally in (37) F refers to the future of the moment when Bob's mentioning took place. This is precisely what we found to be peculiar to the different readings of 'would' in (9).

In Part I of this paper, we found (21) to be four-ways ambiguous. (Cf. (22)–(25).) We can now formalize these readings as follows:

(38) $PSays_{Joe}P[(Ev_1)(v_1$ is a child $\wedge$ v_1 is born $\wedge$ $F(v_1$ becomes ruler of the world) $\wedge$ $F(v_1$ is widely recognized))].

(39) $PSays_{Joe}P[(Ev_1)(v_1$ is a child $\wedge$ v_1 is born $\vee$ $F(v_1$ becomes ruler of the world) $\wedge$ $D_PF(v_1$ is widely recognized))].

(40) $PSays_{Joe}P[(Ev_1)(v_1$ is a child $\wedge$ v_1 is born $\wedge$ $D_PF(v_1$ becomes ruler of the world) $\wedge$ $F(v_1$ is widely recognized))].

(41) $PSays_{Joe}P[(Ev_1)(v_1$ is a child $\wedge$ v_1 is born $\wedge$ $D_PF(v_1$ becomes ruler of the world) $\wedge$ $D_PF(v_1$ is widely recognized))].

Again, what is essential here are the moments the future of which the futurity operators refer to. The reader can easily ascertain that (38)–(41) differ from each other precisely in the way found characteristic of the different readings of 'would' in (21).

Other 'would'-sentences considered in Part I are only more complicated versions of (21). The reader can formalize them himself or herself without much difficulty.

Methodological Considerations

The reader may feel tempted to ask why we used game-theoretical (and not e.g. the more customary Carnap-Tarski type) semantics for spelling out the semantics of backwards-looking operators. There are important reasons for our choice which we shall now put forward.

In customary intensional logics, the basic semantical concept is that of truth (or falsity) of a formula at a possible world, moment of time, etc., (in a model). This concept is taken as well-defined and, in particular, the concept is not relativized to an evaluation. Thus we completely abstract from the dynamics of evaluation, for the basic concept is independent of it.

What we have to do when defining explicit semantics for backwards-looking operator is to generalize our semantical perspective and somehow bring the concept of a stepwise evaluation into the picture. In Hintikka's game-theoretical semantics, which we have used in this paper, the problem of assigning a well-defined and non-trivial meaning to the idea of an evaluation process is particularly simple to answer. Indeed, one can simply say that this semantical approach has the concept of a step-by-step evaluation built in. This concept also plays a natural and intuitively clear role in the game-theoretical framework.

In contradistinction, the classical Carnap-Tarski approach to semantics is not sufficiently flexible in this respect. Admittedly, one could generalize the approach so as to yield semantics for backwards-looking operators. From a philosophical point of view the resulting semantics for the new type of operators is nevertheless *ad hoc* and weakly motivated. The basic concept is now truth (or falsity) of a formula at a point u with respect to another point v (in a model), or more generally, truth (or falsity) of a formula at a point u with respect to points $v_1, \ldots, v_n$. There are two arguments against this methodology or approach to backwards-looking operators.

First, we do not seem to have any kind of pre-theoretical intuitions about the basic concept of this approach. This observation is further confirmed by the fact that a sentence like

(42)   Every man who was ever introduced to Marilyn Monroe now thinks that he should have kissed her then.

is certainly true or false at the present moment. It is weak, and intuitively incorrect, to argue that this would not be the case and that the truth value of (42) cannot be firmly established since we are not told with respect to which moments of time (in addition to the present moment) the sentence is being considered. Yet if we wish to do justice to the intuitive force of 'then' in (42) we should take this particle as 'looking back', referring back to that moment when the introduction took place. Thus we have to take 'then' in (42) as a backwards-looking operator. In the customary semantical framework its semantics would have to use the concept of truth (or falsity) of a formula at a moment of time with respect to another time as a primitive. But, as we have just argued, this is not in accordance with our intuitions about (42). Whatever our native intuitive semantics is they do not employ such notions, since the truth value of (42) is well established once we are given a moment of time for (42) to be considered at.

Game-theoretical semantics in this respect constitutes a more natural framework than Carnap-Tarski semantics. For the game-theoretical approach allows us to both have our cake and eat it, by providing a possibility both for defining explicit semantics for backwards-looking operators and, by employing the usual and intuitive notion of truth (or falsity) of a formula at a possible world or moment of time (in a model), for dispensing with all relativization to other possible worlds or moments of time.

Second, the idea of an operator referring back to a world, moment of time, etc., is tied up with the notion of a (stepwise) evaluation. It is thus typical that the most natural and intuitive characterization for operators of this kind is in terms of the concept of an evaluation (or a comparable concept, say that of an attempted proof or disproof). In game-theoretical semantics we have a straightforward and natural counterpart to the concept of a step-by-step evaluation. This means, if we give the semantics for backwards-looking operators in the natural way, that these operators are made to do just what they were intuitively intended to do, viz. to refer back to an earlier stage of a stepwise evaluation.

The situation with Carnap-Tarski semantics as a framework for backwards-looking operators is quite different. There is no natural counterpart to the notion of a stepwise evaluation in this approach, even if modified along the lines suggested by Kamp, Vlach, and others. Again, the basic semantic concept – truth of a formula at a point with respect to perhaps many other points – is independent of any evaluation and stands on its own. Admittedly, one can *interpret* the notion in a suitable way and think that the new points have been introduced at earlier stages of a stepwise evaluation. But this is an interpretation to which we need not adhere to.

One intuitive observation also illustrates that the new type of operators are seen in quite a different perspective in the light of game-theoretical semantics as compared to that of the Carnap-Tarski framework. The notion of a *backwards-looking* operator seems to be new in the literature, even though the term describes the intuitive nature of the new operators rather well. Scholars working in the Carnap-Tarski semantical tradition have spoken of *multi-dimensional* operators. The term is well chosen in view of the semantics that these scholars have used. Literally taken, their 'backwards-looking operators' do not look backwards but rather they look at dimensions, i.e., they look at the points with respect to which truth and falsity at a point is relativized. Thus it seems justified to maintain that while the idea of backwards-looking operators has been well-known for some time, their true nature has been blurred by the selection of a wrong general semantical framework.

GENERAL CONCLUSIONS

There is a more general moral which can be drawn from the above discussion. This moral can be expressed in the form of the following general conclusions:

Conclusion 1. Prior type analysis of natural language tenses is essentially defective, at least in being insufficient.

Comment: The basic idea of Prior-type analysis of natural language tenses is to take them as operators. (See e.g. Prior, 1957; 1967; and 1968a.) This is not defective in itself, but it is defective together with the kind of semantical analysis of operators adopted by Prior. Prior's semantics for tenses do not satisfy even limiting thesis 1. And from limiting thesis 1 there is a long step to limiting thesis 5.

Conclusion 2. Even though Prior-type tense analysis is defective and too restricted, we need not analyse tenses as explicit quantifiers.

Comment: Paul Needham (1975; 1976) has also argued for conclusion 1. His argument is based mainly on the claim that there are sentences of English that cannot be expressed in Prior-type tense logic with tenses analysed as operators. From this observation Needham draws the conclusion that tenses should be analysed as explicit quantifiers. This conclusion is nevertheless unjustified. For it is the *semantics* that is defective in Prior, not the *syntax*. In other words, we can analyse tenses syntactically as operators if we make the semantics of the operators powerful enough. Backwards-looking operators are syntactically operators while they are powerful enough to account for the phenomena on which limiting thesis 5 is based.

Conclusion 3. There is an essential similarity between the semantical behaviour of pronounc anaphora and tense anaphora.

Comment: Lauri Carlson has put forward a convincing treatment of pronoun anaphora. The framework Carlson is using is Hintikka's game-theoretical semantics, as developed for natural language directly. (See Carlson, 1975; 1978; and Hintikka and Carlson, 1978.) The game-theoretical import of Carlson's rule for anaphoric pronouns is precisely the same as that of my rule for backwards-looking operators. Backwards-looking operators were put forward above to capture in a formal language the behaviour of certain aspects of tense anaphora.

What has just been said has bearing on the methodological question discussed in the previous section. There we put forward reasons for using game-theoretical semantics for spelling out the semantics of backwards-looking operators. Further evidence in the same vein is now in the offing. Instead of game-theoretical semantics, we could have used a variable-dimensional intensional logic (which meets limiting thesis 5). However, then the connection between tense anaphora and pronoun anaphora would have been missed. (The connection of variable dimensional logics to usual quantification theory is a nontrivial one.)

It could also be claimed that we have not 'really' solved the problem of the 'would'-sentences of part I because we have not given any formalization rules. In other words, we have not explained as to how to arrive on formulas of $\mathscr{L}(\mathcal{O}, \mathscr{D})$ on the basis of the natural language sentences and knowledge of syntax only.

This criticism of our discussion is correct but points beyond the tasks of this paper. We quite agree that in the last analysis, if we want to study a natural language by trying to translate it into a formal language, we must of course make the connection between the two explicit. One particularly convincing way to do this is game-theoretical semantics, as developed for a natural language directly. We did not try to develop game-theoretical semantics in this way for the sentences of part I mainly because this would have necessitated discussion of the game-theoretical treatment of English tenses. This in turn is a large problem-area which contains a number of open problems not of direct relevance to tense anaphora. It seems quite obvious, however, that once a game-theoretical treatment of English tenses is developed, our observations on tense anaphora can easily be incorporated into it.

Academy of Finland

BIBLIOGRAPHY

Åqvist, Lennart (1973), 'Modal Logic with Subjunctive Conditionals and Dispositional Predicates', *Journal of Philosophical Logic*, **2**, 1–76.
Carlson, Lauri (1975), *Peliteoreettista semantiikkaa*, unpublished thesis submitted in partial fulfillment of the requirements for the fil. kand. degree in University of Helsinki, Helsinki.
Carlson, Lauri (1978), 'Strategic Anaphora', forthcoming.
Gabbay, Dov M. (1974), 'Tense Logics and the Tenses of English', in J. M. E. Moravcsik (ed.) *Logic and Philosophy for Linguists*, Mouton, The Hague, 177–186.

Gabbay, Dov M. (1976a), 'Two Dimensional Propositional Tense Logics', in Asa Kasher (ed.) *Language in Focus: Foundations, Methods, and Systems*, D. Reidel Publishing Company, Dordrecht, 569–586.

Gabbay, Dov M. (1976b), *Investigations in Modal and Tense Logics with Applications to Problems in Philosophy and Linguistics*, D. Reidel Publishing Company, Dordrecht.

Gale, D. and F. M. Stewart (1953), 'Infinite Games with Perfect Information', *Annals of Mathematical Studies* **28**, 245–266.

Hintikka, Jaakko (1962), *Knowledge and Belief: An Introduction to the Logic of the Two Notions*, Cornell University Press, Ithaca.

Hintikka, Jaakko (1968), 'Language-Games for Quantifiers', in N. Rescher (ed.) *Studies in Logical Theory*, Basil Blackwell, Oxford. Reprinted with revisions as Chapter III of Jaakko Hintikka, *Logic, Language-Games, and Information*, Clarendon Press, Oxford, 1973.

Hintikka, Jaakko (1969), *Models for Modalities*, D. Reidel Publishing Company, Dordrecht, Holland.

Hintikka, Jaakko (1974), 'Quantifiers vs. Quantification Theory', *Linguistic Inquiry* **5**, 153–177. Reprinted in the present volume, pp. 49–79.

Hintikka, Jaakko (1975a), 'Impossible Possible Worlds Vindicated', *Journal of Philosophical Logic* **4**, 475–484. Reprinted in the present volume, pp. 367–379.

Hintikka, Jaakko (1975b), 'On the Limitations of Generative Grammar', in *Proceedings of the Scandinavian Seminar on Philosophy of Language*, Philosophical Studies published by the Department of Philosophy, University of Uppsala, Uppsala, 1–92.

Hintikka, Jaakko (1976), 'Quantifiers in Logic and Quantifiers in Natural Language', in S. Körner (ed.) *Philosophy of Logic*, Basil Blackwell, Oxford, 208–232. Reprinted in the present volume, pp. 27–47.

Hintikka, Jaakko (1977), 'Quantifiers in Natural Language. Some Logical Problems, II', *Linguistics and Philosophy* **1**, 153–172. Reprinted in the present volume, pp. 81–117.

Hintikka, Jaakko and Lauri Carlson (1977), 'Pronouns of Laziness in Game-Theoretical Semantics', *Theoretical Linguistics* **4**, 1–29.

Hintikka, Jaakko and Lauri Carlson, 'Conditionals, Generic Quantifiers, and Other Applications of Subgames', in A. Margalit (ed.) *Meaning and Use*, D. Reidel, Dordrecht, 1978. Reprinted in the present volume pp. 179–214.

Hintikka, Jaakko and Esa Saarinen (1975), 'Semantical Games and the Bach-Peters Paradox', *Theoretical Linguistics* **2**, 1–20. Reprinted in the present volume, pp. 153–178.

Hintikka, Jaakko and Veikko Rantala (1976), 'New Approach to Infinitary Languages', *Annals of Mathematical Logic* **10**, 95–115.

Jespersen, Otto (1933), *Essentials of English Grammar*, George Allen & Unwin Ltd., London.

Kamp, Hans (1968), *Tense Logic and the Theory of Linear Order*, UCLA dissertation, University Microfilms, Ann Arbor, Michigan.

Kamp, Hans (1971), 'Formal Properties of "Now" ', *Theoria* **37**, 227–273.

Kuhn, Steven (1976), *Many-Sorted Modal Logics*, Stanford dissertation, University Microfilms, Ann Arbor, Michigan.

Moravcsik, Julius M. E. (1975), *Understanding Language*, Mouton, The Hague.

Needham, Paul (1975), *Temporal Perspective*, Philosophical Studies published by the Department of Philosophy, University of Uppsala, Uppsala.

Needahm, Paul (1976), 'The Speaker's Point of View', *Synthese* **32,** 309–327.

Owen, Guillermo (1968), *Game Theory*, W. Saunders Company, London.

Prior, A. N. (1957), *Time and Modality*, Clarendon Press, Oxford.

Prior, A. N. (1967), *Past, Present and Future*, Clarendon Press, Oxford.

Prior, A. N. (1968a), *Papers on Time and Tense*, Clarendon Press, Oxford.

Prior, A. N. (1968b), ' "Now" ', *Nous* **2,** 101–119.

Rantala, Veikko (1978), 'Extension of Partial Isomorphism and Game-Theoretical Semantics', in J. Hintikka, I. Niiniluoto and E. Saarinen (eds.) *Essays on Mathematical and Philosophical Logic*, D. Reidel, Dordrecht.

Saarinen, Esa (1977), 'Game-Theoretical Semantics', *The Monist* **60,** 406–418.

Segerberg, Krister (1973), 'Two-Dimensional Modal Logics', *Journal of Philosophical Logic* **2,** 77–96.

Vlach, Frank (1973), *'Now' and 'Then'. A Formal Study in the Logic of Tense Anaphora*, UCLA dissertation, University Microfilms, Ann Arbor, Michigan.

ESA SAARINEN

INTENTIONAL IDENTITY INTERPRETED: A CASE STUDY OF THE RELATIONS AMONG QUANTIFIERS, PRONOUNS, AND PROPOSITIONAL ATTITUDES*

INTRODUCTION

A problem in philosophical logic has puzzled philosophers, linguists and philosophically-minded logicians. This is the problem which Peter T. Geach (1967) has called the problem of 'intentional identity'. This problem arises for sentences which contain two propositional attitudes, one of them syntactically dominating a quantifier phrase and the other dominating a pronoun whose antecedent is the quantifier phrase.

In this paper, my purpose will be twofold. On the one hand, I shall present a semantics for sentences of this Geachian form in their full variety. On the other hand, I shall put forward a solution to Geach's puzzle in the sense that I shall present semantics for the kind of reading which, I will argue, was intended by Geach. In both these problem areas the discussion is (to the best of my knowledge) the first systematic study available in the literature.[1]

The discussion will also yield a number of other results as by-products. Among the most prominent of these is an observation to the effect that the juxtaposition of propositional attitude contexts and quantifier phrases gives rise to no less than five different kinds of ambiguities. I shall also apply game-theoretical semantics to the natural language sentences studied and demonstrate how the right representations can be obtained in this semantical framework. This will involve further developments within game-theoretical semantics.

GEACH'S PROBLEM STATED

Geach's problem of intentional identity can be best appreciated by

245

E. Saarinen (ed.), Game-Theoretical Semantics, 245–327. All Rights Reserved.

considering a representative example. The one that Geach discusses is
essentially this:

(1)   Hob thinks that a witch has blighted Bob's mare, and Nob
           believes that she (the same witch) killed Cob's sow.

(The original sentence of Geach's contained *wonders whether* where I have
believes that. This is an inessential detail. I have selected the *that*-con-
struction because it is simpler to handle and because *whether*-constructions
are the more narrow, being reducible to *that*-constructions. See Hintikka,
1976a.)

Under the reading of (1) which Geach recognizes, (1) says that Hob and
Nob have attitudes towards one and the same focus (in some sense);
however, neither Hob nor Nob needs to have any particular individual in
mind to serve as that focus. Consequently, there seem to be two conflicting
ideas embedded in (1). On the one hand, both Hob and Nob have an
attitude directed to an individual *de dicto*, non-specifically or non-referen-
tially. On the other hand, their attitudes have an identical focus. But in
modern philosophical logic there does not seem to be any way of fulfilling
the two requirements at the same time.

THE GENERAL PROBLEM OF THE SEMANTICS OF GEACHIAN SENTENCES

The problem created by (1) is a special case of a more general problem:
what is the semantics of sentences which contain two propositional attitudes, the first of which syntactically dominates a quantifier phrase, and the
second of which syntactically dominates a pronoun which refers to that
quantifier phrase?

Knowing that in propositional attitude contexts, as well as in intensional
contexts in general, certain ambiguities are present, it is natural to expect
that sentences of the Geachian form will admit several different readings.
We shall see later that this expectation is fulfilled. It will also turn out that
some of these readings are simpler to handle than others and that in certain
sentences only some readings are natural. Because intuitions about
sentence (1), especially on the reading intended by Geach, seem not very
firm, I shall adopt the strategy of working towards (1) and its intended
reading from simpler sentences.

SEMANTICS FOR INTENSIONAL LOGIC

I shall base the discussion of the sentences of the Geachian form on possible worlds semantics for propositional attitudes. This semantical approach has been advocated by Jaakko Hintikka in his seminal works *Knowledge and Belief* and 'Semantics for Propositional Attitudes'. (Hintikka has later pursued his points in a number of directions. See Hintikka 1969b; 1974a; 1975a; 1976a).

The basic ideas of this approach to the semantics of propositional attitudes are the following ones. Phrases *a knows that, b believes that, c thinks that*, etc. are syntactically analysed as sentential operators (i.e. syntactically they map sentences to sentences). In the semantics, the crucial notions are those of a possible world and of an alternativeness relation. 'Possible world' is often understood as a possible course of events, sometimes as a stage of such. The exact content of this term is left unanalysed here.

For each propositional attitude, there corresponds an alternativeness relation defined on a set of possible worlds. If the attitude we are discussing is 'O_a' (where a is an individual) and the corresponding relation is R, then the relevant truth definition runs[2]

> $O_a p$ is true in the possible world u (in model M) iff for all possible worlds v in the universe of M, if uRv then p is true in the possible world v (in model M).

The following intuitive characterizations can be given for some alternativeness relations:

> a knows that p = in all possible worlds compatible with every-
> thing a knows, p
> b believes that p = in all possible worlds compatible with
> everything b believes, p
> c thinks that p = in all possible worlds compatible with every-
> thing c thinks, p.

The juxtaposition of quantifiers and propositional attitudes is of crucial importance for the problem at hand. The basic situations can be seen by considering representative examples. Let 'F' be some non-intensional one-place predicate and 'b' a singular term. Consider now the following formulas:

(2) $O_a F(b)$

(3) $O_a(Ex)F(x)$

(4) $(Ex)O_a F(x)$

(5) $(x)O_a F(x)$.

Given a possible world u, 'O_a' will introduce a set of possible worlds; let us call this set of worlds the O_a-alternatives to u, or simply the O_a-worlds.

(2) says in the kind of semantics we are here employing that in each O_a-world, the individual who is b in that world is F there. Notice that 'b' can refer to different individuals in different possible worlds.

(3) says that in each O_a-world, there is an existent individual who is F in that world. Again, there is no guarantee that we deal with one and the same individual in the different possible worlds.

(4) says that some individual has the property F in each O_a-world. Here we follow the same individual through a set of possible worlds.

(5) says, finally, that all individuals who exist in all O_a-alternatives, are F in those alternatives.

As a logic for propositional attitudes with quantifiers, this kind of semantics suffers from a number of defects. Some of these defects will be analysed below, with cures suggested for them. We have chosen this customary basis as a starting point in order to avoid too many assumptions the reader might find dubious and unmotivated.

TENTATIVE FORMALIZATIONS OF GEACH'S INTENDED READING

How could we try to formalize the reading of (1) intended by Geach in the above kind of intensional logic? *Prime facie*, the following formula (6) may seem to capture the meaning of (1):

(6) $T_H(Ex)$ (x is a witch & x has blighted Bob's mare) & $B_N(Ey)$ (y is a witch & y killed Cob's sow).[3]

The reason that this formalization seems to work is that here the two attitudes are clearly *de dicto*. They are not directed to any specific individual. However, (6) is not an adequate representation of the meaning of (1) but rather of the meaning of

(7)   Hob thinks that a witch has blighted Bob's mare and Nob believes that a witch has killed Cob's sow.

Clearly (7) and (1) differ in meaning; in (7) there is no guarantee that it is the same witch. This shows also that *she* in (1) cannot be taken as a pronoun of laziness, i.e. as a mere substitute for its antecedent.[4]

Since (7) does not work, one might try instead

(8) $(Ex)(T_H$ (x is a witch & x has blighted Bob's mare) & $B_N(x$ is a witch & x killed Cob's sow)).

However, this formalization will not do the job, either. For (8) speaks about some particular, specific individual (the two attitudes are *de re*), and hence does not symbolize the intended reading of (1) but instead symbolizes the sentence

(9)   In respect to someone, Hob thinks that she is a witch and she has blighted Bob's mare, and Nob believes that she is a witch and she killed Cob's sow.

What is good in formula (8) as symbolization of (1) is that it relates the two witches to each other, something lacking in (6). But as we have seen, (8) does this in a way that makes the formalization defective in other respects.

Even though (8) surely characterizes one reading of (1), it is quite clear that this is not the reading which interests Geach. Indeed, the natural language statement corresponding to (8), i.e. (9), is ruled out by Geach because "it would imply that Hob and Nob has some one person in mind as a suspected witch; whereas it might be the case, to the knowledge of our reporter, that Hob and Nob merely thought there was a witch around and their suspicions had not yet settled on a particular person" (Geach 1967, p. 148). This shows that what makes (8) and (9) defective as representations of the intended reading of (1) is that the former are *de re* whereas the latter is *de dicto*.[5] Hence something more is needed for an adequate analysis of (1) in addition to the use of a Hintikka-type quantified intensional logic.

Although (8) fails one could propose instead something like the following:

(10) $T_H((Ex)\,(x$ is a witch & x has blighted Bob's mare & $B_N(x$ is a witch & x killed Cob's sow))).

This seems *prima facie* better than (8) because now Hob's thoughts are directed to a non-specific witch and the attitude in question is accordingly *de dicto*. However, there are again implications of (10) that make it defective as a formalization of (1). First, in (10) the operator 'B_N' is in the scope of the operator 'T_H'. Thus (10) does not speak of Nob's beliefs as such but as thought by Hob. This is of course undesirable. Second, even though Hob's beliefs are directed to a non-specific individual, Nob's beliefs presumably are not. It seems that (10) forces Nob to have some particular, specific witch in mind.

A somewhat different approach to sentence (1) is to consider *she* as a substitute for a definite description. Accordingly, one might try to paraphrase (1) as follows:

(11) Hob thinks that a witch has blighted Bob's mare, and Nob believes that the witch who blighted Bob's mare killed Cob's sow.

A moment's reflection shows, however, that neither will this approach do. It is customary to observe that there are two possible readings for the definite description in (11); it has either a large or a small scope there. The large scope reading can be more adequately paraphrased as follows:

(12) Hob thinks that a witch has blighted Bob's mare, and the witch who in fact blighted Bob's mare is such that Nob believes of her that she killed Cob's sow.

From this we see immediately that the large scope reading of (11) will not do as an explication of (the intended reading of) (1). For one thing, in (11) the speaker must himself assume that there are witches – an assumption lacking in (1). Moreover in (11) Nob's beliefs have a definite object, they are *de re*, and this is again not the case in (1).

The small scope reading of the definite description in (11) is not much better as an explication of (the intended reading of) (1). This small scope reading can more explicitly be written out as follows:

(13)   Hob thinks that a witch has blighted Bob's mare, and Nob believes that the witch who blighted Bob's mare, whoever she is, killed Cob's sow.

But the truth-conditions of (13) clearly differ from those of (1), under the intended reading. For (1) can be true also in a situation where Nob does not have anything to do with Bob. In particular, Nob need not have any ideas or beliefs about *the witch who blighted Bob's mare*. This possibility is ruled out in the small scope reading of (11). Furthermore, in (13) there is no guarantee that the focuses of Hob's thoughts and Nob's beliefs are identical. In fact, it is questionable whether there is any proper 'focus' of Nob's beliefs in (13).

These observations show that (11) will not do as an explication of (1). Perhaps the reason is that we have been trying to analyse the pronoun *she* in (1) as a substitute for the wrong definite description. For example, one might think that we could paraphrase (1) as follows:

(14)   Hob thinks that a witch has blighted Bob's mare, and Nob believes that the witch Hob had in mind killed Cob's sow.

This proposal, however, creates problems rather than solves them. Indeed, how could the clause *the witch Hob had in mind* be interpreted? (Furthermore, if we interpret the definite description in (14) *de dicto*, then this sentence makes the assumption that Nob has beliefs about Hob and what he had in mind. Such an assumption is lacking from (1).)

We are now starting to see the problem involved in (1). In modern philosophical logic there just does not seem to be any way to represent the intended meaning of (1).

THE PROBLEM SUMMARIZED

The difficulties found above with the reading of (1) intended by Geach could perhaps be summarized in the following way.

Problem 1. In (1) the pronoun *she* is in the scope of the operator introduced by *Hob thinks that* (because the antecedent of the pronoun *she* is in the scope of this operator). Nevertheless, the pronoun *she* is also in the scope of the operator introduced by *Nob believes that*, but this operator is NOT in the scope of the operator first mentioned. In other words, there is a problem of crossing scopes. (On this point, see e.g. Hintikka 1973, p. 201.)

Problem 2. In (1) the focuses of the two attitudes (the witches) are introduced *de dicto*; both attitudes are directed to a non-specific individual. But somehow the two focuses are identical. How is this possible?

Problem 1 is mainly of a technical character whereas Problem 2 involves interpretational and semantico-philosophical aspects. One should also notice – and this will become clearer in what follows – that though both problems are exhibited in intentional identity, they are strictly speaking separate and independent problems.

PROBLEM ONE SOLVED: BACKWARDS-LOOKING OPERATORS

Let us consider Problem 1 first. This problem of 'crossing scopes' can be handled easily by means of the backwards-looking operators which I have discussed elsewhere. (See Saarinen 1977a; 1978.) The idea of a backwards-looking operator is to enable reference back to a possible world (or, more generally, to a point of reference or a feature of a point of reference) that has been considered earlier. I shall not go into the details of the behaviour of the backwards-looking operators here. Their semantics can be spelled out very naturally in Hintikka's game-theoretical semantics. Here it is sufficient to recall just the basic idea. The syntactical form of backwards-looking operator is D_O, i.e., D with a subscript. The subscript can either be an intensional operator of the usual kind (say a necessity or an epistemic operator) or else another backwards-looking operator. The GRAMMATICAL ANTECEDENT of an occurrence of a backwards-looking operator D_O in a formula S is that occurrence of O in S which has as small a scope as possible, which is not the grammatical antecedent of any D with a larger scope than the occurrence of D_O in question, and which has, further, the occurrence of D_O in question in its scope. For instance, consider

(15) $K_a(p \& K_a(q \& D_{K_a}(r \vee D_{K_a}s)))$.

Here the grammatical antecedent of the first occurrence of '$D_{K_.}$' (as counted from left to right) is the second occurrence of 'K_a'. The grammatical antecedent of the second occurrence of 'D_{K_a}' is the first occurrence of 'K_a'.

Let us call the world with respect to which an occurrence of an operator is evaluated the world of that operator. For instance, the world of the first occurrence of 'K_a' in (15) is the actual world. When this logical particle is evaluated, an epistemic alternative of a's (with respect to the actual world) is selected, say v, and the formula immediately following 'K_a' in (15) is considered in v. Thus the world of the second occurrence of 'K_a' is v, etc. These considerations indicate that given an evaluation of a sentence S, the world of (an occurrence of) an operator O occurring in S is uniquely determined. But for different evaluations of the sentence, the world of that occurrence of O may be different. For instance in (15) the first 'K_a' will introduce all epistemic alternatives of a's with respect to the actual world. The world where the second 'K_a' is then considered (the world of that operator) will vary in different evaluations through all epistemic alternatives of a's with respect to the actual world.

The semantics of the backwards-looking operators can be spelled out by stipulating that AN OCCURRENCE OF A BACKWARDS-LOOKING OPERATOR ALWAYS REFERS TO THE WORLD OF ITS GRAMMATICAL ANTECEDENT. For instance in (15) the first 'D_{K_a}' refers to the world of the second 'K_a', i.e. to the world where the formula

(16) $K_a(q \& D_{K_a}(r \vee D_{K_a}s))$

was considered. Similarly for the second 'D_{K_a}' and the first 'K_a' in (15).

In presenting an explicit semantics for backwards-looking operators, I used Hintikka's game-theoretical semantics. In this semantical framework the semantical evaluation process takes place from outside in. The semantical vocabulary also contains a perfect 'memory' in the sense that all earlier stages of an evaluation can always be recalled. These two facts indicate two important differences between the game-theoretical semantics and the customary Carnap–Tarski semantics (as extended to intensional languages by Stig Kanger, Saul Kripke, and others).[6] From the point of view of the backwards-looking operators the two facts are of vital importance. They have the consequence that backwards-looking operators naturally 'fit in' the game-theoretical framework in contrast to the customary Carnap–Tarski semantics in which they do not belong.

My treatment of backwards-looking operators can be generalized in an obvious way to cases where we deal with points of reference with several co-ordinates rather than with possible worlds. Then we can develop backwards-looking operators which refer back to some co-ordinate of a point of reference considered earlier. (In an analysis of the semantics of natural language such points of reference with several co-ordinates are needed, anyway. See Lewis 1972 on this matter. We shall make use of points of reference with two co-ordinates in some of the examples below.)

Consider again the problem of sentence (1). It arose because the operator introduced by *Nob believes that* is in the scope of a quantifier which in turn is in the scope of the operator introduced by *Hob thinks that.* Consequently the former operator is (syntactically), but should not be (semantically), in the scope of the latter operator. The backwards-looking operators present a solution to the problem. All we have to do is to put the *Nob*-clause in the immediate scope of a backwards-looking operator that refers to the world where the *Hob*-clause was considered. By this procedure the *Nob*-clause is drawn out of the scope of the operator introduced by *Hob thinks that* while the pronoun in the *Nob*-clause is still bound by the quantifier phrase *a witch* of the Hob-clause. In other words, we can remedy (10) as a formalization of (1) by writing instead of (10) the following:

(17) $T_H(Ex)$ (x is a witch & x has blighted Bob's mare & $D_{T_H}B_N$ (x is a witch & x killed Cob's sow)).

Here 'D_{T_H}' refers to the original world, the world where the whole evaluation started. This makes (17) immune to the first kind of criticism levelled against it as a formalization of (1).

In describing (1) Geach points out that (1) raises the difficulty that "a pronoun in our indirect speech clause is on the face of it bound to a quantified phrase in ANOTHER such oblique context; the scope of the quantified phrase thus seems BOTH to lie wholly within the earlier oblique context AND to cover something in the later context. I cannot even sketch

a structure of operators that would make good logical sense of this..."
(Geach 1967, p. 150). The new operators for which Geach is hunting here
come close enough to the backwards-looking operators. Their interplay
with quantifiers and usual operators is precisely what Geach describes. The
reader can ascertain this for himself by considering (17).

By way of a historical remark, it may be observed that in addition to
Hans Kamp's (1971) *now* operator, backwards-looking operators are a
generalization of an idea briefly suggested by David Kaplan (1972) in
homework problem 19. There Kaplan considers an ill-formed formula
whose truth conditions are natural enough and can be readily grasped. The
crucial point there is that the import of Kaplan's meaningful but ill-formed
formula can easily be expressed in terms of a well-formed formula if that
new formula is allowed to contain backwards-looking operators. We could
here illustrate the import of backwards-looking operators by observing
that the following Kaplanesque ill-formed formula is 'equivalent' to (17):

(17)′ T_H [(Ex) (x is a witch & x has blighted Bob's mare] & B_N[x is a witch & x killed Cob's sow]).

The first two brackets here indicate the scope of 'T_H' and the parentheses
the scope of the existential quantifier.

(While this example illustrates the behaviour of backwards-looking
operators it may be misleading in another respect. For it may suggest that
all uses of backwards-looking operators can be dispensed with in terms of
ill-formed formulas with obvious truth conditions. This is not the case,
however.)

Even though backwards-looking operators solve the technical problem
involved in Problem 1, they do not automatically yield any solution to
Problem 2, which is the really interesting problem here.

For instance, as far as Geach's problem is concerned, it is far from clear
that (17) did come close to capturing the intended truth conditions. Indeed,
it seems that (17) cannot serve as a semantical representation of (1), for
(17) seems to force Nob's beliefs to be *de re*, not *de dicto*. (17) would seem
to commit Nob to have some particular, specific witch in mind as the
suspected killer. But this would seem to show that (17) differs from the
intended reading of (1).

THE INCLUSION REQUIREMENT AND THE SEMANTICS OF GEACHIAN SENTENCES OF THE SIMPLEST KIND

I will not tackle Problem 2 directly but will rather try to sharpen our intuitions on it by working towards the solution from simpler cases. Let us therefore first consider certain sentences of the troublesome Geachian form which semantically turn out to be surprisingly simple. Consider

(18)   Joan believes that someone stole her car. Joan also believes that he (that person) tried to break into her house.

Essentially, this sentence is syntactically similar to (1). What marks a difference is that in (18) we deal with only one attitude of only one person. For this reason, the intuitive meaning of (18) is easy to grasp, and could be expressed in the customary notation as follows:

(19) $B_J(Ex)$ (x stole Joan's car & x tried to break into Joan's house).

Even though (19) unmistakably characterizes the truth-conditions of (18), (19) does not solve all our problems here. For one thing, how could we arrive at (19) on the basis of (18) and syntax only? The syntax of (18) differs in an essential respect from that of (19); (18) contains two belief-operators whereas (19) contains only one. Moreover, notice that in customary logical notation we could not replace (19) with

(20) $B_J((Ex)$ (x stole Joan's car & $D_{B_J}B_J$ (x tried to break into Joan's house))).

(Here 'D_{B_J}' is a backwards-looking operator that refers to the world where 'B_J' was considered.) The truth-conditions of (20) differ from those of (19). The difference between the two is most easily seen by observing that (20), but not (19), demands that each value of x is such that Joan believes of him that he tried to break into Joan's house. This is the case because in (20) we quantify into a belief-context – something we do not do in (19). (Thus (20) makes the second belief in (18) *de re*.)

GAME-THEORETICAL SEMANTICS FOR ENGLISH

An answer to the question of how to arrive at (19) on the basis of (18) and syntax only is forthcoming in game-theoretical semantics. For a reader familiar with the results already achieved in game-theoretical semantics for English, it probably is not a surprise that game-theoretical ideas are also fruitful for he analysis of the problems discussed in this paper. We are discussing certain recalcitrant cases of the interplay of quantifiers, intensional verbs and anaphoric expressions. Game-theoretical semantics has already achieved impressive results as a theory of these phenomena.

It would be helpful if the reader were acquainted with the basic ideas of game-theoretical semantics. (See the writings of Hintikka, Carlson and myself cited in the bibliography.) In order to make the discussion as self-contained as possible, I shall nevertheless briefly state the main ideas of game-theoretical semantics and also present a list of all the game-theoretical rules and principles that will be used in this paper.

The key concepts of game-theoretical semantics are that of a two-person semantical game $G(S)$ associated with a sentence S and that of the strategies of two players (to be called the defender and the opponent) in such a game. At each stage of a game, a sentence is being considered at a possible world. Furthermore, since in game-theoretical semantics we are working with an interpreted language, we assume that a model of a suitable kind is given. In the case of (18), for instance, such a model will be of the form (U, u, D, R, V), where U is a non-empty set of possible worlds; $u \in U$ is the actual world; $D(u)$, for each $u \in U$, is a non-empty set of individuals existing in u; $R \subseteq U \times U$ is the doxastic alternativeness relation of Joan's; and V is an interpretation function which interprets all nonlogical symbols of the fragment of English we are studying in $D(u)$, for each $u \in U$. Because of the dependency of a semantical game on the model given, it is more appropriate to talk not of a game $G(S)$ associated with a sentence S but of a game $G(S, M)$ associated with a sentence S and model M (of a suitable kind). The structure of the game will depend on the sentence under investigation, according to the rules to be given below. A finite number of applications of the game rules will lead the players to consider an 'atomic' sentence to which no game rule applies. The pay-offs of the players are thereupon defined. If the sentence is true (false) at the possible world and in the model considered, then the defender (the opponent) has won the game.

The semantical properties of the original sentence S are now defined by reference to the player's strategy sets in $G(S, M)$. In particular, S is true (false) at u in M iff the defender (the opponent) has a winning strategy in $G(S, M)$.

The game rules that we shall use in this paper can be presented as a list of the following game rules which are special cases of more general rules:

($G.and$)   Assume the game has reached a possible world v and a sentence of the form
$$S_1 \text{ and } S_2.$$
Then the opponent may choose either one of the conjuncts and the game is continued with respect to v and the sentence selected.

($G.or$)   This game rule is similar to ($G.and$) except that the relevant selection is made by the defender.

($G.some$)   Assume the game has reached a possible world v and a sentence of the form
$$X - \text{some } Y \text{ who } Z - W.$$
Then the defender may choose an individual (from the domain of discourse), give it a name, say 'a', and the game is continued with respect to v and the sentence
$$X - a - W, a \text{ is a(n)} Y \text{ and } aZ.$$
(Here '$X - S - W$' indicates that expression 'S' occurs in context $X - W$.)

The reader can easily construct the corresponding rule for the indefinite article a, thus formulating rule ($G.an$).

($G.believes that$)   Assume the game has reached a possible world v and a sentence of the form
$$X - a \text{ believes that } S - Y.$$
Then the opponent may choose a possible world w such that w is a doxastic alternative of a's with respect to v. The game is continued with respect to w and the sentence
$$X - S - Y.$$

Corresponding rules ($G.thinks that$), ($G.knows that$), etc. for other intensional verbs can also be readily given. (This is left to the reader.)

In (*G.some*) we have spoken of picking out an individual 'from the domain of discourse'. Such a domain of discourse will of course depend on the model we are working with in that semantical game, as well as on the world in which (*G.some*) is applied. In a precise treatment we would have to account for both of these facts, but here we shall be content with the informal rule (*G.some*). (Below, we shall nevertheless discuss in some more detail the import of this and other quantifier rules.)

The order in which the game rules are applied is determined by ordering principles, the most fundamental ones of which are the following:

(*O*.comm)   If an expression O_1 commands (occurs in a higher clause than) another expression O_2, a game rule must be applied to O_1 before one is applied to O_2.

(*O*.LR)   If an expression O_1 precedes another expression O_2 in the left-to-right order, a game rule must be applied to O_1 before one is applied to O_2.

Over and above these basic principles, a number of more specific ordering principles must be given. One observation that is relevant for the present study concerns the ordering principle (*O.an*) governing the indefinite article. According to it, (*G.an*) normally has precedence over (*G.believes that*) and the other rules governing intensional verbs. (Similarly for (*G.some*) and rules governing intensional verbs.) This ordering principle takes care of the familiar Russellian scope ambiguity that arises when considering the quantifier phrase '*a X who Z*' in intensional contexts.

Normally we require that (*G.and*) and (*G.or*) cannot be applied if there is a pronominal reference between the conjuncts (disjuncts) (see e.g. Hintikka 1974b). Once rule (*G.pron*)* is put forward below, the requirement can be dropped, however.

One important further development of game-theoretical semantics, put forward by Carlson and Hintikka, has to be acknowledged. This is the possibility of using 'supergames', games consisting of several SUBGAMES. Subgames are here games in the sense explained above; supergames are ordered sequences of such subgames, with a special definition of winning and losing. Only such special cases are of interest to us here as those in which we use supergames to explicate the semantics of independent sentences, and these sentences are adjoined by some such device as conjunction, full stops or partial stops.

The relevant definition of winning and losing states, in the special case that interests us here, that the defender (opponent) has a winning strategy in a supergame G iff he has one in each of the subgames G_n of which the supergame consists (the opponent has one in at least one of the subgames G_n). Carlson and Hintikka have formulated the following principle which governs the order in which the subgames are played:

Progression Principle: If G_1 and G_2 are subgames in a game G, then G_1 has to be played before G_2 if the sentence associated with G_1 occurs earlier in the left-to-right order than the sentence associated with G_2.

Why the order of the subgames is important will become clear later on.

GAME-THEORETICAL SEMANTICS FOR SENTENCES SATISFYING THE INCLUSION REQUIREMENT

Consider again:

(18)   Joan believes that someone stole her car. Joan believes he tried to break into her house.

Because (18) consists of two sentences, it is natural to analyse it as two independent though related semantical units. In terms of game-theoretical semantics, this means that (18) is taken to involve a supergame G which consists of two subgames G_1 and G_2. Because of the progression principle, the supergame will proceed from left to right and subgame G_1 will thus be the semantical game associated with the sentence

(21)   Joan believes that someone stole her car

and the given model (U, u, D, R, V).

Because of the familiar scope ambiguity, G_1 will either start with an application of $(G.some)$, and only after that proceed with $(G.believes\ that)$, or else the other way round. The former possibility will produce a *de re* reading of (18), and it is therefore disregarded here. Thus G_1 starts with an application of $(G.believes\ that)$. Accordingly, the opponent selects a world

$v \in U$ such that uRv and the game G_1 is continued with respect to the world v and the sentence

(22)   Someone stole Joan's car.

(Here we assume that the pronominalization of *her* by *Joan* in (21) is unproblematic.) G_1 continues by an application of the rule (*G.some*) and thus marks a choice of an individual by the defender. In consequence, he will pick out an individual, say Jack, from $D(v)$, and the game G_1 is continued with respect to the world v and the sentence

(23)   Jack stole Joan's car.

Now the game G_1 ends (we do not analyse tenses here). If (23) is true at v in model (U, u, D, R, V), then the defender wins G_1; if false, then the opponent wins it. It can now be determined which one of the two players has a winning strategy in G_1. If it is the opponent who has it, she has one also in the supergame G, and the game thus ends. For if the opponent has a winning strategy in G_1 this means that sentence (21) is false in the model considered. In consequence the sentence (18) is also of course false. If the defender has a winning strategy in G_1, then the players go on to the subgame G_2. For if the defender has a winning strategy in G_1 this means that sentence (21) is true in our model. This does not yet establish that the whole sentence (18) is true, however. Thus the players have to go on to consider subgame G_2.

Subgame G_2 is a game associated with the sentence

(24)   Joan believes that he tried to break into her house.

But what is the model this game is associated with? The two obvious candidates are (U, u, D, R, V) and (U, v, D, R, V) i.e. the original model and this model with the world v as the original world. (Here v is the world which was selected when (*G. believes that*) was applied in G_1.)

If we chose the latter alternative, it would in effect mean that in (18) the latter sentence would be BELIEVED by Joan rather than stated to hold of the actual world as such. Since this is not how things are intuitively in (18), this excludes the possibility of taking v as the original world for G_2 to start from.

Similar criticism cannot be levelled against taking u as the world for G_2

to start from. Generalizing the observation, we shall put forward the following SENTENCE BOUNDARY PRINCIPLE according to which a non-initial subgame G_n in a supergame G is always started with respect to the same world as was the initial subgame.

It will not take long to observe that this principle cannot be anything but a first approximation. The dynamics of a text are more complicated than our simple model suggests. However, a more adequate study would take us to the central problems of text linguistics and thus too far from the main problem area of this paper. We shall therefore be content with the above admittedly roughly formulated principle.

Thus G_2 is the semantical game associated with (24) and model (U, u, D, R, V). Because of $(O.comm)$ and $(O.LR)$ we have to apply first $(G.believes\ that)$. Hence the opponent may select a world $w \in U$ such that uRw. The game G_2 is continued with respect to the world w and the sentence

(25)   He tried to break into Joan's house.

(Again, we consider the pronominalization of *her* by *Joan* in (24) unproblematic.) Now we have to interpret the problematic pronoun *he*. How is this done?

The most convincing treatment of anaphoric pronouns we have seen is that put forward by Lauri Carlson. (See Carlson 1975; Carlson 1978, and Hintikka and Carlson 1978.) In the above case, we are dealing with what Carlson has called 'strategic anaphora'. On the basis of what has been assumed, we know that the defender has a winning strategy f in G_1. Essentially, strategy f is a function which in each doxastic alternative of Joan's with respect to u picks out an individual who stole Joan's car in that world. But the world w, where (25) is considered, is a doxastic alternative of Joan's with respect to u. Accordingly, it is already known that f will pick out an individual in that world. Hence, what is more natural than to interpret the *he* of (25) to refer to that uniquely determined individual which f picks out for w in G_1? Assume that the individual is Bob. Then we end up considering at w the sentence

(26)   Bob tried to break into Joan's house.

The truth or falsity of (26) at w in (U, u, D, R, V) is assumed to be given. If the sentence is true, then the defender has won G_2; if false, then the opponent is the winner.

It can now be determined which one of the players has a winning strategy in G_2. If the defender has one, then he also has one in G. This shows that sentence (18) is true in the model considered. If the opponent has a winning strategy in G_2, she has one in G also, and sentence (18) is thus found to be false in the model considered.

The above semantical game can be 'translated' into a higher-order logic. The output is something like the following:

(27) $(Ef)(v \in U)(w \in U)(uRv \supset f(v)$ stole Joan's car in v & $(uRw \supset f(w)$ tried to break into Joan's house in $w))$.

(Here we assume that the existential quantifier ranges over functions of the appropriate sort, i.e., for each $u \in U$, $f(u)$ is a member of $D(u)$.) Notice that (27) corresponds to (19) in the sense that the truth-conditions of the two are the same. Because of the functional character of f, if $v = w$, then of course $f(v) = f(w)$. Together with the trivial fact that $R \subseteq R$ this secures the identity of the one who stole the car with the one who tried to break into the house. Also we get an explanation of why (19) could serve in a first-order logic with intensional operators as the semantical representation of (18).

These observations show that in order to handle the semantics of (18) in game-theoretical semantics, we just have to apply Carlson's notion of strategic anaphora in a straightforward way.

It is obvious that the above kind of treatment of intentional identity can be generalized to cover all cases which are otherwise syntactically like (18) but which contain other intensional verbs in the place of Joan's beliefs. Sentences that can thus be handled include, for example:

(28) John wants to write a book. He wants to publish it in Holland.

The treatment can be generalized to some other, less obvious cases, too. Consider the semantical game described above. We had to consider the problematic pronoun only when the defender had a winning strategy f in the subgame associated with the first statement on (18), i.e., with sentence (21). Given a doxastic alternative world w, the pronoun he of (25) then refers to that uniquely determined individual which f selects for w. The strategy f is defined for each world that the opponent could possibly select, for we are dealing with the same worlds here in the latter clause as in the first one.

This suggests a way to generalize the treatment. For obviously what we just said holds *a fortiori* when in the second conjunct we are dealing with a SUBSET of those worlds which we considered in the first conjunct. Somewhat more precisely, the existence of the defender's winning strategy in the first subgame implies that for all $v \in U$, if uRv, then $f(v)$ is defined. But then it is a trivial set-theoretical point that f is also defined for all $w \in U' \subseteq \{v \in U : uRv\}$.

This observation implies that some cases of intentional identity become quite as easy to handle in game-theoretical semantics as (the most natural reading of) (18). One case in point is

(29)   Joan knows that Hank has written a book. She believes that it was a best-seller.

Here we assume – as is natural – that knowledge implies belief. As a consequence, each doxastic alternative of Joan's (with respect to a given world) is also an epistemic alternative of hers (with respect to the given world).

It is of course the *de dicto* reading of (29) that interests us here. The semantical game G associated with (29) is defined once a suitable model is given. The model now must be of the form (U, u, D, R_1, R_2, V), where U, u, D, and V are as before, but $R_1 \subseteq U \times U$ is the epistemic alternativeness relation of Joan's while $R_2 \subseteq U \times U$ is her doxastic alternativeness relation.

G will again consist of two subgames G_1 and G_2. Only in case the defender has a winning strategy in the subgame G_1 will the subgame G_2 be considered. Since it is the second subgame in which the anaphoric pronoun is interpreted, we assume that the defender indeed has a winning strategy f in subgame G_1, i.e., in the semantical game associated with the given model and the sentence

(30)   Joan knows that Hank has written a book.

(This semantical game is quite straightforward and can be easily constructed on the basis of the subgame G_1 described above.) From our assumptions it readily follows that for each world $v \in U$ such that uR_1v, $f(v)$ is a book written by Hank at v. Because (29) satisfies what we will call the INCLUSION REQUIREMENT (i.e., the worlds introduced by the latter intensional verb are a subclass of those introduced by the former) it follows that $f(w)$ is defined also for each world w that the opponent possibly could select in subgame G_2.

The semantical representation of (29) is, again using a higher-order formula, something like the following:

(31) $(Ef)(v \in U)(w \in U)(uR_1v \supset f(v)$ is a book in v & Hank has written $f(v)$ in v & $(uR_2w \supset f(w)$ is a best-seller in w)).

(We assume again that the existential quantifier ranges over functions of the appropriate sort.)

Strategy f can of course pick out different individuals in the different possible worlds that we shall have to consider in (29). This shows that both the attitudes in (29) are properly *de dicto*. Nevertheless the interpretation of the anaphoric pronoun is quite straightforward.

The above kind of treatment of intentional identity can be given when the second intensional verb introduces worlds which are a subclass of worlds introduced by the first verb. The theory also seems to give an explanation for certain grammatical constraints on the intentional identity statements. Consider the following:

(32)   It is certain that Sam will find a girl and possible that he will kiss her.

(33)   It is possible that Sam will find a girl and certain that he will kiss her.

These examples are due to George Lakoff (1972). (32) can be handled in the same way as (29) because the principle

(34)   If it is certain that p then it is possible that p

is intuitively valid. For (33) similar analysis cannot be given because the converse of (34) is not valid. Lakoff suggests that (33) is ungrammatical and that the fact just quoted is the explanation for the ungrammaticality. That (33) is ungrammatical does not strike me as self-evident. Indeed, below I shall suggest a natural way to interpret sentences such as (33).

The kind of treatment of intentional identity just put forward seems to be due to George Lakoff (1972). The same point has been made more precisely in game-theoretical framework by Lauri Carlson in Carlson

(1975). In what follows, we shall call the above kind of approach to intentional identity the LAKOFF-TYPE APPROACH.

LIMITATIONS OF THE LAKOFF-TYPE APPROACH

The Lakoff-type approach presents an extremely natural treatment of some cases of intentional identity. The limitations of this kind of approach are nevertheless quite obvious. Indeed, the very idea of the approach rules out quite a number of statements exemplifying intentional identity. Every sentence that does not satisfy the inclusion requirement is *per definitionem* beyond the limits of this approach. Moreover, contrary to what the Lakoff-type approach suggests, not all sentences which fail to satisfy the inclusion requirement are ungrammatical. Hence the kind of explanation of the ungrammaticality of (33) *vis-à-vis* the grammaticality of (32) does not work in all cases and seems *ad hoc* here.

Counterexamples to the Lakoff-type approach are not hard to come by. Consider for instance the following:

(35)   Ernie believes that he will find a proof for the theorem. He is sure it will not be an elegant proof.

For this sentence one cannot give a Lakoff-type semantics because certainly one is not sure of everything one believes to be the case. On the other hand, (35) is quite acceptable syntactically and also has clear intuitive meaning.

This shows that the Lakoff-type inclusion requirement does not give a satisfactory general characterization of intentional identity. It is simply false to claim that an intentional identity statement which does not satisfy the inclusion requirement is automatically ungrammatical. (That is, it is false to claim that if the worlds introduced by the second intensional verb are not included in those introduced by the first one, then the sentence is ungrammatical.)

Other counterexamples to the Lakoff-type approach include the following:

(36)   It is probable that Larry danced with some girl. It is certain that she was good-looking.

(37)   Ed believes that Larry kissed some girl last night. Ed is certain
        that she was pretty.

(38)   Herb intends to publish a paper. Sam is sure that it will be
        weak.

(39)   Mary wants to marry a young man. He must be rich.

These observations suffice to show that the kind of treatment of intentional identity presented above does not give us a general characterization of the situation.

SECOND SOLUTION: THE 'UNIVERSAL' READING OF THE PROBLEMATIC PRONOUN

In order to see how to handle the above counter-examples to Lakoff-type analysis, let us consider (40):

(40) = (37) Ed believes that Larry kissed some girl last night. Ed is certain
             that she was pretty.

Because belief does not imply certainty, this sentence cannot be handled using the Lakoff-type approach.

One natural reading of (40) can be intuitively approached thus. Assume Ed believes that Larry kissed either Joan, Jill or Janet last night but Ed is not sure which one Larry actually kissed. Assume further that Ed is certain that each of these girls is pretty. According to our lights, we could then truly assert (40). This suggests a more general moral which yields the following formalization of (40):

(41) $B_E((Ex)$ (x is a girl & Larry kissed x last night) & $D_{B_E}C_E$ (x
        was pretty))).

Here 'D_{B_E}' is a backwards-looking operator that refers to the world where 'B_E' was considered.

In this analysis, (40) comes close to being synonymous with the following sentence

(43)   Ed is certain that any girl Larry could, for all that Ed believes,
        have kissed last night was pretty.

Yet there is a slight difference between (40) and (43). For (43) presupposes that of each girl such that Larry kissed her last night (for all that Ed believes) Ed is certain that she was pretty. This is not presupposed by (40). The 'universality' involved there is of a slightly different kind; for each belief-alternative of Ed's there must be a girl that Larry kissed last night, and of each of these girls Ed must believe that she was pretty.

The difference between (40) and (43) would vanish if for each belief-alternative of Ed's there would be just one girl kissed by Larry last night. One might think *prima facie* that in fact the use of the singular pronoun *she* in the latter conjunct of (40) entails such an assumption. Nevertheless, this is not the case. To see the point compare (40) and (43) with

> (44)   Ed believes that Larry kissed at least one girl last night. Ed is certain that she was pretty.
>
> (45)   Ed believes that Larry kissed precisely one girl last night. Ed is certain that she was pretty.

(44) shows that the singular pronoun *she* does not impose a 'uniqueness' condition on is antecedent. Thus it in effect demonstrates the inadequacy of the above proposal concerning (40).

Intuitively, there is a difference in meaning between (40), (44) and (45). Furthermore, it seems that the difference is the same as the one exhibited in the difference between (46), (47) and (48):

> (46)   Larry kissed some girl last night. She was pretty.
> (47)   Larry kissed at least one girl last night. She was pretty.
> (48)   Larry kissed precisely one girl last night. She was pretty.

These observations perhaps make it clear that (41) indeed captures the most natural reading of (40).

Even though we thus have characterized the truth-conditions of (40), we can ask how we could arrive at (41), or something equivalent, on the basis of (40) and syntax only. This problem will be discussed in the next section.

GAME-THEORETICAL SEMANTICS FOR THE 'UNIVERSAL' READING

Again, I shall present a solution to the problem just stated using game-theoretical semantics. The semantical game associated with (40) is defined once a model of a suitable kind is given. In the case of (40), such a model will be of the form (U, u, D, R_1, R_2, V), where U, u, D, and V are as before and $R_1 \subseteq U \times U$ is the doxastic alternativeness relation of Ed's and $R_2 \subseteq U \times U$ is his certainty alternativeness relation.

Let us consider the semantical game associated with (40) and the given model first from a general level.

One relevant observation is that associated with (40) we have a super-game consisting of two subgames. This is the case because (40) consists of two separate sentences. We must also keep in mind the progression principle of Carlson and Hintikka according to which the supergame proceeds from left to right. Furthermore, a relevant principle is the sentence boundary principle, formulated above.

Let us now consider the game associated with (40) in more detail. Because of the progression principle, game G starts with subgame G_1 which is the game associated with the given model and the sentence

(49)   Ed believes that Larry kissed some girl last night.

As far as the ordering principles are concerned, we have a choice between two different games here. Either we start with (*G.some*) and only after that apply (*G.believes that*), or else we proceed the other way round. The first possibility would produce a straightforward *de re* reading of (40) and is therefore not of interest here. Thus G_1 starts by an application of the rule (*G.believes that*). Hence the opponent selects a doxastic alternative of Ed's with respect to u, say her choice is v. (We assume that the given model is (U, u, D, R_1, R_2, V).) The game G_1 is continued with respect to v and the sentence

(50)   Larry kissed some girl last night.

We shall not analyse tenses here. For this reason, the next step in game G_1 is an application of the rule (*G.some*). Hence the defender selects an individual, say Barbara, from $D(v)$, and the game G_1 is continued with respect to v and the sentence

(51)   Larry kissed Barbara last night and Barbara is a girl.

An application of the rule (*G.and*) will now run the game G_1 into an end, for it involves a choice of either one of the conjuncts of (51), and the game ends in considering at v the conjunct selected. If the sentence is true at v in model (U, u, D, R_1, R_2, V), then the defender has won the game G_1; otherwise the opponent has won. It can now be determined which one of the two players has a winning strategy in G_1. If the opponent has one, the supergame G ends and she wins it. If the defender has a winning strategy in G_1, the game G is continued by subgame G_2.

Subgame G_2 is the semantical game associated with the sentence

(52)   Ed is certain that she was pretty

and the model (U, u, D, R_1, R_2, V). (Notice that because of the sentence boundary principle, the relevant model is the one just given rather than (U, v, D, R_1, R_2, V).) G_2 starts with an application of the rule $(G.is\ certain\ that)$. Hence the opponent selects a world $w \in U$ such that uR_2w. The game is continued with respect to w and the sentence

(53)   She was pretty.

Now we have to interpret the recalcitrant pronoun.

The novelty as compared to previous cases lies in the fact that now there is no (semantically) well-defined reference for *she* in (40). The syntactical antecedent of *she* in (40) is *some girl*. But for different possible worlds, the defender's winning strategy picks out different individuals. Which one of these does *she* in (40) refer to?

The answer is: to each and every one. In other words, we allow *she* in (40) to refer to each individual that the defender's winning strategy may pick out in G_1.

These observations show how to continue subgame G_2. Assume that we are given a winning strategy f of the defender's in G_1. Assume that Iris is a girl that f picks out in game G_1 when *some girl* is evaluated. Then G_2 is continued by considering at w the sentence

(54)   Iris was pretty.

Winning and losing in G_2 are now defined as usual. Thus it can be determined which one of the players has a winning strategy in G_2. Winning and losing in G are now defined as has already been mentioned above. Thus the defender has a winning strategy in G only if he has one in G_1 AND

G_2. The opponent will have a winning strategy in G as soon as she has one in either G_1 or G_2.

'UNIVERSAL' INTERPRETATION AND DUMMETT'S EXAMPLE

We can illustrate the 'universal' reading in terms of a somewhat different example. Michael Dummett has been concerned about the semantics of the following sentence:

(55)   There were more people at the party than I expected.

The interesting reading here is the one where I do not have any particular number in mind of which I would expect that there would be that number of people at the party. I expect only that the number will fall within certain boundaries, but I do not have any particular number inside these limits in mind. It is thus obvious that the intended reading cannot be expressed by

(56) $(Ex)(Ey)$ (x is the number of people at the party & E_I (y is the number of people at the party) & $x > y$).

The right symbolization calls for backwards-looking operators, to wit:

(57) (Ex) (x is the number of people at the party & $E_I(Ey)$ (y is the number of people at the party & $D_{E_I}(x > y)$)).

This formalization of Dummett's sentence (55) is extremely natural, it seems to me. In different possible worlds compatible with my expectations there is a different number of people at the party. I expect the number to fall within certain limits, between, say, n_1 and n_k. Thus the number of people at the party will vary from n_1 to n_k in the various expectation worlds. Yet the actual number of people at the party is n, for some natural number n greater than ANY of the n_i's ($1 \leq i \leq k$). This is how things ought to be intuitively, and this is how they are according to our symbolization. This shows that our symbolization of (55) captures precisely the intended natural reading of (55).

This reading for (55) is analogous to the 'universal' readings for sentences of the Geachian form, as the reader will readily notice. It seems to me that the naturalness of the reading in the case of (55) can be interpreted as indirect evidence for the 'universal' reading in general.

'UNIVERSAL' READING NOT UNIVERSAL

When we introduced our 'universal' interpretation of (40), the reader might well have asked whether (40) is synonymous with

(59)   Ed believes that Larry kissed some girl last night. Ed is certain that each girl Larry kissed last night was pretty.

The representation of (59) in logical notation is

(60) $B_E(\mathrm{E}x)$ (x is a girl & Larry kissed x last night) & $C_E(y)$ (y is a girl & Larry kissed y last night $\supset y$ was pretty)).

A moment's reflection shows, however, that (60) does not capture the meaning of (40). To see this, consider the following:

(61)   Ed believes that Larry did not kiss Joan last night, but is not certain about it. Ed is certain that Joan is not pretty.

Intuitively, (40) is compatible with (61), for Joan is not among the girls Larry kissed in any of Ed's doxastic alternatives. However, (59) is not compatible with (61). This shows that (59) is not synonymous with (40).

Even apart from the above argument, if (40) were analysable as (60), it would not be easy to explain just why this is so. In other words, it is not easy to see how we could arrive at (60) on the basis of (40) and syntax only.

OTHER APPLICATIONS OF THE 'UNIVERSAL' READING

The above kind of treatment works for a number of other sentences of the Geachian form also. Cases in point are for instance the following:

(62) = (35)   Ernie believes that he will find a proof for the theorem. He is sure it will not be an elegant proof.

(63)   The Professor believed that he would figure out a solution to the problem. Joe thought it would be false.

(64)   Bob thought he could visualize a cardinal greater than $\aleph_0$. Junior thought that he could visualize a cardinal greater than that.

In these examples, it is natural to analyse the anaphoric pronouns to be pronominalized by the indefinite quantifier phrase in the same way as in (40). The semantical games associated with (62)–(64) will accordingly be quite analogous to that associated with (40).

Perhaps the best semantical representations for (62)–(64) are the semantical games associated with them. If we want to express these games in a more customary way, the following formulas of a formal language could do the job:

(65) $B_E \diamondsuit((Ex)$ (x is a proof for the theorem & Ernie finds x) & $D_{B_E} S_E D'_{D_{B_E}}$ (x is not an elegant proof))).

(Here 'D_{B_E}' is a backwards-looking operator which refers to the time and world where the first operator of (65) is considered. '$D'_{D_{B_E}}$' is in turn a backwards-looking operator which refers to the time where 'D_{B_E}' was considered. '$\diamondsuit$' is of course an ordinary futurity operator.)

(66) $B_P \diamondsuit((Ex)$ (x is a solution to the problem & the Professor figures out x) & $D_{B_P} T_J D'_{D_{B_P}}$ (x is false))).

(Here 'D_{B_P}' is a backwards-looking operator which refers to the time and world where the first operator of (66) was considered. '$D'_{D_{B_P}}$' is a backwards-looking operator which refers to the time at which 'D_{B_P}' was considered.)

(67) $T_B((Ex)$ (x is a cardinal greater than $\aleph_0$ & Bob can visualize x) & $D_{T_B} T_J((Ez)$ (z is a cardinal greater than x & Junior can visualize z))).

(Here 'D_{T_B}' is a backwards-looking operator which refers to the time and world where the operator 'T_B' was considered.)

The semantical representations of (62)–(64) are somewhat complicated because we have tried to take into account not only the propositional attitudes but also the tenses involved.

Consider now (65) as a semantical representation of (62). It is trivial that the following need not hold at any time in the future when Ernie finds the proof, for all that he believes:

(68) $S_E((x)$ (x is a proof for the theorem $\supset x$ is not an elegant proof)).

This is how things ought to be intuitively. What (68) says is something like the following (if we take also the tense involved into account):

(69)   Ernie was sure that any proof for the theorem would not be an elegant proof.

Again, it is of interest to observe that our 'universal' reading differs from the corresponding universal statement. Compare e.g. (62) with

(62)'   Ernie believed that he would find a proof for the theorem. Ernie was certain that every proof for the theorem would not be elegant.

Consider now (62) and (62)' against the model described partly thus:

(70)   Ernie believed that he would find a proof for the theorem. He was sure it would not be an elegant proof. Nevertheless, Ernie was not sure that no one could find an elegant proof for the theorem, but he believed that every proof he himself could possibly find would not be elegant.

In this situation, (62)' would be false and yet (62) could be true. This shows that (62) does not imply that Ernie would have to be sure that each and every proof for the theorem would be inelegant.

The basic trick with sentences like (62) is that the anaphoric pronoun is interpreted to refer to a whole set of individuals. Notice, however, that as applied for instance to (62), this idea does not imply that Ernie would have to be sure that there are several proofs for the theorem, each of them inelegant. In (62), the relevant set of proofs are those proofs that are proofs for the theorem found by Ernie in at least one of Ernie's doxastic alternatives with respect to the actual world. The 'universal' interpretation of the second clause of (62) commits us to the view that all members of this set are such that Ernie is sure that they are inelegant proofs. But there is nothing to require that each of them is such that Ernie is sure that it is a proof of the theorem. Again, this is how things ought to be intuitively, as is witnessed by the consistency of the following statement:

(71)   Ernie believed that he would find a proof for the theorem. He was sure that it would not be an elegant proof. He was also sure that there would be only one proof for the theorem.

Our semantics for (62) can account for this phenomenon, for (65) does not of course imply the following:

(72) $B_E \diamondsuit((Ex)(x$ is a proof for the theorem & Ernie finds x & $D_{B_E} S_E$ (x is not an elegant proof & x is a proof for the theorem))).

Similar observations can be made regarding (66) and (67) as representation of (63) and (64).

We have thus managed to make sense of certain kind of intentional identity statements.

Or have we? For it might be pointed out that even though our semantics for (63), (64), (65), etc. captures the most natural reading of them, at least as far as readings where the first attitude is purely *de dicto* are concerned, we have not really solved Geach's puzzle of intentional identity. The point is that in our analysis of these sentences, the first attitude is surely enough *de dicto* but the second one apparently is not. But in the reading intended by Geach both the attitudes should in some sense be *de dicto*.

It is of course true that in our analysis the second attitude in the sentences is not *de dicto* in the sense that the relevant quantifier would be in the scope of the relevant propositional attitude. Nevertheless we hold that the second is *de dicto* and that it is not directed to any particular individual. This is the case for two reasons, I want to suggest.

First, the 'universal' reading, being of the form

(73) $O_a[(Ex)(P(x)$ & $D_{O_a} O'_b Q(x))]$

(where 'O_a' and 'O'_b' are propositional attitudes) does not imply

(74) $(Ex)[O'_b Q(x)]$.

The reason is that in the kind of natural and generally accepted semantics for intensional logic we are employing here (74) would require that there be some actual object to serve as the focus of the relevant attitude. But no such existential presuppositions are involved in the 'universal' reading.[7] (The reader can verify this by considering the truth conditions of the formulas expressing the 'universal' readings. Reflection on the corresponding natural language sentences shows that the point is also intuitively motivated.)

Second, we can argue that the second attitude is *de dicto* because it is
about SEVERAL objects. Thus, there being several objects for the attitude
to be about, there is no one PARTICULAR object which it is about.

'UNIVERSAL' READING FOR GEACH'S SENTENCE

Does the 'universal' reading yield a natural reading for Geach's sentence
about witches? It seems it does not. The 'universal' reading of (1) can be
expressed by

(17) $T_H((Ex)$ (x is a witch & x has blighted Bob's mare & $D_{T_H}B_N$ (x
         is a witch & x killed Cob's sow))).

Above I put forward this sentence as a formalization of the intended
reading of (1). What was defective in (17) as such a formalization was that
(17) seemed to force Nob's beliefs to be *de re*. This criticism is however
now seen to be ill-founded for I have just argued that there is a very good
sense in which the second attitude of (17) could be said to be *de dicto*.

An even more important point is the following. What does (17) really
mean? Assume for instance that the individuals that are witches blighting
Bob's mare in some of Hob's thought-alternatives do not exist. What
would it then mean to say that of each of them Nob believes that she is a
witch who killed Cob's sow? Failing a clear answer to this question, more
analysis is called for before the import of the 'universal' reading is fully
understood.

COUNTER-EXAMPLES TO THE THEORY: FIGMENTS
AND WAX FIGURES

Another observation further confirms the point that more analysis is
needed before we can hope to understand the semantics of intentional
identity sentences. For consider the following sentence which is due to
Merrill Provence:

(82)   Joan believes that a man tried to kill her last night. She believes that he was employed by her ex-husband but the police officer believes that he was a figment of her imagination.

Here the two Joan clauses are of course quite straightforward. They can be handled by a Lakoff-type treatment. The difficulty is created by the police officer-clause. It is obvious that none of the treatments for intentional identity presented above works in this case. Nevertheless, (82) is natural and grammatical.

For another example, consider the following quotation from Husserl's *Logical Investigations* (p. 609):

> "Wandering about in the Panopticum Waxworks we meet on the stairs a charming lady whom we do not know and who seems to know us, and who is in fact the well-known joke of the place: we have for a moment been tricked by a waxwork figure."

Consider now the following sentence against the background of Husserl's story:

(83)   Bill believes that the lady on the stairs knows him, but John knows she is only a wax figure.

(83) is natural and grammatical, but the intended reading cannot be explicated in any of the ways put forward above.

Working towards an analysis of these examples, let us first consider (83) from the intuitive point of view.

It seems that in the paradigmatic case the relevant connection between the problematic pronoun *she* and its antecedent *the lady on the stairs* is secured by two facts. First, there is an actual object which stands in a causal relation to that belief of Bill's reported in (83). Second, the same individual is such that John knows of it that it is a wax figure.

This intuitive description of the semantics of (one reading of) (83) matches well enough the model depicted by Husserl's description. It is also intuitively clear that (under suitable interpretation for the proper names) (83) would be true in the model characterized.

How could these intuitive observations be made more precise? How could we make any clear-cut semantical sense out of them?

DUALITY IN CROSS-IDENTIFICATION METHODS

The best answer to these questions and to the ones made towards the end of the previous section can be given by first considering one *prima facie* unrelated question. How is the cross-identification between different possible worlds carried out? In all of the above discussion, we have tacitly assumed that this question is unproblematic or at least irrelevant for our present concerns.

However, as has been argued by Hintikka, the problem of cross-identification is far from being trivial. (See e.g. Hintikka 1969b; 1975a.) Indeed, Hintikka has argued that in our conceptual framework we actually cross-identify in TWO essentially different ways. Hintikka has called these two individuation methods the descriptive or physical method and the demonstrative, perspectival or contextual method.

As has been observed by Hintikka, what these two different methods amount to "is both so obvious in its general features and so problematic in its details that there is little point in discussing it here at great length" (Hintikka 1976c, p. 82). A general characterization of the distinction will also be sufficient for our purposes.

The purpose of the descriptive or physical method of individuation is to pin down from different possible worlds we are considering the SAME CONCRETE PHYSICAL INDIVIDUAL. To use Hintikka's own characterization, these individuation methods "can be described briefly by saying that they are just the kind of methods we use in trying to cross-identify between real life and a *roman à clef.* . . . To describe these methods a little bit more fully, one can say that they often rely on the continuity of individuals in space and time" (Hintikka 1975b, p. 218).

Hintikka's characterization of the perspectival or contextual individuation method tells us, in turn, that this method

relies on the role [position] of the person whose attitudes we are discussing. Let us suppose that that individual is myself and that the propositional attitude in question is memory. Then my own firsthand memories of persons, times, places, and objects create a framework which serves to cross-identify people, places, objects, etc. AS LONG AS THEY PLAY THE SAME ROLE IN MY PERSONALLY REMEMBERED PAST, I CAN TREAT THEM AS IDENTICAL . . . even though I do not remember enough of them to say (truly) that I remember who, where or what they are, and although they therefore are not well-defined individuals by descriptive criteria. (Hintikka 1975c, pp. 218–219, my emphasis.)

Perspectival cross-identification between two alternatives is not on a par with that between the actual world and an alternative. In the latter case CAUSAL considerations play a crucial role. An actual object and an inhabitant of an alternative world are perspectively cross-identified in case there is a causal relation of an appropriate kind standing between the two.

All these points concerning the nature of cross-identification are controversial and prompt a number of further questions. In this paper it is not our purpose to clarify the nature of cross-identification; we will therefore disregard these questions, important though they are. It seems to us, however, that the Hintikkian notion of trans-world identity is sufficiently well-established and that no further analysis of the notion will affect our discussion in an important way.

Hintikka's point concerning the duality in cross-identification methods can also be put by saying that because of it, an adequate logic of propositional attitudes containing quantifiers should contain two pairs of quantifiers. Accordingly, in what follows we shall reserve '(Ex)', '(Ey)', '(x)', '(y)' etc. for the quantifiers based on physical (descriptive) transworld identity criteria, and '(∃x)', '(∃y)', '(∀x)', '(∀y)' etc. for the quantifiers based on the perspectival trans-world criteria. We shall also often speak about physical (descriptive) and perspectival quantifiers, respectively.

'UNIVERSAL' READING RECONSIDERED

Hintikka's insights concerning cross-identification readily yield an answer to one important question which was left unanswered by the preceding discussion. When presenting the 'universal' reading for Geach's puzzling sentence (1), we asked what that reading interpretationally really amounted to. The reading is depicted by the formula

(17) $T_H(Ex)$ (x is a witch & x has blighted Bob's mare & $D_{T_H}B_N$ (x killed Cob's sow))).

What we asked was what (17) really means, for instance, in a situation where the values of the existential quantifier in (17) are non-existent individuals.

One thing should be made clear immediately. Is (17) – a formula with a descriptive existential quantifier – really the only possibility? In other words, shouldn't the corresponding perpectival quantifier formula be discussed as well? The answer to this question is in the negative. The reason is that at least in our judgement there is just no clear sense in the perspectival quantifier counterpart (84) of (17). Syntactically, the relevant formula would be

(84) $T_H(\exists x)$ (x is a witch & x has blighted Bob's mare & $D_{T_H}B_N$ (x killed Cob's sow)).

What is crucial here is the nature of perspectival cross-identification involved in (84). In (84), we would have to draw perspectival world lines from a thought alternative of Hob's (with respect to the actual world) to each doxastic alternative of Nob's with respect to the actual world. The only kind of perspectival cross-identification that would make even *prima facie* sense here is the kind of perspectival cross-identification we use when cross-identifying between the actual world and a given alternative. This kind of cross-identification relies on causal considerations. But such causal considerations seem to be impossible when we discuss a thought-alternative of Hob's and a doxastic alternative of Nob's, both being alternatives with respect to the actual world. There just cannot be any causal relations between the two, and thus even this attempt to make clear sense of the perspectival cross-identification presupposed by (84) collapses. (Notice that the situation might be drastically different if the relevant alternatives of Nob's were doxastic alternatives with respect to the given thought-alternative of Hob's.)

We conclude that the only formula that deserves our attention here is (17), where the existential quantifier is a descriptive one.

The import of (17) can now be spelled out by keeping in mind the import of descriptive cross-identification. Pick out any thought-alternative of Hob's with respect to the actual world; say the choice is v. There will have to be a witch i in that world who has blighted Bob's mare (there). It is stated in (17) that Nob believes of him or her that he or she killed Cob's sow. Since we are relying on descriptive cross-identification here, this means that we have to be able to follow i from v to all doxastic alternatives of Nob's by relying on descriptive criteria. Because of this, it is thus necessary that v and all doxastic alternatives of Nob's are similar enough in relevant descriptive respects. Keeping in mind that v was just one of Hob's many thought-alternatives, and that the same argument can be restated for each and every one of them, we conclude that in general a necessary condition for the truth of (17) is that Hob's thoughts and Nob's beliefs are sufficiently alike in their relevant aspects.

These remarks will hopefully give enough interpretational import to (17). On the basis of our observations, we can in any case conclude that the reading thus imposed on (1) is not a natural one.

PERSPECTIVAL *DE RE* READING: HUSSERL'S WAX LADY ANALYZED

Armed with these tools, let us now retackle the problematic Husserlian sentence (83). It is instructive to observe why the following formalization of (83) is inadequate:

(85) $(Ex)\,[B_B\,(x = (1y)\,(y$ is a lady & y is on the stairs) & x knows Bill) & $K_J\,(x$ is a wax figure$)]$

Here we have used the physical (descriptive) existential quantifier. (85) is impossible as a formalization of the relevant reading of (83) simply because it presupposes that an actual object be physically cross-identified with a lady and a wax figure. But it is impossible that the same physical object could in one world be a human being and in another a wax figure.

Thus (85), which represents a kind of *de re* analysis of (83), is inadequate to represent the truth conditions of (83).

The situation is quite different if we employ instead of the physical (descriptive) existential quantifier the corresponding perspectival one:

(86) $(\exists x)\,[B_B(x = (1y)\,(y$ is a lady & y is on the stairs) & x knows Bill) & $K_J\,(x$ is a wax figure$)]$.

Keeping in mind the nature of perspectival cross-identification, we can see that (86) indeed comes close to capturing the intended truth conditions of (83). What (86) says is that there is some actual object (say i), and in each doxastic alternative of Bill's there is a lady who is on the stairs such that i

and the lady are in an appropriate causal relation with each other, and the lady knows Bill (in that world). Moreover, in each epistemic alternative of John's there is a wax figure which is in an appropriate causal relation with i.

This uncovering of the semantical import of (86) shows that even though we clearly are on the right track, in one sense (86) does not yield the most natural representation of (83). For it seems that in (83) the most natural interpretation takes John's knowledge to be *de re* not only in the perspectival sense but in the physical sense. If so, then we are tempted to favour the following formula over (86) as the representation of (83):

(87) $(\exists x)\,[B_B\,(x = (\text{Ꞁ}y)\,(y$ is a lady & y is on the stairs) & x knows Bill) & $(Ey)\,(x = y$ & $K_J\,(y$ is a wax figure$))]$.

It can readily be seen that (87) does not suffer from the drawbacks found in (86). In (87), John's knowledge is *de re* in the physical sense and yet of that individual introduced by the perspectival existential quantifier '$(\exists x)$'. Thus both Bill's beliefs and John's knowledge are of the same individual, as is intuitively required by (83).

That the most natural formalization of (83) requires the use of both the existential quantifiers is peculiar to the example we are studying. A closely related sentence where we can most naturally do with only one quantifier is for instance

(88)   Bill believes that the lady on the stairs knows him, and John believes she knows him, too.

The most natural reading is now

(89) $(\exists x)[B_B(x = (\text{Ꞁ}y)\,(y$ is the lady & y is on the stairs) & x knows Bill) & $B_J\,(x$ knows John$)]$.

Neither one of the attitudes is now directed to any physically cross-identified individual, a fact faithfully reflecting our intuitions about (88). Both the attitudes are of the wax lady and yet all the relevant individuals in the doxastic alternative worlds are not wax ladies but human beings, which readily excludes the possibility of physical cross-identification.

It is necessary to get rid of one possible source of misunderstanding. Notice that a pronoun of laziness analysis would not capture the intended reading of (83) or of (88). Consider for instance (88). The pronoun of laziness analysis takes (88) to be synonymous with

(90)   Bill believes that the lady on the stairs knows him, and John believes that the lady on the stairs knows him, too.

Assume now that the wax work has been displayed on the stairs only recently; before that it was in a hall, and that is where John saw it and formed the opinion that she is a lady who knows him. Then there would be nothing to secure reference by the second occurrence of the definite description *the lady on the stairs* to the right individual. Accordingly, (88) could be true and yet (90) false. Similar argument will show that the pronoun of laziness analysis will not work for (83), either.

DIFFICULTIES WITH GAME-THEORETICAL SEMANTICS FOR THE PERSPECTIVAL *DE RE* READINGS

The readings proposed above for (83) and (88) suggest a more general moral, for a natural reading for some intentional identity sentences can obviously be obtained along the same lines. Thus we interpret the problematic sentences to be *de re* in the sense that the relevant quantifier has a larger scope than either one of the intensional verbs. That both the attitudes have the same focus is secured by the fact that the relevant individuals are introduced by one and the same quantifier. However, both the attitudes are *de dicto* in the sense that they are not (necessarily) directed to any physically (descriptively) cross-identified individual.

How could this kind of reading be obtained from the problematic sentences by relying on the knowledge of syntax only? We shall answer this question by pointing out how the right representations could be obtained in the game-theoretical framework.

For the game-theoretical treatment of a sentence like (83) or (88), we need a game rule for the intensional verbs, definite article, and anaphoric pronouns. The rules (*G.believes that*) and (*G.knows that*) have already been mentioned. The game rule (*G.the*) for the definite article has been given in Hintikka and Saarinen (1975):

(*G.the*) Assume the game has reached a possible world v and a sentence of the form

$X - $ the Y who $Z - W$.

Then the defender may choose an individual (call it 'a') and the opponent an individual (call it 'b') different from a. The game is continued with respect to v and the sentence

$X - a - W$, a is a(n) Y who Z, and b is not a(n) Y who Z.

We shall not bother to state the constraints on this rule, nor the more general formulations one can give for it. (Some aspects of these questions have been discussed in Hintikka and Saarinen 1975 and in other papers on game-theoretical semantics.)

What is important for our purposes is that even though (*G.the*) works in a large number of cases, it does not yield the correct representation for sentences (83) and (88). Because of the Russellian scope ambiguity, we immediately face two possibilities in the game associated with it. Either we apply (*G.believes that*) before (*G.the*), or conversely. In the former game we get the (pure) *de dicto* reading (the 'universal' reading) which is not of interest here. Let us therefore concentrate on the game starting with an application of (*G.the*). In the beginning of this game, the defender may choose an individual (call it 'Jane') and the opponent another individual (call it 'Janet'), and the game is continued with respect to (the same possible world and)

(91)   Bill believes that Jane knows him, and John believes she knows him, too, Jane is a lady on the stairs, and Janet is not a lady on the stairs.

An application of (*G.and*) will now allow a choice of a conjunct by the opponent. Assume she picks out the third conjunct whereupon we end up considering the following sentence

(92)   Jane is a lady on the stairs.

But in the model imagined, this sentence would be false. The focus of the two attitudes is a wax figure, not a human being, much less a lady. Thus if the defender is to win in the game, he will have to pick out the wax figure as Jane. But if so, then (92) will be false.

A NEW AMBIGUITY: TWO KINDS OF *DE RE* READINGS

It will not take us long to make a diagnosis of the situation. The difficulty is that the clause *Jane is a lady on the stairs, and Janet is not lady on the stairs* should be INSIDE the scope of the intensional expression *Bill believes that*, not outside it as in (91).

Simple though this observation is, it has far-reaching consequences. For one thing, it suggests that another type of ambiguity is present in intensional contexts, over and above the Russellian scope ambiguity and the Hintikkian ambiguity concerning cross-identification methods.

In particular, the point suggests that in fact there are TWO different *de re* constructions, depending on the location of the descriptive nouns of the quantifier phrase in question. We shall not pursue our point concerning the ambiguity in the *de re* readings much further here. We shall however discuss it in somewhat greater detail below in the last section of this paper.

Here we shall be content with pointing out how the ambiguity could be handled in game-theoretical framework.

The ambiguity can be formally stated by saying that a sentence of the form

(93) $OF(a)$

where 'O' is an intensional expression, 'F' a predicate, and 'a' a singular term or a quantifier phrase, have four *de re* readings which can be represented by

(94) $(Ex)(x = a \,\&\, OF(x))$

(95) $(\exists x)(x = a \,\&\, OF(x))$

(96) $(Ex)O(F(x) \,\&\, a = x)$

(97) $(\exists x)O(F(x) \,\&\, a = x).$

How readings (94) and (95) can be obtained in game-theoretical framework should be obvious. If 'a' is a definite description, for instance, this is done by first applying $(G.the)$ and only after that the game rule for the intensional expression 'O'. (Also, the fact that this kind of readings exist has been documented well enough in the literature, and no further arguments are needed.)

One neat way to handle readings (96) and (97) game-theoretically is to use another game rule for the definite article (assuming of course that '*a*' in (96) and (97) is a definite description). In addition to (*G.the*) we would use the following rule:

(*G.the*)* Assume the game has reached a possible world v and a sentence of the form

$$X - \text{the } Y \text{ who } Z - W.$$

Then the defender may choose an individual (call it '*a*'), and the opponent may choose an individual distinct from a (call it '*b*'). The game is continued with respect to the same possible world and the sentence $X - a - W$; X (a is a(n) Y who Z, and b is not a(n) Y who Z).

It is clear that a number of constraints on this rule are needed before it is really workable. We shall not bother to state these constraints here.

What is important here is that (*G.the*)* produces the right semantic representations of (83) and of (88). Consider for instance the game associated with (88). The interesting reading starts with (*G.the*)* whereupon the defender may choose an individual, say Jane, and the opponent may choose some other individual, say Janet. The game is continued with respect to the same possible world and the sentence

(98)   Bill believes that Jane knows him, and John believes she knows him, too; Bill believes that Jane is a lady on the stairs and Janet is not a lady on the stairs.

From (98) we immediately see that the semantical game associated with (88) will not suffer from the defects found above. As far as the domination relations are concerned, the semantical game based on (*G.the*)* will yield the right semantical representation (89) for (88).

The choice between (*G.the*) and (*G.the*)* will take care of the ambiguity located in the *de re* constructions in those cases where we deal with quantifier phrases which are definite descriptions. The same ambiguity however arises with other quantifier phrases also, for instance, with the indefinite article. To wit:

(98)′   Bill believes that a lady on the stairs knows him, and John believes that she (the same lady) knows him, too.

Because of this ambiguity, we shall need also a pair of rules *(G.an)* and *(G.an)** for the indefinite article. Knowing the import of *(G.an)*, rule *(G.an)** can easily be constructed in a way analogous to what we did above with *(G.the)*. We shall not bother to state the rule here.

GAME-THEORETICAL SEMANTICS AND DUALITY IN CROSS-IDENTIFICATION METHODS

One problem, however, has to be discussed. We have seen that Hintikka's point about the duality of cross-identification methods plays an important role in the semantics of intentional identity. It is thus obvious that if game-theoretical semantics is to yield the correct semantics for the problem, one must somehow be able to mirror the duality in the semantical games.

But how could the duality of the cross-identification methods be built into game-theoretical semantics? So far the problem seems to have been neglected. Individuals are typically introduced when game rules for various quantifiers are applied. The individuals being selected are thereupon named. Now what is the true nature of these names? Even though the point has never been discussed in greater detail, it is implicit in the literature that these names are used in the semantical games as Kripkean rigid designators; terms which refer to the same individual in each and every possible world. The only explicit statement we are aware of is that of Hintikka and Carlson (1977): "When modal or epistemic concepts are considered, the selection of the worlds as a member of which we are considering *a* in the output of *(G.some)* matters. The name '*a*' must be required TO PICK OUT ONE AND THE SAME INDIVIDUAL IN ALL SUCH WORLDS" (p. 5, emphasis added).

What this means is that in effect the whole problem of trans-world identity is begged; the whole notion of a rigid designator presupposes that a criterion of cross-identification is given.

One might think that it would be possible to incorporate the duality in cross-identification methods into game-theoretical semantics simply by stipulating that each game rule involving a choice of an individual is ambiguous; the rule can either involve a choice of a descriptively cross-identified individual, or else of a perspectively cross-identified one.

This simple scheme does not work, however. Consider for instance (83) and its semantical representation given by formula (87). The major difference between the two is obviously that (83) contains just one (explicit) quantifier in the surface, whereas (87) contains two. The presence of the two quantifiers in (87) allows Bill's beliefs to be of a perspectivally cross-identified individual and John's knowledge of the same individual descriptively cross-identified. Because of the former fact, when we apply (*G.the*)* in the semantical game associated with (83), the defender cannot pick out a descriptively cross-identified individual. Yet because of the latter fact, the defender cannot pick out a perspectivally cross-identified individual, either.

These observations on (83) show that the simple model of incorporating the duality in world lines into game-theoretical semantics will not work.

ANAPHORIC PRONOUNS INVOLVE AN IMPLICIT QUANTIFIER

The problem we are now discussing is large enough for a separate work. While we cannot here argue in detail for our position, we wish to put forward our suggestion of the way the duality of world lines should be incorporated into game-theoretical semantics.

Let us start from the simple model suggested above where each selection of an individual means the selection of a descriptively or a perspectivally cross-identified individual. For this purpose it is necessary that two sets, $I_d(v)$ and $I_p(v)$, are assigned to each possible world v. This means that in general our models will take the form $(U, u, R_1, \ldots, R_n, D, I_d, I_p, V)$, where $U, u, R_1, \ldots, R_n, D$ and V are as earlier and I_d and I_p are functions from U. For each $v \in U$, $I_d(v)$ and $I_p(v)$ will represent, respectively, the set of descriptively drawn world lines (from the point of view of v) and the set of perspectivally drawn world lines (from the point of view of v). A number of conditions should be imposed on the two sets. Even though the import of these conditions has been studied in numerous writings of Hintikka and others, it is again clear that the exact nature of them is a topic large enough for a separate work.

The most important conditions on $I_d(v)$ and $I_p(v)$ can nevertheless be stated.

Each member f of $I_d(v)$ and $I_p(v)$ will be a (possibly partial) function from the set of possible worlds. Given a possible world w, the value $f(w)$, if defined, will be a member of $D(w)$. Thus each member f of $I_d(v)$ and $I_p(v)$ is a world line while $f(w)$, for each possible world w, is the manifestation of f in w.

We now have to define quantifier rules in such a way that each selection of an individual at a certain stage of a game will mean a selection of a member of $I_d(v)$ or $I_p(v)$, where v is the possible world assigned to that stage of the game. Furthermore, we have to require that whenever a member i of $I_d(v)$ or $I_p(v)$ is named in the course of the game, the name 'a' for i which is being given to i is such that whenever w is a possible world, 'a' refers to $i(w)$ in w, if i is defined in w. If not, the reference of 'a' is undefined in w.

Notice that the possibility of picking out a member of $I_d(v)$ or $I_p(v)$ implies an ambiguity for the quantifiers only in intensional contexts.

These suggestions will not yield a satisfactory game-theoretical treatment of a sentence like (83). To rectify the situation, we shall propose a new treatment of anaphoric pronouns and leave the above simple model of quantifiers untackled.

Accordingly, we shall reformulate the rule for anaphoric pronouns. In game-theoretical semantics, it is customary to work with the following natural rule for anaphoric pronouns. When we face at a stage of a game a sentence of the form $X - \text{pron} - Y$ (where 'pron' is the singular pronoun *he, she,* or *it*), we go backwards in the game tree until we come to the antecedent of that occurrence of 'pron' (the antecedent is determined by syntactical considerations). Then we give a name to that individual which was selected when the antecedent was played away, say 'a'. (In other words, the name is given to that individual which was picked out when a game rule was applied to the antecedent.) The game is continued with respect to the sentence $X - a - Y$.

The import of this rule, even in its sketchy form, is not hard to appreciate. It has been applied satisfactorily to the analysis of several puzzling phenomena of natural language pronouns. The above rule for pronouns is intended for singular pronouns only. Again, the extension of the analysis to the plural case does not bother us here.

The new rule for anaphoric pronouns we want to propose will contain the import of the earlier one. Our rule could roughly be put thus:

(G.pron)* Assume the game has reached a possible world v and a
sentence of the form

   $X - \text{pron} - Y$.

(Here 'pron' is the singular pronoun *he*, *she*, or *it*.) Determine
the individual to which 'pron' refers as earlier. Say the individual is i. The defender may choose an individual from $I_d(v)$ or
$I_p(v)$, say j. If $i(v) = j(v)$, then the game is continued with
respect to v and the sentence

   $X - a - Y$,

where 'a' names rigidly j. If $i(v) \neq j(v)$, then the game ends and
the opponent has won it.

A number of ordering principles govern (G.pron)*. Among them, the
following is the most important one for our purposes:

(P1)   (G.pron)* has to be applied before (G.*knows that*), (G.*believes
         that*), (G.*thinks that*), etc.

AN EXAMPLE OF A GAME WITH THE NEW PRONOUN RULE

We can illustrate the import of the new pronoun rule best by means of an
example. Let us therefore play the semantical game associated with (83),
which was the sentence that caused the difficulties in the first place.

The pure *de dicto* reading of (83) does not interest us here. We shall
therefore disregard that game associated with (83) which starts with an
application of (G.*believes that*).

As for the *de re* readings, we face two possibilities: we can start the game
either by an application of (G.*the*) or (G.*the*)*. The former game does not
interest us. (In the intended model there is no lady on the stairs, but only a
wax figure.) So our game will start with an application of (G.*the*)*. But
even here we face two possibilities; the defender can choose either a
member of $I_d(u)$ or of $I_p(u)$ (where u is the world from which the game
starts). Again, we exclude the former possibility because the reading we are
trying to obtain is one where Bill's beliefs are directed to a perspectively,
not descriptively, cross-identified individual (cf. (87)).

Thus our game will start by a selection of an individual by the defender (say he picks out an individual i) and by a selection of some other individual by the opponent (say she picks out j). The game is continued with respect to u (the world where the game started from) and the sentence

(99) Bill believes that Jill knows him and John knows she is only a wax figure, Bill believes that Jill is a lady on the stairs and that Janet is not a lady on the stairs.

Here *Jill* names i and *Janet* names j. (The names should be of the rigid kind described above.)

We could now use the rule $(G.and)$ to detach the last two conjuncts of (99), but their import is clear and of secondary interest here. Assume therefore that the opponent selects the following conjunct when we apply $(G.and)$ to (99):

(100) John knows she is only a wax figure.

Our intention is to guarantee that John's knowledge becomes directed to a descriptively cross-identified individual. This is what created the problem with (83) in the first place.

Because of (P1) we have to apply now $(G.\text{pron})^*$. Thus we first have to check who the referent of *she* is. This is i. Then we face a choice. If the defender selects a member of $I_p(u)$, the result will be that John's attitude becomes directed to a perspectively cross-identified individual. This is not the intended reading. Therefore assume the defender selects a member of $I_d(u)$, say i'. If then $i'(u) = i(u)$, we end up considering at u the following sentence

(101) John knows Ann is only a wax figure.

where *Ann* is a name for i'.

The game thus described will produce precisely the right semantical representation of (83). The game corresponds to formula (87), as can be easily seen. Bill's beliefs are directed to a perspectively cross-identified individual because i was a member of $I_p(u)$. John's knowledge is directed to a descriptively cross-identified individual because i' was a member of $I_d(u)$. And the two attitudes were of the same individual because $i(u) =$

$i'(u)$ (i.e., the manifestation of i in u was identical with the manifestation of i' in u).

MORE APPLICATIONS OF THE NEW PRONOUN RULE

We have managed to show how a sentence like (83) can be handled in game-theoretical semantics. Our example suggests a more general moral. It suggests a natural way to analyse game-theoretically sentences involving quantifiers and propositional attitudes, where one and the same quantifier takes as values individuals which presuppose different kinds of cross-identification *vis-à-vis* different propositional attitudes.

The general treatment can be extracted from representative examples. Consider

(102)   Bill believes that the wax figure on the stairs represents lady X while John believes it represents lady Y.

Here the natural reading takes both Bill's beliefs and John's beliefs to be directed to a descriptively cross-identified individual. (Whether or not the descriptive elements of *the wax figure on the stairs* are outside or inside the scope of *Bill believes that* is immaterial here.) How this reading is obtained in the game-theoretical framework is obvious. We first pick out a member of $I_d(u)$, when applying $(G.the)$ (or $(G.the)^*$). And then we apply $(G.pron)^*$ and pick out again a member of $I_d(u)$.

A different situation arises with

(103)   Bill believes that the lady on the stairs knows him, and John believes she knows him, too.

Here the natural 'Husserlian' reading takes both attitudes to be directed to a perspectivally cross-identified individual. The right semantical game picks out a member of $I_p(u)$ when we first apply $(G.the)^*$. (In the natural reading *the lady on the stairs* is not totally outside the scope of *Bill believes that*. Hence we cannot apply first $(G.the)$.) In applying $(G.pron)^*$ we then select again a member of $I_p(u)$.

In

(104)   Bill believes that the wax figure on the stairs represents a lady
while John believes it is a (real) lady

the most natural interpretation is to take Bill's beliefs to be directed to a
descriptively cross-identified individual and John's beliefs to be directed to
a perspectivally cross-identified individual. (Again, it is immaterial whether
the wax figure on the stairs lies completely outside the scope of *Bill believes
that*, or it is only partly outside the intensional expression.) The semantical
game that will produce this reading involves a selection of a member of
$I_d(u)$ when $(G.the)$ (or $(G.the)^*$) is applied, and a selection of a member of
$I_p(u)$ when $(G.pron)^*$ is applied.

A fourth possibility is exemplified by (83) where Bill's beliefs are directed to a perspectivally cross-identified individual, and John's knowledge to
a descriptively cross-identified one. As already mentioned, the relevant
semantical game will involve a selection of $I_p(u)$ first, and then of a
member of $I_d(u)$.

A couple of comments on the above examples are in order. First, when
we have spoken about 'the natural readings' we have tacitly had in mind a
model of the Husserlian kind. Thus for instance the most natural reading of
(103) is what was stated even though this may not generally be the case.
Second, all the above examples are ambiguous between various readings.
We have deliberately concentrated our attention on only some of them.

FRASER'S CIRCLES AS AN EXAMPLE

A well known experiment of J. Fraser's nicely confirms our discussion.
Fraser has presented a picture where one seems to see a spiral which opens
to the right. In reality there is no spiral but a number of cleverly displayed
circles. Even after one has verified this fact by following the relevant lines
with one's finger, one still tends to see there the spiral just as before.

Against this background, consider now

(105)   Bill believes that the spiral on the board is right twisted while
John knows it is a set of concentric circles cleverly displayed.

(Again, we wish to exclude the pronoun of laziness reading. This can be
done analogously to what we have done above. It is enough to assume that

John saw the figure somewhere before it was displayed on the board and does not know it is there.)

An open spiral cannot be descriptively cross-identified with a set of concentric circles. It is yet clear that the most natural way to take (105) is to analyse both the attitudes to be *de re*, i.e., to be of the real figure.

Thus the sentence calls for an analysis which directs Bill's beliefs to a perspectivally cross-identified individual and John's knowledge to a descriptively cross-identified one. In a formal language the intended reading can be expressed by

(106) $(\exists x)[B_B(x = (\gamma y)\ (y$ is a spiral & y is on the board) & x is right twisted) & $(Ey)\ (x = y$ & $K_J\ (y$ is a set of concentric circles cleverly displayed))].

This example further illustrates our point that in natural language a quantifier can introduce individuals which are neither perspectival nor descriptive individuals but rather combinations of the two. In a game theoretical analysis of (105) we will thus have to use $(G.\text{pron})^*$, thereby providing further evidence for the rule. Furthermore, this example yields evidence for our observation concerning an ambiguity in *de re* readings. The usual *de re* reading

(107) $(\exists x)\ (x = (\gamma y)\ (y$ is a spiral & y is on the board) & $B_B\ (x$ is right twisted) & $(Ey)\ (x = y$ & $K_J(y$ is a set of concentric circles cleverly displayed)))

is impossible here. There is no spiral on the board.

PERSPECTIVAL *DE RE* READINGS IN GEACH'S SENTENCE: PRELIMINARIES

The above discussion has, I hope, revealed that in certain problematic sentences exemplifying intentional identity the two perspectival *de re* readings are the most natural ones. It is therefore appropriate to ask whether these readings would do justice to Geach's intuitions about the original witch-sentence. In spelling out the import of the perspectival *de re* readings of Geach's sentence (1), one must keep in mind that two possible sources of ambiguity are present there: both the location of the clause *is a witch* and the nature of the *de re* belief of Nob's (it can be either descriptive or perspectival). Recalling these facts, we can see that the different possible readings are given by the following formulas:

(108) $(\exists x)$ (x is a witch & $T_H(x$ has blighted Bob's mare) & B_N (x killed Cob's sow)).

(109) $(\exists x)[T_H$ (x is a witch & x has blighted Bob's mare) & $B_N(x$ killed Cob's sow))].

(110) $(\exists x)$ (x is a witch & T_H (x has blighted Bob's mare) & (Ey) ($x = y$ & $B_N(y$ killed Cob's sow))).

(111) $(\exists x)[T_H$ (x is a witch & x has blighted Bob's mare) & (Ey) ($x = y$ & B_N (y killed Cob's sow))].

Of these formulas (108) and (110) clearly cannot represent the intended reading of (1), since they would commit us to the existence of witches, and this Geach does not acknowledge (1) to do.

As far as (109) and (111) are concerned, one wonders whether they could be expressed in natural language as follows:

(112) As regards somebody, Hob thinks that she is a witch and has blighted Bob's mare, and Nob believes that she killed Cob's sow.

But (112) is a reading of (1) Geach rejects: "For [(112)] would imply that Hob and Nob had some one person in mind as a suspected witch; whereas it might be the case, to the knowledge of our reporter, that Hob and Nob merely thought there was a witch around and their suspicions had not yet settled on a particular person" (Geach 1967, p. 148).

This would suggest that if (109) and (111) can be represented as (112) – and *prima facie* this seems to be the case – then (109) and (111) do not capture the intended reading of Geach's.

But a closer look at (112) shows that it is far from obvious that it expresses the import of (109) or (111). Keeping in mind Hintikka's point about the duality of cross-identification methods, we know that (112) is ambiguous. For various reasons it is plausible to assume that in putting forward (112) Geach has in mind THAT reading of it which bases the relevant quantifier on descriptive criteria. If so, Geach's criticism levelled against (112) as a paraphrase of (1) is correct. But no matter what one thinks about (109) and (111), it is clear that their meaning is quite different from the meaning of (112) thus explicated. In these formulas we are not working (at least exclusively) with the descriptive cross-identification criteria.

In case the quantifier *somebody* in (112) is based on perspectival cross-identification criteria we get a reading to which Geach's criticism does not speak. In this case it might very well be that neither Nob nor Hob has settled his suspicions on a particular person. It is only presupposed, first, that from the point of view of Hob's thoughts there is some specific individual who is a witch that has blighted Bob's mare. Second, it is presupposed that from the point of view of Nob's beliefs there is some specific individual who has killed Cob's sow.

Both these conditions can be fulfilled without Hob or Nob knowing who has blighted Bob's mare or who has killed Cob's sow.

If we now pay attention for a while to (111), we can see that in fact it will not do as an explication of the sense Geach wants to give for (1). The reason is that (111) directs Nob's beliefs to a descriptively cross-identified individual. Thus Nob has to have some particular individual in mind as the suspected killer. In consequence, even if (111) did explicate one possible reading of (1), this reading is not the one Geach is hunting for.

Thus we are left only with (109). Now it is natural enough to think that (109) could NOT be translated into English as (112), IF we stick to that reading of (112) which presupposes descriptive cross-identification. Since it was just pointed out that Geach's criticism against (112) holds only when the descriptive reading of (112) is presupposed, we seem to be on firm ground in claiming (109) to capture the intended reading, at least as far as (112) is concerned.

However, before the import of (109) can be fully appreciated, we must discuss two apparently unrelated points of a more general nature.

EXISTENTIAL PRESUPPOSITIONS DISPENSED WITH

Consider

(113) $(\exists x)T_N$ (x is a witch & x has blighted Bob's mare).

What is the semantics of this formula? One thing is clear: it implies that from the point of view of Nob's thoughts, there is someone who is a witch and who has blighted Bob's mare. But does (113) imply that this someone is an EXISTENT individual?

It seems to us that if we wish to mirror natural language faithfully, we must not demand that the existential quantifier in (113) carries existential presuppositions. This point again would deserve careful analysis. We shall be content with a few relatively sketchy remarks.

Consider

(114)   The person Joan believes tried to kill her is a figment of her imagination

is most naturally analysed as

(115) $(\exists ! x) [B_J(x$ is a person & x tried to kill Joan) & x is a figment of Joan's imagination)].

For clearly it is natural to think that from the point of view of Joan's beliefs, the person who tried to kill her plays a specific role. But if the whole thing is just a figment of her imagination, and no one in fact tried to kill her, then Joan's relevant beliefs cannot be predicated of any existent individual. This strongly suggests that in the representation (115) or (114) the existential quantifier should not carry existential presuppositions.

Our present point could also be put as follows. In propositional attitude contexts, an existential quantifier has two roles. First, it is a device to state that something exists which has certain properties. Second, it is a device to state that in all the various possible worlds we may have to consider, we are to consider the same individual. These two functions are clearly quite independent of each other. We can imagine that sometimes we would like to impose on a sentence a requirement of the second kind, without making a requirement of the first kind. We have suggested that in natural language this actually happens.

Notice that what has been proposed is intended as a thesis of the logic of propositional attitudes only. The situation may be quite different in tense logics and in the logics of pure (impersonal) modalities.

We shall assume in what follows that existential quantifiers do not necessarily introduce any existential presuppositions.

It is appropriate to observe how game-theoretical semantics should be augmented to accord with the present new development. In fact, this will be quite simple. If we look at the characterization of the game rules above, we observe that they invite us to select members of either $I_d(v)$ or $I_p(v)$, where v is the world at which we are considering a given sentence. We have stipulated that members of these sets are (perhaps partial) functions which assign to each possible world v an element of $D(v)$. Because world lines are thus allowed to be only partially defined, there is nothing, in particular, to require that a world line f in $I_d(v)$ or $I_p(v)$ is defined in v. If this is not the case, then f does not exist in v and, yet, it is possible for a player to select f when quantifier rules are applied in v. This shows that the possibility of having existential quantifiers which do not carry existential presuppositions is, as it were, built into our game-theoretical model. Thus the only further development that is needed is to reformulate the game rules for quantifiers slightly. Whenever a quantifier rule $(G.Q)$ invites a player to select an individual, we must recognize two possibilities. Either the selection is made from those subsets of $I_d(v)$ or $I_p(v)$ which contain only functions defined for v, or else the selection is from $I_d(v)$ or $I_p(v)$. We shall not go into the obvious details of reformulating the game rules here. In what follows we shall however assume that such game rules are at our disposal and we shall refer to them by $(G.an)_e^*$, $(G.the)_e^*$, etc.

TWO PERSPECTIVAL INDIVIDUALS CROSS-IDENTIFIED

Consider now

(116) $(\exists x)(B_a P(x) \,\&\, (\exists y)(B_b Q(y) \,\&\, x = y))$.

Here we have two *de re* statements which report that a's beliefs are directed to a perspectivally cross-identified individual and that that individual is believed by a to be P. Also, (116) reports that a perspectivally cross-identified individual is believed by b to Q. Furthermore, there is a requirement in (116) which demands that the values of '$(\exists x)$' and '$(\exists y)$' are one and the same individual, in other words, that the two attitudes are directed to one and the same (perspectivally cross-identified) individual.

Philosophically speaking, how could we satisfy such a requirement? How could two perspectivally cross-identified individuals be one and the same?

These questions might strike the reader as puzzling, for it seems that the perspectival cross-identification method cannot in any way be extended so as to admit comparisons between worlds introduced by the attitudes of TWO DIFFERENT persons. This seems to be excluded by the very idea of the perspectival cross-identification method.

Moreover, the literature on the two cross-identification methods is not of direct use here. The problem seems to have been neglected so far.

One insight of Hintikka's is nevertheless helpful here. As has been mentioned, Hintikka has argued that perspectival cross-identification between someone's, say, perceptual alternatives and the actual world is of a different character than that between two perceptual alternatives of his. (It is here assumed, of course, that the actual world itself is not one of the perceptual alternatives.) Hintikka's suggestion is that perspectival cross-identification between an actual object a and one of the perceiver's 'visual objects', say b, takes place when there is some sort of appropriate CAUSAL connection between the two.

Hintikka's observation suggests an answer to the question put forward above. We can cross-identify two perspectivally identified individuals i and j of two different persons BY GOING VIA THE ACTUAL WORLD. For we can cross-identify each of the perspectivally identified individuals with an actual object separately, using Hintikka's causality-criterion. The two perspectivally identified individuals are then stipulated as identical (cross-identified in the perceptual or perspectival sense) if and only if there is some individual in the actual world bearing an appropriate causal relation to both of them. In other words, the two perspectivally identified individuals are cross-identified if and only if they can be traced back to the same individual in the actual world.

These observations suggest a way to answer our question concerning the identification of two perspectivally cross-identified individuals.

Because of the point made in the previous section, the existential quantifiers in (116) can have an existential import or may lack it. Assume first that they do make an existential statement of the actual world. Then it is clear what the causality-criterion which forms the basis of the identity statement in (116) here amounts to; namely, that an actual existing object has a causal relation to a perspectivally cross-identified individual i, given by a's beliefs, and to a perspectivally cross-identified individual j given by b's beliefs. It is clear that if Hintikka's point of the causal element in perspectival cross-identification has any truth in it at all, then we are on safe ground; for we are putting forward just one simple application of Hintikka's general point.

Fraser's 'spiral' provides a good example of the present case. Assume we are considering Fraser's picture and we state

(117)   Joe saw a spiral and Bill saw the same spiral, too.

As a matter of fact, there is no spiral. The only base for the identity of the two spirals is provided by the concentric circles of Fraser's picture. Those circles stand in an appropriate causal relation to the spirals of Joe's and Bill's visual alternatives.

The situation is more complicated when the existential quantifiers in (116) do not have any existential presuppositions. Then Hintikka's point does not seem to yield a solution to our problem for how could a non-existing individual be in a causal relation to anything?

The truth of

(118) $(\exists x)B_a P(x)$

secures that from the point of view of a's beliefs, there is an individual playing a specific role and he is believed by a to be P. Now even though that individual does not exist, he can have causal connections to various aspects of the actual world. This is because he is an individual from the point of view of a's beliefs and a's beliefs are something which take place in the actual world. Other people may become aware of a's beliefs and of the fact that from the point of view of a's beliefs, there is something which counts as an individual and which has certain properties.

Thus causal considerations are of vital importance in determining the truth conditions of (116) as well as in a case where the existential quantifiers do not involve existential presuppositions.

An example could be helpful here. Consider

(119)   Bert believes that a mysterious force is operating in the Bermuda triangle, and Mort believes that it (the same force) is operating in the Caribbean sea, too.

Assume now there is no such mysterious force as is mentioned in (119). Nevertheless, we may assume that from the point of view of both Bert's and Mort's beliefs such a force counts as a well-defined individual. Our suggestion is that the two forces are perspectivally cross-identified with each other, if there is a causal relation of an appropriate sort between the two.

One situation where the condition just laid down comes close enough to obtaining is the actual world – at least if we believe Graham Massey in his recent *New Scientist* article:

The Triangle stories are undoubtedly intriguing, but are they true? What first makes one suspicious of the stories of disappearance is that almost every single book and article on the Triangle uses the same old incidents and almost identical words and phrases to describe them. Most can be traced back to an article written by one Vincent Godds in 1964 for the men's adventure magazine *Argosy*: since then, like Topsy, they've just growed and growed. (*New Scientist*, 14 July 1977, p. 74.)

Let now Bert be Mr. Godds and Mort some later scholar of the field. It seems to us that in such a situation (119) could naturally be maintained, even if one insisted that there are no mysterious forces in the Bermuda Triangle or anywhere.

This illustrates our thesis that the truth conditions of sentences like (116) are essentially tied up with causal considerations, irrespective of the existential presuppositions of the existential quantifier.

PERSPECTIVAL *DE RE* READINGS FOR GEACH'S SENTENCE ANALYSED

Above, we considered the various possible perspectival *de re* readings for Geach sentence (1), but only the following one could stand a closer look:

(109) $(\exists x) (T_H(x$ is a witch & x has blighted Bob's mare) & $B_N (x$ killed Cob's sow)).

What does (109) amount to?

Again, we have a choice since '$(\exists x)$' may or may not have existential presuppositions. Assume it does make an existential claim about the actual world. If so, then an analysis of (109) and, accordingly, of Geach's sentence (1) is as follows:

(120)   There is a perspectivally cross-identified individual i in Hob's
          think-alternatives such that in each of those worlds she is a
          witch and she has blighted Bob's mare. There is a perspectivally
          cross-identified individual j in Nob's belief-alternatives such
          that in each of those worlds she is a witch and she killed Cob's
          sow. Moreover, i and j can be traced back in the actual world to
          one and the same individual which bears an appropriate causal
          relation to both i and j.

(120) does NOT imply that there are witches in the actual world. What is
demanded is only that in the actual world there is something which has an
appropriate causal relation to entities which are witches in certain other
worlds. The 'causal origin' of the witches could for instance be a particular
woman with no special properties in addition to the usual ones.

In our opinion, (109) thus understood captures one possible and natural
reading of (1). It seems, however, that this reading does not do justice to
Geach's intentions, because it is implicit in his discussion that the intended
reading of (1) should not make ANY claims about actual objects, neither of
witches or of any other objects. If this is the case, then of course the present
analysis of (1) will not capture Geach's intended reading.

But what happens if we drop the assumption that the existential
quantifier in (109) has an existential import? According to the previous
section, the meaning of (109) could then be spelled out more fully thus:

(121)   There is a perspectivally cross-identified individual i in Hob's
          think-alternatives such that in each of those worlds she is a
          witch and she has blighted Bob's mare. There is a perspectivally
          cross-identified individual j in Nob's belief-alternatives such
          that in each of those worlds she is a witch and she killed Cob's
          sow. Moreover, i bears an appropriate causal relation to j.

A few comments on (121) are in order. The only difference between
(120) and (121) is in the last clause which describes the nature of the causal
element involved. In (121) the causal element does not (necessarily)
connect the two objects i and j by going via the set of actual existing
objects. It connects them as it were indirectly, as individuals from the point
of view of Hob's thoughts and Nob's beliefs. On the other hand, just like in

(119), such a causal relation can obtain because Hob's thoughts as well as Nob's beliefs are part of the vocabulary of the actual world. Hob's thoughts and Nob's beliefs may interact with the course of the actual world in various ways.

To spell out the import of (121) a bit more fully, assume that it was in Hob's mind that the witch mania first arose. It was he who started to speak about witches and it was in his mind and from the point of view of his beliefs that the witches first started to take shape. From the point of view of his thoughts, there is a certain witch who blighted Bob's mare. Of that, from his point of view, particular witch he has talked to Nob; Nob who relies on Hob's authority, also gets caught up in the witch mania, indeed to such an extent that from the point of view of his beliefs, the witch that killed Cob's sow is a particular witch.

This example provides a situation where the relevant conditions laid down by (121) are satisfied. It is of interest to observe the differences to the condition set forth by (120).

According to our lights, the reading depicted by (121) for (1) yields a solution to Geach's puzzle in the sense that it captures the truth conditions of that reading of (1) hunted for by Geach.

It may be asked whether (109), in the sense of (121), could be expressed in English also as (112). We have already pointed out that (112) is ambiguous. *Somebody* can be based on descriptive cross-identification or else on the perspectival cross-identification. If the former reading is imposed on (112), then of course it could not express the import of (109). But even in the latter case, (109) does not seem to come close to expressing the import of (112). The reason seems to be that *somebody* in (112) could be paraphrased as *somebody existing*. Thus the quantifier in (112) seems to contain an existential presupposition, excluding the possibility of its being a natural language representation of (109) in the sense of (121).

Notice that in this solution to Geach's puzzle we do not assume that Hob's thoughts or Nob's beliefs were directed to a specific witch (or a specific individual). Admittedly, the two attitudes are directed to a specific perspectivally identified individual. In other words, from their point of view there is a specific witch (a specific individual) towards which the attitudes are directed. But there need not be any descriptively identified individual of the kind, and so, in the most common sense of the phrase, the two attitudes are not of a particular individual. In that sense, they are not *de re*.

Also, it is fairly obvious that the semantical game associated with (1) looks like which produces the right semantical representation. Assume a model of the form $(U, u, R_1, R_2, D, I_d, I_p, V)$ is given. The relevant semantical game is a game associated with this model and sentence (1). It starts with an application of $(G.an)_e^*$ whereupon the defender selects a member f of $I_p(u)$ such that $f(u)$ is not defined, and the game is continued with respect to u and the sentence

> Hob thinks that Jill has blighted Bob's mare, and Nob believes that she killed Cob's sow, and Hob thinks that Jill is a witch.

Here *Jill* is a name of the appropriate kind for f. The game rule $(G.and)$ now would allow us to detach the first and the third conjunct. What both these conjuncts amount to semantically is clear and we will therefore disregard them here. Assume thus that the opponent picks out the second conjunct when applying $(G.and)$ and that we thus consider at u the sentence

> Nob believes that she killed Cob's sow.

Because of (P1) we have to apply now $(G.pron)_e^*$. The antecedent of *she* is *a witch* and Jill (i.e., f) was the individual that was selected when $(G.an)_e^*$ was applied to this quantifier phrase. Thus $(G.pron)_e^*$ says that the defender may select an individual g from $I_p(u)$ such that $g(u)$ is not defined, and $g(u) = f(u)$. The game is continued with respect to u and

> Nob believes that Jane killed Cob's sow.

where *Jane* names g. After these steps, the game is continued in the standard fashion by an application of $(G.\ believes\ that)$.

One comment on this semantical game, which clearly produces the intended semantical representation for (1), is in order. The reader might feel that there is something like a paradox involved in our semantical game described above. For how could $g(u)$ be identical with $f(u)$ in u, if neither g nor f is defined in u? There is however no paradox here. That f and g are not defined in u means that they do not exist in that possible world. Since g and f are both perspectively cross-identified individuals (perspectival world lines), it follows that our problem reduces to the problem of cross-identifying, in a world, two perspectivally cross-identified individuals which do not exist in that world. But we have already shown above how this question can be answered.

GEACH'S PUZZLE AND DEFINITE DESCRIPTIONS

Our solution to Geach's puzzle is supported by another observation. Consider the following paraphrase of (1):

(122)　Hob thinks that a witch has blighted Bob's mare and Nob believes that the one whom Hob thinks to be the witch who blighted Bob's mare killed Cob's sow.

This sentence is ambiguous, and it is readily apparent that several of the readings of (122) could not possibly do justice to Geach's intentions. First, the definite description

(123)　the one whom Hob thinks to be the witch who blighted Bob's mare

cannot have smaller scope than the intensional expression *Nob thinks*. For if (123) occurs inside the scope of this expression, then there is no guarantee of the identity of the focuses of Nob's beliefs and Hob's thoughts. (What Hob thinks and what Nob believes Hob thinks may be quite different.)

Thus if we want to claim that (122) paraphrases Geach's intended reading of (1), we must assume that (123) occurs outside the scope of *Nob believes*, making (122) synonymous with

(124)　Hob thinks that a witch has blighted Bob's mare, and Nob believes of the one whom Hob thinks to be the witch who blighted Bob's mare that she killed Cob's sow.

This explication of (122) shows that we there quantify into an opaque context. Keeping in mind Geach's intentions and Hintikka's point of the duality of cross-identification methods, we see that Nob's beliefs reported in (122) cannot be of any individual as descriptively identified. Thus they have to be of the one Hob thinks to be the witch who blighted Bob's mare as perspectivally identified.

This assumption is immediately seen to be harmless. For we have argued earlier that (109), in the sense of (121), captures the reading of (1) intended by Geach. In (124) also Nob's beliefs are directed to a specific perspectivally cross-identified witch.

But does the use of the definite description (123) commit us to taking Hob's thoughts *de re*? Again, we must keep in mind the ambiguity located by Hintikka and notice that the following formulas explicate the two possible readings of (123):

(125) $(E!x)T_H$ (x is a witch & x blighted Bob's mare)

(126) $(\exists!x)T_H$ (x is a witch & x blighted Bob's mare).

If we understand (123) in the way depicted by (125), we force Hob's thoughts to be *de re* in the most straightforward sense of the word. Thus we will not do justice to Geach's intentions.

Situation with (126) is quite different. As far as cross-identification is concerned, we are making only the assumption that Hob's thoughts are directed to a specific perspectivally cross-identified witch. This assumption is made by (121) also; so the two will here stand or fall together.

Two more points deserve attention. First, does the use of (126) commit us to making a factual claim of some existent individual? On the basis of what we have argued earlier, we know that there is a choice here. If we impose the non-existential interpretation of the quantifier on (126), we do not make any factual claims about existent individuals. Thus again (124) and (121) would stand or fall together.

There is however, one further possible source for a difference between (124) and (121). The reason is the claim made in (126) that there is just one perspectival individual of the relevant kind. In (121) it is only asserted that there is such an individual but the possibility for several such individuals remains, at least *prima facie*.

The truth of a statement like

(127) $(\exists x)T_H P(x)$

secures that from the point of view of Hob's thoughts there is a specific, well-defined individual who is thought by Hob to be *P*. Being a specific individual means here that there is a specific role the individual is playing, in Hob's thoughts. Could there be several different individuals playing the same role? Clearly not. Thus if the predicate '$P(x)$' defines a specific role for an individual in Hob's thoughts, then the following is valid:

(128) $(\exists x)T_H P(x) \supset (\exists ! x)T_H P(x)$

In the case of (1), it does not seem too unnatural to think that the role in Hob's thought stated to exist in (126) is secured by the predicate *is a witch who has blighted Bob's mare*. But if this assumption is indeed made, then the last source of difference between (124) and (121) vanishes.

Let us restate somewhat more explicitly the intended reading of (124):

(129) $T_H(Ex)$ (x is a witch & x has blighted Bob's mare) & $(\exists ! x)$
         $[T_H(x$ is a witch & x has blighted Bob's mare) & $(\exists y)$ $(x = y$ &
         B_N (y killed Cob's sow)]

Making the at least apparently harmless assumption mentioned above will be sufficient for the equivalence of (129) and (109) in the sense of (121). (121) explicates one possible reading of (1). If we are working with quantifiers with existential presuppositions, then we see that (129) also captures what we have claimed is Geach's intended reading.

What is interesting here is that this shows there is one possible reading in (122) which makes it synonymous with the reading of (1) intended by Geach. It seems to us that, from the intuitive point of view, this yields further evidence for our analysis, for (122) surely represents one natural paraphrase of (1).

Furthermore, notice that the reading of (1) I have put forward goes together very well with one intuitive observation about (1). Above, we noted that (1) could *prima facie* be interpreted as

(130)   Hob thinks that a witch has blighted Bob's mare, and Nob
         believes that the witch Hob had in mind killed Cob's sow.

What was found to be defective in this analysis was that there did not seem to be any reasonable way to analyse the definite description *the witch Hob had in mind*. Our present analysis suggests immediately a natural way to interpret this definite description, i.e., as synonymous with the definite description (123), as analysed in (126). For if Hob has in mind an individual, then it is natural to think that there is a perspectival world line picking out that individual from all the relevant worlds. (Notice, however, that in this analysis (130) paraphrases Geach's intended reading only when *the witch Hob had in mind* has wider scope than *Nob believes*.)

Even though we have already explicated the reading of (1) intended by Geach, it is appropriate to discuss here one important question related to (1). If we set apart Geach's intentions, what other readings can be naturally found for (1)?

One possible reading is obviously the 'universal' reading. What it amounts to in this case has already been pointed out above.

The various perspectival readings have also been mentioned. Of these (108) and (110) are not of interest because they commit us to the existence of witches. On the other hand, in (109) and (111) the existential quantifier does not carry an existential presupposition, and they are therefore more natural formalizations of (1) than (108) and (110) are. (Here we are relying on collateral information, shared by our community, which makes some readings more natural than others. A similar strategy will be used in what follows.)

What about the descriptive *de re* readings? Of these readings only the following ones deserve closer attention:

(131) $(Ex)(T_H$ (x is a witch & x has blighted Bob's mare) & B_N (x killed Cob's sow)).

(132) (Ex) $(T_H$ (x is a witch & x has blighted Bob's mare) & $(\exists y)$ ($x = y$ & B_N (x killed Cob's sow))).

(The corresponding descriptive *de re* readings with the clause *x is a witch* outside 'T_H' will not do as long as we insist that there are no witches.)

Again, (131) and (132) are strictly speaking ambiguous, because of the ambiguous nature of the existential quantifier '(Ex)'.

If we assume that '(Ex)' involves an existential commitment, then the meaning of (132) is analogous to that of (111). There has to be some actual object a descriptively cross-identified with a witch through Hob's thought-alternatives and bearing a causal relation to a perspectively cross-identified individual in Nob's belief-alternatives.

But if we assume that the values of '(Ex)' need not exist, the situation is somewhat more complicated. Again there has to be a causal relation to a perspectively cross-identified individual in Hob's belief-alternatives. The other component of the causal relation is the descriptive individual towards which Hob's thoughts are directed. (How this is possible has been spelled out above.)

As for (131), if we attach existential presuppositions to '(Ex)', then the two attitudes are of a particular individual in the most straightforward sense of the word. For this condition to be satisfied it is necessary that there has to be some actual individual Hob and Nob believe is a witch, i.e., that they have an opinion as to who the relevant witch involved in (1) is.

If we do not attach existential presuppositions to the existential quantifier in (131), a more interesting situation arises. Since there is no actual object for Hob's thoughts and Nob's beliefs to be of, there is at least one sense in which we can say the attitudes are not *de re*: they are not of any particular actual object. The fact that we are using a descriptive existential quantifier implies that Hob's thoughts and Nob's beliefs must be sufficiently alike. This is necessary because otherwise we could not follow the same witch throughout all the relevant thought- and belief-alternatives by relying on descriptive criteria.

This reading not only provides a natural reading of (1) in general, but comes close to capturing Geach's intended reading. For it seems that (131) could NOT be translated into English as

(112)   As regards somebody, Hob thinks that she is a witch and she has blighted Bob's mare, and Nob believes that she killed Cob's sow.

The reason is that as we have already mentioned (112) seems to make an existential claim of the actual world; i.e., (112) seems to imply that Hob's thoughts and Nob's beliefs are of some ACTUAL existing object.

Also, even though the present reading of (1) presupposes that we can follow, by relying on descriptive criteria, the relevant individual throughout Hob's and Nob's relevant alternatives, this is not yet to say that there is some particular individual they have in mind as a suspected witch. For as already stated, there is no particular EXISTING object for the attitudes to be about.

It thus seems to us that (131), with '(Ex)' interpreted free of existential presuppositions, captures Geach's intended reading of (1). Together with our earlier observations, this means that in fact there is no one reading which is THE reading intended by Geach. One can fulfill his requirement in two essentially different ways.

Notice also how naturally the kind of reading we have here suggested for (1) works in the case of the sentence (119), discussed above:

(119)   Bert believes that there is a mysterious force operating in the Bermuda Triangle, and Mort believes it is operating in the Caribbean Sea, too.

We suggested above that one natural reading is to take both attitudes here to be *de re* of a perspectivally cross-identified individual whose world line cannot be extended to the actual world.

Another, perhaps still more natural reading of (119) is depicted by the following formula which corresponds to (131):

(133)   (Ex) [B_B (x is a mysterious force & x is operating in the Bermuda Triangle) & B_M (x is operating in the Caribbean Sea)].

Here '(Ex)' has to be understood not to involve existential presuppositions. Because of the descriptive quantifier used in (133), we must be able to extend, by descriptive criteria, the world line drawn through all belief-alternatives of Bert's to all belief-alternatives of Mort's. For this to be possible we have to assume that Bert's and Mort's beliefs are sufficiently alike, at least as far as forces operating in nature are concerned.

These observations show how natural (133) is as a reading of (119). Because (133) intuitively closely resembles (1) as an example of intentional identity, this yields further evidence for our analysis of (1).

Our present observations also yield a natural treatment of the following sentence which has puzzled scholars:

(134)   Jones worships a god and Smith worships him, too.

It is often suggested that in (134) the pronoun cannot be interpreted anaphorically unless some gods exist.[8] This suggestion does not accord with one's intuitions about (134). It appears that one can assert (134), meaning that we are considering the same god in both cases, and yet not commit oneself to the existence of any dubious entities.

Our analysis of (134) would bind *a god* and *him* to one and the same quantifier, not involving existential presuppositions, and occurring outside both the intensional expressions in (134). The quantifier would most naturally be based on descriptive cross-identification. Thus Jones' and Smith's beliefs would have to be in relevant respects sufficiently alike, in order for us to be able to draw a world line throughout all these alternatives on descriptive criteria.

The adequacy of our treatment of (134) is further supported by observing how the truth conditions of our reading for (134) differ from those of

(135)   Jones worships a god, and Smith worships a god, too.

Here (135) would result from (134) by a pronoun of laziness analysis. In (135) there is thus no guarantee of the identity of the two gods. In consequence, (135) could be true in a situation where Jones is a Christian while Smith is a Moslem.

There is surely a reading of (134) under which it would not be true in the situation envisaged. This reading of (134) is captured by our proposal for it. (134) would not be true in this situation because we cannot draw a descriptive world line connecting the relevant gods through Jones' and Smith's belief-alternatives. Their religious beliefs are too different for this to be possible.

It is easy to see what the semantical games which will produce the intended readings of (119), (134) and (1) (in the sense of (131)) look like. We shall therefore not state them explicitly here.

INTENTIONAL IDENTITY AND FIGMENTS
AND HALLUCINATIONS

One further problem remains to be explored. This problem is created by Professor Provence's sentence

(82)   Joan believes that someone tried to kill her last night. She believes that he was employed by her ex-husband, but the police officer believes that he was a figment of her imagination.

Our discussion above does not seem to yield any natural reading for this sentence. The 'universal' reading is obviously impossible here. It would not make any sense to think that anybody who could be the attempted murderer, for all that Joan believes, is believed by the police officer to be a figment of her imagination.

Likewise, all the various *de re* readings appear unnatural here. It seems impossible that one could believe OF anybody that he is a figment of someone's imagination, in any reasonable sense of the word.

It seems to us, however, that the problems involved in (82) are not due to our analysis of intentional identity but rather to the character of the predicate *is a figment of Joan's imagination*.

That the problems arising with (82) are not due to intentional identity are further supported by another observation. Consider

(136)   Macbeth believes that he sees a dagger but Lady Macbeth believes it is only an hallucination.

A moment's reflection shows that this sentence is analogous to (82) and provides a similar counter-example to our theory. But again, the 'counter-example' involves a curious predicate, this time *is an hallucination*.

We believe (82) or (136) are not proper counterexamples to our theory of intentional identity. We shall present natural semantics for these sentences below, but before that we will have to discuss the semantics of such predicates as *is a figment* or *is an hallucination*.

Inspired by Hintikka's logic of perception and Robert Howell's (1972) treatment of 'Seeing as', Ilkka Niiniluoto (1978) has presented the following natural treatment of seeing an hallucination. Consider

(137) $(\exists x)(\sim(Ey)(x = y) \,\&\, S_a(Ez)(x = z))$

Here it is relevant that the first existential quantifier is taken not to involve existential presuppositions. In Niiniluoto's analysis, (137) says that a sees an hallucination. This is natural because (137) implies that from the perspective of a's visual impressions there is a specific individual such that a sees it exists. Yet the world line of that individual cannot be extended to the actual world; it does not exist in the actual world.

We want to suggest that *it* in (136) is most naturally taken as a kind of pronoun of laziness, and that (136) is most naturally analysed as synonymous with

(138)   Macbeth believes that he sees a dagger but Lady Macbeth believes the dagger Macbeth believes that he sees is only an hallucination.

Here the definite description *the dagger Macbeth believes that he sees* has to be analysed in the following way

(139) $(\exists!x)B_M$ (x is a dagger & Macbeth sees x)

where '$(\exists!x)$' does not involve existential presuppositions. The overall analysis of (136) is then

(140) $B_M(Ex)$ (x is a dagger & Macbeth sees x) & $B_L(\exists!x)(B_M$ (x is a dagger & Macbeth sees x) & $\sim(Ey)(x = y)$).

A few clarifying comments are in order. First, our analysis presupposes that Macbeth's visual impressions are believed by Lady Macbeth to be vivid enough to differentiate the dagger from all other individuals there are in his visual field. This assumption seems most harmless.

Second, in (140) there is no guarantee of any kind of identity of the 'focuses' of the two attitudes. This reveals that the pronoun *it* in (136) is not analysed as a properly anaphoric pronoun.

This analysis of the problematic pronoun seems to accord well with facts. For if Lady Macbeth believes that x is an hallucination, then obviously x cannot count as an individual from her doxastic point of view.

(Notice, however, that this is not to deny conscious hallucinations or illusions. Analogously to what we did with (136), we can analyse (141) as (142):

(141)   I believe that I see a dagger but I know it is only an hallucination

(142) $B_I(Ex)$ (x is a dagger & I see x) & $K_I(\exists!x)(B_I$ (x is a dagger &
          I see x) & $\sim(Ey)(x = y)$).

In (142) the hallucination counts as an individual from my doxastic but not
from my epistemic point of view.)

A similar analysis is natural for (82) also. Again, the natural analysis is to
take *he* not anaphorically but as a substitute for

(143)   the person Joan believed tried to kill her last night.

This definite description has to be analysed analogously to what we did
with (136).

Our analysis of (82) is accordingly

(144) $B_J(Ex)$ (x tried to kill Joan last night & x was employed by
          Joan's ex-husband) & $B_P(\exists!x)$ [B_J (x tried to kill Joan last
          night & x was employed by Joan's ex-husband) & $\sim(Ey)$
          $(x = y)$]

Here '$(\exists!x)$' should not involve any existential presuppositions.

In (144), there is no guarantee of the identity of the focuses of the two
attitudes. This reflects the fact that *he* in (82) is not analysed as an
anaphoric pronoun. Again this is how things ought to be intuitively. For it
seems that in (82) the police officer's beliefs are not *de re* in any sense of
the word.

The crucial thing in (144) is that it says that the perspectival individual
cross-identified through Joan's belief-alternatives with respect to a given
belief-alternative of the officer's does not exist in the latter world. In other
words, given a belief-alternative u of the police officer's, there is a
perspectival world line going through all belief-alternatives of Joan's with
respect to u, but that world line cannot be extended to u.

This shows what our analysis of the clause *he is a figment of her imagination* is. One could perhaps object to our analysis by saying that strictly
speaking we should not in our analysis of this clause consider Joan's
belief-alternatives but rather her imagination-alternatives, or something of
the kind. This objection could very well have a grain of truth in it.
However, we shall not pursue the point any further here, for two reasons.
First, the problem clearly concerns only the finer aspects of the predicate *is*

a figment of her imagination, and thus it is not of direct relevance for a discussion of intentional identity. Second, the general lines of an analysis of the problematic predicate are not affected by the suggestion. Whatever the right intensional verb turns out to be, the right analysis of (82) will be (144) with the right verb plugged in for the second occurrence of 'B_J'.

QUANTIFIER PHRASES ARE FIVE WAYS AMBIGUOUS IN INTENSIONAL CONTEXTS

One result which is implicit in the foregoing discussion is interesting enough to deserve to be put forward explicitly. This result states that quantifier phrases are (at least) five ways ambiguous in intensional contexts.

(a) *Russell's Scope Ambiguity*

The first ambiguity that arises in intensional contexts has been well documented in the literature. This is the scope ambiguity often associated with Bertrand Russell. (We shall not explore the history of the distinction here. It is clear that the distinction is much older. See e.g. Knuuttila 1978.) Following Russell, it is customary to observe that a sentence like

(145)   Bill thinks that Marlon Brando's latest film is excellent

has two readings, more explicitly given by

(146)   Of Marlon Brando's latest film, Bill thinks that it is excellent.
(147)   Bill thinks that Marlon Brando's latest film (whatever it is) is excellent.

(b) *Hintikka's Ambiguity of Duality in Cross-identification Methods*

Another ambiguity arising in intensional contexts that has been documented in earlier literature is Hintikka's ambiguity involved in cross-identification methods. This ambiguity affects a sentence like

(148)   Of the figure in front of him Jimmy believes that it is a lady who knows him.

In the first case, the phrase *the figure in front of Jimmy* is based on descriptive cross-identification. The definite description (148) refers to the figure in front of Jimmy which has descriptive and physical properties which make possible to cross-identify it with a lady (a human being). Thus it is e.g. necessary that the figure in front of Jimmy IS a human being but not that she knows Jimmy. In the second case, where the relevant definite description relies on perspectival cross-identification, it is required that the figure in front of Jimmy bears an appropriate causal relation to that belief of Jimmy's reported in (148), and that from the point of view of Jimmy's beliefs the figure counts as a well-defined individual.

(c) *Ambiguity in Existential Quantifiers*

Our third ambiguity relies on the observation that in intensional contexts an existential quantifier can be understood in two different ways, either to involve an existential presupposition or else not to involve one. More precisely, sentences of the form

(149)   Of some x a believes that $P(x)$

can be understood in two different ways: either (149) is taken to be a statement of an existent individual, or else of an individual not perhaps existing in the actual world, but an individual from the point of view of a's beliefs. (It goes without saying that we could have used almost any other intensional verb in the place of *to believe* in (149).)

We thus observe that the present ambiguity concerns only *de re* readings. It can be stated by saying that a *de re* construction is sometimes of an existent individual, sometimes not.

To illustrate the point, consider

(150)   Nob thinks that a witch has blighted Bob's mare.

According to our intuitions, there are two *de re* readings, the first one of which could more explicitly be expressed as follows

(151)   Of some (real) witch Nob thinks that she has blighted Bob's mare.

That this kind of reading of (150) exists is well documented in the literature. In fact, this reading of (150) follows once Russell's ambiguity (a) is acknowledged. What is important for our purposes is that since it is natural to take the predicate *witch* to be satisfied in a world by only such individuals as exist in that world, it follows that (150) is about some existent individual. Likewise, the *de re* reading of (151) upon investigation is about an existent individual.

Another *de re* reading of (150) emerges as follows. If (150) is *de re* it means that it is of a particular individual. In what sense? One very good sense is that from the point of view of Nob's thoughts there is a particular individual of the relevant kind. In other words, Nob thinks that a PARTICULAR witch has blighted Bob's mare because Nob thinks that there is a witch who is using such-and-such clothes, doing mysterious deeds of such-and-such kind in such-and-such a way, etc. Clearly we can thus imagine a situation where Nob's thoughts are, in a natural sense, about a particular witch, particular, that is, from his point of view. As for ourselves, we do not believe any such things exist, and it indeed may be that there is no existing individual Nob's thoughts to be about.

A *de re* reading of this second kind is accordingly of somebody in particular and yet that somebody does not exist.

How could we disambiguate the situation, and, in particular, could express more explicitly the present *de re* interpretation of (150)? It seems to us that the non-existential interpretation cannot naturally be imposed on a sentence

(152)   Of someone in particular Nob thinks that she is a witch who has blighted Bob's mare.

One explication which comes close to the reading is

(153)   Nob thinks of someone in particular that she is a witch who blighted Bob's mare.

An even better explication of the intended reading is

(154)   Of someone whom Nob takes to be a particular witch Nob thinks that she has blighted Bob's mare.

One powerful argument for the existence of the present ambiguity is the fact, and here our intuitions seem to be particularly unequivocal, that there is an intuitive difference between (152) and (154).

One further argument for the present ambiguity is of an indirect nature. It seems that the most natural interpretation of a sentence like

(155)   John sees that the woman in front of him is wearing a hat, but in fact she is only an hallucination

presupposes that we are working with existential quantifiers without existential presuppositions. (Cf. our discussion above.)

Gail Stine (1976) has lucidly argued for the present point. One example of Stine's involves a comparison between (156) and (157):

(156)   Ralph believes that the particular man who he has in mind as Moses led the Jews out of Egypt.

(157)   Ralph believes that Moses, whoever he may be, led the Jews out of Egypt.

Stine argues as follows:

Now let us consider what would count as Ralph's being able to identify Moses, to have him in particular in mind. Let's say he believes that Moses was the man who as an infant was found in the bulrushes, raised in the Pharaoh's house, led the Jews out of Egypt into the Promised Land, receiving the Ten Commandments on the way, and, in general, whose deeds are as recorded in the Old Testament. Then [(156)] is true. Now let us suppose the whole Old Testament story is legend only, that Moses never existed. This supposition is irrelevant. If Ralph has all those beliefs with respect to Moses, then [(156)] is true, as distinct from the case in which the nonexistent Moses is only a name to Ralph and he believes that Moses led the Jews out of Egypt only because he heard someone whose word he trusts say so, in which cᵣ only [(157)] is true. (p. 496)

Stine's point seems to us to be well taken. The same point has also been put forward by Hintikka (1974a).

Further evidence for the same point is reported without analysis in Ioup (1977). Ioup refers to Fodor (1970) for a similar and earlier account, but we have not been in a position to study Fodor's unpublished MIT thesis. An example of Ioup's is

(158)   Alberta believes that a dragon ate her petunias.

Ioup correctly points out that this sentence "is ambiguous with respect to specificity, even though no referent of the indefinite exists ontologically . . . [for] . . . whether or not dragons exist, Alberta may believe they do and [(158)] is ambiguous as to whether Alberta maintains a belief about a particular dragon or about some unspecified dragon" (Ioup 1977, p. 235).

These observations show, as Ioup puts it, that "the ambiguities concerning specificity appear to be independent of ontological existence entailments". In other words ambiguity (a) and (c) are two different things.

(d) *Ambiguity in* de re *Readings*

The first ambiguity which seems to be novel in our discussion arises when considering a sentence like

(159)   Bill believes that the lady in front of him knows him.

The only readings that we are here interested in are the *de re* readings. (They are the most natural ones here anyway.)

The two readings which illustrate the present ambiguity can more explicitly be stated thus:

(160)   Of the lady in front of him Bill believes that she knows him

and

(161)   Of somebody Bill believes that she is the lady in front of him and that she knows him.

Since in (160) and in (161) the quantifiers can, according to the ambiguity pointed out in (b), be understood in two different ways, it follows that the present ambiguity affects both the perspectival as well as the descriptive *de re* readings.

One could explicate one important aspect of the distinction in possible worlds semantics in the following way. It is often observed that the difference between the *de dicto* and *de re* readings of a sentence like

(162) a believes that $P(b)$

is that in the *de dicto* reading 'b' may refer to different individuals in the different possible worlds a *believes that* introduces us to consider. In contradistinction, in the *de re* readings 'b' is supposed to refer to the same individuals in all these worlds. But should the actual world be counted among these alternatives? By looking strictly at (162), one must answer in the negative, thus yielding the following explication for the *de re* reading:

(163)   There is an x such that a believes both that $P(x)$ and that $x = b$.

If we count the actual world among the relevant alternatives, then we end up with the customary explication

(164)   There is an x such that $x = b$ and a believes that $P(x)$.

Our analysis yields an explanation for the present ambiguity. The point is that readings (163) and (164) for (162) really arise from quite different bases. (163) is a reading which arises from certain SEMANTICAL considerations. It arises because, in the strict semantical motivation for the *de re* reading of (162), we can restrict our attention to the doxastic alternatives of a's – and these do not necessarily contain the actual world.

In contradistinction, (164) is really the reading a Russellian scholar would come up with. Since the Russellian ambiguity (a) is a scope ambiguity and thus a SYNTACTICAL one, we can see that the two *de re* readings located are really of quite different facts.

These observations, if we are right, in fact yield further evidence for possible worlds semantics as a theory of the semantics of propositional attitudes. For as we have pointed out, the reading (163) is precisely the one that results if we reflect (162) in terms of possible worlds, whereas (164) results from syntactical considerations (considerations concerning relative scopes). It seems, furthermore, that no good motivation for (163) could be given in terms of relative scopes.

It is also of interest to observe that natural language contains a very neat way to disambiguate sentences which are ambiguous in the way described. Consider for instance

(165)   Bob believes that the person who first proved the incompleteness of arithmetic is now in Cambridge.

Assume that Bob mistakenly believes that Russell is still alive, in Cambridge and that he was the first to prove the incompleteness. The usual *de re* reading

(166)   Of the person who first proved the incompleteness of arithmetic, Bob believes that he is in Cambridge

would be false, provided Bob knew Gödel is not in Cambridge. Yet there is a *de re* reading of (165) that is true at the situation envisaged, viz.

(167)   Of the person whom he believes to have been the first to prove the incompleteness of arithmetic Bob believes that he is in Cambridge.

This would indeed be true: there is a particular person (Russell) whom Bob believes to have been the first to prove incompleteness and of whom Bob believes he is now in Cambridge.

It is interesting to note that the ambiguity discussed under (c) can naturally be understood in terms of the present observations. To see the point, consider

(168)   Nob thinks that some particular witch has killed Cob's sow.

Our discussion has shown that there are two different *de re* readings of (168), depending on the location of the descriptive elements of the NP *some particular witch*. The two readings can be explicated as the difference between (169) and (170):

(169)   Of some particular witch Nob thinks that she has killed Cob's sow.
(170)   Of something that Nob thinks is a particular witch Nob thinks that she has killed Cob's sow.

What is striking here is that in (170) there is nothing to require that we were there speaking of an existent, actual individual. Nob may be mistaken in thinking that witches exist and hence also in his further more specific thoughts concerning witches. But irrespective of the degree to which Nob's thoughts match reality, (170) can be true. In contradistinction to this, in (169), where *some particular witch* is outside the scope of *Nob thinks that*, we are forced to consider existent individuals only. (This is due to the nature of the predicate *to be a witch*.)

Thus we get ambiguity (c) as a special case of the present more general ambiguity.

Again, a powerful argument for the existence of the ambiguity here argued for is given by the unmistakeable intuitive difference between (169) and (170). What is even more striking is the fact that a closer reflection on (169) shows that in fact it is ambiguous, too. Indeed, (170) gives one possible way to interpret (169). Another, perhaps more natural reading is the one we have tacitly assumed in the above discussion of (169), where *some particular witch* is completely out of the scope of *Nob thinks that.*

Thus we have a striking contrast between the actual semantical practice and the usual semantical theory here. For the second reading of (169) just mentioned is usually put forward as THE *de re* reading of (168) while the first reading, depicted by (170), is completely disregarded. Yet in natural language there is a perfectly straightforward and unequivocal way to paraphrase (in terms of *of-* constructions and relative scopes) reading (170) but not the second reading of (169). This observation should further reinforce our view that we are after a real distinction here and that a *de re* reading of the form (168) really exists.

What was just stated has to be qualified in one way which will neverthe-less not affect our point. For obviously the usual *de re* reading of (168) could unambiguously be written out as

(171)   Of some particular real witch Nob thinks that she has killed Cob's sow.

This does not affect the overall point, however, for (171) does not represent the way the common *de re* reading of (168) is usually put forward. For it is commonly thought that the *de re* reading of (168) (in the sense of (171)) can be written out merely in terms of *of*-constructions and relative scopes. We hope to have shown above that this simple idea is drastically mistaken.

Still another way to put the present ambiguity is to point out that the following two unmistakeably non-equivalent sentences paraphrase a *de re* reading of (168):

(172)   Concerning some particular witch: Nob thinks that she killed Cob's sow.
(173)   Concerning something that Nob thinks is a particular witch: Nob thinks that she killed Cob's sow.

Here (172) and (173) both seem to be unambiguous, and (172), in par-ticular, does not have a reading which would make it synonymous with (173). Thus the situation here is different from that of the *of*-construction.

(e) *Ambiguity in the Construction of Individuals*

The last ambiguity that we shall discuss here is closely connected to, and yet independent of, Hintikka's ambiguity (b). The present observation can formally and schematically be expressed thus: whenever a quantifier quantifies into several propositional attitude contexts, then each of those

contexts can presuppose either perspectival or descriptive cross-identification *vis-à-vis* the quantifier.

An example will illustrate the point. Consider

(174)   There is something of which Bill believes that it is an attractive woman wearing a large hat, and of which John believes it is a wax figure.

Here the quantifier *there is something* quantifies into two propositional attitude contexts. Either one of these contexts can presuppose either perspectival or descriptive cross-identification *vis-à-vis* the quantifier. Thus there are four possible combinations here, even though only two of them are natural here. In a situation of the Husserlian kind, discussed above, the natural reading takes the first attitude to be a belief about a perspectivally cross-identified individual and the second to be about a descriptively cross-identified individual.

But a situation where the converse reading is natural (first attitude about a descriptively cross-identified individual, second about a perspectivally cross-identified one) may arise e.g. when Bill and John are in an audience watching a play where what is really an excellent actress stands completely still wearing a large hat.

Examples of two (or more) attitudes, all of which are *de re* of a descriptively (resp., perspectivally) cross-identified individual are easy to come by. We will not bother to state them here.

GENERAL MORAL

A more general moral can be drawn from our discussion. It is a commonly accepted point among philosophers, logicians, and linguists that sentences like

(175)   Dick Tracy believes that a man with the third finger of his right
          hand missing killed the Painted Lady

or

(176)   John would like to marry a girl his parents don't approve of

are ambiguous. It is sometimes suggested, along the lines of Fillmore
(1967) and others, that the ambiguity could be captured in terms of
specificity/non-specificity distinction. Another suggestion is to follow
Russell and propose that the distinction be captured in terms of relative
scopes of the existential quantifier (or whatever quantifier is involved)
vis-à-vis the relevant intensional verb. And still another suggestion is to
use Donnellan's (1966) distinction between attributive and referential uses
of noun phrases. (For works relevant here, see e.g. Bach 1968; Karttunen
1971; Partee 1972; Hintikka 1973.)

We shall not try to review the literature on this topic. Suffice it to point
out the following important general moral which affects all the work in this
direction: THERE IS NO ONE DISTINCTION WHICH IS THE DISTINCTION
CHARACTERIZING THE AMBIGUITY INVOLVED WHEN NOUN PHRASES ARE
MIXED WITH PROPOSITIONAL ATTITUDES. Rather, as we hope to have
shown above, there are several independent, though related, ambiguities
involved in these cases.

Academy of Finland

BIBLIOGRAPHY

Bach, Emmon (1968) 'Nouns and Noun Phrases', in Emmon Bach and Robert T. Harms
   (eds.), *Universal in Linguistic Theory*, Holt, Rinehart and Winston, New York.
Baranse, G. (1969) 'Identity in Indirect Discourse', *Journal of Philosophy* **66**, 381–382.
Carlson, Lauri (1975) *Peliteoreettista semantiikkaa*, unpublished thesis submitted in partial
   fulfillment of the requirements for the fil. kand. degree in the University of Helsinki,
   Helsinki.
—— (1978) 'Strategic Anaphora', forthcoming.
Cohen, L. Jonathan (1966) *The Diversity of Meaning*, Methuen & Co., London.
—— (1968) 'Geach's Problem About Intentional Identity', *Journal of Philosophy* **65**,
   329–335.
Dennett, D. C. (1968) 'Geach on Intentional Identity', *Journal of Philosophy* **65**, 335–341.
Donnellan, Keith (1966) 'Reference and Definite Descriptions', *Philosophical Review* **75**,
   281–304.

Geach, Peter T. (1962) *Reference and Generality*, Cornell University Press, Ithaca, New York.

Geach, Peter T. (1967) 'Intentional Identity', *Journal of Philosophy* **74**, No. 20, reprinted in P. T. Geach, *Logic Matters*, Basil Blackwell, Oxford, 1972. (Page numbers in the text refer to the latter edition.)

Fillmore, C. J. (1967) 'On the Syntax of Preverbs', *Glossa* **1**, 91–125.

Fodor, Janet D. (1970) *The Linguistic Description of Opaque Contexts*, unpublished MIT thesis.

Hintikka, Jaakko (1957) 'Modality as Referential Multiplicity, *Ajatus* **20**, 49–64.

—— (1962) *Knowledge and Belief*, Cornell University Press, Ithaca, New York.

—— (1969a) 'Semantics for Propositional Attitudes', in Hintikka (1969b).

—— (1969b) *Models for Modalities*, D. Reidel Publishing Company, Dordrecht, Holland.

—— (1973) 'Grammar and Logic: Some Borderline Cases', in K. J. J. Hintikka, J. M. E. Moravcsik and P. Suppes (eds.) *Approaches to Natural Language*, D. Reidel Publishing Company, Dordrecht, Holland.

—— (1974a) 'On the Proper Treatment of Quantifiers in Montague Semantics', in Sören Stenlund (ed.) *Logical Theory and Semantic Analysis*, D. Reidel Publishing Company, Dordrecht, Holland.

—— (1974b) 'Quantifiers vs. Quantification Theory', *Linguistic Inquiry* **5**, 153–177; reprinted in the present volume, pp. 49–79.

—— (1975a) *Intentions of Intentionality and Other New Models for Modalities*, D. Reidel Publishing Company, Dordrecht, Holland.

—— (1975b) *Knowledge and the Known*, D. Reidel Publishing Company, Dordrecht, Holland.

—— (1976a) *The Semantics of Questions and the Questions of Semantics* (Acta Philosophica Fennica Vol. 28, No. 4), North-Holland Publishing Company, Amsterdam.

—— (1976b) 'Quantifiers in Logic and Quantifiers in Natural Language', in S. Körner (ed.) *Philosophy of Logic*, Basil Blackwell, Oxford. Reprinted in the present volume, pp. 27–47.

—— (1976c) 'Information, Causality, and the Logic of Perception', *Ajatus* **36**, 76–94.

Hintikka, Jaakko and Lauri Carlson (1977) 'Pronouns of Laziness in Game-Theoretical Semantics', *Theoretical Linguistics* **4**, 1–29.

Hintikka, Jaakko and Carlson, Lauri (1978) 'Conditionals, Pronominalization by Quantifiers, and Other Applications of Subgames', pp. 179–214 in the present volume.

Hintikka, Jaakko and Esa Saarinen (1975) 'Semantical Games and the Bach–Peters Paradox', *Theoretical Linguistics* **2**, 1–20. Reprinted in the present volume, pp. 153–178.

Howell, Robert (1972) 'Seeing As', *Synthese* **23**, 400–422.

Husserl, Edmund (1970) Logical Investigations, translated by J. N. Findlay, Routledge & Kegan Paul, London.

Ioup, Geogette (1977) 'Specificity and Interpretation', *Linguistics and Philosophy* **1**, 233–245.

Kamp, Hans (1971) 'The Formal Properties of "Now"', *Theoria* **37**, 227–273.

Kanger, Stig (1957a) *Provability in Logic*, Stockholm Studies in Philosophy, Vol. 1, Stockholm.

—— (1957b) 'The Morning Star Paradox', *Theoria* **23**, 1–11.

—— (1957c) 'A Note on Quantification and Modalities', *Theoria* **23**, 133–134.

—— (1957d) 'On the Characterization of Modalities', *Theoria* **23**, 152–155.

Kaplan, David (1973) 'Bob and Carol and Ted and Alice', in K. J. J. Hintikka, J. M. E. Moravcsik and P. Suppes (eds.) *Approaches to Natural Language*, D. Reidel Publishing Company, Dordrecht, Holland.

Karttunen, Lauri (1971) 'Discourse Referents', Indiana University Linguistics Club, mimeo.

Kripke, Saul (1959) 'A Completeness Theorem in Modal Logic', *The Journal of Symbolic Logic* **24**, 1–14.

—— (1963a) 'Semantical Considerations on Modal Logic', *Acta Philosophica Fennica* **16**, 83–94.

—— (1963b) 'Semantical Analysis of Modal Logic: I, Normal Modal Propositional Calculi', *Zeitschrift für mathematische Logik und Grundlagen der Mathematik* **9**, 67–96.

—— (1965) 'Semantical Analysis of Modal Logic: II, Non-Normal Modal Propositional Calculi', in J. W. Addison, L. Henkin and A. Tarski (eds.) *The Theory of Models*, North-Holland Publishing Company, Amsterdam.

Knuuttila, Simo (1978) 'Time and Modality in Scholasticism', to appear.

Lakoff, George (1972) 'Linguistics and Natural Logic', in D. Davidson and G. Harman (eds.) *Semantics of Natural Language*, D. Reidel Publishing Company, Dordrecht, Holland.

Lewis, David (1972) 'General Semantics', in D. Davidson and G. Harman (eds.) *Semantics of Natural Language*, D. Reidel Publishing Company, Dordrecht, Holland.

Montague, Richard (1973) 'The Proper Treatment of Quantification in Ordinary English', reprinted in Richard Montague, *Formal Philosophy*, edited and with an introduction by R. H. Thomason, Yale University Press, New Haven and London, 1974.

Niiniluoto, Ilkka (1978) 'Knowing That One Sees', to appear.

Partee, Barbara Hall (1972) 'Opacity, Coreference, and Pronouns', in D. Davidson and G. Harman (eds.) *Semantics of Natural Language*, D. Reidel Publishing Company, Dordrecht, Holland.

Saarinen, Esa (1977a) 'Backwards-Looking Operators in Intensional Logic and in Philosophical Analysis: A Summary', Reports from the Department of Philosophy, University of Helsinki, No 7/1977.

—— (1977b) 'Game-Theoretical Semantics', *The Monist* **60**, 406–418.

—— (1978) 'Backwards-Looking Operators in Tense Logic and in Natural Language', in J. Hintikka, I. Niiniluoto, and E. Saarinen (eds.) *Essays on Mathematical and Philosophical Logic*, D. Reidel Publishing Company, Dordrecht, Holland. Reprinted in the present volume, pp. 215–244.

Stine, Gail: (1977) 'Intentional Inexistence', *Journal of Philosophical Logic* **5**, 491–510.

NOTES

* I wish to thank Lauri Carlson, Jaakko Hintikka, Ilkka Niiniluoto, Merrill Provence, and the anonymous referee of *Linguistics and Philosophy* for helpful comments on earlier versions of this paper.

[1] Primary exceptions to this rule are Cohen (1968) and Dennett (1968) which discuss the reading intended by Geach. Both these sketchy treatments are unsatisfactory. Cohen's analysis applies to this problem a general approach to indirect discourse which he has developed elsewhere (Cohen 1966). There are a number of reasons speaking against the general approach, however. For one thing, it involves explicit quantification over such problematic objects as propositions or speech acts.

Dennett's analysis of the troublesome sentence (1) is a negative one. He claims that there is no such reading as that claimed by Geach. He argues that "so long as we hold out the hope or conviction that the object or person or witch under discussion exists, questions of identity are substantive and serious, but as soon as we become sceptics like our reporter, and disavow transparent renderings of our discussion, questions of identity and diversity become idle if not outright meaningless" (Dennett 1968, p. 337). This kind of approach to intentional identity seems to us ill-founded. We hope to be able to show below that the kind of reading put forward by Geach does exist and, what is more crucial here, to show what such intentional identity semantically amounts to.

[2] Throughout this paper, we shall often disregard the distinction between metalanguage and object language in discussing formal languages.

[3] Here T_H is the operator *Hob thinks that* and B_N the operator *Nob believes that*. Similar self-explanatory notation will be used in what follows.

[4] For a discussion of pronouns of this kind, see e.g. Geach (1962).

[5] It has been suggested by G. Baranse (1969) that the reason we used to rule (9) out as a reading of (1) is ill founded. Baranse attacks Geach's point that (9) would commit Hob and Nob to have some ONE person in mind as a suspected witch. According to Baranse this is mistaken, for he claims that (9) is implied by

(177)   As regards Jil or Hil, Hob thinks that one (he knows not which) is a witch and has blighted Bob's mare, and Nob believes that she (the same witch) killed Cob's sow.

This argument of Baranse's is mistaken. (177) does NOT imply (9). To see the point, consider the following analogous, clearly invalid inference from (178) to (179)

(178)   As regards Ford or Carter, Hob thinks one (Hob knows not which one) will be the next president of U.S.
(179)   As regards somebody, Hob thinks he will be the next president of U.S.

[6] See Stig Kanger (1957a; 1957b; 1957c; 1957d). Saul Kripke's classical works are Kripke (1959; 1963a; 1963b; 1965). For Hintikka's works in this area, see Hintikka (1957) and various papers collected in Hintikka (1969b).

[7] We shall later modify our intensional logic so as not to attach existential presuppositions to a sentence like (74). In the modified framework the point will however hold *mutatis mutandis*.

[8] This is for instance how the sentence would be treated in Montague semantics, at least as far as Montague's own proposals are concerned. See Montague (1973) for a discussion of parallel examples. (We are not claiming, of course, that Montague semantics could not be rectified in this respect.)

JAAKKO HINTIKKA

THE ROSS PARADOX AS EVIDENCE FOR THE REALITY OF SEMANTICAL GAMES

In a number of earlier writings, I have outlined what may be called a game-theoretical semantics.[1] This semantics can be applied both to formal (but interpreted) first-order languages, with or without modalities, and to certain fragments of English. The strategy on which this semantics is based is to associate with each sentence S under consideration a two-person game $G(S)$ by reference to which the basic semantical attributes of S can be defined.

The two players are called Myself and Nature. The game starts from S and from world W with respect to which we are trying to determine the truth-value of S. At each stage of the game, a sentence S' is considered in relation to some possible world W'. The rules of the game can be understood on the basis of the idea of considering the game as an attempted verification of the original sentence against all the counter-examples which the malicious Nature might produce. Thus these rules might include the following.

(G.some) When the game has reached a world and a sentence of the form

$$X - \text{some } Y \text{ who } Z - W,$$

then I can choose an individual, give it a proper name (if it does not have one already), say 'a'. The game is then continued with respect to the sentence

$$X - a - W, a \text{ is a(n)}Y, \text{ and } a \text{ Z}.$$

An explanation is needed here. In order to verify X – some Y who $Y - W$ I have to produce an individual of the required sort. This requirement is obviously that the individual in question be an Y who Z and satisfy $X - W$. Hence I must be able to defend the conjunction of these sentences in the rest of the game.

Certain qualifications are needed here. In 'who Z' the pronoun 'who' must occupy the subject position, and the main verb must be in the

329

E. Saarinen (ed.), Game-Theoretical Semantics, 329–345. All Rights Reserved.
Copyright © 1977 by the Hegeler Institute, La Salle, Illinois.

singular. Some further clauses will also be needed in order to handle certain pronominalization problems.

My formulation of (G.some) above can easily be generalized so as to dispense with most of these qualifications. It can also be generalized so as to apply to other wh-words than 'who'. What was just given is in effect a special case of the real rule (G.some) which nevertheless is representative enough to enable us to grasp the general form, even if the latter is not explicitly written out.

Similar rules can be formulated for other quantifiers. The following is a case in point.

(G.every) When the game has reached a world and a sentence of the form

$$X - \text{every } Y \text{ who } Z - W$$

then Nature may choose an individual, give it a proper name (if it did not have one already), say 'b'. The game is then continued with respect to the same world and with respect to the sentence

$$X - b - T \text{ if } b \text{ is a(n)} Y \text{ and if } b \text{ W}.$$

The same qualifications are needed as in (G.some). The motivation needed here is similar to that given to (G.some) earlier. In order to defend

$$X - \text{every } Y \text{ who } Z - W$$

I must be able to defend any substitution-instance of $X - W$ with respect to the name 'b' of any potential counter-example that Nature might select. In order to qualify as a counter-example, b naturally must be an Y such that b Z. Hence (G.every).

We can likewise formulate rules for propositional connectives.

(G.or) When the game has reached a world and a sentence of the form

$$X \text{ or } Y$$

then I can choose one of the disjuncts. The game is then continued with respect to it and to the same world.

A restraint on the applicability of (G.or) is needed here. It says that all pronominalization between X and Y must be done by proper names. In applying (G.or), each pronoun in the disjunct chosen which is pronominalized by a noun phrase in the other disjunct will then have to be replaced by the corresponding proper name.

(G.and) The same for conjunctions except that Nature does the choosing.

Negation can be handled in many different ways. One of the simplest is the following one.

(G.not) When the game has reached a negated sentence, say neg + X (where 'neg +' denotes the negation-forming operation), and a world, the players switch roles (as defined by the game rules and the rule for winning and losing) and the game is continued with respect to X and the same world.

I shall not try to specify here the negation-forming operation neg +.[2]

Many cases of the phrasal 'and' can be handled by means of the following rule.

(G.phrasal and) When the game has reached a sentence of the form

$$X - Y_1, Y_2, \ldots, \text{and } Y_k - Z$$

where 'Y_1', 'Y_2',..., and 'Y_k' are singular noun phrases, then Nature may choose Y_i ($i = 1, 2, \ldots, k$) and the game is continued with respect to

$$X - Y_i - Z.$$

Exception: If '$Y_1, Y_2, \ldots,$ and Y_k' is the subject of a clause in the input sentence, then in the output the main verb of this clause is changed from the plural to the singular.

For disjunctive phrases, a similar rule, called (G.phrasal or), can be set up. It is like (G.phrasal and) except that (i) the choice is made by Myself and not by Nature and (ii) the exception is omitted.

Rules for deontic words involve choices of worlds instead of choices of individuals. Not surprisingly, permission is analogous with existential quantification and obligation with universal quantification.

(G.may) When the game has reached a world W' and a sentence of the form

$$a \text{ may X},$$

where 'a' is a proper name, I can choose a deontic a-alternative to W', say W''. The game is then continued with respect to W'' and X', where X′ is obtained from X by changing all the main infinitives into third person singular, and by prefixing '*a*' to them.

(G.must) Likewise for sentences of the form

> *a* must X

except that the choice is made by Nature.

These are of course special cases of certain more general rules which are here left unformulated. For other notions (e.g., for 'if', 'knows', 'any', etc.) other rules are needed.

For any *S* containing only words for which the game rules have been formulated, plus simple verbs and proper names, the game will come to an end after a finite number of moves. The outcome is an atomic sentence with respect to a certain world. Since we are dealing with an interpreted language, this atomic sentence is either true or false in that world. If the former, the winner is Myself and the loser Nature; if the latter, *vice versa*. (Please note that the interpretation of our language includes the specification as to what individuals there are in each world and also how they are cross-identified.)

The concept of truth for atomic sentence is thus presupposed in my definition of truth for nonatomic ones. Its availability here is a corollary to the assumption that we are dealing with interpreted languages (including natural ones.) The first main result of our game-theoretical conceptualizations is to extend the concept of truth to nonatomic sentences. This can be done as follows: *S* is true in the world *W* iff there is a winning strategy available in G(*S*) to Myself in a game starting from *S*. And once we have defined the notion of truth (in a world), the rest of semantics can be built up in the usual way.

One of the most important questions concerning the kind of approach to the semantics of natural languages which is illustrated by the game rules above is whether these games and their rules enjoy any sort of psychological reality in our understanding of language. The purpose of this paper is to produce some indirect evidence for an affirmative answer.

The evidence I have in mind is hypothetico-deductive in character. It can be obtained by deriving a prediction from the assumption that my game rules really enjoy some sort of psychological reality, and then verifying this prediction. The 'derivation' in question is most straightforward. If the moves made by my two idealized players are in some sense real, then we are entitled to expect that they will sometimes get confused with the choices of actual people, for instance with the choices of the people our sentences speak of. And of this there are in fact concrete examples. A case in point is the following sentence which is an instance of the so-called Ross' paradox (Alf Ross, not Sir David) of deontic logic.[3]

(1)   John must mail the letter or destroy it.

Later we shall consider stronger variants of essentially the same paradox.

The peculiar nature of (1) can be illustrated by comparing it with

(2)   John must mail the letter.

What is unexpected about the natural-language sentence (1) is that its semantical force is quite different from the apparently straightforward formalization.

(3) O (John mails the letter $\lor$ John destroys the letter)

where O is the operator for obligation ('must'). For instance, (3) is implied by

(4) O (John mails the letter)

while (1) is clearly not implied by (2) even though (4) is an equally straightforward formalization of (2).

Paradoxes of this type have provoked an extensive literature. From the vantage point of game-theoretical semantics, the solution is nevertheless surprisingly simple. In order to see it, let's examine how the game-theoretical semantics of (1) works out. Starting out from a given world W, Nature will choose a deontic alternative W' to W by (G.must), and the game is then continued with respect to W' and with respect to the sentence.

(5)   John mails the letter or John destroys it.

Now according to (G.or) I ought to be able to choose between

(6)   John mails the letter

and

(7)   John destroys the letter

in each such W' so as to produce a true sentence. But – and here is the crucial idea – everybody keenly feels it to be wrong for me to pretend to make a choice on behalf of another agent, in this case John, of what he is to do. Hence John's real-life choice is naturally transmuted into a choice by him in my semantical games. This of course radically changes the resulting semantics. In every deontically admissible world John must either mail or destroy the letter, but since the choice is his, not mine, John must among other things be permitted by (1) to do either. This observation alone suffices to explain why (1) is not implied by (2).

If this explanation of the peculiarities of (1) is correct, several consequences ensure. Verifying them provides further support for my thesis.

For one thing, the same situation can be expected to arise with 'may' as with 'must'. And indeed it does. For consider, instead of (1), the sentence

(8)   John may mail the letter or to destroy it.

This sentence embodies in fact a stronger form of Ross' paradox.[4] Its semantics is different from that of

(9) P(John mails the letter $\vee$ John destroys the letter)

where 'P' is the permission-operator ('may'). In fact, (8) is almost equivalent with

(10) P(John mails the letter) $\wedge$ P(John destroys the letter).

Be this as it may, (8) is not implied by

(11)   John may mail the letter.

A solution is obtained *a fortiori*. The semantical games connected with (8) are just like those connected with (1) except that the world W' is chosen by Myself, not by Nature. This explains the difference between the semantics of (8) and (9). But the confusion between my choices and John's arose only after W' was selected. The way in which we arrived here does not matter. Hence the explanation for the paradoxical character of (1) immediately covers (8), too.

One can say even more than this, however. In our semantical games, a move by John affects my strategies pretty much in the same way as a move by Nature. This in effect changes the disjunction into a conjunction in (8). Moreover, in the semantical game connected with (8),

John's choice between mailing the letter and destroying it is presumably prior to my choice of the world W'. If so, it has the effect, as the reader can easily see, of giving (8) precisely the force of (10).

Furthermore, in the case of a permission given to John (as in (8)) it must appear especially perverse, perhaps even self-defeating, to deprive him of the choice just permitted to him and to assign the choice between his mailing the letter and his burning it to anyone else. This gives the paradox a special poignancy in connection with permissions, which explains why we perceive it even more clearly in connection with (8) than in connection with (1).

This seems to me a much better solution to Ross' paradox than any of the ones found in the literature. It also is a strong indirect evidence for the psychosemantical reality of my semantical games.

The solution I am proposing may be tested by seeing what it implies for related sentences. One prediction it yields deals with the case in which we have an existential statement instead of a disjunction inside a deontic operator. A case in point might be

(12)   You must vote for a Labour candidate

in its relation to

(13)   You must vote for someone or else.

The line of thought adumbrated above goes through without changes in such cases. Hence according to my lights a paradox is expected to arise here. And in fact it does. As Anthony Kenny has in effect pointed out (*Will, Freedom, and Power*, Basil Blackwell, 1975, pp. 73, 82), (13) does not seem to follow from (12) at all.

Another pair of examples illustrating the same point might be the following.

You must vote for the most experienced Labour candidate.

You must vote for some Labour candidate or other.

These verified predictions offer further support for my explanation. The paradox clearly is not endemic to disjunctions.

Another prediction which the game-theoretical solution of Alf Ross' paradox yields is relevant to some of the competing accounts of the paradox. Attempts have been made to explain away the paradox in terms of conversational (pragmatic) implicatures.[5] It has been pointed out, among other things, that whoever utters (8) or (1) when he is in a position to utter (11) or (2), respectively, violates the conversational presupposition that a speaker does not make a weaker (less specific) statement when he is in a position to make a stronger (more specific) one. This observation is of course correct, and sometimes it has been taken to offer us – suitably developed – a solution of Ross' paradox.

There is no need to deny that a violation of the conversational principle just indicated does in fact contribute to the Ross paradox. However, it follows from my account that it is not the whole story. It also follows from that account we actually have a genuine paradox only in some of the many cases in which the conversational principle is violated. This principle is independent of the subject matter, whereas the kind of confusion between game choices and real choices can arise only in contexts in which some agent's choices are being discussed, and indeed only when a disjunctive or existential clause represents a number of options of some agent (as distinguished, say, from a disjunctive choice between two agents).

These predictions are readily tested by means of evidence. One particularly illuminating course we can follow here is to concentrate on the valid implications which are intuitively seen to hold between different sentences. It seems to me that the importance of the idea of logic as a regimentation of valid inferential relationships between sentences or statements is vastly exaggerated. The semantical properties of sentences are incomparably more important. However, this does not mean that considering inferential relationships is always pointless. What makes such a tactic useful here is that focusing on inferences helps us to disregard largely the disturbing conversational implicatures. One way of heightening this effect is to replace the 'therefore' of inference by 'a fortiori'.

One remarkable thing here is already the fact that the Ross paradox is not eliminated by considering only inferential (entailment) relationships. We would *never* argue as follows.

(14)   John may mail the letter
       Therefore: John may mail the letter or destroy it.

(15)   John must mail the letter.
       Therefore: John must mail the letter or destroy it.

However, my account predicts that in otherwise analogous cases where we are not discussing what some agent does we obtain inferences which are not unnatural in the way (14)–(15) are. What is especially important, we obtain natural inferences in spite of a violation of the conversational implicatures mentioned above. Examples to this effect are the following.

(16)   We may have showers to-morrow.
        Therefore: We may have showers or drizzle to-morrow.

Here 'may' may express either epistemic or natural (meteorological) possibility. On either interpretation, (16) is a perfectly natural inference. Yet it goes against the same conversational implicatures as the inferences (14) and (15). Hence these implicatures cannot explain the unnaturalness of the latter inferences, either.

The same applies to epistemic concepts, as witnessed by the obvious validity of the following inference.

(17)   I know that the party will be on Tuesday.
        Therefore: I know that the party will be on Tuesday or Wednesday

This may be compared with the following.

(18)   For all that I know, the party may be on Tuesday.
        Therefore: For all that I know, the party may be on Tuesday or Wednesday.

The greater unnaturalness of (18) as compared with (17) arises through an interpretation of 'for all that I know' as 'to the best of my knowledge'. However, this unnaturalness is not surprising. It is not surprising that something unnatural ensues if the conversational presupposition which is being violated by all our recent inferences (12)–(13) is promoted to an explicit element of the propositions considered. After all, one way of expressing the presupposition we have been discussing is precisely to say that there is a tacit claim that what is said is 'to the best of my knowledge' every normal declarative statement.

It is also predicted (in some sufficiently loose sense) by our game-theoretical treatment of the Ross paradox that it arises in its most acute form in connection with permission, for there it is clearest that the choice between options is left to the agent. Even when we are discussing what some agent does, we may not obtain the full force of the paradox, for instance when we are focusing not on his decisions but impersonally on the different options open to him. Thus

(19)   John may come on Tuesday.

is felt to imply

(20)   John may come on Tuesday or Wednesday

only if the 'may' is taken to be the 'may' of possibility. Then the
inference is equivalent to the step from

It is possible that John should come on Tuesday to

to

It is possible that John should come on Tuesday or
Wednesday.

However, when the 'may' in (19) is taken to be the 'may' of permission, the inference from (19) to (20) is felt to be invalid. Yet on the
basis of the conversational principles the relative unnaturalness of the
inference ought to be independent of the choice of the two senses of
'may' in (19).

Another implication of my analysis of the Ross paradox is that there
will be nothing deviant about the corresponding negative sentence

(21)   John must not mail the letter or destroy it.

Here a choice by Nature takes the players to a deontic alternative in
which they are invited to consider the sentence

(22)   John doesn't mail the letter or destroy it.

Here (G.not) necessitates a reversal of the roles of the two players,
whereupon they consider the sentence (5). Here the choice between
disjuncts is now up to Nature, not Myself, in virtue of (G.not). Of
course, we very well may feel that Nature should not presume to make
moves on John's behalf any more than I should. But this will not make
any difference to the existence of my winning strategies, and since it is
these strategies that determine the semantics of a sentence, nothing out
of the ordinary happens in (22) semantically. It's logical force is
therefore to be expected to be that of

(23) $O \sim (p \lor q)$.

And this is indeed clear intuitively.

As further evidence, we have an obvious equivalence between (22) and the following natural-language sentence.

(24)   John must not mail the letter, and he must not destroy it, either.

This parallels the trivial equivalence of (23) and

(25) $O\sim p \wedge O\sim q.$

Another corollary to the game-theoretic treatment of the Ross paradox is that the 'paradox' arises only when a disjunction *between different options of an agent* is present. Other kinds of disjunctions do not create the Ross phenomenon. A case in point is illustrated by the obvious validity of the following inference.

(26)   John may mail the letter.
        Therefore: John or Bill may mail the letter.

Again the predictions of my scheme square very well with evidence.

It might be thought here that what makes a difference between (8) and (26) is the relative position of 'or' and 'may'. In the former it occurs in the object term, in the latter in the subject term. Perhaps this is what counts here?

It is not, as shown by the following examples.

(27)   Gardenias may be picked by visitors.
        Therefore: Gardenias or chrysanthemums may be picked by visitors.

This inference (27) is obviously invalid, unlike the following.

(28)   This letter may be mailed by John.
        Therefore: This letter may be mailed by John or Bill.

This inference is clearly valid. Again, the difference between (27) and (28) is readily explained on basis of game-theoretical semantics. In view of the contrast between (27) and (26) as well as between (28) and (8), we nevertheless cannot explain the difference between (27) and (28) on the basis of simple structural properties of 'may' sentences.

This also suggests that another attempted explanation of the Ross paradox which is found in the literature is inadequate. Expressed in crude terms, this type of attempted explanation takes off from the fact that 'or' sometimes seems to do duty for 'and' in English. This is taken to explain in some way or other the apparent transmutation of 'or' into an 'and' in (8).

Such an account is unsatisfactory, however, as long as an account is not given of the linguistic contexts in which the or-and switch takes place.

Another point which counts against this type of attempted explanation of the Ross paradox but which is in agreement with the game-theoretic account is the fact already mentioned that we do not have the paradox with sentences which are like (8) except that the 'may' is in them the 'may' of possibility and not the 'may' of permission. In order to see this, witness the following example.

(29)   You may meet John at the party.
          Therefore: You may meet John or Bill at the party.

Moreover, it was seen earlier that a variant of the Ross paradoxes can arise even when no disjunctions are presented. Hence no account of the paradox in the sole terms of an or-and assimilation can be an exhaustive one.

Along more constructive lines, it may be pointed out that many of the natural-language sentences in which 'or' seems to do the job of 'and', or *vice versa*, can be accounted for in terms of our rules for phrasal conjunctions and disjunctions. (Cf. above for a rough formulation of such rules.) For instance, in

(30)   All men and all women over twenty-one must have a social security number

'and' seems to serve to express disjunction, for (30) is equivalent with

(31)   Everyone who is either a man or a woman and is over twenty-one must have a social security number.

Now (G.phrasal and) immediately takes care of the situation. For it follows from it that (30) is equivalent with the conjunction of

(32)   All men over twenty one must have a social security number.

and

(33)   All women over twenty-one must have a social security number.

However, no such explanation is forthcoming for (1) or (8). This strongly suggests that the phenomena we have studied cannot be accounted for in terms of the semantics of 'or' and 'and'.

Another explanation works for sentences like

(34)   Every published book or paper helps John to get tenure.

An application of (G.every) yields a sentence of same form as

(35)   'Deep Truths' helps John to get tenure if 'Deep Truths' is a published book or paper.

Since 'or' occurs here in the antecedent of a conditional, it clearly has the right (conjuctive) force.

It is also explained easily why (34) can have the same force as

(36)   Every published book and paper helps John to get tenure.

All we have to do here is to apply (G.phrasal and) first so as to see that (36) is equivalent to a conjuction of

(37)   Every published book helps John to get tenure

and

(38)   Every published paper helps John to get tenure.

This is as it should be. But why are our rules to be applied to (34) and (36) in a different order? If they are applied to (34) in the other order, we obtain a weaker statement which is ruled out by the conversational principle of maximal specificity. If they are applied in the opposite order to (36), we obtain a nonsense result. Hence preference in ordinary discourse for the rule orderings we have presupposed.

None of these semantical and semi-pragmatical explanations works for (1) or (8), however.

All this does not amount to knockdown argument against the type of solution of the Ross paradox I have been discussing. However, it is strongly suggested by my observations that it may be more appropriate to explain some of the apparent reversals of 'or' into the role of 'and' in terms of the game-theoretical treatment of the paradox than to use of the alleged fact of such reversal as a basis of an explanation of the paradox.

A weak point in my line of thought might seem to be betrayed when we apply the solution outlined above to first-person statements.[6]

Clearly, the same paradoxes arise in this case as we saw earlier to arise in the third-person case. For instance, from

(39)   I may mail the letter

we do not seem to be able to infer

(40)   I may mail the letter or destroy it.

If anything, the paradox is even more poignant here than in the third-person case.

Yet our explanation of the paradox seemed to turn on a tempting confusion between my moves in a semantical game and choices made by a real-life person, viz. the agent mentioned in the paradoxical sentence. If this person is myself, no confusion appears to be in the offing.

The answer to this *prima facie* objection is implicit in what has been said. What is confused when the paradoxes arise according to my account is not just the choices of two different persons. What is really been replaced is a move by one of the players of a semantical game with an action of an agent typically engaged in actually changing the world. The deep contrast is thus not between persons, but between two types of activity, two different 'language-games'.

Now this latter contrast is even more easily forgotten if the two language-games are played by the same person. Far from eliminating the paradox, a shift to the first person may thus be expected to enhance the paradox, precisely as we saw the case to be.

My game-theoretic treatment of Ross' paradox, which I have defended in the last few pages, shows that the apparently paradoxical phenomenon is of the nature of an anomaly. The game rules are in it twisted by the pressures of nonlinguistic reality. In so far as we want to use a suitable logical symbolism as our medium of semantical representation, it is not advisable to try to change our logical rules for the purpose of coping with Ross' paradox. If we do so, the anomalous character of the paradox is betrayed by the ensuing difficulty of obtaining a simple, accurate set of axioms and rules of inference. (The existing literature on Ross' paradox amply illustrates these difficulties, it seems to me.) The paradoxical sentences are bound to remain exceptions, not typical cases, and have to be treated as such.

However, this does not detract from the naturalness of our game-theoretical explanation of the paradox. Assuming the reality of the moves of our semantical games, it would be amazing if these moves were not sometimes supplanted by real people's actual or potential choices. It is for this reason that Ross' paradox, by exemplifying such a shift, serves as evidence for the reality of semantical games.

At the same time, the analysis of the Ross paradox outlined above offers us an instructive object lesson in the methodology of philosophical and linguistic analysis of language. It is not only hopeless but misconceived to try to develop a theory which would automatically explain all the *prima facie* phenomena of language, including our intuitions concerning relations of entailment. There will always be exceptions which only can be explained, not in the sole terms of the underlying theory, but in terms of the interaction of this theory with various pragmatic forces. In the example we have considered, the main force was the tendency to confuse moves in a semantical game with the choices of real-life persons. What is especially interesting here is that the pragmatic explanation is not an *ad hoc* one but is closely geared to the basic theory which thus almost predicts its own exceptions of the kind we have considered. (It predicts them jointly with suitable pragmatic assumptions.)

This kind of two-level methodology was defended in the first chapter of my *Models for Modalities* (D. Reidel, 1969). The present essay serves as an additional example of the view argued for there.

What makes the view worth re-iterating is the unfortunate fact that it is still being neglected by linguists and philosophers of language, even though the same view is old hat for all experimental physicists. No physicist ever expects to account for a complex experimental situation by the sole means of the theory governing it. Some discussion, sometimes a great deal of discussion, of the specific situation (including the measurement techniques employed) is needed. Apparent exceptions to the fundamental laws are explained in ninety-nine case of hundred (to give a conservative estimate) by reference to the vagaries of the particular experimental setup rather than to exceptions to the underlying theory.

Since there is *a priori* much less reason to expect the laws of language to be context-independent than to expect the laws of physics to be, it is intensely puzzling to me to see many linguists and philosophers to behave as if any proposed linguistic theory ought to explain all relevant phenomena in one fell swoop. I have actually seen a theory of questions being criticized and rejected because it did not (among other phenomena) automatically yield an explanation why expletives like 'the hell' are (linguistically) acceptable only in certain types of questions but not in others. While agreeing with the impatient critic about the potential relevance of such phenomena to any putative theory, I cannot but find the use of swear-words one of the top candidates for a pragmatic rather than semantic explanation.

It seems to me that many linguists are laboring under a methodological misconception. This misconception is seen especially keenly when we consider a physical theory which from its very inception was known to be only an approximation. Bohr's original model of the hydrogen atom yielded a prediction concerning the wavelengths of the relevant spectral bands which was wrong by much more than any conceivable experimental error. Yet the Bohr model was a tremendous theoretical breakthrough because of the theoretical insights it yielded. (They are reflected by the fact that the derivation of the specific predictions from the model is such that it is no small miracle to have them come out with an approximately correct order of magnitude. Factors of the order 10^6 are bandied about in the derivations.) Yet I see almost daily linguists trying to throw out this or that theory because of its failure to explain alone this or that small fact. Such failures are relevant, but much less important than the overall theoretical insights that different theories of language yield or don't yield. It seems to me that linguists have recently been judging these theoretical insights from a perspective which is far too narrow and far too dogmatic.

The fact that in the Bohr example the discrepancies between theoretical predictions and actual data were obviously intended to be explained by theoretical refinements and not by reference to experimental techniques does not spoil my point. Indeed, this feature of the illustration has its own analogues on the linguistic side.

My treatment of the Ross paradox thus yields material for several general methodological observations.

Academy of Finland and Stanford University

NOTES

[1] See especially 'Quantifiers vs. Quantification Theory', *Linguistic Inquiry* 5 (1974) : 2, pp. 153–177 (reprinted in the present collection, pp. 49–79); 'Quantifiers in Logic and Quantifiers in Natural Languages' in *Philosophy of Logic*, Stephen Körner (ed.), Basil

Blackwell, Oxford, 1975, pp. 208–232 (reprinted in the present collection, pp. 27–47); *Logic, Language-Games, and Information*, Clarendon Press, Oxford, 1973.

[2] This problem will be discussed in a forthcoming work of mine on quantifiers in English.

[3] The 'paradox' was first propounded by Alf Ross in 'Imperatives and Logic', *Theoria* **7** (1941), pp. 53–71. There exists an extensive literature on the subject. For samples of it, see, e.g., Alf Ross, *Directives and Norms*, Routledge and Kegan Paul, London, 1968, pp. 160–161; G. H. von Wright, *An Essay in Deontic Logic* (Acta Philosophica Fennica, Vol. 21), North-Holland, Amsterdam, 1968, pp. 20–21, 32, 61, 66; Erik Stenius, *Critical Essays* (Acta Philosophica Fennica, Vol. 25), North-Holland, Amsterdam, 1972, p. 127.

[4] This version is sometimes known as the Paradox of the Free Choice Permission.

[5] The best known attempt of this kind seems to be that made by R. M. Hare in his paper, 'Some Alleged Differences between Imperatives and Indicatives', *Mind* **76** (1967), pp. 309–326. It was rejected by Ross in *Directives and Norms*, p. 161. The general idea of conversational forces has been emphasized and utilized especially by Paul Grice.

[6] I owe this point to valuable critical remarks by Ilkka Niiniluoto.

VEIKKO RANTALA

URN MODELS: A NEW KIND OF NON-STANDARD MODEL FOR FIRST-ORDER LOGIC

1. INCONSISTENCY AND CHANGING MODELS

In present-day logic and philosophy of logic, there obtains a certain disparity between model theory (semantics) and proof theory (syntax). The latter often uses distinctions and conceptualizations which are finer than those that can naturally be made in the former. For instance, in model theory we can classify sentences into contradictory (inconsistent) and satisfiable ones whereas in proof theory we can use all sorts of distinctions between different contradictory sentences depending, e.g., on how their inconsistency can be proved.

In pure logic, this disparity implies restrictions on that parallelism between model theory and proof theory which has proved useful in many directions. (This usefulness is shown, e.g., by such results as the different interpolation theorems.) In the philosophical applications of logic, it entails that model-theoretical conceptualizations cannot in their present form be brought to bear on many important questions, for instance on the question of the nature of contradiction and the question of different kinds of contradictions. For instance, it has been claimed by certain philosophers that there is an intimate connection between contradiction and change. Can we make any model-theoretical (semantical) sense of such a claim? Not in the present form of model theory.

It seems that some of these defects can be straightened out by having a closer look at the relation of semantics to syntax or perhaps rather at the links between a sentence and a model in which it is true. The usual rules of satisfaction and truth deal with this relationship as it were globally, by surveying the whole model in one fell swoop. There is nevertheless a simple and intuitive way of looking at the relation of

347

E. Saarinen (ed.), Game-Theoretical Semantics, 347–366. *All Rights Reserved.*
Copyright © 1975 and 1978 by D. Reidel Publishing Company, Dordrecht, Holland.

language to reality in the case of first-order (quantificational) languages which makes this relation a stepwise affair and hence creates a possibility for finer distinctions (see Hintikka, 1973b). This way is essentially the same as is often employed in the heuristics of elementary probability theory. The world is conceived of as a big box or urn from which we may draw balls (individuals) one by one. The two quantifiers (the existential and the universal one) have their meaning in that they impose restraints on what we may or may not obtain as a result of such draws. The universally quantified sentence $(x)F(x)$ says that each 'ball' (individual) drawn from the urn must satisfy $F(x)$. (This satisfaction will have to be explained in terms of further draws if $F(x)$ contains quantifiers.) An existential sentence $(Ex)G(x)$ says that among the 'balls' (individuals) which we may draw from the urn there is at least one satisfying $G(x)$. Nested quantifiers mark restraints on sequences of 'balls' one can draw, and the difference between draws with and without replacement is precisely the difference between the inclusive and the exclusive interpretation of quantifiers. (For this, see Hintikka, 1973a).

There are two main differences between the familiar urn illustrations of probability theory and the urn interpretation of first-order logic. One of them is obvious. Logic is only qualitative in the sense that there we are dealing with what kinds of balls one can or cannot draw from the 'urn' (model), whereas in probability theory numerical measures (probabilities) are associated with these different kinds of balls.

The other difference is also easy to understand. Since most first-order languages contain words for relations and not just for properties, we cannot establish the relevant attributes of our 'balls' by examining them alone. When a 'ball' (individual) is drawn from the big urn that a model is thought of as being, it comes almost literally with strings attached to it. That is, that individual bears different combinations of relations to the balls still in the urn (i.e., to the so far unexamined individuals of the model).

This implies an important further consequence. Two sequences of individuals drawn from the model may be identical as far as properties of their mutual relations are concerned and yet differ from each other in the kinds of relations they bear to the unknown individuals. Such hidden differences have to be kept in mind in discussing the urn models of first-order logic.

This urn interpretation of quantificational logic can be developed further in two important directions (and also to both of them at the same time). It naturally assigns at once an important role to the constituents, attributive constituents, and distributive normal forms of Hintikka (see Hintikka, 1973a). It can also be made more flexible by letting the composition of the set of balls in the urn vary between the draws. I shall first discuss the former of these two ideas and then the latter.

Let us first suppose we have a fixed first-order language L. For simplicity, we suppose that L includes a finite number of predicate symbols and individual constants but not function symbols.

It is said that a sentence S of L is of *depth* d if the number of layers of nested and connected quantifiers in S is d. It can be expressed by writing $S = S^{(d)}$.

Let $\mathscr{C}_d$ be the set of all constituents of depth d that can be formed in L. We shall only state some properties of constituents, relevant for this discussion:

Each $C^{(d)} \in \mathscr{C}_d$ describes a kind of possible world (model) which can be described by means of the symbols of L when this description is restricted so that it is possible to consider only the sequences of d individuals in their relation to each other. Thus, if $C^{(d)}$ is true in a model M, it gives us a ramified list of all the different kinds of sequences of individuals of length d (i.e., d-tuples) that one can find in M.

If $C_1^{(d)}$ and $C_2^{(d)}$ are different constituents in $\mathscr{C}_d$ (not only notationally different), they are incompatible, that is, they have no models in common. On the other hand, all the members of $\mathscr{C}_d$ taken together give the description of all possible worlds which can be characterized by means of L if only sequences of d individuals are considered. That is, the disjunction $\vee \mathscr{C}_d$ is logically true.

How does a given constituent $C^{(d)}$ accomplish this description of a kind of possible worlds? We shall try to explain this without entering technical details. $C^{(d)}$ includes a certain number of sequences of nested formulas with $1, 2, \ldots, d$ free variables. These formulas are attributive constituents. These sequences of attributive constituents describe the different kinds – all the possible classes – of d-tuples of individuals there exist in a model of $C^{(d)}$. That is, $C^{(d)}$ gives the finest possible partition of the dth direct power of M which can be accomplished by means of the vocabulary of L and by means of d layers of quantifiers. The connection of a constituent (or a sentence in general) of depth d and its model can be explained intuitively as follows: The different sequences of nested attributive constituents specify a process of gradual (stepwise) examination of its model up to a finite number d of steps. They specify the different kinds of individuals one can succes-sively draw from its model up to d draws. If we compare a world to an urn of balls, a constituent specifies what kinds of balls one can draw from this urn after one another.

A constituent $C^{(d+e)}$ of depth $d+e$ greater than d allows us to examine a world by means of the increased number of steps, i.e., it specifies what kinds of sequences of individuals of lengths $d+e$ one can find in its models.

It turns out that each sentence S of depth d can be effectively transformed into a disjunction of some constituents of the set $\mathscr{C}_d$: $C_1^{(d)} \vee \ldots \vee C_n^{(d)}$. This is called the distributive normal form of S (at depth d). Moreover, each constituent $C_i^{(d)}$ can be repre-sented as a disjunction of constituents of depth $d+1$: $C_{i1}^{(d+1)} \vee \ldots \vee C_{ik_i}^{(d+1)}(C_{ij}^{(d+1)} \in \mathscr{C}_{d+1})$, and so on. Thus we obtain the distributive normal forms of S at each depth $d+e$ ($e = 0, 1, \ldots$). The distributive normal form of S at depth $d+e$ is called its expansion at this depth. Hence we obtain a kind of analysis of the sentence S when we expand it into deeper and deeper normal forms. This analysis can be repre-sented graphically by aid of a tree of the following kind:

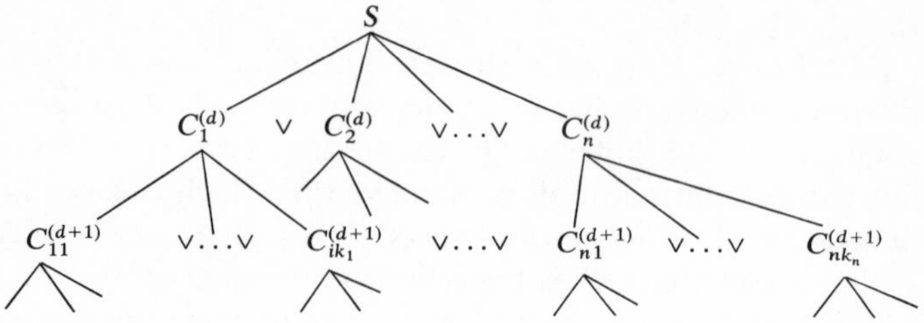

Fig. 1.

Let us now turn to inconsistent (contradictory, non-satisfiable) sen-tences. Since a sentence is inconsistent if all the constituents in its distributive normal form are inconsistent, we can consider mainly constituents.

It appears that there are, in general, two kinds of inconsistent constituents: It may happen that the inconsistency of a constituent $C^{(d)}$ can be found out by comparing its different parts with each other according to certain syntactical rules. So the inconsistency can be seen from the structure of $C^{(d)}$: its different parts *can be seen* to contradict each other. Such a constituent is called trivially inconsistent. But it may also happen that the inconsistency of $C^{(d)}$ cannot be seen from its structure. Then its inconsistency is 'hidden' in it and can be brought out only by expanding it into deeper normal forms. If it is inconsistent, all the disjuncts become *trivially* inconsistent at some depth, that is, there is an expansion $C_1^{(d+e)} \vee \ldots \vee C_k^{(d+e)} (e > 0)$ of $C^{(d)}$ such that each $C_j^{(d+e)}$ is trivially inconsistent.

Before presenting applications, it is useful to consider how inconsistent constituents can be interpreted model-theoretically despite of their inconsistency. A more precise account is in Section 2, below.

We saw that nested sequences of attributive constituents in a given constituent represent the different kinds of individuals one can successively draw from its model when one is examining this model. In ordinary interpretation of a constituent (or a sentence in general) it is assumed, of course, that the model is *invariant* in every respect between the draws. There occur no changes in the model when we are examining it. Now we can easily give up this assumption, i.e., we can allow the world to change between draws. Then we obtain a sensible model-theoretical interpretation of inconsistent constituents. Technically this interpretation can be accomplished, e.g., by modifying Hintikka's game-theoretical interpretation of first-order logic. This is not tied to the special form of a constituent but can be applied to any sentence.

Note here that changing urn models have been used in probability theory for important purposes. The best known case in point is probably Polya's urn model. (For it, see William Feller, 1957.)

By a change in a model we can understand a change in the properties of individuals of the model or a change in its domain (the universe of discourse). However, here we have an important contrast to usual ways of handling change. For example, if I say, 'It is raining', I am uttering a temporally indefinite statement. This statement is sometimes true, sometimes false, and the world is changing independently of my activity in examining the world to find out whether or not it is raining. But in our case change is geared to those interactions of ours with the world which give our language its meaning. If we interpret a constituent game-theoretically as describing the draws of individuals from a model, in the modified version of the game the model can change (as far as my possible experiences are concerned) *with* draws, i.e., it is not independent of the draws.

We shall now give a couple of examples where inconsistent constituents have a proper use.

(A) *Surface information.* This example is connected with the difference between trivial and non-trivial inconsistency of constituents. The concepts involved can be roughly explained as follows (see Hintikka, 1970 and Hintikka, 1973b):

We have seen that all the members $C_n^{(d)}$ of the set $\mathscr{C}_d$ give us the descriptions of all the possible worlds which can be characterized by means of the language L and the depth d. Let the distributive normal forms of sentences S_1 and S_1 be $C_1^{(d)} \vee \ldots \vee C_k^{(d)}$ and $C_1^{(d)} \vee \ldots \vee C_k^{(d)} \vee C_{k+1}^{(d)} \vee \ldots \vee C_{k+h}^{(d)}$ ($h > 0$, $C_i^{(d)} \in \mathscr{C}_d$), respectively. Let W be the class of all models for L.

(a) Suppose first that $C_{k+1}^{(d)}, \ldots, C_{k+h}^{(d)}$ are consistent. Then, if we take randomly a model M from W, it is intuitively clear what we mean if we say that it is more *probable* that M happens to be a model of S_2 (S_2 happens to be true in M) than a model of S_1. Let us say that the probability of S_2 is greater than the probability of S_1. This means that the *information* which S_1 gives us (in some sense) is greater than the information included in S_2:

(b) Suppose next that $C_{k+1}^{(d)}, \ldots, C_{k+h}^{(d)}$ are inconsistent. Then $\vdash S_1 \equiv S_2$, and they have equal probabilities and their informative contents are equal.

But the case (b) can be looked at from a different point of view: Can we compare the probabilities and informative contents of S_1 and S_2 merely by looking at their syntactical structures? Clearly we cannot if some of the constituents $C_{k+1}^{(d)}, \ldots, C_{k+h}^{(d)}$ are *non-trivially* inconsistent. We can only say that S_2 *seems* to admit more alternatives than S_1, so that the probability of S_2 is greater than the probability of S_1, and S_2 is less informative than S_1, as far as we *can know* at the level of analysis of these sentences. Thus the informative content of S_1 is in a sense greater than that of S_2. This is what Hintikka calls *surface information* of sentences. However, when S_1 and S_2 will be expanded into deeper and deeper distributive normal forms, then at some level $d + e$, $C_{k+1}^{(d)} \vee \ldots \vee C_{k+h}^{(d)}$ will become trivially inconsistent, i.e., the constituents of the form $C^{(d+e)}$ in the expansions of $C_{k+1}^{(d)} \vee \ldots \vee C_{k+h}^{(d)}$ at depth $d + e$ are trivially inconsistent. Then we *can see* that the 'real' informative contents of the original sentences are equal. Thus we can say that the information in the sense of surface information becomes greater when we move from level d to level $d + e$.

There is another point to be noticed here, which is due to undecidability of first-order logic in general. If one of the constituents $C_{k+1}^{(d)}, \ldots, C_{k+h}^{(d)}$ happens to be consistent (as in case (a)) it may happen that we can never effectively decide whether it is consistent or inconsistent, that is, whether or not S_2 is more probable than S_1. We have often, so to speak, to build our life upon the surface information of messages as long as we are not able to know the 'real' alternatives these messages give us.

(B) *Definability.* The other example is more special in its nature. It is connected with the theory of definability. It is not possible to present here the notions involved but only to describe the main features of the matter.

We shall consider a first-order language $L = L(\varphi, P)$ whose (finite) set of non-logical constants is $\varphi \cup \{P\}$. $P \notin \varphi$ is a distinguished unary predicate symbol. Let $T = C^{(d)}(\varphi, P)$ be a constituent of L. P is explicitly definable in T in terms of the φ if T implies a sentence of the form $(x)(Px \equiv F(\varphi, x))$ such that P does not occur in F.

Let M be an arbitrary model of T. If we take an arbitrary individual a from M, we can decide whether $M \models P[a]$ or $M \models \sim P[a]$ merely by investigating whether or not a satisfies F, that is, we know how P is interpreted in M on the basis of the interpretation of the members of φ in M if P is explicitly defined in T in terms of φ.

If P is not explicitly defined, it may happen that we can make the decision between $P[a]$ and $\sim P[a]$ for some individuals a of M. But for the other individuals T leaves us in uncertainty whether P or $\sim P$ must be assigned to them.

Now, from T we can construct a certain first-order sentence which describes this uncertainty. This sentence is called an *uncertainty description*. It may be inconsistent but it can be interpreted as follows:

We have seen that the constituent T describes M by telling us what kinds of d-tuples of individuals one can find in M. Let $\langle a_1, \ldots, a_d \rangle$ be a d-tuple of individuals of M. Suppose that we cannot tell on the basis of T and of the interpretation of φ in M whether $M \models P[a_1]$ or $M \models \sim P[a_1]$. Suppose moreover, that the uncertainty concerning P is carried over from a_i to a_{i+1}, so that we cannot tell whether $M \models P[a_{i+1}]$ or $M \models \sim P[a_{i+1}]$ on the basis of the information which can be extracted from T and a_i, a_{i+1}.

Now we can interpret the uncertainty description to describe the different kinds of d-tuples of individuals of M such that the uncertainty concerning P is preserved during the consecutive draws of these individuals despite of all the information which is possible to obtain from T at depth d.

Here we, in fact, have an example of a world which may change between the steps of investigation. This change is due to the fact that the range of individuals of which we do not know whether they have P or P may change from step to step (see Rantala, 1973; 1977). The role to which uncertainty descriptions can be cast as the mainstay of a general logical theory of definability already suffices to show convincingly that urn models (changing models) can be highly useful tools in logic.

If we are carrying out draws without replacement (i.e., opting for an exclusive interpretation of quantifiers), the 'urn' (domain) already changes a little bit at each draw.

2. URN MODELS

To understand the difference between an invariant model and the kind of changing model we have in mind, we again compare a model with an urn containing a number (possibly infinite) of balls with the following specifications. Different balls may have different properties and they may be in different relations to each other. How these properties and relations are manifested is not essential. The only requirement is that different kinds of balls and sequences of balls can be discriminated, some way or other, from each other.

To such an urn we associate one or several players who are allowed to draw from the urn balls one after another. Let us imagine that an urn has a change mechanism which before each draw regulates which balls are obtainable at this draw. We may think that this mechanism removes balls from the urn before certain draws, but brings them back before certain other draws or we may think that it may in some other way prevent a player from picking certain balls. We suppose that the players are informed, some way or other, of the functioning of this mechanism. So the players have the complete information of the relevant properties of the urn before the draws. How this information is transmitted to the players is not specified here. We can suppose that the properties of the balls and the relations between them are characterized in a first-order language, and the functioning of the mechanism is characterized by set-theoretical terms. Thus the players know, on the basis of this information, what kinds of draw they can perform, that is what kinds of sequences of balls they can draw from the urn.

If the mechanism of an urn does not impose any restrictions at all on the players, that is, if any balls are obtainable at each draw, we have an analogue of a completely invariant (usual) model for a first-order language.

The following variation gives us an analogue of a model for a second-order logic: The players are allowed to draw also sets of balls. Then we obtain an analogue of standard or non-standard second-order model according to whether or not the draws are restricted to a proper subset of the set of all subsets of balls in the urn.

The above characterization can be made more precise by the following definitions. We shall define a kind of changing models.

Let L be an arbitrary first-order (elementary) language. Let M be a model for L with the domain D. Let $c = \langle \mathscr{D}_i / i \in \omega \rangle$ be a countable sequence where $\mathscr{D}_0 = D$ and $\mathscr{D}_1, \mathscr{D}_2, \ldots$ are non-empty subsets of the cartesian powers $D, D^2, \ldots$, respectively, such that

(σ) $\langle a_1, \ldots, a_i \rangle \in \mathscr{D}_i$ iff $\langle a_1, \ldots, a_i, a_{i+1} \rangle \in \mathscr{D}_{i+1}$

for some a_{i+1}.

A pair of the form $\mathscr{M} = \langle M, c \rangle$ is called an *urn model* for the language L. $\mathscr{M}$ is called *invariant* if $\mathscr{D}_i = D^i$ for every i, otherwise *changing*.

We shall define the notion of *obtainable individual* of $\mathscr{M}$. An element a of D is *obtainable relative* to $\langle a_1, \ldots, a_{i-1} \rangle$ iff $\langle a_1, \ldots, a_{i-1}, a \rangle \in \mathscr{D}_i$ ($i \geq 1$. If $i = 1$, we shall identify $\langle a_1, \ldots, a_{i-1} \rangle$ with the empty sequence). Let $O^{\mathscr{M}}(a_1, \ldots, a_{i-1}) = \{a / \langle a_1, \ldots, a_{i-1}, a \rangle \in \mathscr{D}_i\}$ and $\mathscr{O}_i^{\mathscr{M}} = \{O^{\mathscr{M}}(a_1, \ldots, a_{i-1}) / \langle a_1, \ldots, a_{i-1} \rangle \in \mathscr{D}_{i-1}\}$, for $i \geq 1$, and $\mathscr{O}_0^{\mathscr{M}} = \{D\}$.

If a is obtainable relative to some $(i-1)$-tuple, it is an ith *obtainable individual*. The set $O_i^{\mathscr{M}} = \cup \, \mathscr{O}_i^{\mathscr{M}}$ of the ith obtainable individuals is the ith *domain* of $\mathscr{M}$. It should be noticed that the $O_i^{\mathscr{M}}$'s may be identical with D although $\mathscr{M}$ is not invariant.

We shall define what it means for a sentence $S = S^{(d)}$ of L to be *true* in an urn model $\mathscr{M}$ for L. We shall modify Hintikka's game-theoretical interpretation of truth (cf. Hintikka, 1973a). The moves of such a game are divided into two parts: the moves which consist of the possible choices of substitution instances of subformulas of S (cf. the rules $(G \cdot \vee), (G \cdot \wedge), (G \cdot \sim)$ in Hintikka, 1973a) and the moves which consist of the possible choices of members of D (the rules $(G \cdot E)$, $(G \cdot U)$): The latter kind of moves may thus include an infinite number of choices.

The rules of our game $\mathcal{G}(S, \mathcal{M})$ are otherwise similar to the rules of Hintikka's game but the rules $(G \cdot E)$ and $(G \cdot U)$ are modified as follows: For convenience, we stipulate that the first move (chance move), which is assigned to neither of the players, consists of the choice of D. The choices of members of D and the choice of D are here called simply *draws*.

$(\mathcal{G} \cdot E)$ If F is of the form $(Ex)F_0$ and $D, a_1, \ldots, a_i$ ($i = 0, \ldots, d-1$) have been drawn earlier, I draw an $a \in D$ which is obtainable relative to $\langle a_1, \ldots, a_i \rangle$. The game is continued with respect to $F_0(a/x)$.

$(\mathcal{G} \cdot U)$ If F is of the form $(x)F_0$ and $D, a_1, \ldots, a_i$ ($i = 0, \ldots, d-1$) have been drawn earlier, Nature draws an $a \in D$ which is obtainable relative to $\langle a_1, \ldots, a_i \rangle$. The game is continued with respect to $F_0(a/x)$.

It is obvious that S is true in an invariant urn model $\mathcal{M} = \langle M, c \rangle$ iff S is true in M. Then we can 'identify' $\mathcal{M}$ with M.

We shall denote $\mathcal{M} \models \approx S$ when S is true in $\mathcal{M}$, and $\models \approx S$ if S is true in every urn model for L. It follows from the remark just made that if $\models \approx S$, then $\models = S$. A formula F is *non-strandardly satisfiable* ($\approx F$) iff its existential closure has an urn model. $F \approx G$ iff F and G are non-standardly satisfiable in the same urn models. $F \approx G$ iff both F and G are non-standardly satisfiable or neither of them is non-standardly satisfiable.

It can be seen now what was meant when we spoke above of a changing world whose changes are not entirely independent of our intervention in it. For this purpose we shall consider two examples of different types of urn models.

Suppose that M is given.

(i) Let $D_1, D_2, \ldots, D_i \ldots$ be fixed subsets of $D, D^2, \ldots, D^i, \ldots$, resp. We define the sets $\mathcal{D}_i$ inductively as follows: $\mathcal{D}_0 = D$; $\mathcal{D}_1 = D_1$; $\langle a_1, \ldots, a_i, a_{i+1} \rangle \in \mathcal{D}_{i+1}$ iff $\langle a_1, \ldots, a_i \rangle \in \mathcal{D}_i$ and $\langle a_1, \ldots, a_i, a_{i+1} \rangle \in D_{i+1}$ ($i > 0$). Let the corresponding urn model be $\mathcal{M} = \langle M, c \rangle$ and its ith domain $O_i^{\mathcal{M}}$.

(ii) Let $D_1', D_2', \ldots, D_i', \ldots$ be fixed subsets of D, and $\mathcal{D}_0' = D$, $\mathcal{D}_i' = D_1' x \ldots x D_i'$, and $c' = \langle \mathcal{D}_i'/i \in \omega \rangle$. The corresponding urn model is $\mathcal{M}' = \langle M, c' \rangle$ and its ith domain $O_i^{\mathcal{M}'}$.

A difference between $\mathcal{M}$ and $\mathcal{M}'$ will become apparent if we ask whether a given member a of D belongs to the ith domain of $\mathcal{M}$ or $\mathcal{M}'$ (with a fixed i).

In case (ii) we can decide whether a is in $O_i^{\mathcal{M}'}$ merely by examining whether it is in the given set D_i', that is, no reference to other individuals is needed. In fact, $O_i^{\mathcal{M}'} = D_i'$ and hence the set $O_i^{\mathcal{M}'}$ is recursive (in some generalized sense) in D_i' and thus in $D_1', \ldots, D_i'$.

But in case (i), to decide whether a is in $O_i^{\mathcal{M}}$ we are possibly obliged to find out whether *there exist* individuals $a_1, \ldots, a_{i-1}$ such that $\langle a_1, \ldots, a_{i-1}, a \rangle \in \mathcal{D}_i$. Thus it is possible that $O_i^{\mathcal{M}}$ is only recursively enumerable (in a generalized sense) in the sets $D_1, \ldots, D_i$ which have been used to define $\mathcal{M}$. We could say that in case (i) the decision concerning the ith domain is, in general, less effective than in case (ii), although in both cases the corresponding urn model is well-defined in the sense that c, c' and the $O_i^{\mathcal{M}}, O_i^{\mathcal{M}'}$ are explicitly defined in terms of the 'primitive' sets $D_1, \ldots, D_i$ or $D_1', \ldots, D_i'$, resp. In fact, $O_i^{\mathcal{M}'} = D_i'$ and $O_i^{\mathcal{M}} = \{y \in D/(Ex_1) \ldots (Ex_{i-1})(x_1 \in D_1 \wedge \langle x_1, x_2 \rangle \in D_2 \wedge \ldots \wedge \langle x_1, \ldots, x_{i-1} \rangle \in D_{i-1} \wedge \langle x_1, \ldots, x_{i-1}, y \rangle \in D_i)\}$.

There are other ways to view informally this difference between $\mathcal{M}$, $\mathcal{M}'$. Let us suppose that the numbers $1, 2, \ldots, i, \ldots$ refer to certain instants of time. Then the above difference amounts to asking what can be known in advance about the state of the universe of the world at a moment i, that is, to what degree this state is effectively predictable from the set-theoretical structure of the change mechanism (c or c') and the initial state (D) of the universe.

We can try to view changes of a world as they are experienced by a person who is investigating this world step by step. In case (i), unlike case (ii), the possibilities that are open to him to find out the state of the universe at a moment i may depend on which individuals he came upon at the earlier moments $j < i$. It is perhaps appropriate to say that from his subjective point of view changes of the universe depend, in addition to the *a priori* conditions (c), also on his own activity. ('Nature is positively malicious', one might perhaps say of such situations.)

Game-theoretically the difference between $\mathcal{M}$ and $\mathcal{M}'$ is important. The game $\mathcal{G}$ defined above is supposed to be a game with perfect information. This supposition is necessary for an urn model like $\mathcal{M}$ in (i) (in the case that $\mathcal{M}$ is really changing, not invariant in the sense defined above). But as to $\mathcal{M}'$ in (ii), or an invariant model, the rules of the game can be modified so that this supposition can be given up in connection with the successive draws. The game with $\mathcal{M}'$ can be played in complete ignorance of (that is, independently of) the earlier draws, except for the chance draw, of course. Hence it is possible that both players are restricted to strategies in which no draw is conditional on the previous draw. Then it may happen that although a sentence S is true in $\mathcal{M}'$, that is, I have a winning strategy in the corresponding game $\mathcal{G}$ with perfect information, no such strategy exists in the modified game $\mathcal{G}_0$.

3. NON-STANDARD SATISFIABILITY

We shall state the condition for non-standard satisfiability of a formula.

It is a straightforward consequence of the above non-standard definition of truth (since the interpretation of the connectives is standard) that for every $\mathcal{M}$ and for every sentences S_1, S_2:

$$\mathcal{M}|\approx S_1 \wedge S_2 \quad \text{iff} \quad \mathcal{M}|\approx S_1 \quad \text{and} \quad \mathcal{M}|\approx S_2,$$
$$\mathcal{M}|\approx S_1 \vee S_2 \quad \text{iff} \quad \mathcal{M}|\approx S_1 \quad \text{or} \quad \mathcal{M}|\approx S_2,$$
$$\mathcal{M}|\approx \sim S \quad \text{iff not} \quad \mathcal{M}|\approx S.$$

Hence we obtain Theorem 1, below (the strict proof goes by an easy induction).

THEOREM 1. If a formula F is a substitution instance of a tautology of propositional calculus, then $|\approx F$.

LEMMA 1. If $|= F \equiv G$ by propositional calculus, then $F \approx G$.

LEMMA 2

    (i) $(x)F \approx \sim(Ex)\sim F,$

    (ii) $(Ex)F \approx \sim(x)\sim F,$

    (iii) $(Ex)(F \vee G) \approx (Ex)F \vee (Ex)G,$

    (iv) $(x)(F \wedge G) \approx (x)F \wedge (x)G.$

LEMMA 3. If x and y are different variables and x is not free in G and y is not free in F, then

    (i) $(Ex)F \wedge (Ey)F \approx (Ex)(Ey)(F \wedge G),$

    (ii) $(x)F \vee (y)G \approx (x)(y)(F \vee G).$

LEMMA 4. If $x_1, \ldots, x_k$ are the free variables of F, then

(i) $(Ex_1) \ldots (Ex_k)F \approx (x_1) \ldots (x_k)F,$

(ii) $(Ex)F \approx (x)F.$

LEMMA 5. $(Ex)F \wedge (x)G \approx (Ex)(F \wedge G).$

LEMMA 6. If z is a variable not in F and F' is a formula obtained when one or more bound variables in F, such that the corresponding quantifiers are not nested, are replaced by z, then $F' \approx F.$

LEMMA 7. $t_1 = t_2 \wedge F(t_1) \approx F(t_2/t_1)$, where t_1, t_2 are terms.

Of these results, Lemma 1 follows from Theorem 1. Lemmas 2, 6 and 7 are obvious. Lemma 3 can be proved by a similar construction as Lemma 4(i). Lemma 4(ii) is an immediate consequence of Lemma 4(i).

Proof of Lemma 4(i). It suffices to show that $\approx (EX_1) \ldots (Ex_k)F$ implies $\approx (x_1) \ldots (x_k)F.$

Consider first an arbitrary formula F with free variables $x_1, \ldots, x_k$ and an arbitrary urn model $\mathcal{M}$ of its closure $(Q_1 x_1) \ldots (Q_k x_k)F$. Let $\mathcal{M} = \langle M, c \rangle$ where $c = \langle \mathcal{D}_i / i \in \omega \rangle$. Consider such a play of the game $\mathcal{G}((Q_1 x_1) \ldots (Q_k x_k)F, \mathcal{M})$ where the k first individuals drawn are $a_1, \ldots, a_k$ (in this order) and which is played according to one of my winning strategies. Then $a_1 \in \mathcal{D}_1$, $\langle a_1, a_2 \rangle \in \mathcal{D}_2, \ldots, \langle a_1, \ldots, a_k \rangle \in \mathcal{D}_k$. We now denote $\mathcal{M} \mid \approx (Q_1 x_1) \ldots (Q_k x_k)F\{a_1, \ldots, a_k\}$. Define an urn model $\mathcal{M}a_1 \ldots a_k$ as follows:

$$\mathcal{M}a_1 \ldots a_k = \langle M, c' \rangle \text{ where } c' = \langle \mathcal{D}_i' / i \in \omega \rangle \text{ such that } \mathcal{D}_0' = \mathcal{D}_0,$$
$$\mathcal{D}_1' = \{a_1\}, \ \mathcal{D}_2' = \{\langle a_1, a_2 \rangle\}, \ldots, \ \mathcal{D}_k' = \{\langle a_1, a_2, \ldots, a_k \rangle\}, \ \mathcal{D}_i' =$$
$$\{\langle a_1, \ldots, a_i \rangle \in \mathcal{D}_i / \langle a_1, \ldots, a_k \rangle \in \mathcal{D}_k'\} \text{ when } i > k.$$

With these denotations in mind, we shall prove by induction on the length of F that

(*)   If $(Ex_1) \ldots (Ex_k)F$ is the existential closure of F, then for every $\mathcal{M}$, $\mathcal{M} \mid \approx (Ex_1) \ldots (Ex_k)F\{a_1, \ldots, a_k\}$ implies $\mathcal{M}a_1 \ldots a_k \mid \approx (x_1) \ldots (x_k)F.$

Then Lemma 4(i) follows from (*).

Proof of (*). (1) Let F be an atomic formula $P(x_1, \ldots, x_k)$ and $\mathcal{M} \mid \approx (Ex_1) \ldots (Ex_k)P(x_1, \ldots, x_k)\{a_1, \ldots, a_k\}$. Thus $M \mid = P(x_1, \ldots, x_k)$ $[a_1, \ldots, a_k]$. Consider the game $\mathcal{G}((x_1) \ldots (x_k)P(x_1, \ldots, x_k), \mathcal{M}a_1 \ldots a_k)$.

There exists only one play in this game and in this play Nature can draw only the individuals $a_1, \ldots, a_k$ (in this order). Since $M| = P(x_1, \ldots, x_k) [a_1, \ldots, a_k]$, then $\mathcal{M}a_1 \ldots a_k |\approx (x_1) \ldots (x_k) P(x_1, \ldots, x_k)$.

The case that F is of the form $x_1 = x_2$ is treated similarly, as well as the cases where the formulas include other terms.

Suppose (*) holds for formulas G and H.

(2) Let F be of the form $G \wedge H$ and $\mathfrak{M}| \approx (Ex_1) \ldots (Ex_k)(G \wedge H)$ $\{a_1, \ldots, a_k\}$. Then $\mathcal{M}| \approx (Ex_1) \ldots (Ex_k) G\{a_1, \ldots, a_k\}$ and $\mathcal{M}| \approx (Ex_1) \ldots (Ex_k) H\{a_1, \ldots, a_k\}$, and by induction hypothesis, $\mathcal{M}a_1 \ldots a_k |\approx (x_1) \ldots (x_k) G$ and $\mathcal{M}a_1 \ldots a_k |\approx (x_1) \ldots (x_k) H$, whence $\mathcal{M}a_1 \ldots a_k |\approx (x_1) \ldots (x_k) G \wedge (x_1) \ldots (x_k) H$. Thus by Lemma 2, $\mathcal{M}a_1 \ldots a_k |\approx (x_1) \ldots (x_k)(G \wedge H)$.

(3) Let F be of the form $G \vee H$ and $\mathcal{M}| \approx (Ex_1) \ldots (Ex_k)(G \vee H)\{a_1, \ldots, a_k\}$. Then $\mathcal{M}| \approx (Ex_1) \ldots (Ex_k) G\{a_1, \ldots, a_k\}$ or $\mathcal{M}| \approx (Ex_1) \ldots (Ex_k) H\{a_1, \ldots, a_k\}$.

Assume the first alternative. Then by induction hypothesis, $\mathcal{M}a_1 \ldots a_k |\approx (x_1) \ldots (x_k) G$, whence $\mathcal{M}a_1 \ldots a_k |\approx (x_1) \ldots (x_k)(G \vee H)$.

(4) Let F be of the form $\sim G$ and $\mathcal{M}| \approx (Ex_1) \ldots (Ex_k) \sim G\{a_1, \ldots, a_k\}$, that is, $\mathcal{M}| \approx \sim (x_1) \ldots (x_k) G\{a_1, \ldots, a_k\}$. Suppose $\mathcal{M}a_1 \ldots a_k |\not\approx (x_1) \ldots (x_k) \sim G$. Then $\mathcal{M}a_1 \ldots a_k |\approx (Ex_1) \ldots (Ex_k) G$, whence $\mathcal{M}a_1 \ldots a_k |\approx (Ex_1) \ldots (Ex_k) G\{a_1, \ldots, a_k\}$ by the construction of $\mathcal{M}a_1 \ldots a_k$. If $\mathcal{M}a_1 \ldots a_k = \mathcal{N}$, then $\mathcal{N}a_1 \ldots a_k = \mathcal{N}$ and it follows from induction hypothesis that $\mathcal{N}| \approx (x_1) \ldots (x_k) G$, whence $\mathcal{M}| \approx (x_1) \ldots (x_k) G\{a_1, \ldots, a_k\}$, contrary to the assumption.

(5) The case F is $(Ex)G$ follows from the induction hypothesis and the fact that $\mathcal{M}| \approx (Ex_1) \ldots (Ex_k)(Ex) G\{a_1, \ldots, a_k\}$ implies $\mathcal{M}| \approx (Ex_1) \ldots (Ex_k)(Ex) G\{a_1, \ldots, a_k, a\}$ for some a.

(6) Similarly when F is $(x)G$.

Proof of Lemma 5. It is obvious that $\approx (Ex)F \wedge (x)G$ implies $\approx (Ex)$ $(F \wedge G)$. Suppose $\approx (Ex)(F \wedge G)$. By Lemma 4 (ii), $\approx (x)(F \wedge G)$, whence by Lemma 2, $\approx (x)F \wedge (x)G$. If $\mathcal{M}| \approx (x)F \wedge (x)G$, it is obvious that also $\mathcal{M}| \approx (Ex)F \wedge (x)G$.

If a formula F is transformed into a formula G using only Lemmas 1–7, we say that the transformation is *permissible*.

THEOREM 2. For every formula F, the following conditions are equivalent.

(i) $\not\approx F$.

(ii)   There is a permissible transformation of F into a formula of the form $(Ex_1)\ldots(Ex_k)G$ where G is either a substitution instance of an inconsistent propositional formula or a conjunction including a formula of the form $\sim(t=t)$.

Proof. We first show by induction on the maximum length l of the sequences of nested quantifiers in F that (i) implies (ii).

1^0. Let F be a quantifier free formula ($l = 0$) with free variables $x_1, \ldots, x_k$, and $\not\approx(Ex_1)\ldots(Ex_k)F$. Then $|\approx(x_1)\ldots(x_k)\sim F$ which implies $|=(x_1)\ldots(x_k)\sim F$. Hence $\sim F$ is a quantifier-free theorem of predicate calculus. By a known result (cf. Church (1956), pp. 184, 284), $\sim F$ is a substitution instance of a propositional tautology or a disjunction including a formula of the form $t = t$. Hence (ii) holds for F.

2^0. Suppose (i) implies (ii) for all formulas with $l \leq n$. Let F be a formula with $l = n + 1$ such that $\not\approx F$. We must consider separately different ways of constructing F from formulas with $l \leq n$. The cases (1)–(7) in the below suffice to establish (ii) for all such formulas.

(1) F is of the form $(Ex)G$. $\not\approx G$, since $\not\approx F$. Thus (ii) holds for F since, by induction hypothesis, it holds for G.

(2) F is of the form $(x)G$. Then by Lemma 4(ii), $\not\approx(Ex)G$, and we are reduced to case (1).

(3) F is of the form $(Ex)G \wedge (Ey)H$. Let z and u be distinct variables not in F. Then by Lemma 6, $\not\approx(Ez)G(z/x) \wedge (Eu)H(u/y)$, and Lemma 3(i), $\not\approx(Ez)(Eu)(G(z/x) \wedge H(u/y))$. Hence (ii) holds for F by induction hypothesis.

(4) F is of the form $(Ex)G \wedge (y)H$. By Lemmas 6 and 5, $\not\approx(Ez)(G(z/x) \wedge H(z/y))$ (z not in F), so (ii) holds for F by induction hypothesis.

(5) F is of the form $(x)G \wedge (y)H$. Then by Lemmas 6 and 2(iv), $\not\approx(z)(G(z/x) \wedge H(z/y))$ (z not in F), and we are reduced to case (2).

The 'dual' cases where F is of the form

(6) $\sim(Ex)G$ or $\sim(x)G$,

(7) $(Ex)G \vee (Ey)H$, etc.

are reduced to cases (1)–(5), as well as the cases where one of the components does not include a quantifier.

The proof from non-(i) to non-(ii) proceeds similarly by induction but we must notice the following: The induction step from $l = n$ to $l = n + 1$ produces only a finite number of permissible transformations in each case (1)–(7). Thus if non-(ii) holds for the formulas with $l \leq n$, it holds for the formulas with $l = n + 1$.

Consider now an arbitrary formula F of L. Since the number of permissible transformations applicable to F is finite and that property of G which is expressed in (ii) is effectively testable, we have a decision procedure for non-standard satisfiability (hence also for non-standard validity) of the formulas. In fact, we have seen that a formula is not non-standardly satisfiable only if inconsistency in it is in a certain sense very 'transparent' and obtains between the same 'levels' of the formula.

Since the structure of a constituent and attributive constituent is very clear-cut, and their import for certain methodological considerations is great (as we saw in Section 1), we shall now study their non-standard satisfiability and present a certain urn model construction for them. Since this study will be based intensively on the syntactical properties of constituents and it is not possible to present these properties here, we refer to Hintikka (1973a).

Let $C = C^{(d)}$ be a closed consistent constituent of L. Let s be an i-tuple $(1 \leq i \leq d)$ of nested attributive constituents (with the free variables $x_1; x_1, x_2; \ldots; x_1, x_2, \ldots, x_i$, respectively) occurring in C. Let s^k be the kth co-ordinate of s. We denote $\bar{s} = s^i$ iff s is an i-tuple. Let $\mathfrak{s}$ be a non-empty subset of the set of all such i-tuples $(1 \leq i \leq d)$ such that if $s \in \mathfrak{s}$ is an i-tuple, then $\langle s^1, \ldots, s^k \rangle \in \mathfrak{s}$ for all $k < i$. Let $d_0 \leq d$ be the maximum length of the elements of $\mathfrak{s}$.

We construct a sentence $S_C = S^{(d_0)}$ as follows. An attributive constituent of the form $Ct^{(d-i)}(x_1, \ldots, x_i)$ may occur in C as part of several deeper attributive constituents, that is, it may be $\bar{s}_1$ and $\bar{s}_2$ where $s_1 \neq s_2$. Now, for every attributive constituent of the form $Ct^{(d-i)}(x_1, \ldots, x_i)$ $(i = 1, \ldots, d)$ occurring in C, we omit from C all its occurrences $\bar{s}$ for which $s \notin \mathfrak{s}$.

Next, we construct an urn model $\mathcal{M}_C$ as follows. Let M be a model of C with the domain D. The sets $\mathcal{D}_i$ are defined as follows. $\mathcal{D}_0 = D$. $a_1 \in \mathcal{D}_1$ iff there is a $Ct^{(d-1)}(x_1) \in \mathfrak{s}$ such that a_1 satisfies it in M. Let $i > 1$. Suppose $\langle a_1, \ldots, a_{i-1} \rangle \in \mathcal{D}_{i-1}$. If there is an i-tuple $s \in \mathfrak{s}$ such that $\langle a_1, \ldots, a_k \rangle$ satisfies s^k in M $(k = 1, \ldots, i-1)$, then $\langle a_1, \ldots, a_{i-1}, a_i \rangle \in \mathcal{D}_i$ iff $\langle a_1, \ldots, a_{i-1}, a_i \rangle$ satisfies $\bar{s}$ in M. If there is no such s, then $\langle a_1, \ldots, a_{i-1}, a_i \rangle \in \mathcal{D}_i$ iff $a_i = a_{i-1}$. Let $\mathcal{M}_C = \langle M, c \rangle$, where $c = \langle \mathcal{D}_i \mid i < w \rangle$.

LEMMA 8. $\mathcal{M}_C \mid \approx S_C$.

Proof. We show that I have a winning strategy in the game $\mathcal{G}(S_C, \mathcal{M}_C)$. This winning strategy is best explained inductively as follows:

Suppose that $D, a_1, \ldots, a_{i-1}$ $(i \le d_0)$ has been drawn so that all the corresponding substitution instances of atomic formulas or their negations (in S_C) are true in M (more exactly: in the corresponding expansion of M). Suppose the possible choices after the draw of a_{i-1} will lead to a formula of the form

(a) $\quad (Ex_i) Ct_\ell^{(d-i_\ell)}(a_1, \ldots, a_{i-1}, x_i)(i \le i_\ell \le d),$

or to a formula of the form

(b) $\quad (x_i)(Ct_1^{(d-i_1)}(a_1, \ldots, a_{i-1}, x_i)$
$\quad \vee \ldots \vee Ct_m^{(d-i_m)}(a_i, \ldots, a_{i-1}, x_i))(\ell \le m).$

Case (a). Let

(*) $\quad Ct_\ell^{(d-i_\ell)}(x_1, \ldots, x_{i-1}, x_i) = A_\ell(x_1, \ldots, x_{i-1}, x_i)$

$\quad \wedge \bigwedge_{k \in K} (Ex_{i+1}) Ct_k^{(d-i_k-1)}(x_1, \ldots, x_i, x_{i+1})$

$\quad \wedge (x_{i+1}) \bigwedge_{k \in K} Ct_k^{(d-i_k-1)}(x_1, \ldots, x_i, x_{i+1})(i \le i_k \le d-1),$

where $A_\ell(x_1, \ldots, x_i)$ denotes a consistent conjunction which for each atomic formula which can be built up of the non-logical constants of S_C and the variables $x_1, \ldots, x_i$ and which contain x_i, contains either this atomic formula or its negation. Possibly $K = \phi$.

Since $Ct_\ell^{(d-i_\ell)}(x_1, \ldots, x_{i-1}, x_i)$ occurs in S_C, there is a member

(**) $\quad Ct_0^{(d-i)}(x_1, \ldots, x_{i-1}, x_i) = A_0(x_1, \ldots, x_{i-1}, x_i)$

$\quad \wedge \bigwedge_{k \in K_0} (Ex_{i+1}) Ct_k^{(d-i-1)}(x_1, \ldots, x_i, x_{i+1})$

$\quad \wedge (x_{i+1}) \bigvee_{k \in K_0} Ct_k^{(d-i-1)}(x_1, \ldots, x_i, x_{i+1})$

of s, for some $s \in \mathfrak{s}$, such that $A_0(x_1, \ldots, x_{i-1}, x_i) = A_\ell(x_1, \ldots, x_{i-1}, x_i)$. Hence by the definition of $\mathcal{D}_i$ there is an $a_i \in O_i^{M_c}$ such that $\langle a_1, \ldots, a_{i-1}, a_i \rangle$ satisfies $A_\ell(x_1, \ldots, x_{i-1}, x_i)$, that is, every atomic sentence and negation of an atomic sentence in the conjunction $A_\ell(a_1/x_1, \ldots, a_{i-1}/x_{i-1}, a_i/x_i)$ is true in M. I shall draw this kind of individual $a_i \in O_i^{M_c}$.

Case (*b*). Suppose Nature will draw an $a_i \in O_i^{M_c}$. By substituting a_i for x_i, the following sentence will result:

$$(***) \quad Ct_1^{(d-i_1)}(a_1/x_1, \ldots, a_{i-1}/x_{i-1}, a_i/x_i)$$
$$\vee \ldots \vee Ct_m^{(d-i_m)}(a_1/x_1, \ldots, a_{i-1}/x_{i-1}, a_i/x_i).$$

Since $\langle a_1, \ldots, a_{i-1}, a_i \rangle \in \mathcal{D}_i$, there is a formula $Ct_\ell^{(d-i_\ell)}(x_1, \ldots, x_{i-1}, x_i)$ of the form (*), for some $\ell \leq m$, such that $\langle a_1, \ldots, a_{i-1}, a_i \rangle$ satisfies in M some member (**) of a $s_j \in \mathfrak{s}$.

Hence $A_\ell(a_1/x_1, \ldots, a_{i-1}/x_{i-1}, a_i/x_i)$ is true in M. I shall choose this disjunct $Ct_\ell^{(d-i_\ell)}(a_1/x_i, \ldots, a_{i-1}/x_{i-1}, a_i/x_i)$ of (***). This is my winning strategy, for all the atomic sentences and the negations of atomic sentences which will emerge are true in M for every strategy of Nature. Thus $\mathcal{M}_C \mid \approx S_C$.

Let us denote by $C^{(d+e)[-e]}$ the result when the e *last* layers of quantifiers are omitted from $C^{(d+e)}$.

LEMMA 9. *If* $C^{(d+e)[-e]} = C^{(d)}$, *then* $\mathcal{M} \mid \approx C^{(d+e)}$ *implies* $\mathcal{M} \mid \approx C^{(d)}$.

Proof. Analogous to the proof of Lemma 8.

It should be noticed that S_C of Lemma 8 may be inconsistent, even trivially inconsistent, although C is consistent. Despite of its possible inconsistency S_C describes, in a definite way, all the i-tuples of individuals of M which are in the set $\mathcal{D}_i$ with $i = 1, \ldots, h_0$. If S_C is consistent, it may nevertheless be incompatible with C (as, e.g., in the case $d_0 = d$). Then M is not a model of S_C since it is a model of C.

The way in which S_C is obtained from C is precisely the same as the construction of an uncertainty description discussed in Section 1, above. This construction can be also characterized in terms of surface models. Let $\tilde{M}$ be a surface model in which C is true in the sense of Hintikka (1973b). When we omit from C certain nested sequences of attributive constituents to obtain S_C, this amounts to omitting from $\tilde{M}$ those proper parts which correspond to these omitted sequences. What we obtain is a tree-like figure $\tilde{M}_C$ which is like a surface model except that there may be branches of different lengths and the truncation requirement and the repetition requirement do not necessarily hold (as in $\tilde{M}$). This kind of generalized surface model can thus be considered as finitary graphic representation of the experiences a person can have in a world whose domain is changing between the steps of the investigation.

A constituent or attributive constituent of the first kind is called *empty* if all its outermost (existential) quantifiers are negated. When it is transformed into the second form, its existential part disappears and the universal part is inconsistent on the basis of propositional logic, that is, the formula quantified by the universal quantifier is a substitution instance of an inconsistent propositional formula. Also in some other trivial cases the main conjunction of a constituent or attributive constituent may contain a substitution instance of an inconsistent propositional formula. This kind of constituent or attributive constituent is also called empty. A constituent is called *proper* iff it has no empty parts.

THEOREM 3. A closed constituent has an urn model iff it is proper.

Proof. (1^0) If C has empty parts, it has no urn model by Theorem 2.

(2^0) Let $C = C^{(d)}$ be a proper closed constituent. If C is consistent, it has an invariant urn model. Suppose C is inconsistent. Let $\mathscr{C}_d^{\sim}$ be the set of all inconsistent constituents (in the vocabulary of C) of depth d. There is a depth $d + e$ at which all the subordinate constituents of every member of $\mathscr{C}_d^{\sim}$ are trivially inconsistent. Since C is inconsistent, at least one of its subordinate constituents at this depth is proper (even though L would contain identity). Let $C_1^{(d+e)}$ be such a subordinate constituent of C at this depth. The fact that $C_1^{(d+e)}$ is trivially inconsistent can be thought to be due to the absence of some attributive constituents from $C_1^{(d+e)}$ (see (A)–(C) in Hintikka, 1973a, pp. 259–262). More exactly: by inserting certain attributive constituents into the tree structure of $C_1^{(d+e)}$ we obtain from $C_1^{(d+e)}$ a completed constituent $\bar{C}_1^{(d+e)}$ of depth $d + e$ such that $\bar{C}_1^{(d+e)}$ is either consistent or non-trivially inconsistent. Since $\bar{C}_1^{(d+e)}$ is not trivially inconsistent and is of depth $d + e$, $C_2 = \bar{C}_1^{(d+e)[-e]}$ (which is of depth d) is not in $\mathscr{C}_d^{\sim}$. Thus C_2 is consistent. Let Ct be an arbitrary attributive constituent occurring in C. Since $C = C_1^{(d+e)[-e]}$, there occurs in $C_1^{(d+e)}$ an attributive constituent Ct_1 such that $Ct_1^{[-e]} = Ct$. By the construction of

$\bar{C}_1^{(d+e)}$, Ct_1 occurs in $\bar{C}_1^{(d+e)}$, whence Ct occurs in C_2. Thus every sequence of attributive constituents in C is in C_2. It follows that C is of the form S_{C_2} with C_2 consistent. Then by Lemma 8, C has an urn model of the form $\mathcal{M}_{C_2}$.

Academy of Finland

BIBLIOGRAPHY

Church, Alonzo (1956) *Introduction to Mathematical Logic*, Vol. I., Princeton University Press.

Feller, William (1957) *An Introduction to Probability Theory and Its Applications*, John Wiley, N. Y. (Vol. I, pp. 109, 131, 225, 246, 370 and 434; Vol. II, pp. 211, 226 and 237).

Hintikka, Jaakko (1970) 'Surface Information and Depth Information', in Jaakko Hintikka and Patrick Suppes (eds.), *Information and Inference*, D. Reidel, Dordrecht.

Hintikka, Jaakko (a) (1973) *Logic, Language-Games, and Information: Kantian Themes in the Philosophy of Logic*, The Clarendon Press, Oxford.

Hintikka, Jaakko (b) (1973) 'Surface Semantics and Its Motivation', in Hughes Leblanc (ed.), *Truth, Syntax, and Modality*, North-Holland, Amsterdam.

Rantala, Veikko (1973) 'On the Theory of Definability in First-Order Logic', Reports from the Institute of Philosophy, University of Helsinki, No. 2.

Rantala, Veikko (1977) *Aspects of Definability* (Acta Philosophica Fennica, vol. 29, nos. 2–3), North-Holland, Amsterdam.

IMPOSSIBLE POSSIBLE WORLDS VINDICATED

One of the oldest and most useful ideas in the logical and philosophical theory of modality is the concept of possible world. It goes back at least as far as to Leibniz. It allows us to characterize the principal modal notions in a very simple way. On this analysis, necessity equals truth in every possible world and possibility equals truth in some possible world or other.

These characterizations may seem circular, and are so in some sense. For instance, possibility is in them characterized in terms of possible worlds. The circle is not a vicious one, however, but is so large as to bring out a great deal of important structure of our modal concepts. Of course a number of serious philosophical problems remain, some of which were recently discussed by Professor Dana Scott under the heading 'Is There Life on Possible Worlds'? By and large, this application of the possible worlds idea has nevertheless proved to be extremely illuminating.

Less than twenty years ago the same idea was applied for the first time to the analysis of a class of concepts which for a philosopher are bound to be even more exciting than modal concepts. These new targets of possible worlds analysis were in the first place the so-called propositional attitudes, such as knowledge, belief, memory, perception, desire, etc. They could be handled by means of possible-worlds semantics by observing – or assuming – that not all possible worlds are equally good for all purposes. In the form of a slogan, not all possible worlds are equally possible. If I consider a person, let's call him a, in a possible world W, he is obviously not going to accept any old possible world as an alternative to W on the basis of what he knows in W. Only some possible worlds fill this bill. I shall call them *epistemic a-alternatives to W.*

The basic idea of the possible worlds analysis of knowledge is that conversely the totality of these alternatives uniquely determines what a knows in W.[1] Hence to speak of what a knows in W is, in the abstract eyes of modal logician, nothing but to speak of the set of epistemic a-alternatives to W. Intuitively speaking, they are all the worlds

367

E. Saarinen (ed.), Game-Theoretical Semantics, 367–379. All Rights Reserved.

compatible with everything a knows in W. Technically speaking, this means that to have the concept of knowledge is to associate with each individual knower a two-place relation on the class of possible worlds, the epistemic a-alternativeness relation. This *is* the logical type of notions like knowledge, we can now say. The a-alternatives to a given world are then all those worlds that bear this alternativeness relation to it.

The generalization to other propositional attitudes is immediately clear.

Again, this analysis of propositional attitudes has proved immensely fruitful, it seems to me. By its means, we can approach such important and divergent problems as knowledge by acquaintance, sense-data, causal theories of perception, the intentionality of sensation, and the nature of intentionality in general.

However, unlike the original possible-worlds characterization of necessity and possibility, the new analysis is subject to a major difficulty, which – it is only fair to say – has not yet been disposed of. It is my aim in this paper finally to bury this problem for good.

The problem, to give it a label, is *the problem of logical omniscience.* It seems that the possible-world analysis of knowledge forces us to say that everybody always knows all the logical consequences of what he or she knows and likewise for other propositional attitudes. In other words, the following rule of inference seems inescapable.

$$(I) \qquad \frac{p \supset q}{K_a p \supset K_a q}$$

In other words, whenever the implication $(p \supset q)$ is logically true, i.e., whenever p logically implies q, whoever knows that p must also know that q. And analogous problems arise for other similar concepts. For instance, the analogous rule of inference for belief seems equally unavoidable. It is the following.

$$(II) \qquad \frac{p \supset q}{B_a p \supset B_a q}$$

How precisely the problem of logical omniscience comes about will be examined shortly. Meanwhile, it may be appropriate to register our dismay at these apparent consequences of the possible worlds analysis of propositional attitudes. They are not only bad; they seem to be little short of a complete disaster. For surely, you feel like saying, we all know and believe any number of things whose consequences we have no idea of. Euclid did not know everything that is to be known about elementary geometry, nor did Maxwell know everything there is to be known about electromagnetism. The idealization involved in the possible-worlds approach to knowledge does not only seem excessive. It seems to turn the whole theory into nonsense.

The situation can be corrected, however. In a number of papers – most of them included in my *Logic, Language-Games, and Information* (Clarendon Press, Oxford, 1973) – I have in effect shown how to restrict the rules (I)–(II) in an interesting way. The main idea underlying these restrictions is that (I)–(II) are valid only when q can be deduced from p without considering more individuals than are considered in either of them.

The problem with this restriction is that the notion of 'considering so many individuals' has so far been given only a *syntactic* meaning. There exists as yet no decent model theory to back it up. The idea of the number of individuals considered in their relation to each other in a given sentence is highly intuitive, but it has not been incorporated into any honest model theory (logical semantics).

This is one of the many problems which can be illuminated by game-theoretical semantics. For in any play of a given semantical game, a certain definite number of individuals are considered in the literal sense of the word. This gives an instant semantical sense to my syntactical notion. The purpose of this chapter is to see how this idea can be carried out systematically, so as to give a real model-theoretical backing to my syntactical ideas.

First we nevertheless have to see precisely how the alleged commitment to logical omniscience comes about. The possible-worlds analysis of knowledge can be formulated as follows.

(1) A sentence of the form '*a* knows that *p*' is true in a world *W* iff *p* is true in all the epistemic *a*-alternatives to *W*, i.e., in all the epistemically possible worlds which are compatible with everything *a* knows in *W*.

The failure of logical omniscience can be formulated as follows.

(2) There are *a*, *p*, and *q* such that *a* knows that *p*, *p* logically implies *q* (i.e., $(p \supset q)$ is logically true), but *a* does not know that *q*.

The notion of logical truth (validity) employed here is to be analyzed in the usual model-theoretical fashion:

(3) A sentence is logically true iff it is true in every logically possible world.

The criticism mentioned in the beginning of this paper can be taken to allege the incompatibility of (1)–(3). However, these three assumptions are not incompatible yet in the form just given to them. A contradiction between (1)–(3) is in the offing only in conjunction with the following further assumption.

(4) Every epistemically possible world is logically possible. (That is, every epistemic alternative to a given world is logically possible.)

A contradiction between (1)–(4) now comes about as follows. Assume that there are (say, in the actual world) a, p, and q as in (2). In virtue of (1), a's not knowing that q will then mean that there is an epistemically possible world, more specifically, an epistemic a-alternative to the actual world, in which q is false. Let's call this alternative W'. Likewise, a's knowing that p means that p is true in each such alternative world. In particular, p is therefore true in W'. According to (4), these epistemic alternatives are also logically possible worlds. In particular, W' is a logically possible world. According to (3), the assumption that $(p \supset q)$ is logically true means that q is true in each logically possible world in which p is true. Since W' is a case in point, q must be true in W'. But q was already found to be false in W', whence the contradiction.

To this contradiction between (1)–(4) philosophers have in effect reacted in different ways. For instance, the positivistic doctrine of the noninformative (tautological) character of logical truths can be understood so as to imply the denial of (2). Since a already knows that p and since the logical implication from p to q cannot (in view of the tautologicity of logical truth) contribute anything objectively new information to what he knows, he in reality knows whatever there is objectively speaking to be known about q.

This line of thought has recently been thoroughly discredited.[2] However, its rejection still leaves several different *prima facie* options open to us. The criticisms I have referred to amount to blaming the contradiction on the possible worlds analysis of knowledge (1). What has not been pointed out in the literature, however, is that the source of trouble is obviously the last assumption (4). This assumption is usually made tacitly, maybe even unwittingly. It is what prejudges the case in favor of logical omniscience and hence leads into a conflict with the denial (2) of such omniscience.

The reason for this allocation of blame ought to be clear. According to the intended interpretation of the epistemic a-alternatives to W, they are all the contingencies which are left open by whatever a knows in W. Some of these contingencies can of course be merely apparent ones which a has to be prepared for solely because of the limitations of his powers of logical and conceptual insight. To require, as (4) does, that these include only situations ('worlds') which are objectively (logically) possible therefore prejudges the case in favor of logical omniscience. It presupposes that a can eliminate all the merely apparent possibilities. This is blatantly circular, however. Just because people (like our friend a) may fail to follow the logical consequences of what they know *ad infinitum*, they may have to keep a logical eye on options which only *look* possible but which contain hidden contradictions.

Hence the real culprit here is (4), not (2) or (1). The way to solve the problem of logical omniscience is hence to give up the assumption (4). This means admitting 'impossible possible worlds', that is, worlds which look possible and hence must be admissible as epistemic alternatives but which none the less are not logically possible.

Admitting them solves our problem for good. For then we can have (1)–(3) all true together. The option $\sim q$ left open by a's knowledge can be realized is some epistemic alternative U while $(p \supset q)$ is happily true in every logically possible world, as long as the epistemic alternative U is not among these logically possible worlds.

The difficulty now is to give a reasonable account of these strange worlds that are epistemically but not logically possible. How can we accomplish that neat trick?

It is not difficult (I have argued on several earlier occasions) to give an interesting syntactical account of what the descriptions of 'impossible possible worlds' (logically impossible but epistemically possible worlds) might look like.[3] However, it might again seem not only very hard but completely impossible to make honest model-theoretic (semantical) sense of 'impossible possible worlds'. This task is apparently made all the more difficult by the restricted range of options that are at all natural here. Attempts have in fact been made to construct a model theory of impossible worlds by adopting some sort nonstandard interpretation of logical constants.[4] However, this course is very dubious. The very problem was created by people's failure to perceive the logical consequences of what they know far enough. Of course these logical consequences must be based on the classical (standard) interpretation of connectives and quantifiers. Thus an attempted nonstandard interpretation is either bound to be beside the point or else to destroy the problem instead of solving it.

But if we cannot change the interpretation of logical constants, what else can we do here? Precious little, it might seem.

My 'surface models' were intended to supply a model theory for the breakdown of 'logical omniscience' (i.e., for a concept of knowledge satisfying (2)).[5] However, in the form in which the theory of surface models was first formulated, they are not real honest-to-god models at all.

Fortunately, the twist Veikko Rantala has recently given to the theory of surface models (following a hint dropped in my original paper on them) provides a new strikingly realistic type of nonclassical models for first-order sentences. In his theory, the 'impossible possible worlds' are not in the least impossible. They are merely *changing* worlds. Or, more accurately speaking, they are *invidiously* changing worlds: they are models whose domain may change as we investigate it. The basic idea is, as Rantala points out, precisely the same as that underlying the use of urns (boxes) with a changing population of balls occasionally considered in probability theory. The point is not just that the composition of the box may change, but that it changes between one's successive draws of balls from the urn. Rantala accordingly uses the apt term 'urn model' for these new models for first-order sentences.

They satisfy both our main *desiderata*. The interpretation of propositional connectives is precisely the usual one, and in a perfectly good sense quantifiers behave in their wont way, too. Nevertheless, even some logically false sentences can be true in urn models.

A brief introduction to the theory of urn models is given in Veikko Rantala's paper, 'Urn Models: A New Kind of Nonstandard Model for First-Order Logic'.[6] It is especially interesting to see that Rantala is using a game-theoretical truth-definition. Indeed, it is the dynamic (step-by-step) character of a game-theoretical truth-definition that enables Rantala to conceive of the models themselves in a more dynamic way as urn models (changing models). Accordingly, Rantala's game-theoretical truth-definition for urn models is to all practical purposes precisely the same as the game-theoretical truth-characterization for old (invariant) models. No nonstandard interpretation of logical concepts is involved here.

In its general form, the concept of an urn model is nevertheless too broad for my purposes here. In order to see this, and to see how the idea of urn model can be specified so as to be relevant to our present needs, let us recall the basic idea of epistemically but not logically possible worlds: they were worlds so subtly inconsistent that the inconsistency could not be expected to be known (perceived) by an everyday logician, however competent.

This idea has an interesting realization in the realm of urn models. Ordinary models ('logically possible worlds') can be thought of as a subset of the class of all urn models. They are simply the *invariant* urn models ('invariant worlds'). In order to be 'epistemically possible', an urn model must vary so imperceptibly as to be indistinguishable from an invariant model at a certain fixed level of logical acumen.

This prompts the more general question as to what one can in principle observe about the world – whether changing or invariant – in which one is living and which one is investigating. It is here that the ideas of constituent and of surface model come to their own. In so far as the different individuals of an urn model are distinguishable from each other only by their properties and by their relations to the other members of the domain of the urn model (as I shall assume in this paper), the different possible complexes of experience one can have by observing at most d individuals together are represented by the different constituents of depth d.

This is the intuitive epistemological conterpart to the deductive role of constituents as the logically strongest propositions of depth d. To put the same point in another way, a surface model of depth d is not a model at all. It is not an ontological but an epistemological entity. It is the sum total of what we can find out about the world (about a given model, whether an invariant or changing one) by considering only sequences of at most d individuals.

This becomes even clearer if the concept of a surface model is generalized so as to omit the truncation requirement and the repetition requirement. Then there will be one-to-one correspondence between constituents and equivalence classes of urn models of the same epistemological status. Constituents of depth d must then be thought of as the verbal formulations of the maximal information we can gather about an urn model by considering sequences of a most d individuals

What precisely constituents are like is sketched in Rantala's paper and described in some detail in my earlier publications.[7] Roughly speaking, a constituent $C_0^{(d)}$ of depth d is a finite set of finite trees (in the precise mathematical sense of the word), each with a unique lowest element (node), and each of length d. (It is to be observed, and kept in mind, that when constituents are spoken of as trees, much of the customary imagery which is associated with them has to be reversed, with consequent awkwardness of the earlier terminology. For instance, what I have earlier called the *depth* of a constituent and what was just referred to as its *length* would now be called more naturally its *height*.)) Each node (element) of each tree comes with a specification as to how an individual connected with it is to be related to individuals corresponding to the nodes lower down in the same branch (and how an individual corresponding to it is related to itself). The successive nodes of each branch describe, in that order, a sequence of d individuals that one can draw from a model M in which $C_0^{(d)}$ is true, and conversely each such sequence will have to be described by some branch or other. At each node n_0, the top segments (above n_0) of all the branches passing through n_0 describe all the different continuations of the sequence of individuals one has to draw from the model to climb up to n_0. (This is the common lower segment of all these branches)

This explains how it is that constituents of depth d describe all the information we can obtain about a model in d moves at most. They describe it by spelling out which ramified sequences of individuals one can 'draw' from the urn that an urn model can be thought of as being. This urn model can be either an urn model in the narrow sense or an ordinary (invariant) model. My ill-named surface models (generalized so as to omit the repetition requirement and the truncation requirement[8]) are now seen to be simply model-theoretical counterparts to constituents. The constitute the finest partition of different kinds of urn models one can observationally distinguish from each other without considering sequences of individuals longer than d.

Now how can we test whether a constituent as I have described it represents draws from an invariant model or a changing one? Metaphorically speaking: How can one tell whether one is living in an 'invariant' world or a 'changing' one? In either case, all that one can observe are the different ramified sequences of different kinds of 'balls' (individuals) one can 'draw' from the 'urn' (world). If so, surely the hallmark of an invariant world must be that *the supply of different kinds of individuals one can obtain in any one draw must be the same*. Saying this presupposes of course that the draws are draws with replacement. Otherwise a small exception will have to be made for the individuals already drawn. They are no longer available, although some of them were available at earlier draws.

Conversely, if the supply of individuals that confronts us at the different draws is the same, as far as we can tell on the kind of observable evidence that is available to us, then surely we are dealing with an urn (a world) which is either invariant or else varies so imperceptibly as to be indistinguishable from an invariant one.

Let us restrict our attention to evidence that can be derived from the observation of sequence of individuals of length d at most. This means restricting our attention to evidence codified by constituents of depth d, i.e., to those bodies of evidence which *are* the corresponding surface models.

In the tree that such a constituent is, the different kinds of individuals available to us after a sequence of draws of individuals a_1, $a_2, \ldots, a_k$ (which takes us to a given node n_0, corresponding to the individual a_k) are represented by the nodes covering n_0 (i.e., immediately above n_0). Likewise, the different choices available to us when we chose a_k are represented by the nodes covering the node n_1 immediately below n_0. The requirement that the two sets of individuals must be identical now implies that the part of the tree above n_0 (skipping n_0 itself) must be the same as the part above n_1. (The identity refers also to the relations of corresponding nodes to nodes below n_1.) These two parts cannot be quite the same, however, for their heights are different. Hence what can be required here is that the part above n_0 is the same (in the sense explained) as the part above n_1 after the last (highest) layer of nodes in it has been omitted.

However, this is precisely the truncation requirement imposed on my surface models.[9]

If we practice draws with replacement, there must also be, for each given node n_i below n_0 in the same branch (including n_0), immediately above n_0 a 'mirror image' node n_i'. This 'mirror image' character of n_i' of course means that it is related to every node in the same way as n_i. (For the replacement implies that each of the individuals drawn earlier must again be available when we have reached a_k.) This, however, is precisely the repetition requirement I have imposed on surface models.[10]

By examining the joint consequences of the repetition requirement and of the truncation requirement we can see that they pretty much exhaust the consequences of the idea that the supply of individuals must be the same at each draw, as far as evidence codifiable by constituents of depth d is concerned. The two requirements say in effect that what can happen after any sequence of earlier draws looks just the same as what can happen after any other sequence of draws (taking into account the effects of replacement).

But the truncation requirement and the repetition requirement characterize precisely those constituents which are not trivially inconsistent. Hence we obtain a characterization of those urn models which are invariant or vary so subtly as to be indistinguishable from invariant ones on the level of evidence codifiable by constituents of depth d: they are the urn models which satisfy some constituent of depth d which is not trivially inconsistent. Such urn models will be called d-invariant. Urn models which are d-invariant but not invariant *simpliciter* will play the role of the epistemically possible but not logically possible worlds whose desirability was motivated in the beginning of my paper.

It is a truly remarkable fact that many urn models are d-invariant without being really invariant. That is to say, they satisfy the requirement that draws from the 'urn' always seem to be made from the same supply of individuals as far as we can tell on the basis of evidence codifiable by constituents of depth d, and yet fail to be true in any invariant urn model. Hence there in fact are plenty of urn models available for the role to which I have cast epistemically but not logically possible worlds.

My definition of such worlds seems to have the awkward consequence of making my epistemically but not logically possible worlds relative to the parameter d. However, this relativity is neither unexpected nor difficult to understand. The worlds in question were calculated to be the ones which a certain person a envisages as being compatible with everything he knows. Their totality depends naturally on his acumen – and on the level of analysis he is practicing. The more insight he gains, the more merely apparently possible worlds he can eliminate. This is accurately reflected by the fact that a d-invariant world need not be a $(d+1)$-invariant world, even though the converse relation does hold.

More generally speaking, we can see that to identify epistemically possible worlds with d-invariant ones amounts to measuring people's logical insight in a way which is as uniform as it is intuitive. We have seen that an urn model is not d-invariant if its variability is betrayed by a review of all the sequences of draws of d successive individuals from the domain of the model. Translated into the language of epistemically possible worlds this says that a world is not epistemically possible at the dth level of analysis if its impossibility can be seen by considering successive draws of no more than d individuals from the domain of the world in question. It is obvious that, even though this is not the only possible way of gauging people's logical acumen, it is an eminently natural one. One aspect of its naturalness is its model-theoretic import. Unlike many other indices of the difficulty of a logical problem (such as the length of proofs), mine does not depend on any particular axiomatization of first-order logic.

Other reasons for the general theoretical interest of just this measure are indicated in earlier papers and books of mine. Several of them are connected with the fact that the length of the sequence of individuals considered in the game-theoretical truth-definition as applied to a sentence S is an excellent explication of the idea of the number of individuals considered together in S. This also indicates the intuitive connection between my syntactical limitation on (I)–(II) and the concept of a d-invariant model. In the same way as in the excluded cases the validity of $p \supset q$ can be seen only by considering more individuals than one does in p or q, in the same way a d-invariant model can sometimes be seen not to be completely invariant by considering sequences of individuals longer than d. These two phenomena can be considered as identical.

The parameter d is not so difficult to get rid off, either, for many relevant purposes. We started out by considering a failure on the part of a to be aware of the logical consequences of some particular proposition p he was assumed to know. Now p comes to us with a definite level of analysis already associated with it. For it has itself a fixed depth d, i.e., a fixed number of layers of quantifiers at its deepest. In other words, in p we are considering at most d successive draws of individuals from the model which is supposed to make p true or false. Hence the question as to whether a person a who knows that p has to know also a certain logical consequence q of p is naturally discussed by reference to d-invariant urn models, that is, by reference to sequences of at most d draws of individuals from the domain. This many draws he will have to consider in spelling out to himself what p means, whereas there is no logically binding reason why he should consider sequences of draws of any greater length.

Sometimes it is natural to consider the question of logical omniscience as it were also from the receiving end, that is to say, from the vantage point of the consequence a and not only the premise p. In other words, sometimes we may want to require that a understand not only p but also q in answering the question whether he knows that q. Then the relevant worlds are the urn models invariant at the depth of $(p \supset q)$, i.e., at the depth max $[\text{depth}(p), \text{depth}(q)]$.

On this suggestion, the model-theoretically motivated solution of the problem of logical omniscience coincides precisely with the syntactically motivated solution I have argued for earlier. For according to the latter, a logical implication from p to q supports an inference from

a knows that p

to

a knows that q

only if $(p \supset q)$ is what I have called a *surface tautology*. What this means is that all the constituents in the normal form of p but not in the normal form of q at the depth of $(p \supset q)$ are *trivially* inconsistent at this depth. But this is readily seen to be tantamount to the requirement that $(p \supset q)$ be true in all the urn models invariant at its own depth. Hence the *semantical* solution of the problem of logical omniscience obtained here coincides with the syntactical (proof-theoretical) solution examined in my earlier work.

We might summarize the main results of this article as follows.

(i) The only reasonable way of solving the problem of logical omniscience is to countenance worlds that are epistemically possible but logically impossible.

(ii) Such worlds may be identified with those urn models which vary subtly as to be indistinguishable from invariant ones at a certain level of analysis.

(iii) These worlds are the urn models described by inconsistent but not trivially inconsistent constituents.

(iv) Hence my earlier syntactical solution to the problem of logical omniscience receives a genuine semantical (model-theoretical) backing, for the upshot of (i)–(ii) is that only surface tautologies must be known by everybody, which is just what the syntactical solution says.

In (iv), 'everybody' of course means 'everybody who understands the proposition in question'.

Urn models and d-invariant urn models offer interesting possibilities for model-theoretical (semantical) reconstructions of a large number of other ideas, including those of proposition and meaning. However, on this occasion I shall restrict my attention to the problem of logical omniscience.

Academy of Finland and Stanford University

NOTES

[1] For this analysis, see *Knowledge and Belief* (Cornell U.P., Ithaca, N.Y., 1962); *Models for Modalities* (D. Reidel, Dordrecht, 1969); *The Intentions of Intentionality and Other New Models for Modalities* (D. Reidel, Dordrecht, 1975).

[2] Cf. my book, *Logic, Language-Games, and Information* (Clarendon Press, oxford, 1973).

[3] This line of thought is based on the idea of considering only a given fixed number of individuals at the same time which was mentioned earlier. See, e.g., 'Surface Information and Depth Information', in Jaakko Hintikka and Patrick Suppes (eds.), *Information and Inference* (D. Reidel, Dordrecht, 1970), pp. 263–297; 'Knowledge, Belief, and Logical Consequence', *Ajatus* **32** (1970) 32–47; and *Logic, Language-Games, and Information* (note 2 above), especially Chapters 7–8 and 10.

[4] For instance, M. J. Cresswell works with a modified truth-definition for negation in his papers 'Classical Intensional Logics', *Theoria* **36** (1970) 347–372, and 'intensional Logics and Logical Truth', *Journal of Philosophical Logic* **1** (1972) 2–15.

[5] See 'Surface Semantics: Definition and Its Motivation', in Hughes Leblanc (ed.), *Truth, Syntax, and Modality* (North-Holland, Amsterdam, 1973), pp. 128–147.

[6] See above, pp. 347–366.

[7] See especially the last chapter of my book, *Logic, Language-Games, and Information* (Note 2 above). Cf. also 'Surface Information and Depth Information' (Note 3 above).

[8] See 'Surface Semantics' (Note 5 above), pp. 134–136.

[9] 'Surface Semantics' (Note 5 above), pp. 135–136.

[10] Ibid., p. 136.

INDEX OF NAMES

381

INDEX OF SUBJECTS

SYNTHESE LANGUAGE LIBRARY

Texts and Studies
in Linguistics and Philosophy

Managing Editors:

JAAKKO HINTIKKA
Academy of Finland, Stanford University, and Florida State University (Tallahassee)

STANLEY PETERS
The University of Texas at Austin

Editors:

EMMON BACH (University of Massachusetts at Amherst)
JOAN BRESNAN (Massachusetts Institute of Technology)
JOHN LYONS (University of Sussex)
JULIUS M. E. MORAVCSIK (Stanford University)
PATRICK SUPPES (Stanford University)
DANA SCOTT (Oxford University)

1. Henry Hiż (ed.), *Questions.* 1977, xvii + 366 pp.
2. William S. Cooper, *Foundations of Logico-Linguistics. A Unified Theory of Information, Language, and Logic.* 1978, xvi + 249 pp.
3. Avishai Margalit (ed.), *Meaning and Use. Papers Presented at the Second Jerusalem Philosophical Encounter, April 1976.* 1979 (forthcoming).
4. F. Guenthner and S. J. Schmidt (eds.), *Formal Semantics and Pragmatics for Natural Languages.* 1978, viii + 374 pp. + index.
5. Esa Saarinen (ed.), *Game-Theoretical Semantics.* 1978, xiv + 379 pp. + index.
6. F. J. Pelletier (ed.), *Mass Terms: Some Philosophical Problems.* 1979 (forthcoming).